A RADICAL WORKER IN TSARIST RUSSIA

Semën Ivanovich Kanatchikov

A Radical Worker in Tsarist Russia

The Autobiography
of Semën Ivanovich Kanatchikov

Translated and Edited by
Reginald E. Zelnik

Stanford University Press · Stanford, California · 1986

Stanford University Press
Stanford, California
© 1986 by the Board of Trustees of the
Leland Stanford Junior University

Printed in the United States of America
CIP data appear at the end of the book

The map of Moscow that appears on p. xxxi is adapted from Laura Engelstein, *Moscow, 1905: Working-Class Organization and Political Conflict* (Stanford University Press, 1982), p. 44. The map of St. Petersburg
that appears on pp. xxxii–xxxiii is adapted from the endpapers in Reginald E. Zelnik, *Labor and Society in Tsarist Russia: The Factory Workers
of St. Petersburg, 1855–1870* (Stanford University Press, 1971).

This translation is dedicated
to my mother, Salomea Czysz Zelnik,
and to the memory of my father,
Simon B. Zelnik

ACKNOWLEDGMENTS

MANY FRIENDS and colleagues assisted in the preparation of this translation of Semën Kanatchikov's memoirs. Gregory Freidin and Nicholas Riasanovsky, in additon to advising me on many other matters, were always on hand to help me unravel seemingly hopeless puzzles of translation. Portions of the draft manuscript were also read and commented on by Victoria Bonnell, Laura Engelstein, Leopold Haimson, and Gerald Surh. Invaluable assistance was provided by Deborah Pearl, Tony Swift, and Robert Weinberg. The manuscript was beautifully typed (yes, typed!) by Eileen Grammp, whose growing interest in Kanatchikov's life seemed to mount with every character she typed, fortifying my confidence in the value of this venture. The University of California Press has kindly permitted me to include the excerpts from Kanatchikov's autobiography that I previously published as Chapter 1 of Victoria E. Bonnell, ed., *The Russian Worker: Life and Labor Under the Tsarist Regime* (Berkeley, Calif., 1983).

This book could not have been completed without the support of a grant from the National Endowment for the Humanities Translation Program, so ably administered by Susan A. Mango. Support was also forthcoming from the University of California at Berkeley, especially its Center for Slavic and East European Studies, Institute of International Studies, Committee on Research, and Humanities Research Program.

Elaine Zelnik deserves special thanks for many things, not the least of which is her willingness to have received a young and troublesome Russian worker as a permanent though uninvited guest in her home for so many years. Nor am I sure he has gone.

R.E.Z.

CONTENTS

EDITOR'S NOTE

THIS TRANSLATION of the autobiography of Semën Ivanovich Kanatchikov is based on the 1929 edition of the first volume of his memoirs, *Iz istorii moego bytiia* (*From the Story of My Life*, published in Moscow and Leningrad), and the 1934 edition of the second volume, *Istoriia moego bytiia* (*The Story of My Life*, published in Moscow). These are the editions most readily available in the United States and Western Europe. The fullest version of Kanatchikov's memoirs was published in a single volume in Moscow in 1932, under the former title. I have used that volume for my translations of passages absent from the 1929 and 1934 editions, and have indicated in the endnotes precisely where such insertions occur. In almost all cases I have used the author's original chapter titles, the exceptions being where I have broken up some very long chapters into smaller ones and added descriptive titles. Thus there are only 42 chapters in the original memoirs, whereas there are 47 in the translation. These changes too are indicated in the endnotes. Otherwise, the only liberties I have taken with the formal structure of the original work are the addition of chapter numbers and an occasional change in paragraphing, usually the breaking up of a paragraph that seemed excessively long.

In translating these memoirs I have attempted to remain as close as possible to the spirit and tone of the original. What characterizes the original, as I see it, is a very direct, straightforward, rather engaging style, punctuated occasionally by a pretentious rhetorical flourish aimed at displaying the literary accomplishments of an essentially self-educated author. Rather than impose an artificial unity on a book whose stylistic antinomies express and confirm important contradictions in the author's life experience, I have deliberately preserved the contradictory styles that sometimes seem to mar the unity of this work.

Kanatchikov's use of some of the colorful Russian colloquial expressions of his peasant and working-class milieus presented me with another dilemma. To retain something approximating the literal meaning of such expressions would have the advantage of exposing the reader to some of the rich metaphorical images of the Russian people but the disadvantage of sounding uncolloquial in English to the point of disfiguring the text. My solution has been to choose the most natural English translation available (except where it introduces an anachronistic tone), while presenting the literal translation in the notes on those occasions when I find it has particular resonance. Thus, for example, I have translated *medvezh'i ugly* as "remote, out-of-the-way regions" instead of "bear's corners," explaining the literal meaning in a note.

Once in a while the author likes to represent the unusual speech patterns of some of his characters—whether foreign accents, regional eccentricities, or simply expressions of deficient educations—by deliberately introducing orthographic, lexical, or grammatical errors. I have tried my best to find English equivalents for these devices, using the notes to alert the reader only to those instances where my translation fails to convey fully some aspect of the original (e.g., that the speaker was a German, or a peasant from the Volga region).

I have deliberately mixed two systems of transliteration in the pages that follow. In the Bibliography and in bibliographic and linguistic references in the notes, which are intended to provide useful leads to students and other researchers who know Russian, I have adhered to a slightly modified Library of Congress system. In the text itself, for what I believe are valid aesthetic reasons, I have further modified that system in my rendering of personal and place names by using the letter "y," where appropriate, *in the last syllable*, while eliminating the letter "i" or unsightly combinations such as "ii," "ia," or "yi." Thus Vasilii (Library of Congress system) becomes Vasily, Avdotia becomes Avdotya, and Krasnoiarsk becomes Krasnoyarsk. By the same token, I have eliminated all hard and soft signs in the text proper (Mel'shin becomes

Melshin, Tver' becomes Tver). Except for bibliographical and linguistic references, all these modified forms are used in the notes as well, even in discussions of books and authors if they are not intended for reference purposes. Non-Russian names given in their Russianized forms by the author are rendered in their original forms whenever those forms are ascertainable. A small number of well-known names are rendered in the forms familiar to the English-speaking reader (e.g., Leo, not Lev, Tolstoy; Nicholas II, not Nikolay II).

Kanatchikov annotated his memoirs very sparingly. I have used asterisks to indicate his notes and to distinguish them from my own, numbered notes. The author's notes are located at the bottom of the page and followed by the words "Author's note," whereas my editorial notes are endnotes.

I have attempted to gear my editorial notes to two different audiences. Primarily, they are intended for readers who lack real expertise in the history of Russia: beginning students in this field, general readers, and comparative historians of labor who lack a firm background in Russian history. With such people in mind, I have endeavored to use the notes to clarify recondite references, identify obscure historical actors, events, and institutions, set the context for more familiar situations, and correct an occasional inaccuracy or, more rarely still, distortion. Many readers, I trust, will be able to bypass these notes at little or no sacrifice. Other notes, however, are aimed at the more advanced students of Russian social history, those who, whether they prefer to read this book in English or in Russian, might be curious about one scholar's view of some of the interesting historical moments portrayed by the author or feel they would benefit from some bibliographical suggestions and analytical leads in pursuing their own interest in the politics and culture of the Russian working class. In any case, readers from both groups, as well as those who may fall between these somewhat arbitrary stools, should enjoy and profit from these remarkable memoirs even if they choose to read them through without examining the notes or the editor's somewhat idiosyncratic introduction.

Unless otherwise indicated, all pre-1918 dates in the text and in the annotations follow the Julian or "Old Style" calendar, twelve days behind the Gregorian or "Western" calendar in the nineteenth century, thirteen days behind in the twentieth. The Western calendar was adopted in Russia in February 1918.

The name Kanatchikov is pronounced roughly as it appears, with the stress falling on the second syllable. The name Semën (the Russian equivalent of Simon) is best envisioned as Simyon, with the stress also falling on the second syllable.

Introduction:
Kanatchikov's *Story of My Life* as Document and Literature

"Bebel was our ideal, and we wanted to make our worker audience into future Russian Bebels."   —Mikhail I. Brusnev[1]

"Every viable working-class movement has brought to the fore such working-class leaders, its own Proudhons, Vaillants, Weitlings, and Bebels. . . . This 'working-class intelligentsia' already exists in Russia. . . ."   —Lenin (1899)[2]

WHO WAS Semën Ivanovich Kanatchikov? Among other things, I like to think of him as a writer. He was certainly not a major figure in the political history of modern Russia, not even an important link in the chain of Russian revolutionary history. He was not, as the reader will soon see, a profound thinker, perhaps not even a subtle one. With few exceptions, his contemporaries barely took any note of him, or if they did they rarely considered him of sufficient interest to warrant inscribing his name into the historical record they left behind.[3] Of course when he ran afoul of the law, as was his wont, his traces were left, together with those of thousands of others, in the routine entries of the archives of the police, and when he served as a delegate to some public gathering, his presence was recorded in the protocols of the meeting. But, again with a couple of notable exceptions, one searches in vain in the memoir literature and other documentation left by the dozens of political activists who crossed his path for any clear description of his features, analysis of his character, or sense of excitement about his presence—indeed, for anything but the most perfunctory allusion to his participation in the revolutionary circles in which he spent the better part of his youth and early adulthood. In short, at least with respect to the years included in Kanatchikov's memoirs (they break off with the onset of the Russian Revolution of 1905, when he was only 26) it is safe to assume that he was the kind of person who, in the absence of his memoirs, would not be remembered as an individual at all, but only as a member of one of the sociopolitical classification systems so dear to historians of revolution and the labor movement: a "conscious worker," "peasant-worker," "skilled craftsman," or "semi-intellectual." It is his memoirs, then, that bring him to life, giving flesh and personality to otherwise colorless sociological categories, and vividly recreating the different social milieus he inhabited, as they were refracted through the prism of his memory.

Of course our Kanatchikov was not a Gorky. He was not, like Gorky, a provincial plebeian who transformed himself into a professional author, emerging from a cocoon of poverty and ignorance as a glorious literary butterfly, observing his own past from a distance and weaving it into the tapestry of literature. Indeed, our Kanatchikov, though a writer, was never really at home in the world of letters and literary creativity. He learned to read, as he candidly admits in the chapters that follow, only with the most painstaking effort, and even as a young adult found mastering a text that was complex and subtle a challenge almost beyond his reach. Not surprisingly, writing (as well as formal public speaking), came to him with more difficulty still.

His greatest pleasure, and certainly the activity that engaged him with the greatest ease apart from the plying of his trade as a pattern-maker, seems clearly to have been conversation—conversation with his fellow workers, of course, especially his fellow "conscious" workers, but with other social types as well, including members of the radical and liberal intelligentsia at one extreme, and his fellow villagers and the more "backward," nonpoliticized, uncultured factory workers at the other. Even his jailers, whom he often engaged in verbal games of cat and mouse, were grist for Kanatchikov's conversational mill. All these conversations—some of them recalled directly by the author, others secondhand accounts as told to Kanatchikov by one of the many comrades he brings to life in the pages of this book—provide the essential raw material from which his memoirs are constructed. Typically, we find the author seated with some comrades in one of their apartments, taking part in a "circle" (*kruzhok*) led by a revolutionary intellectual or fellow worker, discussing some new experience, debating a new idea, arguing over the meaning of a story or an article, or analyzing the character and personality of a new acquaintance. At some point in his life (exactly when is unclear, though there are hints in the text that it was long before he began to publish these memoirs in the 1920's) it occurred to Kanatchikov that these conversations and experiences, if related in some kind of chronological order, would be of value to posterity. The result is the book before us, the work that temporarily turned a worker into a writer, and that gives us the richest autobiographical account we have of life among the urban lower classes in late Imperial Russia.

Some years ago, in an article entitled "Russian Bebels," I attempted to set forth my own interpretation of the significance of Kanatchikov's life experience from the point of view of the development of the social psychology of the Russian factory worker. I would like to recapitulate my basic line of argument in that article here.

Kanatchikov entered the world as part of a fairly typical peasant family of central Russia, of more or less average means. In the course of the next 25 years there would be many changes, some of them strange and unpredictable, in his life, in his self-image, and in his view of the surrounding world. The kaleidoscope of changing experience with which he presents us may best be grasped by dividing our hero's story into two stages. The first, which begins when Semën (or "Senka") was sixteen, is the story of the village lad's transformation into a city dweller, an urban and urbane youth, a denizen of the modern world of machine technology. Somewhat playfully, we might even refer to this stage as Senka's personal "modernization," the embodiment in microcosm of the process Russian society as a whole was undergoing throughout these years. As a village lad with only the most meager of elementary educations—though even his bare literacy already placed him within the elite sector of peasant society, mak-

ing him more receptive to "modernization" than others—Senka
entered the alien urban environment that was to provide the setting for his metamorphosis into a skilled worker with at least the
outward signs of urban culture.

I choose the words "outward signs" deliberately, for as we observe his painful and often touching attempts to cross the social
frontier that separated urban and rural Russia, we are repeatedly
struck by the circuitousness of his path, the jaggedness of his
course, the bumpy transitions, and, above all, the stubborn way
in which his peasant past accompanied him on his journey as an
unwelcome guest. Although historians of Russian labor have
made some important contributions to scholarship in recent
years by their careful analyses of the Russian worker's changing
place in a continuum of rural-urban or peasant-proletarian existence, they have sometimes failed to distinguish the characteristics of unique historical types who managed to combine peasant
and proletarian, rural and urban features in ways too intricate to
be reduced to finite points on a linear graph of social change. Just
as agrarian Russia's partial transformation into an urban industrial society was a complex process in which traditional and modern elements combined synergistically into a new kind of societal
formation, young Kanatchikov's transformation into an urban
craftsman entailed a complex metamorphosis wherein past and
present gave birth to a new social being whose nature cannot be
grasped simply by measuring the relative weights of its component parts. Indeed, Kanatchikov's memoirs compel us to concep-
tualize new social categories that call into question both the old
regime system of legal estates (gentry, priest, merchant, burgher,
peasant) and the Marxist analytical scheme that Kanatchikov
himself would eventually adopt (capitalist, petty bourgeois, proletarian).

The social type that emerged in the first phase of Kanatchikov's
transformation might be thought of as the new urban dweller
whose consciousness is shaped by the shadows of his rural ancestors, the new factory craftsman whose consciousness is formed
by almost unrelieved struggle with his peasant background.
Whether viewed psychologically as a prolonged identity crisis
based on the inability to resolve his early conflicts with a powerful
and frightening father, or viewed sociologically as a villager's
struggle to adapt to an urban environment for which he is but

poorly prepared by his peasant past—and the two perspectives, as I have tried to show in "Russian Bebels," are quite compatible—Kanatchikov's mental world during his Moscow years (1895–98) suggests a state of perpetual conflict. Almost every challenge of urban life—the acquisition of skills, the mastery of reading, the discovery of fashionable dress and respectable forms of social life, the first hesitant steps into the dangerous world of radical politics—is seen in the light of its power to divest young Senka of his peasant identity and recast him as an urban worker. Similarly, a series of equally powerful challenges from his past—religion, paternal authority, drink, traditional marriage, village holidays—present themselves as almost diabolical temptations to sink comfortably back into the quagmire of what Marx had called "the idiocy of rural life."

In this first phase, to be sure, it is the urban world that triumphs. But the victory, if not exactly Pyrrhic—for Senka's new identity, so painfully won, will never be destroyed—should be seen as only partial. The reader of these memoirs is invited to take account of the moments when our hero feels the need to re-fight old battles, to repossess little pieces of what seemed to be already conquered territory: the atheist's flirtations with religious recidivism, the prodigal son's momentary returns to filial piety, the urban dweller's feeling of warmth when he imagines the lazy pleasures of his village youth, the radical agitator's incapacity to face a crowd of sophisticated intellectuals or his terror at the prospect of putting words to paper. That young Kanatchikov's consciousness remained precariously poised at the social margins of peasant and urban life is all the more striking when we consider that his words were being penned many years after the events described, at a time when the ghosts of his peasant childhood had presumably long since been exorcised. How much more visible must they have been to someone who knew him at the age of eighteen, when his experience was as yet unmediated by time and memory.

In many important respects, Kanatchikov's formative years as an urban worker were typical of those of the first-generation industrial workers who poured into cities like St. Petersburg and Moscow during the great industrial upsurge of the 1890's. Peasant background, movement from factory to factory, struggle to acquire new skills, marginal existence in the interstices of the city's semi-industrial, semirural infrastructure, periodic returns to the countryside on religious holidays and other special occasions—such experiences were common to hundreds of thousands of Kanatchikov's contemporaries. Much less commonplace was the second phase of Kanatchikov's life story: his transformation into what he and his contemporaries liked to call a "conscious" worker, his passage into the much more sparsely populated territory of the revolutionary workers' circle (*kruzhok*) and of the worker-intelligentsia. This too was a marginal area, but one whose open borders were defined not by the substantially differing worlds of the peasant and the worker, but by the even more starkly contrasting worlds of the worker and the radical intelligentsia, the rebellious offspring of Russia's privileged elite.

We begin to observe Kanatchikov assuming some of the characteristics of this new breed of urban worker-intellectual in Moscow, even before his first transitional phase has been completed. This is a worker who takes pride not only in his manual skills—the newly acquired skills that prepare him to believe in his power to refashion himself and recreate his world—but also in his intellectual and verbal prowess, at least when contrasted with that of the average wage earner. He not only knows how to read, he considers the reading of advanced and complex texts one of his most important leisure (i.e., nonworking) activities. But the reading is by no means a private affair; or, more accurately, the reading itself may be private but it is seen as only the first, preparatory step in a prolonged process of interaction with other men (and, very rarely, women) that defines his existence at almost every point of his nonworking life, and sometimes even on the shop floor itself.

Indeed, perhaps the most striking characteristic of this new type of worker is the pleasure he derives from the manipulation of words as he exchanges ideas about the content of his readings with the other members of his circle. He learns to initiate his less "advanced" comrades into the intricacies of complex texts, even texts over which his own mastery may still be shaky. He debates both the finer points and the more basic ideological questions with his peers and even, on occasion, with his social and academic "superiors," his teachers from the privileged strata. Thus a new kind of sociability emerges in tandem with the emergence of a new kind of social group: the sociability of the circle of "conscious" workers. Here the abstract manipulation of symbolic language that normally defines the intellectual is appropriated by the self-educated worker, a mixture of competitive and cooperative intellectual games replaces the easy camaraderie and horseplay of shop-floor sociability, and the sipping of tea in a shabby apartment replaces the rapid downing of tumblers of vodka in the neighborhood tavern. Here even cursing can on occasion make a hardened, veteran worker quite uncomfortable.

Much of this new activity mirrors the culture of the Russian university, which was indeed either its direct source (students serving as tutors and propagandists to the workers) or its source one step removed (workers who had been educated by students replacing them in that instructional role). If in his first transitional phase Kanatchikov struggled to accommodate the peasant village to the urban industrial milieu, in the second, overlapping phase he endeavored to tailor that milieu to the world of the student intelligentsia. As in the first case, Kanatchikov did not alight from his journey at an easily definable point on a social continuum, a continuum ranging in this case from worker to intelligentsia. Instead, he was metamorphosed once again into a new kind of social being: the urban worker whose uneasy consciousness is shaped by the struggle between the urge to emulate the intelligentsia model and the desire to resist assimilation, lest adherence to that model be interpreted as a betrayal of his primary allegiance to the working class he had labored so valiantly to join. Thus we will see the ripened, "conscious" Kanatchikov (sometimes speaking through the less inhibited voice of another character) staking out the conscious worker's territory as his rightful property, defining the areas of overlap and conflict that would allow the conscious worker to share the world of the intelligentsia while continuing to maintain his own honor and integrity. We will sometimes encounter one of these workers ironically referring to another as a "student," but we will never see him using the term to describe himself.

What these memoirs show us, then, is the extreme plasticity of Russian society at the turn of the last century, the difficulty of fitting the life of even a single individual (let alone whole segments

of society) into the mold of a neatly delineated social typology.
The range of Kanatchikov's social experience was much too
broad to allow such simplification. And yet fluidity should not be
equated with arbitrariness, nor should plasticity be mistaken for
infinite possibility. If we look a bit more closely at the range of
symbols and symbolic languages available to Kanatchikov and
the ways in which those languages could be shaped into a relatively organized view of the world, appropriate to his social existence and that of his comrades, it should become apparent that
the building blocks of that cultural system, however imagina-
tively and creatively rearranged, had to be borrowed from the various subcultures (or "local" cultures) he encountered in the
course of his journey. The most important of these subcultures
were the religious world of the peasant community, the secular
world of the citified factory worker, and the political world of the
radical student (or, more succinctly, the village, the city, and the
university). Each of these worlds contained its own set of values,
expressed in its own symbolic actions and imagery.

The values of Kanatchikov's peasant world surface in the de-
scriptions of his visits to his native village of Gusevo and in his
musings—sometimes bitter, sometimes bittersweet—about his
village past. As he presents it to us, it was a fixed world of tradition, routine, and social harmony, albeit a harmony that was
sometimes interrupted by unwelcome intrusions from the outside
world. The unifying elements that bound the community together consisted of the patriarchal family, the solidarity between
relatives, neighbors, fellow villagers, and even peasants from
neighboring villages in the same region (Volokolamsk, in Moscow province). These villagers spoke the same language, shared
the same Orthodox Christian faith (one that left ample room for
pre-Christian household spirits, forest creatures, and water
sprites, as well as for some lighthearted anticlericalism), and pe-
riodically reaffirmed their close bonds by participating in rhythmic cycles of holiday and feast-day festivities and the celebration
of numerous rites of passage centered around birth, death, and
marriage (the latter a condition that Kanatchikov studiously
avoided). It was a powerful enough cultural world to retain much
of its influence over its constituents even when they strayed from
the confines of the village to the alien milieu of the metropolis.
Such traditional institutions as the artel and *zemliachestvo*[+]

helped extend the influence of village ways both temporally and geographically, reinforcing such traditional ritual practices as the keeping of Orthodox dietary laws on fast days and, of course, Sunday church attendance.

And yet the tenacious grip of village culture cannot be understood entirely as the product of institutional coercion. It is the deep impression made on the youthful imagination by village lore, as transmitted through the words and deeds of family members (in Kanatchikov's case, his father above all others) and village authority figures (such as teachers and priests), that stands out in the author's account of his fantasy life as a young urban novice whose view of the world was beginning to come under assault. Young Kanatchikov shared the popular piety of his fellow villagers; he was more than familiar with the Lives of the Saints, well acquainted with the Gospels, and had had ample exposure to Orthodox liturgy; above all, he believed in heaven and, especially, in the eternal torments of hell and the power of the devil. It was only when this last belief, the cornerstone of his cosmology, began to shatter that young Kanatchikov's sense of himself as part of the cultural world of a peasant community slowly unraveled in a series of anguishing and dramatic confrontations.

The new, alien forces that simultaneously challenged the integrity of Kanatchikov's old cultural model and provided him with some of the materials with which to construct a new one were diverse and contradictory. In a sense they began to appear even before young Senka left his village, in the form of his father's countless, exaggerated, and exciting tales of life in St. Petersburg, urban adventure stories that included such exotic fare as encounters with Jewish revolutionaries and attempts on the life of the tsar. Thus Senka's soul had already been gnawed by the worm of curiosity well before his new associates in Moscow began to situate these materials within the structure of a more rationalistic political universe. But once Senka was firmly secured within the walls of the big city, the confused and confusing images conjured up by his father began to multiply exponentially: factories, machines, and tools; taverns, dances, and books; socialists, atheists, and homespun shop-floor philosophers rushed together in a kaleidoscope of shifting impressions, both merging and clashing with the assortment of traditional images he had retained since leaving his village.

All of this chaos had either to be rejected or to be sorted and rearranged into a new cultural pattern, integrated into a revised system of values. If I am right that it was the erosion and eventual crumbling of his religious beliefs that finally severed Senka from his village culture, it should not surprise us that the underpinnings of his new value system would be secular, worldly, irreligious—the more so in that religion was the lever with which his father kept trying to pry him loose from his new temptations, thereby denying him his independence. But the secular, worldly, and irreligious do not necessarily add up to atheism, socialism, and revolution. One of the most appealing features of this book is the author's readiness to share with his readers the temptations he faced at various crossroads in his life to pursue a path other than the one he eventually followed. In this case the tempting path was that of the working-class dandy, the well-dressed (by working-class standards), stylish bon vivant whose abandonment of his village ways took the form not of adopting a new political culture, but of adapting to the preexisting culture of citified petty bourgeois and working-class youth.

What counted in this moderately hedonistic world were clothes, evening entertainments, a slightly dissolute conviviality, a degree of superficial learning, access to young women and other "worldly pleasures," and a modest measure of financial success, based on one's ability to ply a skilled trade. Such young men were as cut off from the village and its ways as their politicized counterparts, but, unlike the latter, they lacked an integrating vision, a coherent, all-embracing worldview or cosmology, however synthetic or syncretic, with which to unite the disparate fragments of their existence. When he was not actually on the job, Senka spent as much of his life in Moscow experiencing and strenuously resisting the temptations of urban dandyism as he did casting off his village cloak. But resist them he did, thanks in part to what proved to be the greater seductive power of the alternative culture he was gradually to adopt.

That alternative was the political culture of the "conscious" revolutionary worker, the cultural world of the Kanatchikov with whom we shall become so familiar in the course of this book. In contrast to the domain of the citified dandy, this was not a world that came to Kanatchikov and his contemporaries ready-made— though antecedents could be pointed to in the previous generation.[5] Instead, it was a culture in the making, in the process of being born, one in which a Kanatchikov could serve simultaneously as beneficiary and midwife. Like the world of the citified dandy, this world gave pride of place to industry, technology, and mastery as the fountainhead of one's dignity and self-esteem, one's ability to create a new identity and abandon one's village past. But this is where the resemblance quickly came to an end. For the "conscious" worker's mastery of industrial skills and the self-isolation from his rural past were integrated into a new, encompassing system of values that could compete with the traditional cosmology of the peasant, place its wavering adherents on firmer ground, and provide them with a central animating vision.

For all its secularized vocabulary and self-description, this new system offered its adherents a millenarian goal that was essentially religious: nothing less than the permanent liberation of the Russian people from the double yoke of autocracy and capitalism. Lest this vision be mistaken for the mere repetition of themes long since echoed by generations of the Russian intelligentsia—from which it clearly drew a great deal of its sustenance—we must take special note of the important role it reserved for the skilled and cultured worker-hero. Though he modeled himself in part on the image of his student tutor, the conscious worker nevertheless retained, and was determined to retain, his identity as a worker, a special kind of worker to be sure, but a worker nonetheless—a *Russian Bebel.*

A meeting of these budding Russian Bebels was a meeting of men who were beginning to assign themselves a special destiny—indeed, a martyr's destiny. They were knights in pursuit of the holy grail of justice, prepared to sacrifice themselves for a higher cause. Their view of society was a highly dramatic or even melodramatic one, replete with villains—heartless capitalists, privileged gentry landowners, cruel police officials, the tsar himself—and revered heroes and heroines of the past and present, including some of the same romanticized revolutionary "nihilists" whom Senka's father had once described in such unflattering but provocative terms. In short, with one important difference, these Russian Bebels were not unlike the university students who provided them with the novels, stories, plays, and poems that they drew upon in order to construct their secular world of saints and sinners.

The critical difference was their determination, as I have already indicated, to retain their identity as workers and to share
the fruits of their self-improvement with the rank and file of less
privileged, less educated workers, even those they sometimes
looked down upon. We see this process at work in Kanatchikov,
but there are moments when we see it even more clearly in his
representations of the ideas and attitudes of some of his comrades. Discrete characters in their own right, they sometimes appear, like the characters in our dreams, as thinly disguised sur-
rogates for the author/dreamer himself. Hence the "conscious"
workers' love-hate relationship with the intelligentsia is most
poignantly displayed whenever Kanatchikov's worker-comrades
reveal their deeply ambivalent attitudes toward that segment of
society that helped them find and organize the materials with
which to construct a new cultural identity.

Seen in this light—seen, that is, from the broader perspective
of the formation of a new subculture within the working class
rather than from the narrower one of the formation of particular
political alignments—it matters little whether such workers
ended up calling themselves Social Democrats (or Marxists), as
Kanatchikov did, or Socialist Revolutionaries, or Anarchists.
These were simply superficial variants of what was becoming a
fairly stable underlying structure. The most durable aspects of
that structure were a worker-centered universe that placed the
skilled, educated, cultivated worker at center stage; the high pre-
mium placed on access to the written word and dexterity in its
verbal exegesis as a visible sign of special selection; delight in the
defiance of constituted authority and the courting of danger; and
some combination of militant atheism (a quasi-religious noncon-
formity such as Tolstoyan nonresistance to evil was also acceptable up to a point) and collectivist goals, combined and welded
into a "socialist" ideology.

There were also numerous institutional settings that emerged
in which characteristics and values such as these could flourish,
the most prominent and permanent being the late-night circle
meeting in a clandestine apartment. Almost as common were
one or more experiences of prison and exile, visits to the homes
and offices of wealthy liberal sympathizers, the frequenting of
radical intelligentsia "salons" (whatever their particular political
orientation), and secret outdoor meetings in protected forest or

island retreats. Apart from the intensive reading and talking already mentioned, concomitant activities included the singing of revolutionary songs (often reworked versions of traditional folk songs and verses), the drinking of tea (spirits were not excluded, but excess could lead to removal from the ranks of the "conscious," both literally and figuratively), and, when the time was ripe, the composition, printing, and dissemination of illegal leaflets in conjunction with protest demonstrations, working-class holidays (especially May Day), or strikes (viewed by the government as criminal acts).

It is true that the radical intelligentsia, the real "students," often joined the workers in these activities, either as participants or in some auxiliary role (such as providing the workers with literature, printing facilities, or assistance in the drafting of the leaflets), but readers of these memoirs are likely to notice the critical role of the workers in these human interactions: except when they were visiting salons or the quarters of liberal sympathizers, the action was always taking place in the workers' own territory, more or less according to their terms, even when those terms were not yet fully defined. And in Kanatchikov's case in particular, whether in St. Petersburg or in exile in Saratov, where his contacts with the intelligentsia grew most intense, readers will surely discern a marked incapacity to become spiritually or emotionally comfortable in the company of even the most friendly representatives of the privileged classes.

In my earlier attempt to interpret Kanatchikov's life history I wrestled briefly (and I believe with only limited success) with the specific problem of explaining his ultimate identification with the Bolshevik wing of the revolutionary movement, that impatient faction of Russian revolutionary Marxism that was least inclined to leave the working class, even the conscious workers, to its own devices and give it space and time to develop without the pressure of the intelligentsia's tutelage.[6] Without recapitulating that particular discussion here, I would simply add that the above attempt to reconstruct the broad outlines of Kanatchikov's unique cultural world as it emerged in the last years of the nineteenth century and the first years of the twentieth renders the question of his Bolshevism even more problematic. For although we know relatively little about the world of Bolshevik committeemen in which he operated in the years immediately subsequent to the end of his

memoirs,[7] it is all but certain that this was a world very far removed from the culture of the workers' circles that he had frequented between the ages of 19 and 25. It was a world, as I have
argued, in which the identity of "professional revolutionary" (the
last two words of Kanatchikov's memoirs) acted as a solvent on
the earlier distinction between intelligentsia and conscious
worker, thereby preparing the ground for yet another political
culture, an underground *party* culture, which included many
workers but is much more difficult to describe as "working-class."
Perhaps for this reason, some of the worker-comrades who frequent Kanatchikov's book failed to follow him into the all-
embracing party that was to become his second home. (Of course
many others did; it is hardly surprising that an author writing in
the USSR some years after the Bolshevik Revolution should have
centered his attention on future Bolsheviks.)

Kanatchikov's memoirs are peopled with a variety of characters
and social types so wide as to defy classification. It is important
as we try to make sense of the broad social and cultural trends
illuminated by his personal story not to lose sight of the dozens
of intermediary characters who inhabited the margins of his
changing world. Not only do these figures enrich our understanding of the texture of Russian social and political life in an
age of flux, they also contribute significantly to our hero's own
development, often serving as the links between Kanatchikov's
narrower world and that of other social types he has not yet encountered. Thus his first experience of antireligious ideas comes
not at the hands of a radical student, but from another worker
(was he a devil in disguise?) whose militant atheism and eclectic
radicalism had already evolved some years earlier. Along with
Senka, we meet such proletarian types as the old, isolated worker
who attacks the status quo with words but never with deeds, the
militant worker who refuses to abandon his religious views, the
Tolstoyan believer in nonresistance to evil, the woman revolutionary who is torn between identification with the working class and
the intelligentsia, the fainthearted worker who folds under pressure and betrays the common cause, the educated worker who is
easily mistaken for a genuine student, the coarse and backward

worker whose presence is an embarrassment to his cultural "superiors." The list is as endless as the author's power to evoke the uniqueness of each of these varied types.

Kanatchikov's evocation of a variety of characters from other, nonproletarian social milieus—the villagers he encounters when exiled to his native region, the students from the privileged classes, the array of government officials, mainly police agents—though informative and valuable, is less successful. A certain homogeneity sets in and the author's powers of observation seem to fade, not because these characters are stereotypical (on the whole they are not), but because, except for a few of the villagers, Kanatchikov's relations with these people lacked the kind of intimacy that facilitates nuanced characterization. Nevertheless, his portraits of the awkward efforts of liberal and radical intellectuals to convey their sympathy to workers with whom they lacked a genuine, personalized rapport are as illuminating as any in the literature, and are surpassed in sensitivity only by his re-creation of the workers' confused reactions to such people and situations. I trust that the reader will find many other fine examples of this kind of social characterization.

To return, then, to my opening assertion, Kanatchikov was a writer, and this memoir, whatever its inconsistencies—possibly a testimony, if any is needed, to its authenticity—stands up as a minor work of literature as well as a major historical source. Most of its characterizations are dense and subtle, and its style, though not elegant, is refreshing in comparison with much of what passes for working-class memoir literature. Though this is certainly no "polyphonic" work—a single authorial voice is dominant throughout—the author does allow other voices to be heard, usually by means of his own imaginative re-creation of their words (presented as both direct and indirect discourse), occasionally by inserting historical documents into the text.

Finally, the work has a definite artistic structure. It is a chronological account of the author's adventures—he is too straight-laced for us to be able to use the modifier "picaresque"—in a wide variety of settings and situations, and of his encounters with diverse characters, each of whom participates in his education, enlightenment, and moral development, whether by negative or positive example. It is, in a sense, a *Bildungsroman*, but one in which the author's respect for authenticity of feeling and description prevents him from presenting the development of his own character too neatly or symmetrically. We not only see his weaknesses, we are almost invited from time to time to take note of the fact that they are not completely overcome. Nevertheless, his development over time is purposeful and is invested by the author with almost teleological meaning. Young Senka emerges from his family hearth as an adolescent in search of an identity. He finds a social identity, but learns that it is unsatisfactory, under the conditions that obtain, unless it is blessed with a higher purpose, unless his "wanderings from factory to factory" are transformed into a heroic Russian "exploit" (*podvig*), more secular than Christian to be sure, but one, in the words of Pierre Pascal, beginning with the "conscientious performance of the simplest duties, developing through asceticism, and culminating in total sacrifice."[8] The vehicle finally chosen for the self-sacrifice by Kanatchikov was complete submergence in the revolutionary movement in its Bolshevik incarnation—his permanent "profession," his priesthood. And yet he also leaves us with the impression of a journey completed, a journey that, if not really circular, was ultimately a disguised return of the prodigal son, when he explains to the reader that, for the politically conscious worker, "a comradely milieu, an organization, and eventually a party become his family home and hearth, and his comrades in struggle take the place of his brothers, sisters, father, and mother." It is sad that the record does not reveal the nature of Kanatchikov's relations with his second family in the last years of his life.

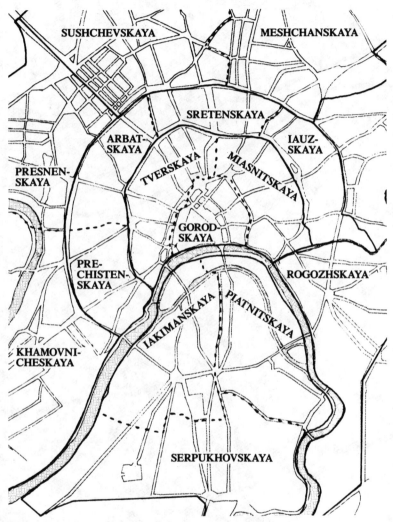

Moscow in the early years of the twentieth century.

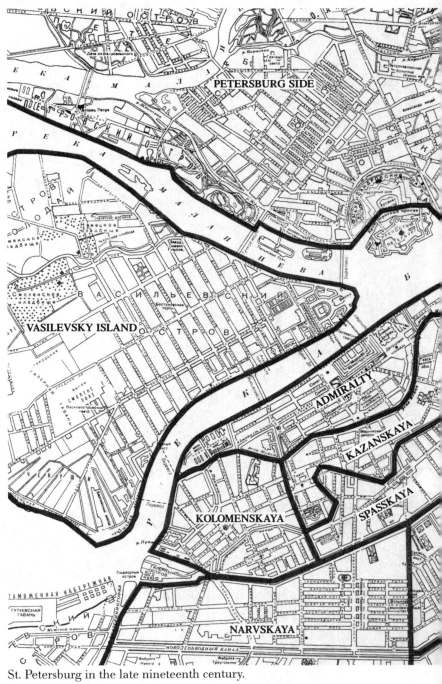

St. Petersburg in the late nineteenth century.

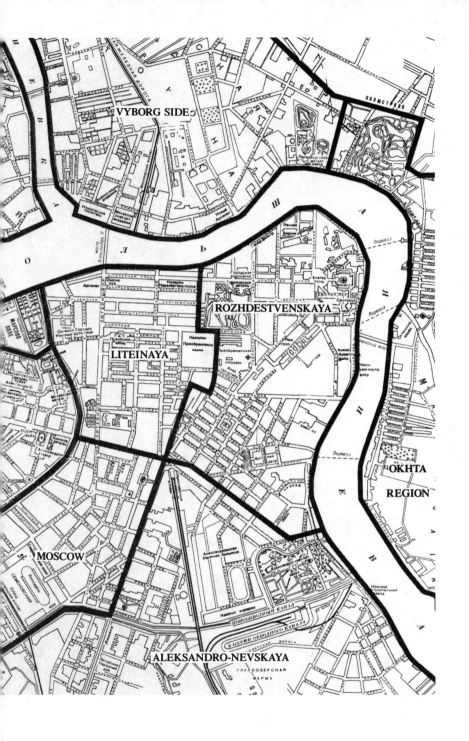

Part One

Moscow

1
My First Years

I WAS BORN in 1879, in the village of Gusevo, in the Voloko-lamsk district of Moscow province.[1] It is the very same district that has recently shifted from an antiquated three-field to a multifield system of crop rotation. As this circumstance suggests, the people of my district have moved along the path of progress more rapidly than their backward neighbors, even in the past. The Volokolamsk district is also remarkable in that, during the period of War Communism, it was the site of our first electric power station, the inauguration of which was attended by Comrade Lenin.[2] And yet the forward march of the people of my district along the path of progress did not stop there. They were also the first to capture the spirit of the policy of NEP; they were quick to liquidate the "vestiges" of War Communism—including the electric power station itself—and were also the first to beget several dozen swindlers in their cooperative organizations, who in turn became the object of the first show trial.[3] Such, then, is the brief but noteworthy history of my region.

My early childhood was not accompanied by any particularly outstanding events, unless one counts the fact that I survived; I wasn't devoured by a pig, I wasn't butted by a cow, I didn't drown in a pool, and I didn't die of some infectious disease the way thousands of peasant children perished in those days, abandoned without any care during the summer harvest season.[4]

For a village child to survive in those times was a rare event. As evidence of this there is at least the fact that my own mother, according to some sources, brought eighteen children into this world—according to others the number was twelve—yet only four of us survived. It is clear from the two figures I have mentioned, even if we take only the second, that I had little choice but to view my presence on earth as a great stroke of fortune.

My father—and this was more than half a century before our era—belonged to the very large stratum of middle peasants.[5] Of course I have no intention whatever of claiming that circumstance as a credit to either my father or me, for we can hardly assume the presence on his part of a carefully thought-out plan to remain a middle peasant all his life. Indeed, to the best of my judgment he had no desire whatever to remain at that rank and he endeavored throughout his life to enter the ranks of the kulaks: he tried to rent land, to engage in trade, and so on. But because he lacked the kulak's tightfisted grasp, because he was a simple peasant, honest and just to the core, he was always defeated in his kulak efforts.

My father's past, to the extent that I can picture it in my own mind on the basis of separate, fragmentary memories, looked something like this. During the days of serfdom, when still a young boy, he was sent to St. Petersburg to work as a servant.[6] He was employed in various big hotels as a bellboy, a room-servant, a billiard-room assistant, and so on. He taught himself to read and write; he was very good at reading aloud but he wrote very poorly. Most of his life was passed "in freedom," that is, away from his home. Nevertheless, he was attached in various ways to his peasant household. He often sent money back to his village, money that he tore away from his scanty earnings; whenever he had the opportunity, he would try to go back to his village or would send for his mother to come visit him in the city. Around the age of 50, having completely ruined his health, he moved back to the village for good. He loved the land and he tried to implant that love in me. "Stick to the land, my son—the land is our provider with water and food," he would often repeat to me. Yet he was not capable of doing peasant work himself; in addition, he was short-winded and couldn't engage in hard work.

Our peasant household was actually managed by my older brother, who already had his own family. During the winter, when the field work was over, he too went off to a factory to earn money.

Our family consisted of nine or ten souls. There was no way we could live off the land alone, for our allotments were very paltry and the winter earnings of my older brother were inadequate. My father tried to sow more flax and to get into commerce, but, as I said earlier, nothing came of these efforts: the land was exhausted, the price of flax was falling, and the commercial endeavor was shattered. In this way he continued to struggle, year in and year out, barely able to make ends meet.

When I was nine they sent me off to attend school in the nearest large village.[7] During the winter, every day they would take us children there by sled, one at a time. For our generation the methods of school instruction in those days were very uncomplicated: the ruler, the birch rod, the teacher's belt, and the simple slap in the face. To be sure, there were also some more humane teachers at our school, teachers to whom the methods of modern pedagogy were not alien; these were the ones who would take us by the nose and put us in a corner on our knees or would make us go without lunch. In our school these teachers were replaced rather often. And, depending on the individual inclinations of the particular pedagogue, their methods of instruction changed as well. We looked upon all these methods as the unavoidable components of pedagogy, recalling the dictum: "Better one man who's been schooled than two who have not been."[8]

Many amusing but at the same time unpleasant moments were provided to us by our religion instructor—an enormous, broad-shouldered, long-haired priest from the neighboring village, who was distinguished by his ferocity toward us and by his great love of horses. His lessons took place after lunch on Fridays, when he usually returned from the open-air market where he liked to wheel and deal; on his return trip he would stop at our school. A bit tight, speaking inarticulately, he would ask us to say the prayers and make us read the Gospels in Church Slavonic and translate them into Russian.[9] After the lesson, which was always accompanied by a large number of thrashings, he would test our "knowledge" by asking his own rather peculiar kind of questions. They were distinguished by their extremely unpredictable quality, such as, for example, how many hands were on the icon called the "three-handed" Holy Mother of God,[10] or, perhaps, does a calf have a soul? Two or three incorrect answers from the same pupil would again produce a thrashing. When the "lesson" was over, our religion instructor would get into his wagon, which was harnessed to a great bay stallion, and drive off madly to his own village until the following Friday.

Yet despite all this, my studies went rather well, which gave my father great pleasure. Often when I came home from school I would read to him aloud, on a long winter's evening, selections from *The Native Word*[11] or else recount from memory some of the entertaining stories from the Old Testament. He would caress my hair, praise me, and in his turn tell me stories of his life in St. Petersburg.

I can still remember individual episodes from those stories, such as how the former artisan-hatter Komissarov, Alexander II's "savior," who, during the attempt on the tsar's life, while standing behind the "nahilist" Karakozov, had jolted the hand with which Karakozov was aiming his revolver at the tsar—how this same Komissarov had stayed at the hotel where my father worked. Alexander II had generously rewarded Komissarov and granted him noble status.[12]

My father also told me stories about the execution of the "Jewess" Perovskaya and the "nahilist" Zheliabov.[13] When I asked him why they were executed, Father replied:

"They wanted to kill the tsar."

"But who were these nahilists?"

"Landowners and students, and they killed the Tsar-liberator because he'd given freedom to the peasants. They are all 'Freemazons,'" he added, "they believe in neither God nor tsar."[14]

Just what these "Freemazons" were, Father himself could not explain with any clarity. From time to time he used the word "pedagogues," which he was also unable to explain. Somehow he thought that this word too meant something akin to atheist and "nahilist."

At the age of thirteen I finished elementary school.[15] My father was now faced with the question of what to do with me next. He lacked the resources to continue my education, and in any case my own heart wasn't in my studies. Nor did Father wish to "set me free" in the city of Moscow where, without paternal supervision, he feared I might cut myself off from our homestead and be corrupted. His real dream was to keep me in the village, to make me into a good peasant. But our peasant farmstead, with its small allotments of land, held no promise for the future. And so two years went by without any resolution of this problem. During that time I grew accustomed to peasant work: I tilled the soil, I harrowed, mowed, and threshed, and in the winter I went to the forest to gather wood.

My father was strict in disposition and despotic in character.

He kept the entire family in mortal fright. We all feared him and did everything we could to please him.

There were times when he would "go on a binge," and when he was on a binge—as they'd say in our village—"he locks the gate." During his drinking bouts Father usually spent his time away from home, in the circle of his drinking companions and hangers-on. At such times he would become kind, merry, generous, and extravagant. Not infrequently he would drink to the point where he was seriously ill, and there were even occasions when he was close to death.

When his binges were over and he'd begun to recover, Father would become gloomy, morose, and demanding. A heavy silence reigned over our home, and everyone would tremble. To compensate for the money he'd squandered on drink, Father would introduce a regimen of economizing and would reduce the family's expenditures: instead of drinking tea twice a day, we'd drink it only once; Mother would stop baking pies and cakes on holidays, and so on.

But the biggest burden at times like this fell upon my unfortunate mother; my father was her deathblow. I loved my mother intensely and hated my father with an animal hate: I would become rude to him, insolent and disrespectful. I passionately took my mother's part and prevented him from beating her. This kind of interference usually ended with Father beating me up as well, unless I managed to dodge his blows in time and run away.

My older brother stood aside from these family tragedies and refused to get involved. Father disliked him very much and any attempt on his part to intervene might easily have led Father to cut him off.

In spite of all these defects, however, my father did have some positive features in his character. He was a religious believer, but he wasn't superstitious. He did not believe in demons, household spirits, or magic spells, he made fun of village wise women and healers, and he didn't like priests. He read many different books and once he even took out a subscription to a cheap newspaper. Observing him when, his iron eyeglasses atop his nose, he sat for days on end fixated on some book, I too developed a passion for reading. I would steal some money from my father and some eggs from my mother and purchase some popular illustrated books in the neighboring village.[16]

When I reached the age of fourteen, a terrible misfortune beset me—my mother took ill with an inflammation of the lungs and died. Before she died we summoned a priest to her, gathered around her, and administered the last sacrament; then she quietly passed away.

For whole nights through, holding a waxen candle over the corpse of my deeply beloved mother, I read aloud from the Psalter, hoping to help her to migrate to the "heavenly kingdom." According to the popular belief of those times, you had to read the entire Psalter forty times over in order to achieve this goal. Great were my bitterness and suffering when, at the twenty-eighth reading of the Psalter, exhausted, worn out by the sleepless nights, I began to fall asleep and stopped reading.

My life in the village was becoming unbearable. I wanted to rid myself of the monotony of village life as quickly as possible, to free myself from my father's despotism and tutelage, to begin to live a self-reliant, independent life. It was not long before the opportunity presented itself, and Father, after long arguments and discussions, decided to let me go to Moscow. My joy and delight were boundless!

My departure was invested with a certain solemnity. In the morning Father gathered the entire family in the cottage and lit the icon lamps in front of the images of the saints. Everyone sat on the benches in solemn silence and waited. Then Father arose and began to pray to the icon. The entire family followed his example. When the prayer was over, Father addressed me with his parting words, once more reminding me not to forget God, to honor my superiors, to serve my employer honestly, and, above all else, to be mindful of our home.

In the spring of 1895, when I was sixteen years old, Father drove me to Moscow where he placed me into apprenticeship at the "Gustav List" engineering works.[17] Since there was no place in the pattern shop, I began in the painting shop.

2
In the "Artel"

I REMEMBER what a stunning impression Moscow made on
me.[1] My father and I, sitting in our cart, walked our gray
horse along the brightly lighted streets. Huge multistoried
houses—most of them with lighted windows—stores, shops,
taverns, beer halls, horse-drawn carriages going by, a horse-
drawn tramway—and all around us crowds of bustling people,
rushing to unknown destinations for unknown reasons. I was not
even able to read the signboards. What struck me most was the
abundance of stores and shops: for every house, there was one
store after another.

"Who buys all these goods?" I asked my father. "Why, there are
more stores here than there are people!"

"Mother Moscow, she feeds all of Russia. Our tradesmen also
come here for merchandise," Father responded, coughing and
moaning from shortness of breath.

Compared with our village hovels, what struck me about the
houses of Moscow was their grandiose appearance, their luxury.

"Am I to live in a house like that?" I asked with delight.

"You'll find out in due course."

And sure enough our gray horse soon turned into a side street,
and the wagon entered the gates of a huge stone house with a
courtyard that looked like a large stone well. Wet linens dangled
from taut clotheslines all along the upper stories. The courtyard
had an acrid stench of carbolic acid.[2] Throughout the courtyard
were dirty puddles of water and discarded vegetables. In the
apartments and all around the courtyard people were crowding,
making noise, yelling, cursing.

My delight was beginning to turn into depression, into some
kind of inexplicable terror before the grandiose appearance and
cold indifference of my surroundings. I felt like a small insignif-

icant grain of sand, lost in the unfamiliar and hostile sea of people that surrounded me.

On the evening of the same day, my father and I, together with our countryman Korovin, who had arranged my job at the factory,[3] went to a tavern. Father ordered tea for three, with rolls and a pint of vodka.

Korovin — tall, round-shouldered, sporting a goatee, in a faded, knitted jacket worn over his shirt — adopted the strict, preceptorial attitude of a teacher with me. But when the pint had taken effect, he began to brag about his closeness to the foreman, his knowledge of his craft, his high wage, and his plan to build a two-story house in the village.

Father sat quietly, nodding his head in approval, occasionally offering advice on the building of the house. At the end of the evening Father asked Korovin to treat me strictly, to keep me from consorting and getting into mischief with the wrong kind of people. And he again admonished me to be obedient to my bosses and superiors and have faith in God.

On the following day, early in the morning, Father departed for the village, and I remained alone. Two feelings were struggling in my soul. I longed for the village, for the meadows, the brook, the bright country sun, the free clear air of the fields, and for the people who were near and dear to me. Here, in the hostile world of Moscow, I felt lonely, abandoned, needed by no one. While at work in the painting shop to which I'd been temporarily assigned, and which smelled of paint and turpentine, I would remember pictures of our village life, tears would come to my eyes, and it was only with great effort that I could keep from crying. But there was another, more powerful feeling that provided me with courage and steadfastness: my awareness of my independence, my longing to make contact with people, to become independent and proud, to live in accordance with my own wishes, and not by the caprice and will of my father.

Awkward, sluggish, with long hair that had been cut under a round bowl,[4] wearing heavy boots with horseshoes, I was a typical village youth. The skilled workers looked down on me with scorn, pinched me by the ear, pulled me by the hair, called me a "green country bumpkin" and other insulting names.

Our workday at the factory lasted eleven and a half hours, plus a one-and-a-half-hour lunch break. In the beginning I would grow terribly tired so that as soon as I got home from work and ate dinner, I would fall into my filthy, hard, straw-filled sack and sleep like a dead man, despite the myriad bedbugs and fleas.

I roomed and boarded not far from the factory, in a large, smelly house inhabited by all kinds of poor folk—peddlers, cabmen, casual laborers, and the like. We rented the apartment communally, as an artel of about fifteen men. Some were bachelors, others had wives who lived in the village and ran their households. I was put in a tiny, dark, windowless corner room; it was dirty and stuffy, with many bedbugs and fleas and the strong stench of "humanity." The room contained two wooden cots. One belonged to Korovin, my countryman and guardian; the other I shared with Korovin's son Vanka,[5] who was also an apprentice and worked in the factory's pattern shop.

Our food and the woman who prepared it were also paid for communally. The food was purchased on credit at a shop; our individual shares were assessed twice monthly. Every day at noon, as soon as the factory's lunch bell rang, we would hurry back to the apartment and sit down at the table, where a huge basin full of cabbage soup was already steaming.

All fifteen men ate from a common bowl with wooden spoons. The cabbage soup contained little pieces of meat. First, they would ladle out only the soup; then, when the soup was almost all gone, everyone tensely awaited a signal. A moment later someone would bang his spoon against the edge of the soup basin and say the words we were waiting for: "Dig in!" Then began the furious hunt of the spoons for the floating morsels of meat. The more dexterous would come up with the most.

Avdotya, the cook, her sleeves tucked up and the hem of her calico-print dress pulled back, would look steadfastly at the bottom of the soup basin, saying:

"Is there anything left, fellows, to dig out of there?"

"Go ahead, Duniakha,[6] dig away!" several voices would sing out in unison.

Avdotya would carry the basin to the oven, refill it with cabbage soup, and return it to the table. After the soup came either buckwheat gruel with lard or fried potatoes. Everyone was hungry as a wolf; they ate quickly, greedily.

After lunch everyone—except the youngsters—would throw himself on a cot to rest without removing his boots or workshirt.

Twice a week—on Wednesday and Friday—Avdotya would prepare the fast-day food: cabbage soup with a fishhead and gruel with vegetable oil.[7]

Twice a month, on the Saturday paydays,[8] our artel indulged in wild carousing. Some, as soon as they had collected their pay, would go directly from the factory to beer halls, taverns, or to some grassy spot, whereas others—the somewhat more dandified types—first went back to the apartment to change clothes.

Somber, cross, often bruised, and in some cases still in a state of undiluted intoxication, the inhabitants of our artel would return home late at night or on Sunday morning.

Korovin was a passionate fisherman; therefore every Saturday he would wind up the line on his fishing rod while Vanka and I prepared his worms, which we gathered at night from other people's gardens at the risk of our lives. Then off he'd go to fish all night in the Moscow River.

Korovin usually returned from his fishing on Sunday morning. Sometimes he brought back two or three grunters or shiners, and usually he came back with nothing at all, but he unfailingly came back smelling of vodka. His goatee would be disheveled, his face inflamed, sweaty, his thinning hair stuck to his forehead.

On Monday he would still be out of sorts—cross, somber, and ill-tempered. Although he normally had little interest in the condition of our intellects, at moments like this he would summon Vanka and me and begin to recite his moral-pedagogical teachings.

"Where did you little pigs go yesterday?" he would begin in a severe voice.

If our conduct had stayed within the confines of our prescribed program we responded truthfully, but if we had gone beyond it we would lie.

"Did you go to mass?"

"We went to the Cathedral of St. Basil the Blessed, and for the early morning service we went to 'St. Nicholas on the Drops.'"[9]

"You probably fooled around more than you prayed, and ogled the girls."

"By the word of God, papa, we stayed through the entire service," Vanka swore.

"And which deacon held the service?" Korovin continued to interrogate us suspiciously.

"The same one again—the big one, with curly hair and a red beard and a bass voice."

Korovin knew the Moscow deacons backwards and forwards. It was hard to fool him.

"Did you see Stogov?"

"No, we didn't."

"Don't you dare get involved with that awful Stogov when I'm not around. He'll take you to the Khitrovka." [10]

This was virtually the entire range of Korovin's moral instruction. After a final threat to "pull our hair," he let us go in peace.

Ivan Stogov, the man whom Korovin had cautioned us to avoid, was a copper smelter by trade and a close relative of Korovin's. I remember his appearance. He was blond, with his hair in a brush cut, of average height, with a worn, emaciated face and gray, thoughtful eyes. At the time I saw him he was about 25 years old. He worked for the so-called "graters" (the owners of tiny workshops operating on subcontract),[11] and often changed employers. As a craftsman he was unusually talented. Even Korovin acknowledged this, saying: "His hands are golden, but his mouth is foul."

He suffered from heavy drinking and during such periods would disappear, no one knew where. People would encounter him at the Khitrov market, in all-night teahouses, in flophouses. From time to time he would be sent back to his home village under police escort.[12] Stogov lived in our artel and paid two and a half rubles a month for his cot, but he rarely showed up. He only appeared at those times when, having spent everything he had on drink, he would divest himself of all his possessions— there was nothing to sell or to hock, and as everyone knows, when he's out of money even a good drunkard gives up drinking. Then he would suddenly show up in our apartment.

At such moments his appearance would be picturesque. Rags of some indescribable color would hang from his body; on his feet were something resembling old worn-out footwear or the high shoes worn by women, trodden down at the heels, with rubbers. Agitated and sullen, he would silently sit down on his cot and remain there for hours without moving. The compassionate Avdotya would serve him some soup with a hunk of bread and tenderly try to scold him.

"Stop it, Avdotya, I already know that I'm a toothless beast.[13] I feel lousy enough without your scolding."

A week would go by, then another. Then Stogov would again get work from some "grater" and would toil like a devil until late at night, sometimes even all night through. Soon he was able to reassemble, piece by piece, the components of his wardrobe, until he again resembled a human being.

He was a good comrade: hearty, sympathetic, always ready to assist a comrade who was in trouble. He disliked Korovin and made no effort to hide this. "The skinflint, the big shot—he'd sell his own father. He is so sanctimonious, but all he really thinks about is how to fleece people, and send them back to their village." That is how he spoke about Korovin.

Merry, witty, and a good storyteller, Stogov possessed an amazing memory and had an inexhaustible supply of tales, jokes, adages, and anecdotes. He was the spirit and the favorite of our artel, though it's true that the older men, whom he often abused, were not very fond of him.

Sometimes our young men would sit at the table after dinner on a rainy day or a winter evening prior to payday, when going to a tavern was pointless, and say with a grin:

"Hey there, Stogov, tell us one of your holy stories, a funny one."

"I've forgotten them all. Nothing comes to mind," Stogov would answer, playing hard to get.

"Try to remember!"

"Don't play hard to get, this ain't your mother-in-law's," could be heard from all sides.

"Well, all right," Stogov would agree, "Now listen to me. Only if I start babbling at some point, don't interrupt!

"Once upon a time, in a certain kingdom some two hundred miles from the place where we fools live, there dwelt a priest. And this priest had a worker. The worker was lazy, and desired nothing more than to eat heartily and sleep. One day it happened that the priest sent him off to plow a distant field. 'But Father,' says he to the priest, with good reason, 'our field is far away and time is precious. Let me first eat lunch so that I need not return home for that purpose.' The priest agreed, thinking: 'A diligent worker indeed!' Right after lunch, the worker again says to the priest: 'Father, now let me eat my supper, so that I need not return home for that purpose and lose the precious time.' The priest thought and thought and once again agreed. Then, after he had supped, the worker made his bed and lay down to sleep. Seeing this, the priest was puzzled: 'Ivan,' says he, 'why don't you go plow the field?' 'Who me, Father?' says the worker, 'Work after supper? Why, everyone goes to bed after supper!'"

A burst of laughter resounds, followed by comments: "He sure put one over on him!"

In the wintertime, when the Moscow River was frozen, we would go to the wall of the dike and have fistfights with workers from the Butikov factory.[14] In the evening we would return home with our black eyes and our broken bloody noses.

But we also had our "cultural" amusements. The artel subscribed to the boulevard newspaper *Moscow Sheet*, in which what interested us the most were the chronicle of criminal cases and the "feuilletons." At that time the paper was running a long, serialized novel called *Bogdan Khmelnitsky*, in which the entire artel became engrossed.[15]

On Sundays we sometimes went to look at the pictures at the Tretiakov Gallery and the Rumiantsev Museum.[16]

In addition, we never missed a Moscow fire, and no matter how tired, we would run at breakneck speed to see these free spectacles.

Once a year, on a winter Sunday, my employer would organize a public prayer meeting at the factory. In the enormous machine shop, a large rostrum was erected which was ascended by all the authorities of the factory: the owner, the director, the chief engineer, the foremen of the various shops, and the clergymen in their gilded sacerdotal holiday robes. Through the dense crowd of workers, the older workers elbowed their way forward and took their places at the tribune, under the eyes of the authorities. They crossed themselves with fervor, kneeled, and bowed down to the ground, especially when the priest prayed for the long life of the factory owner. When the prayers were over, the priest delivered an emotional, moralizing sermon about a negligent slave and a zealous lord. Then we came up to the priest and kissed the cross.

3
In the Pattern Shop

A<small>FTER</small> <small>WORKING</small> for a month in the painting shop, I was transferred to the pattern shop where I was placed under the authority of an unskilled worker named Nikifor. My duties for two or three months were to prepare the glue, paint the pattern models, run to the storehouse for nails, help Nikifor sweep up the shop, and "pay attention" to how the job of patternmaking was carried out.[1]

To learn to do the work properly one had to come to the shop an hour prior to the onset of work, both during lunch break and in the morning. After convincing one of the pattern-makers to let us use his tools and workbench until he arrived at work, we apprentices endeavored with all our might and main to use that short period of time to teach ourselves the skill.

The tools that were placed at our disposal were usually the worst ones: a worn-out, shabby smoothing plane; a paring chisel that had been stitched to its handle; the kind of stump of a round chisel that most pattern-makers themselves would no longer use.

Most of the time the pattern-maker who trained us would use us for various kinds of auxiliary work — at the command of our "teacher," we would carry battens or wooden boards from the drier, cut them up into square beams or segments of various sizes, help him to plane them on the planing machine, joint the edges of the boards and glue them together at the widths indicated by the pattern-maker, and so on.

Depending on the particular character of the instructor, any mistake, oversight, or damage we made in our work usually resulted in a slap in the face, a thrashing, a smack on the back of the head, and—this only rarely—a curse that mentioned our parents.

In those days there were no safety devices, air holes, or fans placed on the machines, since workers were cheap to come by whereas safety devices were all expensive. In the workshop there was usually a thick cloud of dust next to the machinery, and many a worker went around with pink stumps in the place of his missing fingers.

One hour after the beginning of work there was always a fifteen-minute break for breakfast. Nikifor, the unskilled workman, would carry in an enormous piping-hot teakettle made of tin and place it on a workbench, whereupon the pattern-makers would step up to it and pour into their tin and earthenware mugs the hot brown liquid smelling of tin and wisps of leaves that was known as tea.

Before breakfast some of the pattern-makers would send me to an adjoining booth to fetch some Advent pastries. These pastries were inexpensive, but very few workers ate them. Some simply earned too little money, whereas others were saving their money for the village. Nikifor and I belonged to the first category. Together we drank our tea with heavily salted black bread while we gazed with envy at the lucky ones as they greedily devoured their warm, fragrant Advent cakes.

Nikifor treated me in a comradely fashion—he would always joke with me or tell me things about himself, and when he noticed that I was beginning to pine for the village, he would cheer me up.

Nikifor had once been a fine wood engraver; he had worked in the best furniture workshops, but after repeatedly straining his eyes in bad light, he began to lose his vision. He was compelled to abandon engraving and to look for some other kind of work, something not requiring good eyesight. Subsequently, he worked as a sweeper, as a janitor, and as the watchman at a cemetery (or, as he liked to put it, watchman over the closed-eyed ones, i.e., the dead), until finally he got a job as an unskilled laborer at the List factory, for 60 kopecks a day. With a family to support, his life wasn't easy, but he never lost heart.

On the Mondays following payday, when half the workers in our shop were hung over with splitting headaches,[2] Nikifor

would become everyone's idol. Early in the morning a pilgrimage to him would begin. With a swollen red face, with glazed
eyes, one of the "sufferers" would usually come up to him and
ask mysteriously in a drunken bass:

"Well, Nikisha, have you brewed the tea?"

"No, not yet. I'll go to the storeroom in a little while and get
a nice fresh pot."

"Great, old boy, but make it quick, I can't endure it much
longer, my head is splitting so!"

Nikifor would make a compassionate face, shake his head
sympathetically, and say consolingly:

"All right, all right, just show a little patience and your thirst
will grow."

The sufferer would walk off with hope. After him Nikifor
would have several more visitors, with wistful, imploring eyes,
asking him to hurry with the "teapot."

After they went away, Nikifor would reach behind the boards
under a workbench, pull out a tin can filled with an alcohol-
based varnish, which had been prepared on Saturday for painting the models, drop a certain amount of salt into it, shake it,
and return it to its secluded spot.[3]

"In the morning these damn bastards sure make it hard for
you! Just let them get drunk before lunch and the foreman will
catch the scent and ask where they got the drink," Nikifor would
grumble.

After lunch half the shop would be drunk. Some would loaf
on other people's workbenches; others would sit it out in the
lavatory. Those whose morning-after drinking had gone too far
went to sleep in the drying room or in the shop shed.

On such days the lavatory would be transformed into a loud
and lively "club." The latest gossip about all kinds of happenings
was shared there, people quarreled, insulted each other, or
played tricks on someone. The unelected president of the "club"
was almost always its most frequent visitor, the driller Ivan—a
prankster, boisterous and foul-mouthed. The object of his banter
was usually another driller—a Turk named Egor, a huge black-
bearded, good-natured man. At the time of the Russo-Turkish
War,[4] Egor had been taken prisoner. Then he fell in love with a
Russian cleaning woman, converted to Christianity, married her,
and remained in Russia for good.

"Hey there, old buddy," Ivan would say when he saw him, "How come you gave up Mohammed for a woman?"

Egor would smile good-naturedly and calmly sit down on a free place, without reacting at all to Ivan's jokes.

"Well, you played the fool, my friend!" Ivan would continue, encouraged by the friendly laughter of the others. "You could have had seven wives—boom, boom, bang, bang!—and made love to whichever one you wished. You could even have bathed with all of them at once—boom, bang, boom!"

Ivan's erotic fantasy could create the most unusual possibilities in this area.

"But now you're stuck for the rest of your life with one cleaning woman. I could go for the Moslem faith myself," Ivan would resume his banter after a short pause. "Even their paradise is better than ours. With us, even if you make it to heaven there's no reason to rejoice: you can't smoke there, you can't drink or enjoy a bit of cheap tobacco—and you'll be kept for all eternity on a Lenten diet! And how is it in the Moslem paradise? There the heavenly powers take you to a cool spot, give you 77 pretty girls, and you enjoy yourself to your heart's content!"

"But maybe according to their law you're not allowed to touch the girls?" someone would interject in a serious tone.

"They give you the girls to sooth your soul," Ivan would explain with just as much seriousness. "And why put them there at all if they can't be touched?"

Conversations like this could have gone on endlessly but for the fact that from time to time someone from the factory administration would take a look into the "club." Then everyone would make a rapid exit.

After I had been at the factory about four months, Bogdan Ivanovich, a German foreman, summoned me to the office and said: "Simon, your painting has been satisfactory. Go now to joiner's bench. You soon get used to work."[5]

I thanked the foreman, and, pleased and delighted, I went to Nikifor to share my happiness.

"Well, Semën, that means you've risen in the world. You'll be a pattern-maker—remember me, a poor sinner," Nikifor said half jokingly, as he accompanied me to the workbench. "Let's have a drink to your new wages."

My wage had been 25 kopecks a day, but now it was going up

to 40 kopecks. My spirits were rising. I liked the work in the pattern shop, which had a great attraction for me.

In those days pattern-makers still worked with their own tools. A good pattern-maker, when he started work at a new factory, was expected to bring a case of tools along, and some factories even required that he have his own workbench. My first act was to begin to fashion myself a jointing plane and a chisel out of strong beechwood. At first my tools were not completely satisfactory, but they were good enough to use. My hands were still poorly trained; they lacked the dexterity and strength to cut hardwood with care and precision.

I also learned how to use a turning lathe. This work absorbed me greatly since I soon learned to carve all kinds of wooden knickknacks—wineglasses, little tumblers, eggs, pencil cases, and so on. True, sometimes my excessive love for knickknacks cost me a whack across the head from the foreman, but that didn't bother me very much.[6]

During the fall and winter seasons, when the factory received many orders, we were often made to do overtime work, in the evening or at night. After a workday of eleven hours, it was sheer torture to stay for overtime work. But we were obliged to do so, for refusal of overtime work meant immediate dismissal. Those pattern-makers who were physically stronger endured it with relative ease and were able to keep working without leaving their benches. But the majority of the pattern-makers would work without any spirit: they gazed longingly at the booth where the foreman—bent over the drawings with an air of self-importance—was sitting, and awaited his departure impatiently.

No sooner would the foreman abandon his booth than the news would instantly be flying about the entire workshop. Everyone would react in his own way. Some would sit down comfortably on boards or wooden blocks near their workbenches and begin to talk quietly about this or that subject or listen to some entertaining story. Others would gather in some secluded spot and almost always begin to sing a slow and mournful song, at first very softly, but then as the little group grew larger, the singing grew louder and stronger, until the song began to resound powerfully and reverberate against the windows and the doors. At this point someone who had heard us from the courtyard or another workshop would come to warn us to be more cautious, but then, carried away by the mood, he would begin to join quietly in the song and settle in more comfortably.

They sang about "Vanka the Steward," who, for his love for a young princess, was ordered by the fierce prince to be hanged from a "silken sash"[7]; they sang of the ill-starred fate of the poor man; but most of all they sang of the dashing brigands, the "valiant, wonderful fellows," daring and bold, who made merry in the forests and plundered by night.[8]

These tired people, worn out by hard labor and by their dull, dark lives, used their slow, mournful songs to lament their bitter fate and to express their envy of the incorrigible firebrands, the dashing brigands, who roamed the green forests in freedom.

After loitering in this manner until close to midnight, many of the workers could hold out no longer and went off to sleep in some secluded spot. It was my responsibility to find and awaken each one of them on time.

But there were times when it happened like this: tired to the point of complete exhaustion, I too would collapse and fall asleep somewhere under a workbench. And when that happened I was sure to be in for a rude and terrible awakening! It would have been better not to wake up at all!

After a year's experience at the workbench, I already knew how to draw and could design a pattern if it wasn't very complex. My confidence in my own powers was growing stronger. But at the same time, my faith in my old principles was declining. I was becoming bolder and more definite in my opinions. The authority of my "elders" was beginning to lose its effect on me. I already had a critical attitude toward everyday, conventional morality.[9]

Because I had not been accustomed to abstract modes of thinking, there was a long period of time when I was unable to establish a genuine connection between the schematic lines of a technical drawing and the concrete model that was to result. I was unable even to approximate in my mind the future appearance of the model that was traced in complex lines, entangled like a cobweb, on the large, glossy drawing.

For a long time you scrutinize the diagram, which you had spread out on the workbench, while you lean your elbows on it. You examine it in longitudinal section and in lateral section. After looking at it for a while, you begin to sketch the pattern

in its natural dimensions on a large wooden board. At this point
things become clearer in your mind—your mental image of the
completed model, of its different parts, begins to take on specific
contours.

I am seized by a proud and joyful feeling of satisfaction from
my awareness of having overcome these obstacles independently.
Cheerfully and confidently I begin to prepare the blank of the
model, to saw, to plane, to turn on the lathe, to cut with a chisel
along the thin penciled lines. I place both halves of the model
on the pattern dowels in such a way that the center fits in the
middle, so that when the molding is taking place each half of
the model will emerge from the ground freely and easily, without
breaking the mold. Sometimes I go to the foundry to watch how
they cast the model and to consult with an experienced foun-
dryman about the best way to strengthen a tag or some other
piece of the model in order to remove it from the ground more
easily. Using a large and then a small piece of glass cloth, you
polish the finished model until it shines brightly, as if it were
your beloved child; you caress it tenderly with your hand, measure it carefully one more time with a caliper, and begin to paint
it with a strong-smelling varnish mixed with red lead. Then,
when the varnish has dried, you look at it, admire it one more
time, and proudly carry the product of your labor and creative
efforts to the foreman's booth.

These, then, were the feelings and experiences that bright-
ened up my gray, gloomy existence—and that of others like
me—under conditions of capitalist oppression and immeasurable exploitation.

To be sure, my "creativity" and "inspiration" did not always
mean that things worked out so smoothly and ended in such
lyrical, harmonious "chords." There were occasions, especially
frequent during my "conscious" period,[10] when the foreman
would simply look for trouble in my work or else would find
some real defects and exaggerate their significance. And at such
moments it was no longer the sounds of "lyrical chords" that
filled my soul, it was the seething hell of hatred and anger toward the foreman, the owner, the heartless machine, and even
toward the work itself.

The pattern shop was considered to be the "aristocratic" workshop. Most of the pattern-makers were urban types—they

dressed neatly, wore their trousers over their boots, wore their shirts "fantasia" style, tucked into their trousers, fastened their collars with a colored lace instead of a necktie, and on holidays some of them even wore bowler hats. They cut their hair "in the Polish style" or brush-cut. Their bearing was firm, conveying their consciousness of their own worth. They used foul language only when they lost their tempers and in extreme situations, or on paydays, when they got drunk, and not even all of them at that.

It is hard to understand why it was that the pattern-makers gained such an "aristocratic" reputation. True, our work was mentally challenging, and literacy was an absolute requirement, but pattern-makers earned much less than, for example, smelters or metalturners. The basic contingent of pattern-makers almost never changed: they had been working at the List factory for ten, fifteen, and even twenty years. Most of them were family men and were related to various petty bourgeois strata. Some of them had put away savings "for a rainy day."

In general, our lives were peaceful and harmonious, a small paradise. Only one thing was wrong: our workday was too long—eleven and a half hours. But even that problem was soon removed without a struggle. After the St. Petersburg weavers' strike of 1896, our sagacious employer, Gustav Ivanovich List, immediately introduced the ten-hour day at his factory.[11] After that our group of skilled workers began to live as well as could be.

How we experienced those events will be discussed later.

Among the pattern-makers there was one group whose appearance set them off from the rest—the pattern-maker peasants, whose ties with the village were still strong. They wore high boots, traditional cotton-print blouses girdled with a sash, had their hair cut "under a pot," and wore beards that were rarely touched by a barber's hand. Every payday without fail they would send part of their money back to the village. They lived in crowded, dirty conditions and behaved stingily, denying themselves everything in order to accumulate more money for the village. They were always looking for a free drink. On holidays they attended mass and visited their countrymen, and their conversations were mostly about grain, land, the harvest, and livestock. When they weren't able to return to their village on visits, the "missus," that is, their wives, would come to town to visit them; these were fat, big-bosomed women in woolen skirts, in bright red calico sarafans, with whom the men would go to the tavern on holidays to be entertained and listen to the music "machine."

The other pattern-makers did not like these peasants, called them "gray devils," and made fun of them on every possible occasion. Most of the peasant pattern-makers had never passed through a factory apprenticeship but had been village carpenters under a contractor and had done only simple, rough work with an axe. They became pattern-makers only by accident or through someone's protection—either they did some foreman a "favor" or one of their countrymen set them up.

These village pattern-makers had yet another bad trait. They tried as hard as they could to compensate for their ignorance of their craft with extra "zeal." Stalwart and powerful fellows, they would work all the time, never leaving the workbench or straightening their backs.

"Pavlukha! Enough of this drudging! Take a break! The foreman won't see you, he went away," one of the pattern-makers would say in a mocking tone.

But Pavlukha, ignoring the derision, continued to "drudge," for he knew full well that the eyes and ears of the foreman remain in the workshop even in his absence. Of course the shop aristocrats could not forgive the villagers for all of this.

In the workshop one could often hear the following joke, illustrating the carpenter origin of the village pattern-maker.

One mocker turns to another and says:

"Vaniukha, Vaniukha! Did you cut off a length of board?"

"Sure I cut it, but it came out too short!"

"By very much?"

"Just by a straw."

"Well that's all right, it can be stretched with a nail."

"It can't be stretched."

"How come?"

"Because I also cut the other board, the one that it fits against, a straw too short."

All this is spoken in the restrained dialect of Vladimir province. Everyone roars with laughter.

Another equally popular scene was often performed: how the contractor dismisses the workers he does not need in the fall.

"Look, fellows, a bear is crawling on the roof," says the contractor, rushing toward the window.

"What kind of bear is that! It's a cat!" retort some doubters.

"No, it's a bear!"

"It's a cat!"

"You say it's a cat, I say it's a bear. Whoever thinks I'm wrong is fired!"

4
"Sushchy"

NEAR THE WINDOW opposite my workbench worked a tall, redheaded peasant with broad shoulders and a wide beard. The pattern-makers liked to call him "Sushchy."[1] He had a somber look about him that commanded respect, and his gait was measured and smooth. He spoke in a quiet, humble, tender voice, as if he were a saint who had alighted on earth, like the ones I still pictured to myself in those days. This impression was not even spoiled by the fact that he sniffed tobacco, which caused something resembling dregs from the shop floor to form on his mustache under his nose. He was a God-fearing man; he never cursed or used foul language. He would collect money from the other craftsmen to buy oil for the icon lamp, and every morning, crossing himself zealously, with an air of deep veneration, he arranged the lamp before the image of the Savior that hung in our shop.[2]

He took his room and board in the same artel as me. In his part of the room stood a high wooden bed, covered by a dirty quilt made of rags and shreds of various colors. His religious fervor was so extreme that he refused to leave anyone else in peace. Every Sunday, early in the morning, he would awaken the younger men who lived in our artel and take us off to the morning church service. Exhausted from a week of very hard work, we desperately wished to be able to sleep in on Sundays. But the uncompromising "Sushchy" was determined to put us on the path of virtue and save our lost souls, come what may. Motivated by the unpleasant prospect of having to spend the next life in hell and frying there year after year in a frying pan, we suppressed our natural feeling of youthful protest, obediently got up, splashed some cold water from the dirty wash basin on our faces, and donned our holiday jackets.

So it went until the day when my faith began to be put to a serious test and the virtues displayed by Sushchy began to fade and turn dull. This is how it happened.

Once on a Saturday evening, after receiving our pay, when our entire artel had begun to indulge in its usual carousing, we youngsters decided to take a little walk around the Alexander Garden,[3] where we'd frequently chase after the girl stocking-knitters. As we were walking along the embankment near the municipal bathhouses, which in the summertime usually served as a popular trysting place for the deprived working people of this area, the turner Stepka, a joker and a mischief-maker, suddenly called something to our attention:

"Look, look, boys! There's your saintly Sushchy with a girl, and they've been to the bathhouse together."

"Maybe that isn't him?" we demurred, keeping our distance so he wouldn't see us.

"What are you, blind or something!" Stepka retorted angrily.

On the wooden gangway emerged the tall, broad-shouldered figure of Sushchy, with his wide beard and his measured gait, carrying his little bundle, while by his side walked the prostitute Mashka, known throughout the neighborhood.

We had barely begun to recover from our surprise when Stepka rushed off to intercept the departing couple.

"Congratulations for your legal marriage, Vasily Ivanovich![4] Love one another, take a bath, and fear not sin," Stepka said mischievously.

At first Sushchy looked very embarrassed, but then, after a threatening remark to Stepka, he walked home in his usual measured gait.

On the following day all the babblers of our artel sharpened their wits making sport of Sushchy.

"Why Father Sushchy, even you have been led into sin by a harlot," said the planer Ivan mockingly.[5]

"It happens all the time," added another. "When your old woman is back in the village. . . . Only look out Father Sushchy, not to be caught doing it at the wrong time; the clocks don't exactly sing songs but they don't leave you in peace, either."

"When you start loving women in fancy hats, you'll soon end up in rags," commented a third.

At first Sushchy listened to all this meekly and calmly, though he took out his tobacco pouch and inhaled a pinch of tobacco more often than usual. But after a while he apparently could no longer take it. Slowly and deliberately he pulled on his boots, put on his hat, and went outdoors.

Despite his sober appearance and all his humility, Sushchy was feared and disliked in the workshop. We never cursed the factory administration or drank the varnish in his presence. When he approached someone else's workbench, everyone would stop talking and diligently set to work. It was said by some that he misappropriated the money that he collected for the lamp oil, yet no one had the courage to refuse him when he approached them for some change on payday. He was often to be seen at the beer hall in the company of hearty, inebriated people, but no one ever saw him pay for his own beer. According to his fellow countrymen, from the Riazan area,[6] he had purchased some 80 acres of land from a gentry landowner and paid him in cash, but he never talked to anyone about this.

During ceremonial religious services at the factory, Sushchy would always stand in the front with a candle in his hand. He would fall on his knees when the deacon bellowed "long life" to the factory owner.[7] When the service was over he was always the first, pushing the crowd apart with his powerful shoulders, to go up to the priest and, with great veneration, kiss his chubby, priestly hand and the cross.

5
The Beginning of My Apostasy

THE GUSTAV LIST machine-building factory never held a rank-ing position in the struggle of the working class for its eman-cipation. Neither yesterday nor today has a single outstanding event in the annals of revolutionary history been linked to its name. And yet at the same time the factory has not been a back-ward one. It has always participated in all the notable events, and the role of individual List workers in those events has been far from insignificant.

In those days, however, it was the Gopper factory that was con-sidered really advanced. Even in those early years strikes had al-ready taken place there.[1] The leading role in that factory was played by the pattern shop, some of whose pattern-makers had already spent time in exile or under police surveillance. The workers in the pattern shop at my factory used to call the Gopper pattern-makers "students"*—that is, people who are against the tsar and do not believe in God—and they were somewhat afraid of them.[2]

My own conception of these "students" was extremely con-fused. My only encounters with them were on the streets, and my feeling toward them was always one of great admiration mingled with fear and terror. I feared them because they didn't believe in God and might be able to shake my faith as well, which could have resulted in eternal hellish torments in the next world—"not for a hundred years, not for a thousand years, but for eternity without end," where there will be "weeping and the gnashing of teeth"—I often recalled the words of some divine revelation. But

* In those days the word "student" meant the same thing as "revolutionary." (Author's note.)

I admired them because they were so free, so independent, so well-informed about everything, and because there was nobody and nothing on earth that they feared.

The only thing that amazed me was that they were walking freely on the streets instead of being imprisoned in the Peter-and-Paul Fortress.[3] Such tolerance on the part of the authorities was incomprehensible to me.

How great were my surprise and curiosity when I learned one fine day that a pattern-maker from the Gopper factory had joined our workshop.

Just three benches away from mine a thin, sinewy man of medium height, with curly, light-colored hair and huge blue eyes, was fidgeting about. His shirt was tucked in and he wore his trousers outside his boots. In short, his outward appearance was no different from that of most of our pattern-makers. But he struck me as being particularly impetuous and fidgety.

My acquaintance with him began on the very first day.

"Well, my boy, how about giving me a hand with this cabinet," he said, beckoning me with his finger. "What's your name?"

"Semën."

"Have you been working here long?"

"This is my second year."

"I guess you already chase the girls, right?"

I grinned and, to cover my embarrassment, began to lift the heavy cabinet filled with tools.

"Hey, wait a second, watch out or you'll break your back! I have so many tools in there that even two of us can't lift it."

With enormous effort we managed to lift the cabinet. Then he took a brush out of it, brushed the wood shavings off his workbench, tested the stability of its longitudinal screw, and began to lay out his tools while continuing to chat with me.

"What district are you from?"

"Volokolamsk."

"Your father's probably ready to get you married, right?"

"I'm not going to marry until I've done my military service," I replied.[4]

This person was definitely beginning to appeal to me. I was won over by his comradely, jocular tone, a tone that other adult workers assumed with me only rarely.

"What if he has approached me in this roundabout manner in order to convert me to his godless faith?" I cautioned myself.

Other workers too approached him carefully, with a mixture of suspicion and curiosity.

Merry, sociable, and thoroughly skilled in our trade, he quickly overcame the normal workshop hostility with which the old-timers always treat the newcomer. Whenever the foreman left the shop, people would gather around his workbench. Jokes and wisecracks would fly about, anecdotes would be told, and at times a loud, infectious burst of laughter would resound. Obscenities were almost never heard.

Not infrequently, fierce and bitter political or theological arguments would be launched.

In the stories and anecdotes, however, it was always the priests who were given pride of place. Even the older workers listened indulgently to tales about the adventures of priests. But when the talk began to turn to the saints or to God, the mood would change completely: then there would be no end of noise, shouting, and mutual insults. Savinov (that was the newcomer's name) was particularly fond of making sport of the sacred things of Moscow. He would refer to the Iversky icon of the Mother of God, which at the time was being carried about in a carriage harnessed to a team of six horses, as "a priest's tool for gaining money"; he'd refer to monks as "parasites," to priests as a "breed of horses," to Ioann of Kronstadt as "Vaniukha," and so forth.[5]

"Well all right, let's say that the priests really are greedy, dissolute parasites; there's still no point in your sneering at miracles and the relics of saints, Savinov," the venerable and respectable-looking old worker Smirnov, a dogmatist and churchgoer, would say, losing his patience. "Why at the Monastery of the Caves in Kiev[6] I saw with my own eyes how they tended to this very sick man—he couldn't use his legs at all, couldn't take a step—and how they brought the holy relics to his lips. Well no sooner had he kissed the relics and said his prayers than he was up on his feet. He just walked out of the monastery as if nothing had happened! So, what do you say to that?"

"But why do you call that a miracle? If, say, he had no legs at all and you'd seen his legs grow back with your own eyes, then that would be a real miracle," Savinov would reply calmly, his irony barely perceptible. "What you described was simply the effect of hypnotism. Why in the town of Babye they say there's a hypnotist whose miracles are much greater. I've been told of occasions when they brought him people who not only couldn't walk but who were completely paralyzed, and they left his place fully restored. And he can cure people of diseases like alcoholism and female hysteria as with a touch. . . . As for your relics, Smirnov, they're just a priest's trick, and nothing more. What I'd like to hear from you is how many lazy, good-for-nothing monks and priests hang around those relics like parasites, looking for suckers!"

"I suppose you think that relics that never decay are also a trick?" Smirnov would intone passionately, shaking his gray beard as he stepped closer to Savinov. "There's a saint who has been lying in the earth for 300 years. Then he appears in the dream of a truly pious man. So they go to dig up his grave and they find him lying there looking alive and well, as if they'd only buried him yesterday. Why he even smells good. Now could that ever happen to an ordinary sinner?"

"Certainly it could. You just go visit the Historical Museum,[7] old fellow, and take a look around. You'll find Egyptian mummies there, lying under glass. Each one is more than a thousand years old. These people were alive before the birth of Christ and yet they've been preserved to this very day—and with their hair intact. Yet the Egyptians were idol-worshipers. Surely you wouldn't call them saints, would you?" Savinov would parry with a smile, sensing his superiority. "Let's take another example. Not long ago our tsar, Alexander III, died of drink.[8] They took out his intestines and embalmed him. Now they say he can lie there like that for 300 years without decaying. In 300 years will he be taken out and used as relics too?"[9]

"Well, master, does this mean you don't even believe in hell?" Sushchy would inquire meekly, in his quiet voice, his tobacco pouch in his hands, while he pushed in a pinch of snuff out of agitation.

"What in the world do you need hell for? A worker spends his whole life in the torment of hell. If you want to see for yourself just go visit the foundry some evening, when they're carrying the pots filled with castings. Not even a priest could invent a hell like that."

"Does that mean we'll receive no retribution in the next world for the sins we commit on earth?" Sushchy would meekly continue his inquiry.

"Our only retribution is our conscience, inside of us. It punishes us for our bad deeds. Retribution in the next world is something the priests have invented for simple people who aren't conscious. Meanwhile the rich can live here as if they were in paradise, enjoy themselves to their hearts' content, and pay the priests to prepare a paradise for them in the world to come."

After arguments like that were over the older workers would sigh sorrowfully as they dispersed, shake their heads, and whisper to each other: "What a hopeless man: he doesn't believe in God, he's against the tsar, he stirs up the Orthodox faithful, the people. He'll never escape the prison wagon, that's for sure!"

"When I lived in St. Petersburg lots of troublemakers like that got caught," old Smirnov would say. "They'd take the guy away— he'd disappear, no one knew where—without telling his parents, relatives, or anyone else. They wasted no words there: they'd lock him up in a prison-fortress, grind him up in a mill—I've heard there's a mill in every cell—and throw the remains in the Neva River."

The younger workers, on the other hand, listened to Savinov's talk with enthusiasm and interest. Often they would turn to him with questions and requests for clarifications. Nevertheless, it wasn't easy for him to overcome their suspicion—rooted in them from early childhood—of everything that was new, hard to grasp, or unfamiliar.

There were times when I was deeply angered and pained by Savinov's words. Questions that I had long since resolved, so I thought, and which had raised no doubts in my mind, would suddenly begin to drill themselves slowly and steadily into my brain, as if a piece of thin cold steel was being thrust into it. My beliefs, my views of the surrounding world, the moral foundations with which I had lived and grown up so nicely, peacefully, comfortably—suddenly began to shake. Even that which I'd thought to be most solid—the earth itself—was spinning beneath our feet, as Savinov put it, while we, like cockroaches on a flywheel, went crawling along it. Shivers ran up my spine—I became cold and terrified, as if I were preparing to leap across some abyss. But at the same time I felt light and free when I remembered that to-

gether with the old principles would also disappear that terrible
nightmare that threatened me with the tortures of hell "not for a
hundred years, not for a thousand years, but for eternity without end."

Having mastered my rage and indignation over his insulting
remarks about "sacred" things, I timidly, cautiously began to get
into arguments with Savinov. Despite what to me was the obvious
correctness of my positions, my arguments with Savinov invariably ended in defeat. I would be seized with passion, rage, and
indignation, but I had at my disposal neither the facts, the logical
arguments, nor the appropriate words with which to refute his
convictions.

"You say there is no hell, there is no heaven, no holy relics, no
saints; then are you also saying there is no God?" I inquired, my
heart already sinking in anticipation of his answer.

"No God? Of course there's a God, only not the kind that's conjured up by the priests," Savinov answered evasively, alerted by my
passion.

"Then in your opinion who created the first man?"

"Why did he have to be created? He developed by himself.
Those are just fairy tales in the Bible that tell you how God created man from clay, when the fact is that he was created by nature. I can prove it to you with an example, my little friend," Savinov continued, staring fixedly at me with his dreamy blue eyes.

I was taken aback by surprise. "How can he possibly prove it to
me with an example? Could he be some kind of sorcerer or ma-
gician, or perhaps the devil himself in the form of a man?" Ideas
like this flashed in my head.

"What's wrong? Don't you believe me?"

"Of course I can't believe such nonsense."

"All right, then do this: find yourself a little box, say, and fill it
with earth. Take a good close look at the earth, to be sure there's
nothing in it. Then put the box in a warm place for about two
weeks, and you'll see that without fail worms or little insects will
begin to appear there."

"And then what happens?"

"And then other creatures will begin to develop from the insects, and so on. . . . And, in the course of four, five, or maybe
even ten thousand years, man himself will emerge."[10]

At the time this example seemed so convincing to me that later, when I had already become "conscious," I still used those little "worms" and "insects" for many years as one of the most convincing arguments in my debates.

So the ice had been broken. My talks with Savinov became more frequent, more prolonged and detailed. His confidence in me was apparently increasing.

He told me many interesting things about the "Dukhobors," who "would not oppose evil with violent means," and who preached true evangelical love of humanity.[11]

"The tsarist officials want to make them serve in the army, but they refuse to go. They are given guns, but they fling them to the ground. 'We will not make war,' they say, 'we have no enemies; all men are brothers. We wish to live by the gospel,'" Savinov recounted with admiration. "What wonderful human beings!"

Savinov was only about 27, but he had already managed to roam the length and breadth of Russia, wherever he could find work. He had been to Warsaw, had worked in the metallurgical factories of the Ural Mountains and in the South, but he never stayed anywhere very long.

"It bores me to stay in one place, Semën," he would say to me. "I don't like the grass to grow under my feet. So whenever spring comes along, I long to head for new places. I need to look at new people, to see other ways of doing things. But I'll tell you one thing that's for sure: everywhere you go life is just as bad for the worker, who always lives in pitch-black darkness. The only place I haven't worked is Petersburg. They say the people there are much more conscious than our people here. I'll be heading there next year, no question about it."[12]

One evening, as I was approaching my workbench, Savinov stealthily and cautiously thrust some kind of disheveled, grease-stained little book under my bench.

"Read it, Semën, and don't show it to anyone else," he whispered to me.

Tormented by curiosity and fear, I could barely wait for the bell. I finished the book in two sittings. It was Hauptmann's *The Weavers*.[13] At the time it was still an illegal publication. The book made a rather strong impression on me. I soon learned the "song of the weavers" by heart and would recite it to the other apprentices of my age group in the workshop. The words kept echoing again and again in my ears:

So merciful and upright, the court in our land:
To the worker it shows scorn, honor to the gentleman!
Our workers are tormented, as in a torture cell,
They plunder, starve, oppress us, but you are silent, silent! . . .[14]

The book had a very disturbing effect on me, stirring up my animosity toward the rich and my pity for the oppressed and awakening many new, previously unknown emotions, yet it did not really satisfy me. It failed to answer the questions that were tormenting me: how should I live and what should I do? It had nothing to contribute to the formulation of my world outlook.

That task was to be accomplished by yet another little book that I read, also passed on to me by Savinov: *What Should Every Worker Know and Remember?* I don't remember the author's name.[15] Clearly written, in a popular but passionate style, this book produced a total transformation in my ideas. A complete revelation for me was the elegant exposition of its views of the socialist society of the future. Factories, workshops, the land, the forests, the mines—everything would become the common property of the toilers! The organized struggle of the working class against the capitalists, the landowners, and the tsar—that was the meaning of life and work for every conscious worker.

For an entire week I was in a state of virtual ecstasy, as if I were standing up high on some tall stilts, from where all other people appeared to me like some kind of bugs, like beetles rummaging in dung, while I alone had grasped the mechanics and the meaning of existence. My past life seemed completely boring, dull, uninteresting. Every day had been identical, just like clockwork—late to bed and early to rise, again and again, day after day. That was "eternity without end"!

The next book I read was G. Plekhanov's *The Russian Worker in the Revolutionary Movement*, after which many aspects of my father's old stories about the "nahilists" became clear and comprehensible to me.[16] Now my emancipation from my old prejudices moved forward at an accelerated tempo.

I now withdrew from my artel and settled in a separate room with one of my comrades. I stopped going to the priest for "confession," no longer attended church, and began to eat "forbidden" food during Lenten fast days. However, for a long time to come I didn't abandon the habit of crossing myself, especially when I returned to the village for holidays.

Noticing my blatant "apostasy," Korovin made several attempts to lecture me on morality:

"Don't you listen to that heretic Savinov, Senka," he would say. "He's not going to do you any good. They'll kick you out of the factory, and you haven't even learned to do the work properly yet. Where will you go then? Some student you turned out to be! Why the milk on your lips still isn't dry and you're already mixing with wiseacres. I think I'll write to your father; let him burn your back with 25 strokes!"

"But I'm not doing anything illegal, am I?" I replied in self-justification.

"I know just what you've been doing! They're going to put a necktie made of hemp around your neck—you'll hang there with your feet jerking."

However, these admonitions failed to impress me.

Then Korovin would write letters about my apostasy to my father. Alarmed, Father would insist on each occasion that I return to the village for the holidays to hear his parental admonitions. In the intervals between holidays he would write me edifying letters, in which he advised me to say my prayers, attend church, and call on the reigning Mother of God and St. Nicholas for assistance, that they might guard me from atheism and every other horror.[17]

During my visits to the village on holidays, Father and I would quickly get entangled in theological arguments. Because I was already quite well versed in these questions by then I almost always emerged the victor from these arguments with my father. To be sure, not wishing to cause him great pain, I wouldn't pose the question of the "non-existence" of God very sharply and I gladly agreed to grant His existence as a possibility.

Father would then calm down somewhat and would even be proud of me. But this never lasted very long. As soon as I left for Moscow Father was on his own once more and, when he began to receive disturbing letters from Korovin, Father's edifying letters to me would resume.

But none of this was considered by Father to be all that terrible. There was only one thing he was unable to come to terms with—the fact that I was so indifferent to our home and to our peasant farmstead. Once during one of my visits Father summoned me to the barn, where, three years earlier, he had already prepared himself a good hollow coffin, which in the meantime was used to store oats, cabbages, firewood for the winter, and so on.

"I would like to have a serious talk with you," said my father.

"Fine, let's talk."

"As you know," he began in a sad voice, "I'm already growing old and might die quite soon. I've made myself a coffin and there's really nothing more I need, just seven feet of earth. But for me to die in peace I would like to see you settled down."

"But I am already settled down. I'm working at a factory and I'll soon be earning a good wage," I replied, pretending not to understand what Father was getting at.

"No, that's not what I'm talking about. . . . As you know, I don't get along well with your brother. I want to give him a separate property settlement and to have you get married while I'm still alive, so that the house will mean more to you and you'll be better off while you're still young, since if you wait until you're older you won't even marry."

"No, I don't want to marry until I've done my military service; when I'm a civilian again, then I'll get married," I answered fairly decisively.

"But I'll be dead by then."

"Well, I will get married on my own," I declared firmly.

Father, understanding that there was no chance of persuading me, gave up the fight and said with sadness:

"Well, God be with you! Live according to your own lights!"

6
Khodynka

WELL BEFORE the coronation of the new tsar,[1] the authorities had begun to "purge" Moscow of all unreliable elements. In houses inhabited by all kinds of poor people the janitors began to check on the apartments more often than usual; they would verify passports, examine registration forms more closely, and so on.[2] Spies and stool pigeons of all varieties made their way stealthily through the city's outlying neighborhoods, through the working-class quarters, listening attentively for talk that might sound excessive. In our factory rumors abounded that all "suspicious" persons would be banished from the city. But just who these suspicious persons were, no one could say with any precision. However, everyone said: "Now is the time to hold one's tongue." There were stories going round about people who worm themselves into all kinds of places, eavesdrop, play the simpleton, deliberately elicit derogatory comments about the tsar, even get people drunk with vodka and beer—and then, as soon as you weaken, as soon as you begin to chatter, this nice fellow, who turns out to be a detective, grabs you and hauls you off to jail. In short, a tense atmosphere of suspicion and pursuit could be felt everywhere.

About a week before the coronation—it was a non-workday—Korovin, his son Vanka, and I went off to the country to take in some fresh air. We didn't return home until evening. As we were approaching the city we were suddenly accosted by a respectable-looking, distinguished gentleman who appeared to be some kind of professor or lawyer.

"I love the working people," he said to us in a carefree manner, pretending to be a little tipsy. "Say, friends, let's go, let's sing a song to our common cause," he went on, turning to Korovin and slapping him lightly on the shoulder. "La-la-la-la. . . . What's the matter, friends, why aren't you singing along? Go ahead!"

"We don't know that song."

"Well let's just sing—you pick the song. . . . But better still, let's all go to that beer hall."

We refused to pursue his invitation, pleading the fact that we had to arise early the next day to go to work.

For a long time this character refused to take leave of us. First he'd start talking about the "hard lot" of the working man, then he'd attempt to lead the discussion toward the subject of various social problems or to remind us of the tune of some song, apparently thinking we would sing along. Remembering that "now is the time to hold one's tongue," we stubbornly remained silent and responded to all the obsessive demands of the distinguished personage briefly and inconclusively.

Having failed to accomplish anything, the personage gave up on us and, waving his walking stick, moved slowly away.

After this incident Korovin, who was now absolutely terrified, instilled so much fear into us that we not only were afraid to speak on the street, we were even afraid to breathe there.

It was around this time that one of the pattern-makers from our shop disappeared from sight. His disappearance provoked endless rounds of discussion, speculation, and rumor. Some of the men went to his apartment to make inquiries, but there was no sign of him there either. We concluded that he had probably been put in a prison wagon and carted off somewhere or other for having spoken out of turn.

The name of this pattern-maker was Mikhail Afanasev. He had joined us only recently, having previously worked at the Gopper factory. Afanasev dressed neatly, combed his hair toward the back of his head, and usually came to work with a copy of the newspaper *Russian News*, from which he often read individual articles or commentaries to the pattern-makers.[3] At the time he was about 27 or 28; he was of above average height and had rosy cheeks that bore witness to his blooming health. He conducted himself with great self-confidence, even arrogance. In arguments and discussions with others he didn't try to prove his point or to persuade, but simply spoke in a very solemn tone that permitted no disagreement. He too was considered a "student," but in gen-

eral, for reasons I failed to grasp at the time, other workers somehow disliked him.

Unexpectedly, some three days after his disappearance, when
all of us were quite certain that he was riding to parts unknown
in the prison wagon, Afanasev suddenly reappeared in the workshop. Of course this was followed by no end of questions, debates,
and discussions. However, all these discussions were conducted
in a strictly conspiratorial form. During work Mikhail Afanasev
would usually go out on the stairway for "a little smoke" in the
company of three or four other pattern-makers. In order to protect themselves from being surprised by the foreman, they would
leave the door to the stairwell open. That way they could observe
all the foreman's movements. From behind the door one first
heard the sounds of calm conversation, which soon would be followed by fierce and furious arguments. Then Mikhail Afanasev,
flushed and excited, would return to his workbench and, his
hands still trembling, resume his work.

Though I did everything I could to strain my attention and my
hearing, I was unable to learn anything essential about the mysterious disappearance of Mikhail Afanasev. All that was known
was that he had been arrested, held in jail for three days, and
then released. Subsequently, when I was already a revolutionary,
I learned that Mikhail Afanasev had become a zealous partisan
of the famous Zubatov, the "Okhrana" official, and played a
prominent role in the Zubatov movement in Moscow.[4] His arrest
and speedy release on the eve of the coronation in 1896 were evidently the first steps leading to his downfall.

The coronation ceremonies were held in Moscow during the
first half of May. The weather was unusually warm and sunny.
The entire city was illuminated and decorated with a multitude
of flags. The Sofia embankment near the "Gustav List" factory
was lined with guns, which from time to time fired off deafening
ceremonial volleys, causing the air to vibrate. You could hear the
sounds of glass breaking in the nearby houses. In the evenings
Moscow glowed with the light of millions of electric lamps while
multicolored fireworks soared high into the sky. For three days
the streets near the Kremlin were blocked off by the celebrating
public. The Alexander Garden was in an absolute uproar. It was
flooded with townspeople, artisans, and other workers; tall,

handsome hussars and cuirassiers in picturesque costumes, their sparkling swords dragging along the ground, would emerge proudly and pompously with "the ladies of their hearts" while shelling little seeds.[5] Housemaids, cooks, seamstresses, milliners—in those days all these women were the virtual prisoners of the dashing Petersburg guard officers.

"There isn't any female nourishment left for the working man," the skirt-chasers from our factory would complain angrily.

All around the Alexander Garden crowds of people were gathered to enjoy themselves. Some were singing in chorus, songs like "Down Along the Mother Volga," others danced the Kamarinskaya[6] to the shrill sounds of an accordion, and in still another group people were telling entertaining stories. . . . In a word, the people were making merry. The uniformed police were nowhere to be seen.

At our factory, the director announced that during the three days of celebration in honor of the coronation the workers would work only eight hours a day, with a one-hour break for lunch. Our joy was unbounded! In the course of those three days we came to understand for the first time just how sweet was the taste of the eight-hour day and to feel the full weight of eleven and a half hours of work.[7]

After eight hours of work, we still had so much time left over that we didn't even know how to fill our remaining hours: we strolled along the streets and boulevards, gazed at the reveling holiday crowd, attempted to cut through to the front rows and "get a glimpse of the tsar." Admittedly, we tried to do this not out of respect or admiration for the tsar, but from simple curiosity to see royal luxury, the royal suite, and so on. Moreover, we looked upon this business as a kind of sport. Vanka Korovin and I would get all stirred up whenever someone asked us in a tone of surprise:

"Do you mean you still haven't seen the tsar?"

We would reply with embarrassment that we had not.

"But how is that possible! Why, I've already seen him three times. . . . You boys should get up a little earlier in the morning and find a good place to stand," someone would instruct us at the end of such dialogues.

After repeated and persistent attempts to "get a glimpse of the tsar," the last in our series of efforts ended very sadly: when we tried to force our way through to the front rows, Cossack troops drove us back with their whips, hurting us, even tearing apart Vanka's jacket. We ran home with a feeling of shame and disgrace, and never again attempted to "get a glimpse of the tsar."

"Well, boys, eat up and let's go try to see the tsar"—these words continued to resound around us in the workshop for quite some time.

Either on the 14th or 15th of May, a big public celebration was announced, to be held on the Khodynka field.[8] It was said that during the festivities little bundles filled with sausages, rolls, a mug bearing the emblem of the tsar, and a half-ruble piece would be distributed to everyone from special booths. No one could say with any accuracy just what kind of mug it would be: some said copper, others said tin or porcelain.

On the day before the celebration, Krasnitsky, the master mechanic at our factory, gathered together the foremen of all the shops to announce that, in order to avoid the big crush, all our workers were to start off for Khodynka at eight in the morning in a single group led by him, Krasnitsky; the workers shouldn't be worried, since special gifts from the tsar were being prepared for everyone at our factory.

That evening the most contradictory, ominous rumors were already being spread in the house where we lived. Huge masses of people had begun to gather on the Khodynka field on the eve of the celebration. Several people from our house were among them. We began to grow agitated and to speak rudely about the master mechanic, fearing that by the time we got to the field all the gifts would already be distributed. Some of the men proposed to leave immediately and spend the night there. Vanka and I were fully prepared to go in the evening, but Korovin, who had complete faith in Krasnitsky's promises, would not allow it.

It is a clear and sunny morning. Commanded by master mechanic Krasnitsky, we march in a long file to the Khodynka field. The morning air is bracing, the sun shines brightly, there is laughter, joking, animated talk, and, at the end of our path, crowds of joyful people making merry, puppet shows, music, folkdancing, singing, the brash, endless sounds of the accordion, and so on. And then, suddenly. . . .

As we approach the vicinity of Khodynka, we encounter a cabman. In his cab a young woman is tossing about and screaming something incomprehensible at the top of her lungs.

"Nervous hysteria, most likely," we decide, and we continue our procession.

The master mechanic led us to a place that was still pretty far from the celebration and then went off on his own to find out about our gifts. We settled down to await his return. However, we soon began to disperse in different directions.

Then some people approached our group, shouting: "Oh my God, oh my God! How many people have been crushed! They're taking away the corpses by cartloads!"

"Who!? How were they crushed?"

"You can't imagine how many people fell into the wells! There's this deep, deep well; people kept falling into it even when it was already packed," others told us. "They say the wells were left open on purpose!"

"There was this enormous crowd there, swaying from side to side, moving like waves in the sea," says another, "and you could see the steam from the stuffy air hovering over the crowd. And all the people standing there, just as if everyone was still alive, but when the crowd finally gives way, suddenly they fall to the ground by the hundreds: their crushed bodies had been standing up."

"The only reason I'm still alive is because I managed to make my way through by practically climbing over everyone's head. A kind person came by and put me down on a safe, high spot," said a small, skinny man in a visored cap.

We never received our gifts and we were certainly in no mood for them anyway. We were happy and thankful that we hadn't left for the field in the evening and hadn't ended up in that mess ourselves. On the way back home, now and then we would run into military wagons piled with corpses covered with bast mats; arms, legs, and heads could be seen dangling out from under the mats. . . . It was terrifying.

On the following day the crush at Khodynka was the only thing discussed at our factory. The newspapers were beginning to publish lists of the victims. Some of the workers found the names of their friends. A low murmur began to arise. The atmosphere grew tense. The lists that appeared in the papers clearly underestimated the number of victims, placing it at two or three hundred, I can't remember exactly. This evoked enormous outrage.

"The papers are lying. They crushed thirty thousand, not three hundred, the dogs!" the old worker Smirnov, whose friend or relative had been killed, said angrily. "Have you ever heard of anything like it? Thousands of people are crushed to death and they don't even find the guilty party!"[9]

"And who, sir, is the guilty party? Why, we're the guilty ones ourselves. We coveted those gifts, we didn't maintain order, and, well, we crushed one another," Sushchy responded in a meek, sweet voice.

"It's a gift to the tsar, the little father, that's what it is!" Savinov interjected bitterly.

Sushchy remained silent. We were afraid to stay with this theme very long.

Mikhail Afanasev, who had turned a bit pale, lowered his tone and attempted to focus the other workers' attention on the tsar's promise to "compensate" the widows and orphans of those who had perished at Khodynka. Of course that promise was of little consolation to us, but no one would contradict Afanasev. It felt as if each new day contained some new secret, and somehow we all withdrew into ourselves and awaited something.

Little by little our lives began to return to their ordinary daily routines, but for a long time we were unable to forget the pleasure of the eight-hour day, which often served us as a topic of conversation. We still continued to await something and we all hoped that important changes in our life would somehow come about on their own.

One payday Savinov took up some kind of a collection among the pattern-makers. They apparently contributed very enthusiastically, for Savinov was very pleased with the results. But the destination and purpose of these collections were unknown to me. On one such occasion, however, my fellow countryman Novikov—a loud-mouthed drunkard—having used his pay to get himself drunk, began to reproach Savinov for these collections.

"You've been treating us like fools," Novikov blurted out, "you collect money from us and nobody even knows who or what it's for! Maybe you spent it all on drink. . . . Some clever guy you turned out to be!"

At first Savinov shrugged this off lightly, but then, having lost patience over the last remark, he rushed toward Novikov's workbench, grabbed some object along the way, and would have just about massacred him if the neighboring workers hadn't intervened in time.

"You drunkard! You stupid animal! Here, you can choke on your money!" Whereupon Savinov, his hands trembling with rage, hurled some silver coins at Novikov's bench, the coins clattering as they rolled along it.

Evidently Novikov had not anticipated such a stormy protest; suddenly taken aback, he calmed down and stood there in silence, having completely lost heart. His intoxication instantly seemed to vanish.

"Well, all right. . . . That's enough of that! I suppose I've been drinking too much," he said with embarrassment.

At that time I had the impression that Savinov's "collections" were directly connected with the strike of the Petersburg weavers.[10] It seems that shortly after the scene with Novikov that I described above, during one of our lunch breaks, a triumphant Mikhail Afanasev arrived in our workshop carrying a copy of the newspaper *Russian News*. A group of pattern-makers quickly formed near his workbench and he loudly and clearly read them an article about the strike of the Petersburg weavers. Although the article recounted those events in a dry, bureaucratic style, for us it was a complete revelation; we appropriated everything in the article that was related to our daily life and work. Thenceforth the words "strike" and "combination," which were mentioned in the article, would assume a real meaning for us, would truly come alive.[11] Heroic though it was, the unequal struggle of lone individuals—of "students"—who were imprisoned and "ground up in mills," was now transformed into a struggle of the working masses. The terrifying legends that had had such a hold on the workers' imaginations were now losing all their significance. As a practical matter, it was impossible to imprison 30,000 Petersburg weavers in the Peter-and-Paul Fortress and put them through the mill![12]

Shortly after these events our factory changed from an eleven-and-a-half-hour workday to ten hours. We could now breathe more freely and we immediately felt that an enormous burden had been lifted from our shoulders. Granted, in those years there were few of us who knew how to organize and exploit our free time in a rational manner. Yet it was already a wonderful thing that we were now able merely to rest physically and to think about subjects that were unrelated to our work. For our generation this in itself was a great conquest. From here on in it would become much easier for us to engage in organizational work, propaganda, and agitation among the broad masses of workers.

Over thirty years have since passed, but at that time, when my understanding of political questions was still very weak, I could already sense that these three events—Khodynka, the Petersburg weavers' strike, and the shift to the ten-hour day—were closely connected to one another and somehow stood in a state of causal interdependency.

Although it had no direct relation to the shop-floor interests of the workers of our factory, the Khodynka catastrophe greatly weakened the authority of our rulers and undermined the old blind faith in the tsar, even among the older men. What aroused people's indignation most of all was the irresponsibility, the impunity of the authorities who had destroyed thousands of lives.

"Why did these Christian souls have to perish?" one worker would ask.

"For the benefit of tsarist circles."

Remarks and anecdotes like this circulated widely among the workers.

On November 14, the occasion of the half-year anniversary of the Khodynka catastrophe, the students of Moscow University organized a memorial service for the victims that turned into a demonstration. The students were surrounded by the police and driven into the riding academy.[13] This incident had great agitational significance at our factory. Previously, the mass of workers had looked upon students as restless rioters, as atheists who attacked the tsar for obscure reasons and, in any case, stood at a very great distance from the workers' day-to-day interests. But now many workers were beginning to speak sympathetically of students who, unafraid of punishment, "seek after justice."

7
Sergey Petrovich

H<small>E WAS A SMALL</small>, slender man, with long blond hair that was combed back; with his disproportionately long thin legs, covered by narrow, tubelike trousers, his supple body, constantly twisting and turning as if all its bones had been removed and replaced with rubber, he reminded one of some kind of water snake. On his thin face there were small, pointed, reddish whiskers and two beady, gray, mocking eyes. I never saw him conversing with anyone in a serious manner; he was always joking, kidding around, and smiling with his jagged mouth, revealing the gaps from his missing teeth. His family name was of course known to the front office, but in our workshop no one knew it and no one cared. Everyone called him Sergey Petrovich.[1]

Nor did anyone know where he had worked earlier and whence he had come to us. He appeared in our workshop from out of the blue. We come to work one day and what do we see: standing at a lathe, turning a block of wood, is a sickly-looking little dandy. But two weeks later the pattern-makers were already drinking up his "vodka tax" with him and wishing him a "long life" at his new workplace.[2]

He wasn't much of a craftsman and at first his turning was of terrible quality. However, Ivan Fedorovich, our turner—a huge, stout fellow, a real glutton, and a lover of liquor, whom Sergey Petrovich would treat to drinks—eagerly initiated him in the mysteries of the turner's craft, and Sergey Petrovich soon became a pretty decent turner.

The turners' lathes were located at the end of the shop, in the same area as the band and circular power saws. There was a constant noise in that area—the squealing, cutting sound of the saws, the rustle of the driving-belts, the light cracking sound of

wood as it was turned on the lathe. Swarms of sawdust and wood
shavings flew around in the air while fine particles of wood hung
overhead like a cloud. This part of the shop was situated outside
the field of vision of the foreman, who was enthroned in the
middle of the shop in a glass booth. In part for that reason, but
mainly because Sergey Petrovich, who had an inexhaustible supply of humor at his disposal, would always come up with some
kind of novel, unexpected little trick, those workers who liked to
spend their time having fun were very happy to visit that area.

Just one look at Sergey Petrovich's mobile, comical features,
his supple little figure, and you couldn't help feeling cheerful.

> *The rich man drinks champagne,*
> *While the poor man gets by with his vodka.*

He liked to recite this often. To represent the self-satisfaction
of the rich man, he would bend his tiny figure into an arch, push
his belly forward, puff up his cheeks, and make his thin, cock-
roachlike whiskers bristle.

> *The rich man drives about in a carriage,*
> *While the poor man travels by foot.*
> *The rich man buys cigars,*
> *While the poor man picks up cigarette butts.*

When they looked at his figure, his gestures, his mobile features, even the most severe kinds of people were put into a cheerful mood. Sergey Petrovich was well informed about all the latest
theater news. During conversations he often inserted into his
turns of phrase some sharp or funny expression that he'd heard
at the theater. And he sometimes tried to sing an aria in his ridiculous voice.

It was from him that I first learned that on this earth there is
something called a theater, where "actors" and "actoresses" perform all kinds of funny roles in person. Of course this is not completely accurate—I had already heard of the existence of the theater from my father's stories and from newspapers, but as I pictured it, the theater assumed the form of something very abstract
and obscure, where only very rich "gentlemen" would venture. It
was from Sergey Petrovich that I first learned concretely just what
happened in a theater and that it was possible to go there for as
little as 30 kopecks for a gallery seat.

Nevertheless, although my theoretical knowledge of the theater was now enriched, it was only some two years later that I actually had occasion to attend a theatrical performance.

After looking around the workshop for a while, Sergey Petrovich soon put together a "comic choir" in his part of the shop. It consisted of Ivan Fedorovich, the apprentice Egorka, and himself. One day, having heard that Sushchy had received a letter from his wife in the village in which she wrote that their mare had died, Sergey Petrovich, after waiting for the foreman to leave the shop, quickly gathered his "choir" together and organized a memorial service for the dear, departed mare, God's servant.

For the Easter holiday, Sergey Petrovich's "choir" solemnly intoned such paschal songs as this:

> *In defense of God's glory,*
> *On the second story,*
> *Near the ledge you'll catch sight*
> *Of three cats in a fight.*
> *Meow! Meow! Don't leave now!*

Or this:

> *Be hallowed, be blessed,*
> *Be baked, little cake.*

Strange as it may seem, even the religious old-timers listened to this "blasphemous" singing by Sergey Petrovich's "choir" indulgently: it contained so much that was funny and enjoyable. As for the youths, they were literally in raptures over it.

In those days I still had trouble making sense of people, of my environment, of events that were sometimes very significant; yet, under the influence of my own bitter experience, I was beginning to develop a certain "feel" for things. Thus, for example, I was unable to explain, to demonstrate logically, the injustice of a particular wrongdoing, but I immediately and definitely felt antipathy and disgust toward the person who'd done the deed. When Sergey Petrovich first joined us, I was still a long way from having overcome my religious biases. And yet, despite all his "blasphemy," something would draw me to him. It seemed to me that Sergey Petrovich's buffoonery and affectations were only a mask and that behind that mask something more serious and significant was concealed. I could feel the difference, for example, between the buffoonery of Ivan-the-Driller and that of Sergey Petrovich. But what was the nature of that difference? I could not

grasp it logically. Later, when I had already become fully c
scious, it was obvious to me that Ivan's buffoonery was pure n ⌐
chief, whereas that of Sergey Petrovich had a "tendency."[3]

After I had gotten to know Sergey Petrovich better, I heard
some illegal songs from him for the first time; these songs were
rapidly passed from mouth to mouth throughout the factory. I do
not know if he composed these songs himself or adopted them
from someone else.

I still remember one of these songs, which I later taught to the
village youths when I was banished to the country. It was sung to
the tune of "Khaz Bulat the Daring."[4]

> *Fifteen years have now gone by,*
> *Maybe more before me lie.*
> *I was still so young and green*
> *When I first met my machine.*
> *The sun's still shining in the sky,*
> *But I've no rest to get me by.*
> *In this world I've had to stay*
> *'Til my hair has turned to gray,*
> *But not a penny saved of pay*
> *To help me on a rainy day.*
> *What thief or demon came from hell,*
> *What dark magician cast a spell,*
> *Squeezed the worker, sucked him dry,*
> *Takes my money, lets me die?*
> *Why, that's no thief or being from hell,*
> *Or sorcerer who casts a spell,*
> *That takes my money every day*
> *And sucks the worker's blood away.*
> *It's just the merchant and the priest,*
> *It's just the tsar—our father pure.*

This song, only partially reproduced here, would touch the
heart of our young people very deeply in those days.

I never encountered Sergey Petrovich again in the course of my
life, but his memory, closely tied to those first revolutionary
songs, has remained with me for a long time.

8
The Beginning of My Wanderings from Factory to Factory

Two years of my apprenticeship at the List factory passed. By now I was already an accomplished draftsman and designed uncomplicated patterns on my own. I loved my craft, and I put a lot of "spirit" and initiative into it. As everyone knows, the pattern is made for casting the iron and bronze parts of a machine, which is also constructed from forged iron or steel parts that are made, in accordance with a strict division of labor, in different workshops. In order to acquaint myself with the entire process of producing a complete machine, I often made the rounds of the factory's various shops, where I spent hours standing and watching how this or that part of a machine was made.

I especially enjoyed visiting the foundry, where the patterns were sent after being completed in our shop. In the huge, tall foundry building, which was covered by soot and dust, dirty, dark-colored people, whose blackened, soot-covered faces revealed only the whites of their eyes, rummaged like moles in the earth and dust of the earthen floor. The roar of the enormous lifting cranes and turning gears, the clattering of the thick chains, and the mighty breathing of the cupola furnace where the pig iron was smelted—all these sounds constantly filled the foundry building with their din.

In the evening, when the casting began, the foundry would turn into a veritable hell. Pouring out of the furnace on a chute would be an enormous, heavy fire-red stream of molten pig iron, which spewed forth large blazing sparks and illuminated the dark faces of the smelters standing nearby. One after another the molten pots of pig iron were quickly filled, and, two at a time, the smelters carried them on an iron handbarrow across the huge floor, which was littered with molds ready for the casting. The dark floor of the shop would be brightly illuminated by a large number of fire-red points with tails, resembling little blazing comets. Then the smelters slowly poured the molten pig iron from the pots into the earthen molds. The heat near the pots and the furnaces was unbearable and the clothes of the smelters would repeatedly catch fire and have to be doused with water.

On the following day I would watch how the iron parts of the future machines, cast but still not cooled down, were cleansed of earth and cleared of knobs and patches of pig iron by unskilled workers.

Then, after a few more weeks or months, depending on the size of the machine, I could see the workers in the assembly shop painting the powerful beauty—with its polished bronze and steel parts sparkling—the completed steam engine.

Workers would look with a loving glance at its massive iron body as they passed by. As for me, I began to be gripped by the poetry of the large metal factory, with its mighty metallic roar, the puffing of its steam-driven machines, its columns of high pipes, its rising clouds of black smoke that sullied the clear blue sky. Unconsciously, I was being drawn to the factory, to the people who worked there, who were becoming my near ones, my family. I had the feeling that I was merging with the factory, with its stern poetry of labor, a poetry that was growing dearer and closer to me than the quiet, peaceful, lazy poetry of our drowsy village life.

Christmas was approaching. During these holidays the factory would close down for almost an entire week. A large number of workers had ties with their villages: these were the workers from the areas of Mozhaisk, Tula, Riazan, and Volokolamsk.[1] They would await the coming of the holidays with impatience—they saved their money to buy things for themselves and for their village hosts. When it came time for the great departures to the countryside—which happened both at Christmas and at Easter—we were subjected to a medical examination at the factory. It was carried out quite primitively and crudely and it yielded almost no results. On payday, in the paymaster's office, a doctor would be seated next to the bookkeeper while he paid us. We would line up, undo our pants, and show the doctor the part of our bodies he needed to see.[2] The doctor, after tapping it with a pencil, would tell the bookkeeper the results of his "examination," whereupon the bookkeeper would hand us our pay. Although there were probably quite a few workers at the factory who were infected with venereal disease, I do not know of a single instance when the doctor found such a person during these medical examinations.

After the medical "examination" I was given my pay and, along with other workers, I too departed for my village. But this time my voyage turned out to be a fateful one. This is what happened. Korovin had decided that, come what may, he would marry off his son Vanka—who was a year older than me—during this holiday vacation. Korovin decided to carry out all the preliminary marriage procedures—the showing of the bride, the striking of hands, etc.—during the holy period, when priests cannot perform the actual weddings.[3] Then, after the holy period, he would take off three or four additional workdays for the wedding itself. Whether he had received permission from the foreman for this extension in advance or whether the foreman authorized the illegal absence of Korovin and his son after the fact I no longer remember. In any case they were not penalized. For me, however, the story was to have an unhappy ending.

I played a very active role in Vanka's marriage preparations in the village: I went to parties with him, accompanied him to the showing of the bride, and, finally, after we had selected a bride for him, I was his best man at the wedding. In general I had a great time in the village on this visit, though my merrymaking almost led me into getting married myself, to the sister of Vanka's bride. But once again, when all my other arguments had proved useless and vanished into smoke before the verbal onslaught of my sisters and aunts, I was rescued by my impending military service.

From Korovin's point of view, Vanka's marriage was very successful. It seems that he got a dowry of some 200 rubles and all sorts of fine clothing. What is more, the bride herself wasn't bad. Although her face was not pretty, her body was splendid—broadboned, stately, and tall. As our workers would say when she later came to visit her husband in Moscow: "That's not a girl, it's a city!"

But what pleased Korovin the most was that his daughter-in-law was the daughter of a rich kulak, a man of reknown in our district. To be sure, this was of no major material benefit to Korovin, either then or later, but it was still very nice to become the kin of a rich man, and it gave him some hope for the future.

Vanka, the real hero of the festivities, was in seventh heaven. He had never even dreamed he might have a wife like that! People now began to call him Ivan Ivanovich.[4]

At this point I shall make a small digression and say a few more words about Vanka, whom I hardly ever saw again for the rest of my life. At work he was a diligent, assiduous fellow, obedient to the factory administration, deferential to his superiors. His father had known how to bind him to his home and instill in him obedience to his parents. And Vanka, without even stopping to think—if he was capable of thinking at all—submitted to all of Korovin's wishes and blindly followed in his father's footsteps.

Korovin himself, I was later told, ended up as follows. When Bogdan Ivanovich, the old foreman in the pattern shop, died, Korovin replaced him as foreman. In that position he soon became universally disliked and made a lot of personal enemies. He died in a very sad manner. It seems that one day the factory administration had arranged some kind of celebration for the workers. At the festivities, many workers became extremely drunk. Then, when the celebration was in full swing, one of Korovin's "wellwishers" flung a glass of vodka at him, terrifying Korovin so greatly that he died on the spot. I have never been able to learn any more of the details of this story.

Korovin's son Vanka is still alive and well. He is working at the very same factory, having inherited his father's post as foreman and having acquired all his virtues: he never misses a single mass, goes to confession every year, takes Communion, and is very concerned about maintaining the splendor of the neighborhood church.

And now let us return to my own youth. Having celebrated young Korovin's marriage with lots of din and uproar and a good deal of drinking, we headed back to our factory. As I already said, we were three days late. The Korovins got away with it, but the old foreman Bogdan Ivanovich declared categorically that I was fired with two weeks' notice.[5] Korovin and I pleaded with him, but all in vain. The prospect of unemployment confronted me. I became depressed, and my work deteriorated. I was frightened by the unknown.

"Cheer up, Semën, you'll pull through," Savinov said to me with compassion as he slapped me on the back, having come up behind me unobserved.

"How can I, Vasily Egorych,[6] when I have nowhere to go?"

"You sure have been worrying! Don't be afraid. With good hands and a head on your shoulders, you can always find work!" He looked at me with his clear, invigorating gaze and added in a stern, businesslike tone: "Semën, stop feeling sorry for yourself and let's talk some sense instead."

"Vasily Egorych, I always ask your advice about everything," I answered meekly, while feeling reassured.

"Well then everything will be fine. Don't come to work here tomorrow. Instead, go to the entrance of the big Bromley factory[7] first thing in the morning and ask the foreman for a job. I've heard they need pattern-makers there."

On the next day I packed my tools in my beloved gray toolbox and, after all sorts of kind parting words from my friendly fellow pattern-makers, I abandoned the Gustav List factory, filled with joy about the present and anxiety about the future.

9
I Am an Adult

W ITH FEAR and trembling, for the first time in my life I am standing at a joiner's bench as an adult! I lay out my tools and begin to study the designs for the work that has been assigned me as a test of my skills in the pattern shop of the "Old Bromley" factory. The design—which is for a bearing—turns out to be uncomplicated, and, without any help from the older pattern-makers, I am able to cope with the task by myself. Then I hand the completed pattern to the foreman. I wait in a state of excitement, my heart pounding, while the foreman, using calipers and measure, tests the accuracy of the pattern I have made.

In my later wanderings from factory to factory, when I had already acquired real skill in my work as well as confidence in myself, I never experienced any special feelings of agitation. But this time, when my future as an independent craftsman was being decided, I literally trembled like a puppy dog as I stood by the workbench and waited for the foreman to complete his examination of my work.[1]

From stories I had heard from experienced workers, I knew that foremen always preferred to hire reliable, older pattern-makers and would pay them higher wages even if they were less skillful than the younger men. In general, my youthful appearance—I not only had no beard, I did not even have a mustache—was very distressing to me and, at that time, was the source of many unpleasant moments for me. For one thing, the young women—stockingmakers, milliners, dressmakers—with whom my older-looking contemporaries were so successful, refused even to acknowledge me as an adult man. At times like that I regretted very much that I had not taken care of this problem much earlier and corrected my natural deficiency, as my more experienced comrades had advised me, by artificial means: the application of baked onions, at night, to the spots where I wanted to encourage the growth of facial hair.

To my delight, however, this time things worked out all right even without the "baked onions." The foreman summoned me to the office, announced good-naturedly that my work was of acceptable quality and, right on the spot, gave me the drawings for another pattern. Flushed and excited with embarrassment, and afraid that other workers would notice my unrestrained joy, I proudly and confidently marched to my workbench with the new drawings in hand, trying to look as if all of this was the most normal routine for me.

"Well, Kanatchikov, did you make it?" my neighbor asked with curiosity.

"I made it," I answered, trying in vain to conceal my joy with a tone of indifference.

"What'll you be earning, about seventy kopecks a day?"

"Who knows?"

"Listen, if you had a beard, you can be sure the foreman would have offered you a full ruble," said my neighbor, hitting me on my sore spot.

At that time, after the forty kopecks I had been getting at List's, seventy kopecks wasn't a bad wage for me. Secretly, however, I dreamed of more. My neighbor, Sherstiannikov, was much older than me; he was one of those pattern-makers who had been a village carpenter, still had problems in reading a design, and was making only eighty kopecks a day. It was obviously his envy that prevented him from admitting that the foreman could pay more than seventy kopecks to a young greenhorn like me.

There was still a week until payday. I was consumed with impatience to learn just how high a wage the foreman would assign me. It was not that I was greedy for money; the size of the wage concerned me not so much for material as for moral reasons, as an appraisal of my worth as a socially useful person, as measured in money by strangers who did not know me. Of course, given the level of my intellectual development at that time, I was not capable of formulating the feelings and mood that possessed me as clearly as I am doing now, but I distinctly recall that they were something like that.

The size of my wage was also of concern to the other pattern-makers, who loved a free drink and were anxiously awaiting pay-day for me to "treat" them, the size of the treat depending upon the size of my wage.[2]

At last the long awaited Saturday payday arrived. The time-keeper began to distribute the paybooks.[3] He placed mine on the workbench. Trembling, I opened it up. On the first page were my first and last names and my occupation: "pattern-maker."

"This means I am no longer just a little apprentice; I'm a real pattern-maker!" I said to myself proudly. With trembling hands I licked the tips of my fingers, turned to the next page, and read: eighty kopecks per day! I was filled with so much joy that I could hardly breathe, and my head began to throb.

"How much?" Sherstiannikov asked me.

Instead of answering I silently handed him the paybook, at-tempting to conceal my excitement.

That evening, after drinking a cup of tea (I had not yet learned to drink vodka) and treating the others to drinks in a tavern, I hauled my scanty possessions over to the apartment of Sherstian-nikov, who had offered to rent me half a room, and parted with Korovin forever.

As I have already said, Sherstiannikov, whose apartment in the Zamoskvoreche district[4] I moved into, was also a worker at Brom-ley's and earned eighty kopecks a day. He was married and was expecting an addition to the family in the near future. It was hard enough for two of them to live on eighty kopecks, and now, to add to their misfortunes, there was a child in prospect. Hence they were very pleased to provide me with room and board and thereby add to their income. Sherstiannikov was a quiet, sub-dued, poorly educated fellow. His wife Grusha was his exact op-posite—a glib, saucy, tough-talking city girl.[5] She had once been the housekeeper of some great "lords," a source of enormous pride to her. She considered her marriage with Sherstiannikov a failure and was not ashamed to say as much to his face.

"You boor, you lout! You don't even have any education! Why there were once real gentlemen who wanted to marry me!" she would often cry out in a fit of rage.

"Well, then you should have married a gentleman," Sherstian-nikov would answer sullenly.

"Precisely! What a fool I was to disgrace myself with a dope like you. You're not even good enough to clean my shoes. You ought to get down on your knees before me for going for such a lout!"

The more Sherstiannikov would answer back, the more incensed Grusha would become. For this reason he would usually keep quiet during such incidents, and Grusha would gradually calm down.

From time to time Grusha would entertain her girl friends in the apartment. These were workers from the Einem candy factory. They would sit around and drink tea. I would then be invited to join them. Embarrassed and blushing in the presence of girls, I would silently but seriously drink my tea and curse myself in my heart for my incapacity to deal with women. After tea they would move the bed, table, and chairs into a corner and begin to dance without music, either a quadrille or a "pastoral" waltz. Then I would feel my helplessness even more keenly: I simply lacked the real polish of an accomplished dancing partner.

How I used to envy my comrade Stepka, an apprentice turner at the List factory! When he visited me with his fiddle or guitar, our entire apartment would come alive and would soon be filled with the sounds of laughter and merriment. Stepka was a rather good-looking fellow—taller than average, slender, blond, with curly hair and lively, laughing eyes. He played the fiddle and the guitar pretty well, danced all the latest dances, knew a lot of anecdotes, and was able to tell all kinds of entertaining, funny stories. Naturally, he enjoyed enviable success among our young ladies, and, as we used to say, he was "the first fellow in the dancing ring." Not a single party, not a single wedding celebration among the workers we knew could take place without Stepka. He was always a sought-after guest, always the life of the party. In female company he seemed like a fish in water, and he would "pick the flowers of pleasure" unceremoniously. He had no interest whatever in politics and preferred to read the more humorous magazines, from which he drew his witty material. Nor was he especially religious, which meant it would eventually prove relatively easy for me to dissolve the last remnants of his religious prejudices.

It is true that each of us had his own assessment of the harmfulness of religion. At that time I viewed religion as a fabrication contrived by priests, which prevented people from growing intellectually and workers in particular from creating the heavenly kingdom here on earth. Stepka viewed the problem differently. "What others do is not my business," he would say, "but I don't like religion because it bores me: you have to go to church, observe the fast days, keep a somber look on your puss, and spend your whole life in fear of being hung by the tongue or by the feet in your afterlife. I prefer to live and to enjoy myself."

My frequent and close relations with Stepka were bound, of course, to have some influence on me, especially since there was no one around to counteract his influence. Vasily Egorych Savinov, my former teacher, had recently grown very sad about something; he resigned his job at List's and departed for somewhere in the Ural region, probably Orenburg. I began to devote more attention to my appearance. I bought myself a stylish jacket with mother-of-pearl buttons, a "fantasia" shirt, and a visored cap with a velvet band and a leather crown. In order to master the art of dance, I began to go to a dancing teacher.

The business of worldly self-improvement was now so attractive to me that I secretly began to search for books on these matters. "Indeed," I thought, "why shouldn't there be books like that? Why, there are even books on how to write letters!" I had bought just such a book on letter writing, one that I used with some success and that rendered great service to me.

One day, as I was walking by a store on Nikolskaya Street, I noticed in the window display a little book with a poorly painted cover, on which were depicted a lord and lady dancing. The book was entitled: *Self-Teacher of Dance and Good Manners*. I do not remember the author's name. "This is just what I need!" I said to myself with joy. I entered the store and asked to see the book. The price was reasonable—fifteen kopecks. I ran home with the book at full speed in order to learn the secrets of "good manners" without delay. But, alas, the book contained very little that was useful to me. It said that when seated at table, one should not wipe one's nose with the napkin, roll the bread into little balls, eat fish with a knife, or gnaw at the bones of a grouse. It explained how to eat an artichoke or an asparagus. In short, the book dealt with subject matter I had never even encountered; in fact, I did not even know if these things belonged to the animal, vegetable, or mineral world.

The only part of the book of any value to me was the one that contained some pointers on the "theory" of the art of dance. But it did not make me any less timid or any more resourceful in my relations with women, notwithstanding the intensive assistance of my friend Stepka.

In general I spent that winter quite happily, in a manner befitting an adult craftsman: I attended wedding celebrations, went to parties, danced, did the Kamarinskaya, and recited humorous couplets. And at one wedding party, I even took an active part in a brawl, from which I emerged with honor, ending up with some minor bruises under my shirt. In those days such brawls at weddings and parties were a common occurrence. They broke out on the slightest pretext—often even without much drinking. All that was needed was for two rival groups of young men who were competing for the same girls to run into one another, and a battle was sure to begin. Then, on the next day, decorated with "shiners"[6]—as we liked to call our black eyes—the bearers of these "distinguishing" marks became the targets of everyone's mockery and wisecracks at the factory. The usual, predictable response to the foreman's indiscreet inquiry into the origins of these "facial decorations" was this:

"On Saturday when I was at the baths[7] I stepped on the soap, slipped, and banged my snout against the washtub."

"Hey, what happened? Stepped on the soap again, eh?" These were the ironic words that usually greeted the embarrassed fellow with the shiner as he entered the lavatory to have a smoke.

"No, it's a little spot that came off somebody's fist."

"What kind of spot is that? More like a sledgehammer!"

Passing my time in this heady atmosphere, I had failed to notice that the long Easter holidays were again approaching. Grusha would wash and scrub, clean the room, scream, scold her phlegmatic husband Afanasy, and send him off on errands to bazaars and shops, never allowing him any peace and quiet. I too began to prepare for the holidays. I bought a barrel of red wine and all kinds of sweets, with the intention of organizing a little get-together at my place. I had decided not to return to the village this time, but to emancipate myself from my parental home once and for all.

At this point I should make a brief digression in order that the reader not be left with the impression that, carried away by my good fortune, I had lost all interest in political ideas. Despite my strong attraction to the worldly pleasures of city life, the little ember of political awareness that Savinov had implanted in me continued to smolder. This was expressed by the fact that, in the plant, I openly preached my still rather shapeless socialist ideas, engaged in arguments with the older workers, made fun of religion, spoke abusively about the factory administration, and so on. Of course all these speeches were no secret to the foreman. He heard about them through his informers, and for a certain period of time he remained quiet and observed what was happening.

As usual, I loved to read, and I would look to books for answers to all the questions that excited me. I loved to walk to Sukharevka[8] and rummage in the book piles, looking for something, but not even knowing what it was. Along with song books, letter-writing manuals, and the like, I sometimes got hold of books with a "point of view." I would choose these books at random, by their titles, which, of course, did not always correspond to their contents. Using this method, I once bought the book *The Black and the White Clergy*,[9] which did not live up to my expectations. Another time I bought a thick old book called something like *Collection*. This time I was luckier: it contained verses in translation about the exile of Dante as well as a fable by Franko called "The Little Tail."[10] As a rule, I did not read journalistic articles, since they were too difficult for me to understand.

The Easter holidays arrived. The first day in our apartment went rather badly. From the crack of dawn there were big arguments between Sherstiannikov and Grusha about their religious disagreements: when Grusha insisted that Afanasy go off to church to have their Easter cakes blessed,[11] he refused. Then a stormy scene occurred. Grusha scolded her husband with foul language, screamed, stamped her feet, and cried. But Sherstiannikov was unmoved. Grusha understood that I was the cause of Afanasy's apostasy, but she still decided not to extend her anger to me. The rest of the day was passed in painful silence.

After lunch on the following day, arrayed in my holiday best, I went to the Moscow River to watch the ice float by. I recall that the weather was springlike—clear, sunny. The riverbank was filled with holiday animation: laughter, joking, people nibbling on sunflower seeds, and here and there the cursing of drunkards. I ran into Stepka, and we began to wander together without any particular goal. Somehow holidays always seemed to derail us.

We would drift aimlessly from street to street until we finally
ended up in some beer hall or tavern. And so it was on that day.
When it grew dark, we ran into the turner Rezvov, a jolly joker
and an old bachelor, and the three of us went to a tavern. When
I had been working in the List factory as an apprentice, Rezvov
would never condescend to socialize with me. But now I was a
skilled craftsman.

The tavern was stuffy, full of smoke, and noisy. But this was all
drowned out by the powerful, ringing metallic sounds of the "or-
chestrion"—the so-called music machine. We sat down at a
small table. Rezvov would have liked to order a half bottle of
"Smirnovka," but I proudly announced that I did not drink pure
vodka, and we agreed to order ashberry brandy. At the same time,
Rezvov also ordered two bottles of beer. When we had finished
the brandy and the beer, Rezvov again proposed that we drink
"Smirnovka." Once again I began to object and suggested we
drink either ashberry or some other kind of brandy. But Rezvov
began to demonstrate so cunningly that there was no real difference between pure vodka and brandy, that the only distinction lay
in their strengths—namely, you had to drink more of the one
than of the other in order to get nice and tipsy—that I dropped
my objections. Today I cannot say for sure whether I had lost my
sense of taste or whether Rezvov was actually right, but in point
of fact I discovered no essential difference between the ashberry
brandy and the purified vodka.

After we had finished the vodka, Rezvov bought a pack of cigarettes and treated us to a smoke. At the time I still did not
smoke, but for the company's sake I did not refuse the cigarettes,
and I began to puff courageously. This excessive mixing of alco-
hols, in combination with the cigarettes, had a stupefying effect
on an "inexperienced" youth like me. I still cannot recall what we
talked about at the table, under what circumstances we separated, or how I left the tavern.

I came back to my senses when I felt the fresh air out on the
street as I headed back toward my home. As I was later told by
Stepka and Rezvov, they had not even noticed any special change
in me, for I was able to stand firmly on my feet for the entire time.
I lived on the fifth floor. As I ran quickly up the stairs, I could feel
my head turning round in circles and sat down on one of the
stone steps. But I had barely closed my eyes when I was caught in

such a terrifying, dizzying whirlwind that I felt that the building, the stairway on which I sat, everything had begun to spin and whirl around in circles while I was hurtling into some kind of an abyss. I gripped the banisters tightly. Inside of me something began to romp and turn about, as if, within my gut, a huge sickening snake had made its lair and was now coming up into my throat and trying to crawl out of me. For a while I either fell asleep or blacked out. When I came to, I had a strong headache and a tortured, remorseful conscience. I knocked on the door of the apartment and tried my best to appear sober. Then I walked through to my room. Grusha had opened the door, it seemed, without noticing anything. I felt relieved. I was especially afraid of losing my authority with her, for—in view of my sober lifestyle—she called me a "neat little mirror," forgave me my freethinking, and always held me up as an example to her husband Afanasy, who suffered breakdowns from his drinking bouts. And now, suddenly, she might see this "little mirror" in a drunken stupor. Just the thought of this consumed me with shame. Fortunately, however, everything turned out well.

I woke up early the next morning with an unbearable noise crackling in my head. Then I put my dirty outfit in order, destroyed the traces of my crime that had been left on the stairs, and only after that, feeling much more relaxed, did I tell the Sherstiannikovs the story of my first fall into sin. In the wake of this shock I then took a solemn oath never again to touch any vodka. Of course I did not keep to this vow fully and completely, but at least I never again was to find myself in that condition.

The holidays ended badly for me in one other respect. Every year the "Old Bromley" factory would undergo a cleansing of "unsuitable," "unreliable," and generally "undesirable" elements. This operation was carried out rather simply. When the Easter holidays came round, all the workers would be dismissed. Then when the holiday was over the foremen of the various shops would hire their workers anew.[12] In this manner all the workers whom the foremen found objectionable were left outside the factory gates. This was the category I now found myself in. The whole situation was so stupid that you could not even learn the reason for your dismissal. Not that many were interested in knowing.

This time, however, I did not grow sad, the way I had the previous time. First, because I already knew my own worth; second, because it was spring, and in the summer, as we used to say, "every little bush can give you shelter for the night"; and third, because this was a time when industry was beginning to flourish—new factories were being constructed everywhere and workers were in great demand. There were, of course, no labor exchanges in those days, but in spite of this we were very well informed about where workers were needed.

So this time, taking along my traditional tool box, I boarded a train and headed for the Mytishchensk railroad car factory, which had just been built.[13] That morning I "stepped up" to the foreman and was hired.

10
At the Mytishchensk Factory

THE NEW, bright-colored, spacious Mytishchensk factory sparkled like a toy. It was pleasant to look at from every angle. And the roar of its mighty Herculean whistle, with which the trumpets of hosts of archangels could not compare, resounded through the distant meadows and forests, frightening the animals and awakening the shabby, gray villages from their deep, centuries-old slumber. In and around the factory construction work was still in full swing: new factory buildings were being erected, workers' housing was going up in disorder—both little wooden houses and, for the bachelors, enormous barracks.

Our pattern shop was located on the upper floor, above the machine shop, inside a huge, tall building. The shop resounded with the characteristic monotonous metallic din of regularly operating turners' lathes, planing and milling tools, and the rustling noise of an entire cobweb of sliding driving belts. Now and then the screech of a circular saw cutting into strong dry wood would burst into this rhythmic sound.

Since the factory had been functioning for only a few months, no musty workshop traditions had had time to take shape.[1] There were few older workers; merry, cheerful, freedom-loving young men were predominant. I felt at home from the very first day. By now I was not in the least bit troubled by having to perform tests of my skill. I handled these examinations without the slightest difficulty. Despite my youth (I was eighteen), the foreman set my daily wage at a ruble sixty, that is, double what I was paid at Bromley's. I was, as they say, in seventh heaven.

I settled in an apartment that was a half-hour's walk from the factory, in the village of Sharapovo—in a little bungalow with a small front garden. The apartment owner—a metal turner named Vasily Alekseevich Klushin—was a venerable and fully "conscious" man who once had worked at the Gopper factory. He had participated in a strike and knew on a first-name basis all the outstanding workers who had suffered for their convictions. He never attended church, never prayed to God, and ate forbidden foods during Lent. He subscribed to the magazine *Niva*—because of its supplements, as he explained to me.[2]

From the very first time we took tea together Vasily Alekseevich gained my affections, and for a long time to come I retained the fondest memory of him. I would later recall with great warmth the dark summer evenings when, after work, sitting on the terrace over our tea by the sparkling light of a lamp, Vasily Alekseevich in his monotonous, grating voice, but a voice that penetrated deeply into my soul, would tell us about the heroic struggle of the members of the People's Will, about particular episodes from the history of the French Revolution, about the workers who had led the strike in which he took part, and so on. When he told his tales all the actors would quickly come to life; they became big and strong, with unyielding wills and irresistible charms.

Despite the calmness of his tone, I could sense his profound hatred for the "bloodsuckers"—the nobles, the landlords, the priests, and the tsar. When, in the course of some story, the "tsar" happened to come up, Vasily Alekseevich carefully avoided that word, either substituting the word "himself" or else lowering his voice to a secretive whisper.

"The people are dark, ignorant, without consciousness," he would say to me afterward, as if to justify himself, "they believe in the good father-tsar. You can curse the government officials, you can curse the nobles as much as you like—that's just fine, but the moment you try and touch 'himself,' why they'll just stomp on you. 'He's our anointed ruler,' they say, 'don't you touch him!' And who is it that anointed him?! Ignorant, they're ignorant, Seniushka,[3] our working people are slumbering," Vasily Alekseevich would add, shaking his head with a sigh, after a brief pause. "They need to be whacked on the head with something— then maybe they'd wake up a little faster. Or else maybe if some kind of a brigand appeared in our midst, someone like Stenka Razin or Pugachev[4]—then, if you please, everyone would follow him and hang the rich and the nobles from the lampposts, as they

did in France," Klushin would sometimes begin to fantasize, unhappy with the slow awakening of the working people.

Vasily Alekseevich also liked to muse about the future arrangement of a just order for humanity:

"Then everyone on earth shall be equal. There'll be neither
tsars, nor earthly rulers, nor judges, nor gendarmes, nor priests."

> *To the lazy belly we'll give no food,*
> *And a heavenly kingdom we'll create here on earth!*

—he'd love to cite these verses of Heine, which he altered to his
own taste.[5]

It was also from him that I first heard Pushkin's famous aphorism:

> *In Russia there is no law—*
> *There is only a pillar, and on that pillar—a crown.*[6]

There was one thing I didn't like at Vasily Alekseevich's: it was
the times when, on payday, after getting drunk, he would begin
to go into a jealous rage, without any justification, and to beat his
wife—a thin, frail woman, worn out by housework and by her
children. Not infrequently I had to come to her defense and save
her from the blows of the enraged Klushin. Nevertheless, my affection for Vasily Alekseevich did not diminish: in those days
wife-beating was a normal occurrence among workers.

But the presence of a Klushin at our factory was no "normal
occurrence" at all. To be sure, during my subsequent wanderings
I almost always encountered one or two venerable, respected,
conscious workers at each factory, men who were very similar to
Vasily Alekseevich in their spiritual outlook. They usually subscribed to an advanced, "progressive" newspaper, purchased
books with a "tendency," followed political developments, and
didn't believe in God. They kept their distance, however, from
real political activity. They would never get involved in anything,
never get too close to anyone, and would engage in frank discussions only with those workers whom they trusted. In their youths
they had almost all been actively involved in politics, and some
had even paid a price. They had known some of the outstanding
revolutionaries in their day, and they remembered them with
great admiration and told stories about them to us younger men
with great pride.[7]

These men were not attached to any well-defined political

trend, but were always glad to give their advice and share their experience—while maintaining all precautions—with their more youthful conscious comrades.

To jump ahead somewhat, I will say a few words about one such oldster whom I met a year later in St. Petersburg, while working at the Semiannikov factory.[8] I don't remember his family name, but everyone called him Vasily Evdokimych. He was then about sixty, but he was cheerful, healthy, and zestful. Almost all the young revolutionaries who were then working in the factories of the Nevsky Gate region knew him.[9] Everyone in our workshop had great respect for him, although they called him names like "the student" and "the atheist."

Vasily Evdokimych lived to see the Revolution of 1905. They tried to elect him a delegate to the Soviet of Workers' Deputies, to elect him a factory elder, and so on, but he refused.[10]

Somehow it raised your spirits to know that right there, by your side, or else in another shop, there was someone working with whom you could share your thoughts, your doubts, your failures. You knew that this person was sympathetic to you, understood your anxieties. . . . He was ready to help you with his counsel, ready to share his experience. . . . There is no doubt that such cultured worker-loners played no small role in the history of the workers' movement.

Later, enriched by revolutionary and worldly experience, I couldn't help but compare two types of withdrawal from politics and revolution—that of the workers and that of the intelligentsia.[11] When a member of the intelligentsia withdrew from the revolutionary movement it was usually accompanied by disenchantment, the disowning of his own past, nasty criticism of the things he had worshiped, frequently even acts of betrayal, or, at best, absorption in a narrow, useless way of life.

The situation of the worker-revolutionary was very different. He had no way out of the working class—he had to remain, as before, among his comrades, oppressed and exploited by capital, even if he was disenchanted with the revolutionary struggle. The knowledge and experience such workers had acquired in the revolutionary struggle would still remain with them, and their objective circumstances compelled them, albeit with great caution, to share these with the younger, active workers.

Vasily Alekseevich Klushin had great confidence in me, and

was in turn a real authority figure in my eyes. Unfortunately, his knowledge was extremely fragmented and unsystematic, and for this reason he was not always able to satisfy my intellectual curiosity.

One day he advised me to get hold of the works of Shelgunov, which, as he said, were "banned." [12] Undisturbed by that circumstance, I would spend entire days during my Sunday excursions to Moscow city strolling about the Sukharevka market searching in vain for the works of Shelgunov. I was just about ready to give up when all of a sudden I chanced to wander into a secondhand bookshop on Sretenka Street, and, just to clear my conscience, inquired one more time. To my amazement and happiness, the bookseller crawled under the counter and pulled out two large volumes in yellow covers—the works of Shelgunov. Overcome with joy, barely even bargaining with the bookseller, I paid him two rubles and fifty kopecks, headed straight for the railroad station, and returned to Mytishchi, holding my precious acquisition firmly in my hands.

Shelgunov's works interested and excited me for two reasons: first, they were banned, and second, Vasily Alekseevich had told me they contained exhaustive answers to all the questions of working-class life that had been troubling me.

And yet, when, with my heart pounding, I finally began to read the first volume, I experienced great chagrin and disappointment. The abstract language, the long, circuitous sentences, and the foreign words made it impossible for me to comprehend the book. No matter how hard I tried to strain my attention and penetrate into the heart of the text, I got absolutely nowhere. Nor was Klushin's assistance of much use to me. Finally, he somehow got the idea to advise me to buy a dictionary of foreign words. But even this proved futile: the dictionary I purchased for fifty kopecks was too small. I had to buy another. So it was that, by spending the entire evening at it every day for one whole month, I was just barely able to prevail over one article—I think it was "The Situation of the Working Class in Western Europe." [13]

My teachers had always held up the West European working class—the revolutions it had carried out, its forms of political and trade-union struggle—as an example to me. Yet here is Shelgunov describing its terribly hard conditions, its oppression and exploitation by capital, its poor housing, and so on. What could this possibly mean?

When I shared my doubts with Vasily Alekseevich, he tried to quell them, saying:

"That was earlier, a long time ago; today the workers in other countries are living very well. . . . Once we've had our revolution we won't have to listen to those damn bourgeois any more—how they trick us! . . . The workers themselves must learn to be leaders . . . and not to put their trust in outsiders."

But I didn't find these soothing opinions very convincing. The article I had read put me in a pessimistic mood about the fortunes of the revolution.

Real life, however, clearly more powerful than any mind-boggling theories, would not allow me to abandon myself to this pessimistic mind-set, pushing me instead to the real activity of this world. Sufficiently fortified by now by my awareness that I was "adult," "independent," and, what is more, "conscious," I bravely entered into combat with "human injustice." I stood up for the abused and the oppressed, enlightened and persuaded the "unconscious," and argued passionately with my opponents, defending my ideals.

Apart from me there were four or five tenants living at Klushin's apartment; during the summertime they slept in the entrance hall, in the storeroom, and on the terrace. They were young men of about my age or a little older. Two of them, brothers, were foundry workers called Aleksandr and Flegont. They came from Iaroslav province, and therefore pronounced the letter "o" very roundly.[14] They were both very lively and jolly fellows; one of them owned a "Vienna" accordion and played it very nicely. A third, Ivanov, was a machinist. He was a coarse, awkward fellow, who was often the object of mockery. Then there was the turner Volodka Ozeretskovsky, who liked to plume himself before us on his "clerical" background. And finally there was the timekeeper Oslopov, an affected young man with a slanting part in his hair and thin, reddish whiskers, who took great pride in belonging to the factory's administrative staff and was very embarrassed by his name's double meaning.[15] "My family name isn't Oslópov, it's Ós-lopov," he would usually say irascibly, correcting one of our guys and placing the stress on the first syllable, for we deliberately tried to distort his name.

We didn't like Oslopov and we kept him at a distance, and if we occasionally got to talking with him, it was only for the purpose of teasing him and making fun of his membership in the "noble" estate of officialdom. Although his salary was considerably lower than our monthly earnings, he still "looked down" on us workers. When he spoke he held his head aloft and forced his words, pronouncing them partially in his nose, trying to imitate the master mechanic. To impress us with his importance, he often began his conversation with the words: "The master mechanic and I. . . ."

Oslopov had once served as a scribe in the provincial governor's office, and he owned a visored hat that bore an official emblem, which he kept in his trunk and greatly esteemed.

"I still have the right to wear the emblem on the hat; it's just that I don't want to," he would boast to us.

"The emblem isn't going to make you any smarter," Flegont would interject.

Oslopov would get mad and leave the table.

"Come by more often—there's fun when you're not here," the indefatigable Flegont would call after him. Rare was the meal or tea at our place that was not accompanied by a clash between Oslopov and Flegont. But with the exception of Oslopov, we all lived together quite amicably.

Sometimes on Sundays we were visited by girls. The foundry worker Aleksandr would start playing his "Vienna" accordion and we'd begin to dance. My struggle against "human injustice" in no way prevented me from becoming more accomplished in the "worldly" social graces. My *Self-Teacher of Dance* was proving very successful. I no longer experienced any financial needs. I had bought myself a holiday "outfit," a watch, and, for the summer, a wide belt, gray trousers, a straw hat, and a pair of fancy shoes. In a word, I dressed myself up in the manner of those young urban metalworkers of that period who earned an independent living and didn't ruin themselves with vodka.

I shared a room with Ozeretskovsky, the turner I already mentioned. I already knew him from the List factory, where he too had worked as an apprentice. He was what we called a "straightforward" guy. He didn't mind a good drink or a good meal, enjoyed getting together to sing and dance, and loved to dress up and woo the girls. He was also excessively squeamish on matters of cleanliness—he waxed his shoes twice a week, kept his bed extremely tidy, never lay down on a cover in dirty boots and workshirt, and cleaned his teeth with toothpowder every day. Legally,

Ozeretskovsky belonged to the clerical estate—he was the son of a deacon or a sexton—a fact he liked to brag about when drunk.[16]

In spite of my closeness to him, or perhaps because of it, he would not submit to my propaganda. "It is said in the Scripture: neither cast ye your pearls before swine . . ."—he'd retort ironically, when I began to press him. "Look, if all the workers were to rise up, then I would join them, but I'm not about to put my head in the noose all alone, and I advise you not to put yours in either. Stop banging your head against the wall!" Hearing these and other similar stale arguments coming from the mouth of such a young fellow infuriated me at first, but after a while I got used to it and simply gave up on him.

In those days I didn't get to put much effort into antireligious propaganda, for the kind of young metalworker I was encountering was either indifferent to religion or consciously a nonbeliever.

One evening I returned home from work to find a "guest" awaiting me. It was my father. When he saw me, he rose to greet me, embraced me, and kissed me three times. In his long, fading pleated waistcoat, with his beard grown white and his dark thinning hair streaked with gray, he had somehow become stooped, pinched, and aged over the past few months. His voice had grown quiet. I felt sorry for him. The two of us sat together in my room all evening (Volodya Ozeretskovsky was working the night shift that week). Coughing intermittently and breathing heavily, my father spoke in a low voice about the village, about the bad flax harvest, about the loss of two sheep, about our family difficulties, about his quarrel with my older brother, and so on. I understood that in all the family squabbling it was my father himself, with his authoritarian, despotic character, who was guilty, while my brother was the victim. But as I heard his soft, penetrating speech, I was infected involuntarily by my father's mood. I felt an interminable pity for him, for this lonely, suffering old man, forsaken by everyone. But how could I help him? By returning to the village to become a peasant? No, that was out of the question. Even my father understood my state of mind and therefore uttered not a word about my returning to the village.

He stayed at my apartment for three days. He paid close attention to our style of life. All in all, he seemed pleased with me.

My comrades were very attentive to my father. Wishing not to hurt the old man, Volodka even decided to conceal our freethinking: on Saturday evening he lit the lamp before the icon that hung in our closet, although in general it was never illuminated, and on Friday he quietly asked the landlady to prepare Lenten fare for us. Such precautions were superfluous, for my father understood full well that I had "not returned to the Christian faith," that I had indeed become even firmer in my freethinking. And I myself did not conceal this.

Soothed and touched by my attentiveness, Father returned to the village. As we parted, I gave him ten rubles. Evidently, this kind of attention was particularly pleasing to him. Many years later people in the village would tell me how proud of me my father had been. It was not the money as such that was important to him as much as the fact that I had made my own way in life and become independent.

Yet at the same time, judging from his letters and from the accounts of fellow villagers, Father was constantly tortured by some kind of dim anxiety about me and about the fate that awaited me.

"I am amazed at the kind of child I have fathered: he drinks no vodka, smokes no tobacco, doesn't play cards, and doesn't care at all about the peasant," he would say with sadness about me to his friends and neighbors.

"It's all right, Ivan Egorych, he'll turn out right when he gets older," they would answer to console him.

The end of the summer was approaching imperceptibly. I was beginning to think about finding a winter apartment, since our cottage was not suitable for winter living. I did not wish to part from Klushin, so we discussed these problems together. In short, all my thinking was channeled toward my winter amenities. I felt solidly ensconced at the factory: the foreman was well disposed toward me and satisfied with my work; I made no errors in my work and arrived at work on time, missing no days. So it seemed to me.

But one day it happened that the foreman assigned me a very simple task: to make a pattern of the most ordinary straight piece of pipe with flanges. The foreman drew the sketches for the pattern by hand. When the pipe was finished, he came up to me, measured the mold with calipers, and declared that it would have to be thrown away because I had erred by an inch. Then he added that I would be fired because of this. Deeply upset not so much over the announcement of my dismissal as over the insult to my professional pride, I rushed to the workbench to get the sketch and shove it in his face, to prove it was his error and not mine. But, alas, the drawing was not on the bench, and I searched for it in vain. The foreman's sketch, the only proof that I was right, had disappeared, vanished without a trace. The foreman made no effort to locate it, which I found suspicious. And when my anger and resentment had subsided somewhat, everything became clear to me.[17]

After being paid off and saying good-bye to my friends, I headed back to Moscow to find a new job.

11
Working for a "Grater"*

ONCE AGAIN I did not remain without work very long. I found a job at a rather small machine works near the Krestovsk Gate. I believe it was called Vartts and Mak-Gil.[2] At first everything went smoothly and well there. I passed the test, bought everyone a round of drinks, made new friends among the pattern-makers, and even gained a bosom buddy, whom I later brought to Piter.[3]

Vanya Maiorov was my new friend's name. He was my age but still worked as an apprentice. He had a very keen interest in social questions, liked to argue, and struggled passionately against any kind of "injustice." We hit it off in no time at all and soon were sharing a single room.

It was from him that I first learned of the existence of the poet Nekrasov.[4]

"Listen, Senya, if only we could get our hands on Nekrasov's poems, you and I could learn so much! How well that man could write about the poor, and how he hated the rich! He excites you by getting straight to the heart of things," Vanya would say with enthusiasm, his eyes burning and his fists tightly clenched and raised in the air. "Now that was a man! But he lived in poverty, and how he was despised by all the high and the mighty, the idle talkers, those whose hands are steeped in blood!"

At this point Vanya would begin to declaim:

> From exultant idle talkers,
> Whose hands are steeped in blood,
> Lead me to the camp of victims
> For the wondrous cause of love.[5]

* A *rashpil'* is a file with a very large rasp cut. Workers used the term to refer to little subcontractors. (Author's note.)[1]

"And Nekrasov wrote another poem like that, about big shots and simple peasants," he continued. "When you read it, tears will flow from your eyes and your fists will clench by themselves. You've got to read it! It's called: 'At the Main Entrance.'"[6]

Almost every Sunday thereafter Vanya and I would go to Sukharevka market in search of Nekrasov.

On one of those Sundays we were lucky: we located an old, tattered volume of Nekrasov's verse. Filled with excitement, we rushed home with the book. However, we were in for a big disappointment: the page with the poem "Reflections at the Main Entrance" had been torn out.

Still, we refused to give up hope that we would somehow be able to recover it. On one of the following Sundays, Vanya, who was better than I was at writing, went to the Turgenev Library to find the Nekrasov volume and copy "Reflections at the Main Entrance" from it. But here too we were in for a disappointment. It turned out that reading the works of Nekrasov was not permitted at the "people's libraries."[7]

We read other verses by Nekrasov with great enthusiasm. Even though we knew that we would have to arise and go to work at 6 A.M., we often remained awake well past midnight reading aloud the simple, angry verses of Nekrasov, henceforward our favorite, most beloved poet. We learned all his more or less outstanding poems by heart. Thereafter, and for a long time to come, Nekrasov's poetry was a powerful propaganda weapon among workers who were just beginning to open their eyes.

Not a month had gone by since I joined the Vartts factory when I was fired once again, this time without even getting two weeks' notice. I endeavored to obtain "justice" from the factory inspector, but absolutely nothing came of this.[8] Vanya Maiorov was dismissed at the same time I was. Dark and difficult days of unemployment followed. Our savings were running out. We would arise earlier in the morning than usual, walk to some outlying area of the city, and stand at the gates of a factory awaiting the appearance of a foreman. We had long since stopped riding on the horsedrawn trolley, which we could not afford. We lunched in soup kitchens for five kopecks on leftover pieces of tripe and lung. And in the evening we drank tea with bread.

All our efforts to find some sort of job at a factory were fruitless.

We were forced to turn to a "grater." The latter greeted us with distrust and suspicion. Usually the people who came to him for work were inveterate drunkards, ruined from drink, who appeared at work dressed in tattered clothes that "barely covered their privates"; now there suddenly show up two young fellows in nice trousers and high boots, in fancy caps with rivets, and without any signs of unrelieved drunkenness on their faces! This was truly an amazing sight to behold! Winking mischievously with his left eye and looking us over unceremoniously from head to toe, the "grater" picked at his nose with self-importance, scratched himself below the back and asked:

"Do you know how to work?"

"We sure do."

"Show up at work tomorrow then."

Filled with joy, after nearly a month of unemployment, we took our places at the joiner's bench with great delight and set to work with zeal. The "grater" was pleased.

There were only a few workers in the Maliavkin (the "grater's" name) workshop: the two of us, the owner's younger brother, who had just returned from the army—he was a powerful fellow, formerly a joiner and now learning the pattern-maker's trade—and two young apprentices.

Maliavkin's pattern shop was located in Marinaya grove on the basement level of a filthy wooden two-story house. The "grater" Maliavkin—a man of medium height, broad-shouldered, with tiny, constantly squinting eyes that seemed to be taking aim at something, a man with the demeanor of a Iaroslav bartender—did not work in the workshop himself but rushed about somewhere on the outside, getting orders and making all kinds of other arrangements along the way.

Strictly speaking, Maliavkin's "enterprise" could be called a "pattern shop" only with great reservations, since we obtained very few pattern-making orders and therefore mainly carried out the "assignments" of various "inventors."

For a while we worked on a solution to the then fashionable problem of inventing a "nonsplashing" tire: we built various tire covers—shields and casings for the wheels—carving different kinds of notches into them that, according to the inventors, would hold the mud near the wheel and keep it from splashing on pedestrians.

For a long time we also worked on the "invention" of an armchair toilet seat, with various hidden compartments and shelves
that were supposed to give it the appearance of a normal elegant
armchair while curtailing the smell. Whether this invention ever
brought glory and money to its authors I cannot say, but our
"grater" certainly made some money from this affair.

Officially, our workday was supposed to be eleven hours; but to
our misfortune, the "time problem" was decided not by us but by
our inventor-entrepreneur, who, with the aid of his categorical
imperative, also dictated the rules of our behavior. Hanging on
the wall of the workshop was a dusty, flyblown clock, which, obedient to Maliavkin's will, accelerated its pace at the beginning of
the workday and slowed down at the end, thereby transforming
our eleven-hour workday into twelve hours. Our wage was eighty
kopecks a day, a sum we could only accept temporarily. Given my
professional ambition and the standard of living I had already attained, I could not be satisfied with a wage like that.

Unfortunately, our "grater" tried to reduce even this meager
sum. Always short of money, we were forced to borrow small
amounts from Maliavkin in the interval between paydays. On
such occasions he would be unusually accommodating and even,
it seemed to us, generous. When we asked him for two or three
rubles before payday, he usually replied:

"Take even more, my boys—we'll work it out later. For you I
always have money." Sometimes the suggestion that we borrow
from him came from Maliavkin himself.

Then payday would come around. Maliavkin would "balaness"
the books, as he put it, and there would always be an underpay-
ment of one and a half or two rubles for each of us. We would try
by means of frank discussion to establish the rights of objective
truth; however, although we were the majority, the "grater's" subjective truth always gained the upper hand, and the two of us,
furious, clenching our fists and cursing his "virtues," would return
to our wretched hovel. Then we would discuss at length the in-
adequacies of the existing social order, building up our stock of
spite and indignation.

Winter was approaching. Our life at the "grater's" was becoming unbearable. Tired and angry, we would get home late, drink
our tea in silence, and go to sleep. We arose early, dressed hastily,
hurriedly ate our breakfast while still half asleep, and rushed to

work. So it went from day to day. Each of us on his own, at length and tenaciously, was thinking of how he could break away from the powerful clutches of the "grater." But where to go? In Moscow I was already known at many factories. To get work at some tiny plant was difficult and not even interesting. I would dream passionately of moving to Petersburg. I pictured that city as "the promised land," where the majority of workers were "conscious" and lived a cordial, comradely life, supporting one another in their struggle against foremen and owners.

We soon came to a firm decision to move to Piter. I would go first, and then, as soon as I found work, Vanya Maiorov would follow.

Having sold my entire wardrobe for next to nothing, I collected my money for the trip and, in the autumn of 1898, I moved to Piter.

Part Two

St. Petersburg

12
In Piter

ARLY IN THE MORNING, while the street lamps were still
E burning, I descended the platform of the Nikolaev railroad
station, my toolbox in one hand and a canvas bag in the other.
Where was I to go? I didn't know a soul. The streets were dark.
There were only twenty kopecks in my pocket.

After some thought I decided to go to a teahouse to drink tea
and await the dawn. I ordered tea and doughnuts and began to
rack my brains: what should I do next? Then I remembered that
my father used to talk of a distant relative who lived in Petersburg
and who had once been married to his sister (my aunt) and who
had remarried after she died. Father had also told me that this
relative too was a pattern-maker by profession. But I had never
laid eyes on either my deceased aunt or Bykov (my aunt's husband's name) in my life. "Shouldn't I seek out this Bykov?" I said
to myself. "Since he too is a pattern-maker, perhaps he'll be willing to help me out."

I located the city address bureau.[1] There I learned that Bykov
lived on the Smolensk Highway, in the region beyond the Nevsky
Gate.[2] So I boarded the local steam train, took an upper seat—
which was cheaper and gave me a better view—and headed for
the Nevsky region.

There, no matter which way you turned, you saw all kinds of
factories and workshops everywhere. An entire forest of enormous factory chimneys was spewing forth clouds of black smoke,
which covered the already gray Petersburg sky. Factory buildings,
houses, streets, and people moving rapidly about—all were covered by a thick layer of soot. Massive rhythmic noises resounded
from every direction: the rumble of the huge shafts that rolled the
red-hot iron bars; the blows of the steam hammer, which made

the earth tremble; the ponderous sound of panting locomotives.
And suspended in the air above all these other sounds was the
unbroken hum of the riveting of enormous steam boilers, which
lay on the ground like giant caterpillars. Everything here bespoke
the power of human labor and the grandeur of its inexhaustible
creative force.

And even later, whenever I happened to be in that region, I
would always be captivated, elevated, and transported by that
swift and powerful flow of human energy.

The train, rattling onto the siding, soon dragged me to the stop
at the Maxwell factory. I got off involuntarily and began to look
around: this was the very same factory where, two years earlier,
the workers had conducted a heroic struggle for a better future.
We owed our current ten-hour workday to these warriors. They
had fought and suffered for our sake.[3]

With these thoughts in mind, carrying my baggage in both
hands, I found the little two-story wooden house I was seeking
and walked upstairs.

In the corridor by the staircase, I was met by a small chubby
woman whose sleeves were rolled up to her elbows. In one hand
she held a washpail, in the other a dirty dustrag. She was apparently about to wash the floor.

"Bykov? Yes, here! And who would you be?" the woman asked,
placing the pail on the floor as she looked me over curiously.

I explained.

Her face expressed both joy and puzzlement. "How big you've
grown! How in the world did you end up here? Why I knew you
when you were only this high," the woman prattled, holding her
hand less than two feet from the floor. "By God, I would never
have guessed! Chances are if I'd met you on the street I couldn't
have recognized you for all the world. But why am I standing here
like this?" she said, suddenly collecting herself. "Let's go to our
apartment; I'll give you some coffee. You must be tired, poor boy."

We entered the apartment, which consisted of three rooms and
a kitchen. It was stuffy, and reeked of smoke and grease from the
work-clothes that hung there and the smell of swaddling clothes.
Skinny little kids, wearing nothing but small shirts and no pants,
were playing on the floor. With all their noise, shouts, and
squealing, it seemed as if there were eight of them.

"Are they all yours?" I asked.

"Who else's would they be! They're all ours. Their father is planning ahead for his old age. But the kids have gotten the best of us! Little Fedya is two years old and I'm already carrying number six."

It was clear that Avdotya Petrovna Bykova was really pleased by my arrival. She bustled about, ran every which way, made all kinds of fuss, served me coffee, and inquired about my father, our home, the village, and so on.

Engrossed in conversation, we were unaware that the dinner hour was approaching. Then the factory sirens began to roar. Somewhere in the neighborhood a mighty siren bellowed three times, pausing between each cry.

"That's our siren," Avdotya said as she rushed off. "I'll go make dinner before our people get home from work."

About ten minutes later, bending his head so as not to bump it against the door beam, the tall, thin, sinewy figure of Bykov, with his small light-colored beard and somewhat stooped shoulders, made his way into the room.

"This is Ivan Egorych's son—Semën Ivanovich," said Avdotya Petrovna, introducing me to Bykov.

Bykov's stern-looking, wrinkled face was suddenly illuminated by a broad, good-natured smile. He extended me his huge callused hand. We sat down to eat together. Avdotya Petrovna brought a half-bottle of vodka and placed a cup of thick, rich cabbage soup on the table. Bykov asked me about my father, and about the village that Bykov had left some 25 years earlier. I, in turn, told him why I'd come to Piter and asked him to find me work at the Semiannikov metalworking plant.[4]

"At the moment there doesn't seem to be a single free workbench at our factory," he said, "but I'll still ask the foreman. I've heard that pattern-makers are needed at the Rasteriaev factory.[5] Go work there for a while and I'll bring you over to our place when business has picked up there. Do you have your own tools?"

I pointed to my box under the bed.

"That should do for now," he said, "but later you'll have to buy some more. This won't be enough."

Avdotya Petrovna invited me to stay with them until I found work. She set up a cot in the kitchen.

"Now don't be upset with me, Seniushka, but you'll have to sleep with our tenant, Mikhail. As they say, there's no offense in close quarters."

This unexpectedly warm welcome raised my spirits; early the next morning, full of hope and confidence, I headed off to the factories in search of work. Each day, for lack of money, I had to cover on foot a distance of seven to ten miles: to the Vyborg side of the city, to Vasilevsky Island, and so forth.[6]

Within a week I was already at work in a metal factory on the Vyborg side. At first, since I still lived in the Nevsky Gate region, I had to walk all the way to the Vyborg side to get to work. I was terribly tired, but this did not diminish my joy and energy. I managed until my first payday, when I located an apartment near the factory, thanked Bykov for his hospitality, and set off eagerly to work.

Around 100 men worked in the pattern shop of the metal factory. A large number of them were Finns, Estonians, and Latvians—stern and taciturn peoples whom it was very hard to get to know. The routine at the factory was very rigorous; it lacked the patriarchal simplicity one found in the metalworks of Moscow. Let's just begin with the fact that the factory's huge iron gates clanged shut with the precision of clockwork exactly at the beginning of the workday every morning and at the end of the lunch hour. Even if you were only a few seconds late, the heavy gates crashed down right under your nose, leaving you without a half-day's work; on top of this, apart from the lost pay, they hit you with a one-ruble fine. Even the lavatory was located in the workshop itself; it was elevated on a platform, from which anyone who mounted the throne could be surveyed by the foreman.

The foreman, a red-snouted, stocky man with a reddish beard, always loomed large at his table in the middle of the shop, from which he unswervingly observed every motion of the workers. All of this gave me a gloomy and depressing feeling.

Similarly, my apartment, located on Timofeev Street, near the factory, brought me neither calm nor joy. Officially I had rented a half a room for myself, but since I did not own my own bed, I had to share one with a very "gray" fellow,[7] an unskilled laborer from the same factory. My other roommate—a tall, stout Lithuanian with a red mustache—worked in the boiler shop. He was a Catholic and was notable for his great devoutness. During his free

time, even on weekdays, he would sit with his prayerbook, or else
he would get some other religious book from his priest and would
begin to read us quotations from the texts and sayings of Thomas
Aquinas, Socrates, Plato, etc. At the time I had no idea who those
characters were, but I assumed they belonged to the ranks of
Catholic saints.

On holidays both my roommates would put on starched shirts,
get their frock coats from their trunks, and set off for the Catholic
church. Then, after dinner, they would take a nap, following
which they would visit their friends or invite them to the apartment—the friends were the same kind of gray religious types,
without any real interests—to talk about the workshop, about
wages, about high prices, and about how life used to be incom-
parably better. To have conversations with them about "higher
matters," in the absence of which I could no longer survive, was
both useless and possibly dangerous. I didn't have a single close
friend. On non-workdays I would always return to the Nevsky
Gate region and unburden my soul to Ivan Vasilevich Bykov.
True, he was not of my generation, he did not share my romantic
orientation, but he still understood me amazingly well, sympathized with those who struggled for "justice," took pity on them,
and was prepared to render them any kind of support. However,
he did not really believe in the triumph of "the ideals of justice."

Two months went by. I had made the acquaintance of a young
fellow, a pattern-maker named Aleksey Churakov. He lived with
his parents in the Okhta region.[8] Once when, in the course of a
conversation, I expressed my displeasure with my apartment, he
proposed that I move to his place. We grew close very quickly; we
began to have discussions and to read books together, so that little
by little my life began to assume a more sensible character. I sent
for Vanya Maiorov, who came up from Moscow and moved in
with us.

Nevertheless, life on the Vyborg side was rather dull and monotonous. A working man had nowhere to go during his free time
or on holidays. The only place for relaxation was the tavern or the
billiard room. During the two weeks between paydays we usually
stewed in our own juice: we debated, we conversed, we read, but
we were bored by all this and we began to look for some other
kind of distraction. Payday would come, and after getting our
money we sometimes went to a tavern, ordered a double bottle of

vodka, and, in a spirit of foolhardy competition, drank it up without pausing for breath, after which we went to play billiards. We'd return home late in the evening a bit tipsy. Aleksey Churakov's old mother would scold him and we would catch it at the same time. Sometimes we were visited by a tall, thin joiner named Skorodumov, who brought along forbidden books or proclamations. We would read them greedily, argue about them— and that was all.

Our connections and experiences were neither growing nor widening. But meanwhile, at the factory, little clashes with the foreman began to take place—first it was me and then Churakov. We perceived, as did others, that foreman Artemev was mocking us and trying to drive us out. At first we patiently tolerated all his cavils, but when payday came around we noticed that he'd reduced our piece-rates by ten kopecks each. Our patience ran out. We were insulted and outraged by this injustice. The entire workshop knew what had happened; everyone took our side and tensely awaited the outcome. Outraged and indignant, we went up to the foreman, threw our paybooks on the table, and demanded to be paid off. The foreman was taken somewhat aback, but then he calmly accepted our challenge and promised to discharge us in two weeks.[9]

I can no longer recall whether it was before or after this exchange with the foreman that we hatched a plan to teach him a lesson, cost what it may. We confided our plan of revenge to some of our close comrades. They apparently revealed the news to others, which resulted in a shopwide collection of money for use in the event of our arrest. This, in turn, considerably heightened our spirit of revenge. We soon felt like heroes, doing a brave deed in the interest of all people oppressed by the foreman.

It was agreed in advance, after we had weighed all the circumstances and devised a plan, that on Friday morning of Passion Week, three of us—Churakov, Skorodumov, and I—would await the foreman on a quiet street, far away from the police, where, we calculated, he had to pass on his way to work. We knew that Artemev usually went to work a little later than the workers, at a time when the side street was already empty. When the last siren had sounded, the gates had clanged shut, and the side street had emptied, the stocky figure of Artemev came around the corner. When he saw us he evidently understood what we were up to and tried to retreat. But at that moment Skorodumov, who was standing behind him, knocked Artemev down with a deft blow of his fist. He got up, but just at that moment we ran up to him, knocked him off his feet again, bloodied up his face, and then took flight when he cried out. A policeman came running to the scene, but by then we were all gone.

That evening the three of us went to the factory to collect our severance pay. When we got there, however, we were met not by the bookkeeper but by a police inspector. We demanded our money from the workshop supervisor. He declared that we would receive our payoff at the police station.

"We would like to point out that we don't work at the police station!" we replied.

"Knock off the smart talk! Forward march to the station!" the inspector declared rudely.

We obediently accepted his invitation. At the police station they drew up an official report accusing us of having assaulted and beaten the foreman. We denied this and refused to sign the report. After some argument they took us to the basement, where they locked us up with some drunkards who were drying out. In the morning we were each accompanied to our homes by a policeman, who signed us over to the custody of our janitors.[10]

Some two weeks later we were summoned to court. Although we managed to produce the most authentic perjurers, who confirmed our innocence, the justice of the peace still sentenced us to ten days in jail.*

---

* I once tried to record this episode, in 1909, but unfortunately my manuscript was taken from me by gendarmes and was utilized as material evidence by the court in the chambers of the rather well-known judge Krasheninnikov. I recall how, after my defense attorney, Novikov, delivered a speech in which he claimed I was the most honest person in the world, the prosecutor got up and quoted with irony the part of my manuscript that said: ". . . although I managed to produce the most authentic perjurers, the justice of the peace still sentenced me to ten days in jail. . . ." My lawyer was so disconcerted by this circumstance that he wouldn't call any more witnesses in my defense. (Author's note.)

13
Vasilevsky Island

SOON AFTER the incident at the metal factory I obtained a new job at the Siemens-Halske plant on Vasilevsky Island.[1] This factory manufactured electrical machine parts, various kinds of apparatuses, fixtures, etc. The workers there were highly qualified, most of them foreigners. Among them were Germans, Swedes, and Estonians, but we gave them all the same name—"Germans." Working conditions were good there: the workers were not subjected to humiliating searches when they left the factory; each workshop had a cloakroom for your outer garments. The foreign workers came to work wearing starched collars and hats; some of them arrived on bicycles. Then they changed into their workclothes in the shops, where they would hang their streetclothes in the cloakroom before donning their long workshirts. Every workshop had its own washbasin, government-issue soap, and pieces of clean rag for washing the hands. Wages, to be sure, were no higher than at other factories, but these outward conditions were a great attraction for workers. Many a worker dreamed of getting work at Siemens-Halske.

In this respect I was lucky: without any trouble, without any patronage, I was hired immediately, took the test, and was given an hourly wage of fourteen kopecks. There was also supplementary piecework, so that I generally earned around two rubles a day.

At the factory I befriended two young workers—the patternmaker Khristofor Marakasov and the machinist Pavel Smirnov. At first we usually got together at Marakasov's apartment, but the three of us soon rented a large room and moved in together.

Smirnov had connections with some students, who now and then would visit our apartment. We served them tea and conversed with them about various political themes. On one occasion

one of them brought us the book *Underground Russia*, by Stepniak.[2] Much of it was incomprehensible to us, especially the
theoretical discussions, but some of the individual stories, the
episodes from revolutionary life, and the characterizations made
a powerful impression on us. It was all so terrible and frightening,
yet at the same time we wanted to suffer for the common cause,
to sacrifice ourselves in the same way as the heroes described in
the book.

The most frequent visitor was the student Ilya Shendrikov.* Of
average height, thin, with a tiny beard and long hair, lively and
passionate—he would often regale us with the most terrible terrorist plans. One time he would tell us how nice it would be to
invent some kind of electric gun that could smash the gendarmes, spies, and in general the power of the propertied classes,
all without being seen. Another time he outlined a plan to hurl
the most highly explosive bomb at the Council of State[4] or at
some other institution where high officials and privileged society
gathered. Often heated arguments—barely comprehensible to
us—flared up between him and Koriakin, a tall, disheveled student who wore a frock coat.

All this was new to me, exciting and interesting. It soared above
everything else around me; it confronted me with a whole series
of new questions and stimulated my thirst for knowledge. Shendrikov, Koriakin, and the other students, the first students I had
ever met in my life, seemed to me to be extraordinary people,
who gripped all knowledge in their hands and had ready answers
to all questions. I envied them, but at the same time I was afraid
of something, had some kind of misgivings. I did not feel as natural among them as among my fellow workers.

One day during a visit Shendrikov proposed that I accompany
him to the Taitsky Sanitarium, where the student Koriakin was
convalescing. I eagerly agreed, donned my holiday suit and a
starched collar, and set off with Shendrikov for the railroad station. On the way, Shendrikov said to me:

"Since there will be many people visiting the sanitarium, I will
introduce you not as a worker but as a pharmacist."

I had never heard the word "pharmacist" before and had not
the foggiest idea what it meant. But out of a false sense of shame,

---

* This is the same Shendrikov who later played the adventurer-traitor's role in
Baku. In Siberia in 1917–18 he simply became an outright villain. (Author's note.)[5]

I couldn't get myself to ask Shendrikov to explain it and I pretended to understand. At the sanitarium we were met by Koriakin. Delighted to see us, he conducted us on a sightseeing tour of the enormous building. Then we strolled around in the woods and went to the public dining room, where many people were gathered to drink tea and listen to a lady visitor play the piano. Various student friends of Shendrikov would come over and chat with him. He introduced me to each of them, always pronouncing my last name very unclearly. One of them was a medical student in his student uniform, whom I mistook for an officer. We were introduced. He asked me my occupation. I replied: "pharmacent."[5] He smiled, took Shendrikov aside, and exchanged some whispers with him. Then Shendrikov, embarrassed, told me that the student had been intensely interrogating him about who I was, since I had pronounced the word "pharmacist" so badly. By now I was so upset by what had happened that I began to make one blunder after another, until I finally asked Shendrikov to get us out of there as quickly as possible. He tried to calm me down, assuring me that the incident would not lead to any trouble. Shendrikov continued to visit us fairly often after this, and every time he came he would try to drag me to some kind of gathering of educated society, but after the sanitarium incident I always turned him down in no uncertain terms.

Through Khristofor Marakasov we made the acquaintance of Vasily Ivanovich Riabov, a draftsman at the Baltic shipbuilding factory. Riabov was a very lively little man, witty, cheerful, more well-read than we were, who also had connections with students. At his suggestion we decided to form a little circle, which would meet about once a week to discuss the burning issues of the day or to read some article from a magazine or book that Riabov would comment on and interpret. At the time, because we still were ignorant when it came to understanding the various political groupings, we often read articles or stories from the journal *Russian Wealth*.[6]

One day Shendrikov came to our circle and tried to convince us to organize a mutual-aid fund, whose charter he would write himself. As best I can recall, there was nothing really political, let alone revolutionary, in his proposal. But we did not have a very direct sense of the difficult situation of the working class that he would describe to us; our wages were good, our workday was not very long, and we were tired of hearing people talk, whether at home or at the plant, about our problems of daily life. What we wanted to hear from outsiders, from students, was something out-of-the-ordinary, something novel, something that would open new horizons to us. For this reason we were very cool toward Shendrikov's proposal, although, out of tact, we raised no objections and accepted it without debate. We took up a collection on the spot and gave him the money. Later my comrades and I frequently subscribed to mutual-aid funds of this kind, though as such they were of little interest to us. We thought of our contributions as going not to ordinary mutual-aid funds, but to the goal of revolutionary struggle.

It was around this time that our circle was joined by two women workers from the Cheshire textile factory.[7] Both were friends of Pavel Smirnov. They were Olga Nikolaevna Melnitskaya and Anna Nikolaevna (whose last name I don't remember). The former was very intellectually advanced, very well-read, and had a brother—Nikolai Melnitsky (a writer)—who was in political exile.[8]

Until this time, as was customary in a workers' milieu like ours, we had looked upon the woman worker as a creature of a lower order. She had no interest in any higher matters, was incapable of struggling for ideals, and was always a mere hindrance, an encumbrance in the life of a conscious worker. How great, then, was my surprise and admiration when, for the first time, I made the acquaintance of two conscious women workers, women who argued logically and debated just like the rest of us. Henceforth we met with them frequently and joined them on big holiday excursions in the country.

Our life proceeded happily, joyfully, sensibly; we enjoyed the present and looked with hope to the future. Our cheerful mood was not even beclouded by the fact that I was once again dismissed from the factory. I soon found a job at a very tiny machine works, the Mikhael factory, where the workday lasted eleven hours. This was exhausting, but my youth and health conquered all. Though I ran all around the far-flung working-class regions of the city, often exhausted from lack of sleep, I never lost my high spirits.

Thus the summer went by and a new winter approached. I began to visit Bykov's place in the Nevsky region more frequently and again reminded him of his promise to get me a job at his factory. That fall, during one of my visits, he cheerfully announced that his foreman at the Semiannikov factory had sent for me. Overjoyed, excited, I rushed off to share my triumph with my comrades. They were very sorry that we had to part, but I promised them that, even though I'd be living in the Nevsky Gate region, I would surely maintain my close relations with them.

I received two more letters—mailed from the village—from my father; both were full of anxiety. Apparently someone had told him all kinds of fables and horror stories about me. In the first letter he called on me to attend church, to pray to God, to serve my employer with diligence, and so on. As a model of virtue he offered himself as an example: "I lived in Petersburg for 25 years," he wrote. "I changed employers only twice, I was never prosecuted or subjected to criminal investigation, I didn't spend one night in jail. But you, you scoundrel, you haven't been able to find yourself a decent place in society; you change jobs every month. Just wait and see: your employers will soon sweep you out with a broom. . . ."

The second letter was even more ominous. This time my father categorically demanded that I mend my ways: ". . . and if you don't settle down, you scoundrel, I won't renew your pashport. I'll have you brought home by the police, and when they've brought you home, I'll whip you with a birch rod myself, in the district administrative office, in the presence of honest people. . . ."[9]

This threatening letter seriously disturbed me, especially because my passport was about to expire. True, I knew that my father would not carry out his threat, although in those days he definitely had the authority to do so, and I remembered several instances of that kind. I knew my father's hot-tempered yet easily appeased character. So I wrote him a conciliatory letter and sent him ten rubles, after which he calmed down somewhat.

14
The Nevsky Gate Region

THIS IS ONE of the working-class regions that has played an enormous role in the history of the revolutionary movement. Such giant plants as the Nevsky (formerly Semiannikov) shipbuilding factory, the Aleksandrovsk works, the Obukhov factory, the Pal factory, the Maxwell factory, and the Stearine works were located there.[1]

The inhabitants of the region's Smolensk Highway, entirely working-class, lived under particularly crowded, dirty, uncomfortable conditions. Although it collected vast amounts of tax money from the workers, the Petersburg city council did absolutely nothing to provide them with services. The highway area was replete with inns, beer halls, taverns, and churches, but there were no cultural institutions of any kind to be seen. For a population of 60,000 there were only two shabby theaters: the "Vienna" Garden and the little theater at the glass factory.[2]

It is therefore not at all surprising that on holidays, after the workers collected their pay, the area witnessed constant fights, scandals of all kinds, hooliganish gang-beatings of innocent passersby. The local jails were filled with drunks, hooligans, and the victims of violent beatings. Especially notorious for their violent fracases were the so-called "Pskopsies" (a slang term for men from Pskov province)—ignorant, illiterate, tough fellows who did most of the heavy, dirty work in the metal factories.[3]

The workers of the Nevsky region, in both their outer appearances and their inner lives, could be divided into two basic parts: the metalworkers and the textile workers.[4] The former were more cultured, earned higher wages, and, in their overwhelming majority, were not connected to the village.

The workers from textile factories—most of them women[5]—
had low wages, lived in barracks, and were strictly protected from
outside influences by their employer-"benefactors"; although
even textile workers were only weakly connected to the village,
they still retained the peasant biases and the lack of culture that
characterized village life.

However, both groups were subjected to immeasurable exploitation, to the unrestrained arbitrary power of the factory administration, both large and small, inside the workplace, and to the
savage law of the fist enforced by the tsarist police regime on the
outside. Whether innocent or guilty, a worker who landed in jail
was subjected to mockery, curses, and beatings by the police.

For this reason, whenever there were conflicts of any kind
within their own ranks, workers could not tolerate police intervention and tried to resolve them on their own. Even among the
"gray" workers hatred of the police was so great that in their eyes
the normal laws of human society did not extend to the "pharaoh," the "archangel," the policeman in general.[6] To beat up or
even to kill a policeman was considered a great deed, worthy on
this earth of "forgiveness for forty sins."

And yet the mass of workers, taken as a whole, were so ignorant, so politically undeveloped, that one could conduct socialist
propaganda among them only with the utmost caution. You could
inveigh against the factory administration, the police, or the
priests practically out in the open, but to insult either the tsar or
God was out of the question. "You can break the cup, but never
touch the samovar!" you would often hear the older men shout
when one of the conscious young workers said something insulting about the tsar.

In those days one could still observe the most savage scenes of
religious fanaticism in the Nevsky region. I saw with my own eyes
how, in a temperature of 30 below, eight workers who were being
baptized, when the priest had said the prayer and sanctified the
water in a Neva River ice-hole, threw themselves into the icy
water one after the other to "purify" themselves of their sins.
True, the huge crowd standing on the riverbank, as I recall, was
interested not so much in the "purifying" side of the affair as in
the daring and fearlessness of the bathers:

"Those guys are incorrigible!"

"Look, boys, look! The one with the beard not only plunged in,
he even took a swim! Isn't he something!"

"After a dip like that you've got to drink a good half bottle and then sleep it off."

"Why just a half! It'll take more than a bottle to warm them up."

This was followed by all kinds of talk about swimming in the "Jordan" and what that had led to.[7]

"What fools, damn them!" Bykov cursed, when I told him the story of the baptismal bathing. "You see? And you want to get to socialism with this kind of people! Why they'll hang you from the first lamp. First they must be educated!"

"Don't worry, they'll start moving, you'll see," I retorted.

"Maybe if you beat them with something, then they'd rise up, but like this . . . ," he replied despairingly.

I would often hear this kind of negative statement about the working people, about their ignorance, from persons who sympathized with their cause but for one reason or another stood aside. In order to arouse the working masses, you had to "knock them on the head," "strike" them with something extraordinary—that was a constant theme of conversation even among the more impatient workers, who disliked the petty, tedious, day-to-day tasks of organizing and educating workers, and who therefore turned to the SRs or the anarchists in search of "glorious deeds."[8]

Sometimes Bykov and I would engage in yet another kind of dialogue:

"You youngsters are poorly. . . . Well, you're just not serious enough," he would say with distress.

"And what of it? Would you like to paste beards on our faces?" I'd reply, half-jokingly.

"No one will trust you guys—you're too feeble. No solid, reliable worker would follow you. And they're the ones with the power!"

"Well why don't you solid types get down to business yourselves, instead of criticizing us!" I rejoined, stung to the quick.

"Don't get mad! I mean well. But you're wasting your time with the likes of us. I have a heap of kids, each one younger than the next, and Vasily Evdokimov is already too old."[9]

These and similar conversations emerged almost spontaneously from the environment and way of life of the workers of the Nevsky region. An enormous mass of workers was distributed within a rather small area. This was particularly striking on hol-

idays when, abandoning their stuffy "corners," "bunks," and barracks, the working people poured into the streets like a happy
anthill, forming barriers for miles on end, blocking the movement of the train, and incessantly ringing bells. The question
naturally arose in the mind of any conscious worker who viewed
this crowd of peacefully parading workers: "And what couldn't
this mass accomplish if only it were conscious? If by some miracle
one could awaken this powerful force and turn it against the tsarist autocracy, the police, the capitalists?! Why we'd level the old
slave system to the ground!" Such were the thoughts and dreams
of the few solitary revolutionary youths, who, as they observed
this harsh and unattractive reality, continued to founder among
the inert and sometimes even hostile masses.

I was again living at the Bykovs at this time. Besides me they
had four other tenants, also workers from nearby factories. It was
noisy, crowded, and dirty at the Bykovs, but I was happy there:
Avdotya Petrovna treated me with unusual kindness and often
even cited me as an example to the other tenants. At first my old
friends—Marakasov, Smirnov, Vanya Maiorov, and others—visited me pretty often. As before, we would gather together to read
and to discuss all kinds of burning political questions.

Sometimes individual issues of the journal *Workers' Thought*
would come our way, and we would read them with great interest.[10] But despite this interest, we considered the journal not very
suitable to our own needs. True, we were unable to define its
shortcomings analytically, since we were still too ill-equipped intellectually, but to us it simply seemed insufficiently belligerent.
On the other hand, we considered it great material for conducting propaganda among less conscious workers: it contained
much information about the workers' basic needs, it printed correspondence from factories, and it criticized management.

"The people who run the journal must think differently, but
they deliberately write less harshly so as not to frighten away the
less conscious masses"—this is what we would say to ourselves
regarding *Workers' Thought*. The mass of workers, as I would
later have many occasions to learn, eagerly swallowed this shop-
floor bait, but still their political development failed to advance.

One day I brought a poem someone had given me to the pattern shop, a poem I liked very much. I will cite it here as best I
can recall it:

> *The happiness of life does perish.*
> *The people suffer torture.*
> *All day long, from morn to night,*
> *It's "work!" It's "toil!"*
> *The parasites, the bosses,*
> *Beware of them, watch out!*
> *No one appreciates our work,*
> *Our labor's not for us:*
> *He who lives and thrives from it*
> *Is he who tortures us.*
>
> *The working folk are stupid!*
> *To pray for their bosses*
> *They visit the temples.*
> *There, the priest begins*
> *To preach his sermon:*
> *They must be patient, pray,*
> *And learn to suffer.*
> *And so the working folk endure,*
> *Endure their pain in silence,*
> *As they haul their kopecks,*
> *Their last one to the priest.*[11]

These verses were surprisingly successful, even among the older workers. They were read, copied, and memorized. You had to wait your turn to get hold of them. Among the pattern-makers I had my share of enemies, who could not forgive me for having broken the shop tradition when I started working there: I had refused to pay the "vodka tax."[12] Now, since almost everyone knew who had brought in the poem, I anticipated the worst possible outcome. But days went by, then weeks, yet my misgivings proved unfounded. Soon thereafter many of the very workers I had feared began to approach me stealthily to ask if I could give them something to read. I can only explain the success of the poem by virtue of the fact that it insulted neither tsar nor God.

By contrast, I had had to disseminate the proclamations of the "Union of Struggle for the Emancipation of the Working Class" with extreme caution, since they would quickly throw the "solid," "honorable," and backward element of the workers into a state of panic and rage.[13]

Before long I had formed a wide circle of ties with workers from the Nevsky region, including workers from other factories as well as our own. Among them I can recall Dobrovolsky from the Maxwell factory, Petr Mitrofanov from the Pal factory, and the metalworker Mikhail Sergeev.

Within this group Dobrovolsky stood out for his enormous ardor. He always arrived at our gatherings in a state of agitation and alarm and, his voice trembling, would tell us of some new outrage or offense perpetrated by the factory administration against some male or female worker. His wrath and indignation were usually aroused not so much by the administration itself as by the slavish submissiveness and abasement with which the offense was tolerated.

"It's sad to say, but it's obvious that the working people will not awaken from their slumber very soon." With these words he would end his angry, disorderly speech, bitterly and without hope.

Sometimes he would recite the verse of Nekrasov:

"What if the storm broke out? . . ."[14]

Dobrovolsky was older than the rest of us, but he was so passionate, fiery, and honest, he experienced every injustice, every outrage, so profoundly, that we seriously feared he might get carried away and do something absurd.

After we had come to know and trust one another sufficiently, we formed a little circle of six or seven persons. The leader of our circle was a tall student with a small, light-colored beard, who was called Danilov.* He was calm, self-possessed, and thorough. Our lessons were usually on Sunday mornings, either at Mitrofanov's place or at my own. At first Danilov would tell us about the lives and struggles of the workers of Western Europe. We listened to him attentively, but we felt, as he did, that these questions did not really grab hold of us.

When he noticed that we were listening mainly out of politeness, he would say to us: "Comrades, you mustn't hesitate to tell me, which questions really interest you?"

Dobrovolsky replied: "Everybody talks to us about other countries, about how bad it is for the workers there. It would be better to talk to us about whether here in Russia, in olden times, there were any fights for freedom. Our books tell us that Stenka Razin and Pugachev were brigands," he continued, in his own effusive style, "but is this really true? The simple working people don't know anything about this, and even I don't."[16]

---

* This was Postolovsky, who later became a member of the Bolshevik Central Committee, where he was known as "Vadim." During the era of reaction he parted company with us completely. (Author's note.)[15]

Dobrovolsky was very successful in accurately reflecting our common frame of mind in those days, and we supported his request with great enthusiasm. So next time we met, Danilov instructed us for a while on the theme of peasant rebellions. We were so taken by this theme that, not content with the information we acquired in our circle meetings, we began to look for books on Pugachev and Stenka Razin.

As far as I can remember, these propaganda circles—both then and later, when I had become a propaganda leader in my own right—rarely completed their original programs. In the course of time the composition of our circle would change, as would its student leaders.

Our other leader was Sergey Dmitrievich Lvov,* a student of natural science with big blue eyes and a thick blond beard, which he apparently grew to conceal his extreme youth. At the time he struck us as a very learned and widely educated person. In those days most circles would begin by studying political economy.[18] This dry and dull subject usually put the listeners to sleep. Lvov, however, was able to prevent this from happening. He very successfully managed to illustrate each of his postulates with some kind of vivid example or with a story about the lives of foreign workers and their struggle to improve their economic position. We workers became so close to Lvov that we would even invite him to our evening entertainments, an honor we granted to very few intelligentsia.

* Lvov is now Professor of Botany at Leningrad University. (Author's note.)[17]

15
Our Cultural Life

IT USUALLY HAPPENED that no sooner did a worker become conscious than he ceased being satisfied with his social environment; he would begin to feel burdened by it and would then try to socialize only with persons like himself and to spend his free time in more rational and cultured ways. At that moment his personal tragedy would begin. If the worker was an older family man, conflicts would immediately arise within his family, primarily with his wife, who was usually backward and uncultured. She could not understand his spiritual needs, did not share his ideals, feared and hated his friends, and grumbled and railed at him for spending money uselessly on books and for other cultural and revolutionary goals; most of all, she feared losing her breadwinner.

If the worker was a young man, he inevitably came into conflict with his parents or other relatives, who had various powers over him. It was on this basis that conscious workers developed a negative attitude toward the family, toward marriage, and even toward women. They would look upon every contact with girls either as an attack on their personal freedom or as the loss of a comrade for the revolutionary cause. The active, conscious worker saw himself as a doomed man, with prison, exile, want, famine, privations, and often even death looming before him. To settle down to family life meant, at least, to add the sufferings of his dear ones to the weight of his own sufferings, and, at worst, to abandon the revolution under the weight of his family burdens.

And yet, at about this time, here and there some conscious women were beginning to stand out among the female workers, women who participated in the revolutionary life of the advanced workers and became their comrades in struggle.

In the wintertime, on holidays and other nonworking days, we would often organize evening "socials." We would pick the apartment of some conscious worker on the outskirts of town or on some quiet side street, invite fifteen or twenty trustworthy young workers, and set up tea and some snacks; to avert the eyes of the police, we would also buy some vodka. Only a few girls would attend these evenings. Both Olga Nikolaevna and Anna Nikolaevna, whom I mentioned above, were almost permanent frequenters of these events.

The evening program usually consisted of recitations of the poetry of Nekrasov, Apukhtin, or Nikitin;[1] revolutionary songs were sung in chorus and sometimes there was folkdancing, to the sound of an accordian. Most popular of all were Nekrasov's poems "The Railroad" and "Reflections at the Main Entrance,"[2] which were declaimed by a young worker from the Aleksandrovsk factory with great emotion and skill. I also recall an evening when we read Saltykov-Shchedrin's tale "The Nag."[3] In addition to the workers, we would also invite someone from the intelligentsia to these evenings. He would usually deliver a revolutionary speech at the outset, after which the people would split up into little groups and debate various issues among themselves.

Not infrequently our intelligentsia acquaintances would get us tickets to concerts, plays, or to some kind of student parties. We would go to these concerts in groups of three or four, and we always stuck together to keep up our courage. I recall that the music played at the concerts or theaters failed to impress me; we did not understand it and dismissed it as lordly amusement for the privileged. Dramas were more comprehensible. But once we heard the actor Tinsky recite "The Little Tail" and some other "tendentious" poem,[4] and this really had a great effect on us. It was the first time we had ever heard such a magnificent, heartrending recitation. We also attended the theater at the glass factory in the Nevsky region when it was showing *Othello*. That play did not appeal to us, but we were very impressed by a play called *The Workers' Suburb*.[5]

I remember the time we were given tickets to an evening dedicated to the memory of Saltykov-Shchedrin. Two days before the event we were already in a state of excitement, as we impatiently anticipated seeing the writer Korolenko,[6] who was supposed to perform there. We went there as a gang of five people and took seats in an obscure corner, so as not to attract attention.

The celebration included performances by actors and poetry readers and reciters, among them the actress Iavorskaya,[7] the writer Barantsevich,[8] and, finally, Korolenko himself. Korolenko was a man of medium height, broad-shouldered, with a large beard and a thick head of curly hair. At that time we had hardly read any of his work, but from stories we had heard we knew him as a writer-revolutionary who had served time in prison and in exile, and we were filled with enormous esteem for him. His appearance on the platform was greeted by loud applause, which quickly turned into an ovation. We did not lag behind. His cheerful, friendly appearance, his simple, open face seemed so familiar to us that we even began to joke about it:

"Do you know what, boys? He's probably one hell of a folk-dancer. Should we go ask him?"

We all broke into laughter. Then we gathered around Korolenko and chatted with him at great length.

Apparently our appearance and our unusual way of behaving attracted attention. During one of the intermissions a young woman student in a pince-nez sat down by us and began to engage us in conversation; she obviously wanted to "establish connections" with real "workers." Having guessed her intention, we began to pull her leg.

"Comrades, are you workers?" she asked.

"Workers, yes indeed!"

"From which factory?"

"From different factories, in the Nevsky region."

"Do you read books?"

"We read everything," we replied, "even *Workers' Thought* and the proclamations of the 'Union of Struggle'!"

The young woman, taken aback and perplexed, then said in a cautionary half-whisper:

"Comrades, be careful; you shouldn't speak about illegal matters here. You might run up against a spy or a provocateur."

We burst out laughing heartily.

Finally, we had one other form of "cultural" amusement: visits to the homes of liberals, where we were taken for display. In groups of two or three (we refused to go alone), led by one of our intelligentsia acquaintances, we would go to some highly fashionable apartment on Liteiny or Nevsky Prospect,[9] where we felt completely at loose ends. There we'd be warmly received by the well-dressed, well-fed host and his corpulent wife. Our intelligentsia guide would introduce us in a loud voice, emphasizing the words: "Conscious workers." Then we were regaled with tea and all manner of strange snacks that we were afraid to touch, lest we make some embarrassing blunder. Our conversations with such liberals had a very strained character. They would interrogate us about this or that book we had read, question us about how the mass of workers lived, what they thought, whether they were interested in a constitution. Some would ask us if we'd read Marx. Any stupidity that we uttered in our confusion would be met with condescending approval.

After leaving these gatherings we would breathe a sigh of relief and laugh at our hosts' lack of understanding of our lives as workers and at their alien way of life and thinking.

"Then why the hell do we hang out with them?" one of us would ask with indignation. "Why the hell do we play their game? They just want to use us to pull their chestnuts out of the fire. They'll get themselves a constitution and then they'll leave us in the lurch."

The member of the intelligentsia who was accompanying us would try to soften our mood and demonstrate the usefulness of the liberals to the revolutionary cause.

"We must go along with them up to a certain point," he would say, to placate us. "We need to take advantage of them now; later, they can go to hell!"

Though on the surface we agreed that even liberals might indeed be useful to the revolutionary cause, a kind of hostility toward them, a feeling of distrust, was constantly growing inside us.

Sometimes an argument about poetry, music, love, or some other higher matter of this kind would break out in our presence.

At that time our favorite poet was Nekrasov. We recited and sang his verses, which served us as a propaganda weapon. We were less familiar with Nikitin, although his poem "The Boat Hauler," especially the first lines, inspired us so much that we were ready to scale any mountaintop whenever we heard it:

> *Alas, my friend,*
> *You too, I see, have known grief,*
> *If a happy song can make you cry. . . .*[10]

We barely knew any Pushkin at all and we thought that reading him was a waste of time, since he was a gentleman's writer.[11]

Konstantin Langeld, a machinist from the Aleksandrovsk factory who was much older and more intellectually developed than us, would often lose his patience and break into these elevated discussions:

"Love, music, poetry," he would say, "they all may be very fine things, but they aren't accessible to us workers. Right now all those things are for the idlers, parasites, and loafers."

"Pardon me, my dear comrade," he would be interrupted by some honorable lawyer or member of a local governing council,[12] deeply hurt by Langeld's words, "does it follow from what you're saying that we, the advanced, progressive intelligentsia, are parasites and loafers too?"

"That isn't what I said, but you do have something in common with them. You understand them, you sympathize with them, but you don't really understand us workers. You've never been inside our skins," Langeld replied passionately. "Why at the factory this is already my third straight day fitting cylinder plugs that each weigh well over 70 pounds. I have to hold them in my hands all day long. When you get home after a day like that it isn't love, poetry, or music you look for, it's your bed. And there's work that's even worse than mine. How can the worker comprehend your Onegin and your Lensky, who become more enraged as they grow more prosperous. They should have been sent to a factory to fit some cylinders to a vise; and I'd put your Tatiana and your Olga to work at a loom, amid the dust and dirt, and let the foreman make fun of them. Then let's see what kind of songs they'd sing!"[13]

These words would cause confusion among the guests.

"That's nihilism, isn't it!"

"No, he got those ideas from Pisarev," others would say.[14]

"But Marxism doesn't deny aesthetic values!"

"Good boy, Kostya. Today you really gave the liberals what for!" we would say to Langeld approvingly, as we proudly and triumphantly left the building.

We greeted the year 1900 under unusual and, for us, novel circumstances. About three days before the advent of the new year five or six of us were given little pink tickets that bore some kind of secret "Masonic" signs. In a state of high excitement, I awaited the coming of a very promising evening. We were told that Struve and Tugan-Baranovsky would give speeches at the gathering.[15]

In groups of two or three, constantly looking all around us, we stealthily made our way along a very quiet, remote street of the Petersburg side.[16] By the time we reached the apartment it was already filled with people: students in their short, tightly buttoned jackets, or in official blue frock coats, with bright buttons; female students from the special classes for women, with closely cropped hair, wearing simple dark dresses; and a smattering of civilians.[17] Everyone was in motion, loud, arguing, laughing. There was so little room that many people sat on the floor, in extremely relaxed postures. We workers felt rather jolly and relaxed, and we began to saunter among the groups, moving from one room to another. Fortunately, our student acquaintances left us in peace, thereby sparing us from being subjected to inspection as rare examples of "conscious workers."

Looking into one of the rooms, we caught sight of a disheveled student in a blue stiff-collared shirt, over which he was wearing a simple, open, grey coat. He was standing in the middle of the room, hitting himself on the chest, shaking his head, and talking about something. His face was round, snub-nosed, and very serious.

The people sitting and standing around him, however, were laughing uproariously. Two female students seated on the floor were swinging their torsos in a strange manner while holding handkerchiefs to their eyes. We pressed through the crowd and began to listen.

The student was telling a very funny story about the way a populist-socialist engages a simple peasant in conversation in the countryside.[18] Then, with even greater success, he recounted the Biblical story of creation as if it were being told by a slightly tipsy soldier who had returned to his village on leave:

"And then the Lord God said to the Holy Trinity: 'We will create a man out of clay,' says He, 'in My image and likeness.'

"So the Lord God takes a clod of earth, breathes on it, spits on it, and says: 'So be it!' The Holy Trinity looks on with amazement: standing at attention before the Most High is the first man, Adam, who reports to the Lord God: 'God but it's boring,' he says, 'to live on the earth all alone.'"[19]

The laconic, epic quality of the tone in which the story was told, and the full round face of the narrator, without even a trace of a smile, had everyone literally groaning with laughter. I tried to restrain myself, straining every nerve in order to memorize this unusual, "blasphemous" story, which impressed me so much with its boldness, but I was strangled by my suppressed laughter and my throat was squeezed by my tears.

The storyteller continued in the same tone:

"And the Lord God and the Holy Trinity went out on the balcony to breathe the fresh air. But when He looked at his thickly foliaged garden, He saw neither Adam nor Eve there. The Lord God cried out in a loud voice:

"'Ada-a-a-m! Ada-a-mushka! Where are you?'

"'He-e-ere. Here I am,' came Adam's response.

"'Come here to Me, both of you!'

"'We, O Lord, we're naked. . . . We have s-s-sinned!'

"Now the Lord God grew angry, together with the Holy Trinity, and he cries out in a furious voice:

"'Host of angels, heavenly powers! Drive them out of the great garden and into a little kitchen-garden!'

"And they are chased along streets filled with police and gendarmes, while the people look on in surprise. . . .'"

Neither Struve nor Tugan-Baranovsky, the important guests we were awaiting, ever came to the gathering. Filippov, a doctor of philosophy, addressed the guests in the living room, but I have no clear recollection of what he said and I had trouble understanding his abstract speech.[20] Several other orators held forth and the whole affair ended with the singing of "Dubinushka"[21] and "Nagaechka."[22]

All told, it was the "story of creation" that made the biggest impression on me that evening; I memorized almost the entire story and retold it repeatedly at my workshop.

16
At the Kornilov Evening School

I HAD FIRST HEARD of this evening school, where, on evenings and Sundays, workers studied all kinds of scholarly subjects, when I was still working on the Vyborg side.[1] Some of the older workers had told me it was the very best school, but that workers who enrolled there inevitably turned into "students" and then ended up in prison.[2]

So it was only natural that, as soon as I had settled in the Nevsky region, attending the Kornilov school became my dream. Registration in the school took place in the fall. I went to enroll, filled with awe and fear. I was greeted simply and cordially by a middle-aged, tall, graying lady. She asked me to choose between entering the evening technical school, which was a three-year course leading to such and such rights after graduation, and taking individual subjects as electives. I declared my preference for the technical program. It turned out that this lady was the director of the school. Right then and there, without any further ado, she handed me a piece of writing paper, a pencil, and a pen and proceeded to test my knowledge to see if it was adequate for entering the program.

I did just fine in the reading part and in repeating what I had just read in my own words. I also managed to struggle past the dictation fairly well, but the arithmetic, always my weak point, proved very hard for me. I sat there for a long time, pencil in hand, sweating over the solution to the problem of the four basic rules of arithmetic. I did manage to conquer three of the rules, but I completely flunked the division. I was defeated by zeros in the dividend, which I just couldn't handle.

The director shrugged her shoulders, expressed her regret at my weak performance, and advised me to enroll in arithmetic and Russian language courses. As I recall, I didn't even push very hard for acceptance in the technical school, since the other classes looked more interesting and I also had comrades who were taking them.

So I signed up for chemistry and physics, Russian language, arithmetic, and literature. Why did I pick these subjects? The test of my knowledge had revealed the full extent of my illiteracy. The explanation for my ignorance is as follows: as everyone knows, the village elementary school, which I had completed, was very weak in teaching you reading and writing, and in the course of the seven years since I had graduated I had managed to forget even the little I had learned there, except for basic reading. During those years the only practice I had in writing was the few very simple letters that I wrote to my father; my "correspondence" with ladies cannot be counted, since I copied most of my letters and the replies from my letter-writing manual. My helplessness became especially clear to me one day when, in the literature class, the teacher asked us to write down our evaluations of M. Gorky's story "Chelkash."[3] I sat there without budging for three or four evenings in a row, but all I could show for it was a page of scribbling.

Here I was a conscious worker, as I thought of myself, one who was always speaking of the value of enlightenment, and yet I was nearly illiterate myself. I was filled with shame. With redoubled energy I threw myself into self-education. But it was much harder to "crack the nut" of science then than it is now. After a hard and long day's work we would rush home, quickly drink some tea and have a bite to eat, and then rush off to the school, where instruction lasted from 8 to 10 P.M. We cheerfully sat through the first hour, but during the last hour, despite all our efforts, we'd begin to nod off. Either an exceptionally interesting topic or our active participation in the assignment was required to stave off our drowsiness.

There were two subjects that aroused my special interest and that of my comrades—physics and the history of literature. The former was taught by a small, animated man with a blackish, wedge-shaped beard—he was either a professor or a teacher from one of the secondary schools. I have forgotten his name. We enrolled in that class strictly out of intellectual curiosity. I, for example, wanted to learn in great detail, experimentally, the origins of snow, rain, thunderstorms, electricity, and many other natural phenomena. Of course I did not believe in their miraculous or divine origins, but I was unable to give a clear explanation of where they came from when I was arguing with someone.

Our teacher was obviously a broadly educated man, for no matter what question we asked him, even if it had nothing to do with physics, he responded with clarity and thoroughness, using many entertaining examples to illustrate his point, fascinating us and enjoying himself at the same time. He would tell us about the origins of "antediluvian" animals, about the formation of coal, of underground oil deposits, and so on. When we attended his classes and listened to his stories of the many millennia that had passed since the existence of this or that fossilized monster, all our concepts and notions of time would grow confused. Ichthyosaurs, plesiosaurs, and other monsters of that kind filled our entire imaginations. Proud of my erudition, I would return home and strike terror in the imaginations of the superstitious inhabitants of our apartment when, in arguing with them, I contrasted my giants—the ichthyosaurs and the plesiosaurs—with their divine or evil little spirits.

The other subject that captured our attention was the history of literature. Strictly speaking this was not really "history" but an examination of the individual works of various writers concerned with the issues of the day.

This subject was taught by a young, tall, well-proportioned blonde named Vera Nikolaevna, whose last name I cannot remember. She apparently had a good knowledge of literature, but her approach and her explanations did not always please us. To the best of my recollection, her ideas leaned in the direction of Populism.[4]

By that time—albeit mostly just spontaneously, instinctively— we already approached social and political questions from the standpoint of the class struggle; for our teacher, by contrast, the oppression of workers by the ruling classes was merely an "injustice." For her every kind of "poor" human being deserved compassion and help. We, on the other hand, felt and always strongly emphasized the special position of the working class and its special tasks.

"Gentlemen, what is it with all your 'we workers' this and 'we workers' that!" she would instruct us, half-jokingly. "With your way of thinking workers will end up as a privileged group some day. Why, the peasant's life is often even worse than yours; they oppress and abuse him no less than the worker."

"Well, and what of it? The peasant doesn't know how to fight for his rights, while the workers are already awakening," retorted Aleksandr Tolmachev, a machinist from the "Atlas" factory.[5] He was a young, passionate worker with SR inclinations, but in his assessment of the role of the working class he was still on our side.[6]

"Then you'll teach them to fight," said the teacher.

"The Populists have already tried to teach them, but the peasants betrayed them to the rural police."[7]

This kind of polemical debate would take place when the lesson had finished. The entire class would disperse, but our group of ten or so men would usually remain for a while or else we would form into a band and accompany Vera Nikolaevna to the nearest train station.

One day our teacher brought a copy of the journal *Russian Wealth* to class.

"Today, gentlemen, instead of the usual lesson I will read you a story by a young writer from the people, Maxim Gorky," she announced solemnly, holding the book in front of her.

We pricked up our ears. It was the first time we had heard the name of this strange writer.

"Would that be his real last name or did he invent it for himself?" one of the pupils asked.

"It's his pseudonym," Vera Nikolaevna replied.

"Well, his life must sure have been bitter for him to pick himself a name like that," someone suggested.[8]

"That's true enough. His life has been a very bitter one. Although he is still very young, he knows the life of the poor very well," Vera Nikolaevna explained.

The story in question was called "Chelkash." Vera Nikolaevna had not even finished reading us the first page when the noisy class grew completely silent. Not only did we listen, we profoundly experienced the drama between Chelkash and Gavrila; we drew a mental picture of the harbor of the big port city where, in the heat and dust, the dirty, sweaty stevedores, crushed by work beyond their strength, were swarming; we imagined the warm southern night and the phosphorescent glow of the sea. It was even difficult to grasp, at first, the storm of impressions that rushed over us when Vera Nikolaevna, clearly as excited as we were, breathing heavily, closed the book and looked out at the class in puzzlement with her big, sad eyes. Stunned, we just sat there for a long time, unable to find the words to express the feelings and thoughts that were troubling us. It was decided to put off our analysis of the story to the next meeting of the class; in the meantime each of us was supposed to write an account of all the things in the story that had struck us the most and to write our evaluation of the story. This proposal was accepted without any objections.

As I have already mentioned above, it was the attempt to write an analysis of "Chelkash" that revealed the full extent of my illiteracy. Thoughts, feelings, exciting experiences—I had plenty of all these, but they simply wouldn't set themselves down on paper. My crude, unbent fingers, more accustomed to running a chisel or a plane, laboriously produced some kind of scribbling instead of letters. Instead of vivid experiences I came up with some pale scraps of thoughts. What had struck me most of all in the story was the description of the harbor: the sweaty, dirty, weary figures of the stevedores and, close by them, the colossal machines.[9] The words "what they had themselves created enslaved them and robbed them of their humanity" echoed in my ears. Man, who was the ruler of nature, had become the slave of the heartless machine he had created—this was approximately the way in which I then formulated my confused thoughts.

At our next class meeting we began our analysis of the story we had read. When asked which of the heroes we liked best we unanimously declared that our sympathies lay with Chelkash. Speaking with fervor, Konstantin Langeld began to prove that Gavrila was a bad person: he was greedy and dull, he had no interests apart from managing his own little farm, he was incapable of having any kind impulses. "But Chelkash," Langeld said, his eyes sparkling as he raised his soot-covered hands, "why he may be a smooth talker and a crook, but he's still a good person; he's generous, courageous, disdains money, and despises the power of the wealthy."

"Gentlemen, that is not the way to evaluate Gorky's heroes,"

Vera Nikolaevna gently interrupted Langeld. "You should approach them from the social point of view. Now I ask you: who is more useful to society—Chelkash or Gavrila?"

This unexpected way of posing the question threw the class into a state of confusion. Several different voices could be heard:

"Gavrila is more useful, since he gives society bread; Chelkash is a parasite. . . ."

"Not so," came another voice, "it's society that made Chelkash into a parasite, and if you ever made him conscious he'd be a hundred times more useful than Gavrila."

The voices in the classroom began to divide in two: some spoke for Gavrila, others for Chelkash, but only a tiny minority was on Gavrila's side. Vera Nikolaevna intervened, once again trying to weaken our sympathies for Chelkash.

"Gentlemen, I ask you: could a society really consist of people like Chelkash? Certainly not; although it's true that Chelkash has some good features that Gavrila lacks, Chelkash is not useful to society whereas Gavrila is. Gavrila is a peasant, the basis of society."

We argued passionately for a long time, trying to prove Chelkash's superiority over Gavrila, but we were unable to provide a logical basis for our views. We felt very clearly that we were right, but we lacked the words with which to prove it.

There were fewer arguments in our Russian language class, taught by Rubakina.[10] Most of the works she introduced us to were far removed from our real world, and the pupils themselves were very diverse. They expressed themselves infrequently and reluctantly. I recall that on several occasions we had readings from such plays as *Woe from Wit*, by Griboedov, and *Poverty Is No Vice*, by Ostrovsky.[11] After reading aloud we would analyze what we had read. When an exchange of ideas did take place we couldn't help pushing the discussion back toward contemporary realities. And when we did speak up we spoke bluntly, calling everything by its real name. In these discussions we would use such words as bureaucrat, autocracy, gendarmes, factory director, foreman, etc. To cloud our thoughts in literary-legalistic forms was impossible for us. Because the pupils in this class did not know each other well, we preferred to refrain from idle chatter.

Rubakina would often bring us "tendentious" books, which we always read with enormous interest. Most of these books were works of fiction, novels or stories from the annals of the struggles for independence or national liberation of all kinds of nations in many different epochs. I still remember some of these books quite distinctly: *The Garibaldians*, Ezh's book *At Dawn* (a story from the annals of the Bulgarian liberation struggle), *Under the Yoke of Time*, and *The Albigenses*.[12] The last two novels give a very colorful picture of the Netherlanders' struggle with the Inquisition.[13] Despite their highly varied locations and diverse epochs, we would identify the circumstances of all these struggles, as well as the heroic figures of the stories, with our own Russian reality; from them we learned the meaning of selflessness, the capacity to sacrifice oneself in the name of the common good. For our generation that kind of literature played an enormous educational and revolutionizing role.

Nor did it really matter that this literature was not always class-oriented; as *we* interpreted it, even a pacifist poem like this one, printed in one of the Rubakin collections, was transformed into revolutionary verse:

> *The hardest years will pass,*
> *A better age will dawn.*
> *There shall be new ideas*
> *And there shall be new men.*
> *The stern and endless enmity*
> *Will fade from earth forever.*
> *We await the reign eternal*
> *Of science and of labor.*

At the time this poem sounded to us like a battle call to the war against autocracy.[14]

Whether it was Giordano Bruno fearlessly approaching the pyre of the Inquisition for the sake of truth, or the Albigenses battling the Inquisition, or the Garibaldians, or Bulgarian nationalists—we saw them all as our kindred spirits.[15] Our fantasy endowed these heroes with inexorable will and extraordinary intelligence; they knew neither fear nor doubt in their struggle for the liberation of their oppressed peoples.

The Kornilov school deserves an honorable place in the history of the labor movement. It educated more than one generation of worker-revolutionaries. Bolshevik workers who are still alive remember it to this day with feelings of deep gratitude and affection. The tsarist gendarmes, for their part, devoted a good deal of

attention to the Kornilov school, endeavoring by means of prov-
ocation and spying to drain it of everything vital, thoughtful, and
revolutionary.

Here, for example, is the way in which the Chief of Gendarmes, Sviatopolk-Mirsky,[16] appraised the more advanced workers in his report to the tsar at that time:

During the past three or four years the good-natured Russian lad has
been turned into a peculiar type of semiliterate *intelligent*, who considers
it his duty to deny religion and the family, scorn the law, and disobey
and sneer at the authorities.

Fortunately (the gendarme adds soothingly), there are still not many
young men of this kind in the factories; yet this insignificant handful is
dominating the entire remaining inert mass of workers by terrorizing
them. The majority of the worker-agitators and ringleaders of all kinds
of strikes have attended the Sunday schools.[17]

17
My Arrest

D URING MY LAST YEAR in the Nevsky region of St. Petersburg, revolutionary activity there assumed very large proportions. Considering our level of development and the recent vintage of our revolutionary work, my comrades and I made up only a minor part of the existing cadre of advanced revolutionary workers, and we could not, of course, be aware of everything that was happening in that part of the city. Nevertheless, we knew of approximately ten fully organized underground circles there. Predictably, the gendarmes and police intensified their vigilance, our failures grew more frequent, the arrests of our comrades multiplied. We felt certain that our turn was soon to come. More and more frequently, at our circle meetings, we began to discuss such questions as how to behave under interrogation by gendarmes, how to uncover provocateurs, how to elude the shadowing of spies, how to conceal illegal literature, and so on. Those comrades who had already been in trouble shared their experiences, recounted the occasions when they'd managed to put one over on the gendarmes and spies. With regard to such matters as the mastery of self-control or how best to resist the investigatory snares of the gendarmes, we were greatly assisted by a very interesting and clearly written little book called *How to Conduct Yourself During Interrogation*, by Bakharev.[1] We knew it virtually by heart.

By now I had a mysterious feeling that the ring of political surveillance was tightening around me and would soon be ready to enclose me completely.

One day when I returned home from work I saw Avdotya Petrovna waiting for me on the staircase in a state of alarm. Looking secretive, she led me to a separate room and began to speak in hushed tones:

"Something bad is going on here, Seniushka."

"What's happened? Has there been an accident?" I pricked up my ears, fearing that something had happened to her children.

"No, no," she replied, "don't be alarmed. What happened is that one of your countrymen came here looking for you, except that he didn't look at all like a countryman. He asked all kinds of questions about you, like who were your visitors and where did you go yourself. So I say to him: 'I don't know anything. He just rents a room from me,' says I, 'and I don't have time to keep track of his visitors. I can't even keep track of my own kids.' And he left without even saying who he was. If you want my opinion, Seniushka, he was just pretending to be your countryman; I think he was really a gendarme. He was even wearing blue trousers, like the gendarmes wear.[2] And the neighbor woman also told me that a gendarme came to her. 'Petrovna,' she says to me, 'it was a gendarme from the Shlisselburg police office.' She actually recognized him. Seniushka, please, be careful, protect yourself, or something awful will happen to you. They've already grabbed one of the tenants of Terentev, the machinist, my dear, and he's still in prison. And Terentev's wife told me he was a really good guy, the meek and quiet type, she said, who didn't even drink." Thus spoke Avdotya Petrovna, sighing with distress and looking at me with pity, while tears flowed down her round, pale face.

"That's enough, Avdotya Petrovna, nothing bad is going to happen. It's no big deal—if they arrest you, you just serve your time, that's all. Better people than me go to prison, but in the end they're released. Besides, what am I doing that's wrong, anyway?" I tried to soothe her, affecting a carefree air.

During my stay at the Bykovs Avdotya Petrovna became very attached to me; she was affectionate and attentive toward me and clearly felt sorry for me. Later, the actions of the Bykovs would demonstrate again and again their attachment to me, their deep sympathy for the revolutionary cause, and their hatred for the gendarmes and police.

Around this time a situation arose that compelled me and my comrades to be more alert. Sometime earlier, an acquaintance of Mitrofanov's named Mukhin, a draftsman from the Obukhov factory, had begun to call on Mitrofanov regularly. Later Mitrofanov would affirm that he had no recollection of where and under what circumstances he had first met Mukhin, but he had evidently lacked sufficient resolution—nor was there an appropriate pretext—to show him the door and get rid of him.

One day a bunch of us were taking a holiday stroll in the "Vienna" garden[3] when suddenly from out of nowhere a small nimble fellow with long hair, in a wide-brimmed hat, carrying a thick stick in his hand, managed somehow to fly up to us. He quickly bounded up to Mitrofanov and then began to squeeze our hands and introduce himself in a very familiar and impudent manner. At first we thought this must be one of Mitrofanov's close friends so, although he didn't appeal to us, we raised no objections to mixing with him. From then on Mukhin begins to worm his way into our group with great intensity and persistence. For some reason or other he chooses me as the object of his pursuit.

Almost every Sunday, and sometimes even on workday evenings, he would come to my room, seat himself on the bed and, talking in a familiar tone, would begin to brag about his connections with the intelligentsia, speak about his extraordinary revolutionary exploits, recount the clever ways in which he had given the slip to spies and shadows and had outwitted the police. His voice was sugar-coated and musical and his almond-shaped, cunning eyes were always moving, touching his interlocutor, soothing and persistently penetrating his soul. Sometimes he would bring along illegal literature, which protruded carelessly from his pocket, and pass it to me with a look on his face that seemed to say that there was no one and nothing on this earth that he feared, "not even the devil himself."

I asked my comrades' advice. "How should I handle this?"

"Take his illegal literature," they said, "but kick him the hell out."

I took the first part of their advice, but the second was much harder to carry out.

We began to make inquiries about Mukhin. Although no one was able to say anything specific about him, everyone we asked advised us to keep our distance from him. Our most passionate comrades began to entertain the thought: why not dump this Mukhin into the Neva River?! Some of them were already experienced at this kind of thing. But Kostya Langeld, the most calm and restrained among us, intervened at this point:

"You're not talking sense, boys. You'll do in one scoundrel, but you'll lose five good men as a result."

All kinds of impassioned objections to Kostya's position would follow, but for the time being we went along with it. The Mukhin question was temporarily removed from our agenda, though it was not resolved. Then it was settled by the political police. On the night of 31 January, 1900, our entire group was arrested.

18
In Prison

PRISON MADE an unbearably painful impression on me. After long and distressing hours locked up at the gendarme station, it was only on the following evening, around dusk, that I found myself in the famous House of Preliminary Detention.[1]

Physically and morally exhausted, but emotionally stimulated, I lost all my sensations; I had no desire to eat or to sleep. When the thick iron door slammed shut with a loud rumble and I found myself in a small dimly lit cell, I had only one desire—to flee, to rush about, to bang on the door, to scratch and gnaw on the walls.

As a healthy, cheerful, sociable young man, I experienced my solitude, my isolation from life, friends, and normal surroundings very acutely. The thick, cold, naked walls, the heavy iron door, and the small grated window beneath the ceiling crushed your consciousness, enchained your will, restricted your movements, and prevented you from breathing freely.

As I bustled around the cell, I noticed a push button. It was probably a bell. I pressed it. This produced a short ringing sound and, at the same moment, the noise of a bolt being moved. No one came to the door. I have no idea how long I continued to bustle about the cell. Then I suddenly heard the jingle of keys; the little square transom in the cell door swung back and a brusque, stern voice inquired:

"What d'you need?"

"Give me something to read."

No reply. The transom slammed shut; again I heard the jingling of the keys. Once more I rushed about the room in a state of agitation. My face is burning. My head is filled with noise; disconnected thoughts are whirling through my mind—about my arrest, about my comrades, about the interrogation that awaits me, about the identity of the traitor. . . .

Again the transom is opened. Silently, the guard extends his hand through the opening; it holds a tattered book. Greedily, I raise it to the weak light of the electric lamp and then, disappointed, put it down on the table: *A Short Sacred History of the Old Testament.*

I resume my nervous pacing along the diagonal of the cell— six paces forward and six paces back. I feel confused; I'm getting hot. It was only now that I finally noticed that I still hadn't removed my outer garments; I had been pacing the whole time in my galoshes, overcoat, and hat. . . . But in an instant I've forgotten about that.

Then I again hear the promising tinkle of the keys in the door. My heart beats rapidly with joy. The thought flashes before me— perhaps they intend to release me?

"Lie down and go to sleep! The lights are going out soon," the stern voice returns me to sad reality.

I hastily throw off my clothing. I slide under the felt prison blanket and try to sleep. In vain! My thoughts begin to spin around like a whirlwind. The pillow has turned hot. The blanket is stifling. Tossing and turning from one side to the other, I turn the pillow over and throw off the blanket. I long for sleep to deliver me from all my suffering. I begin counting to a hundred, then to a thousand. Nothing helps—sleep flees from me. I again get out of bed, grope about in the dark, put my clothes back on, and resume pacing the cell till I'm ready to drop from exhaustion. Then, still dressed, I fall on my bunk and lie there in semiconsciousness, awaiting the new day. . . .

Suddenly, startled by the rattling of the keys, I leap out of bed. "Take your bread!"

I take a heavy hunk of dark bread from the guard's hands and place it on the cold iron table. So it's morning. The cell is still dark.

The endlessly long, agonizing hours of solitude kept dragging on, occasionally interrupted by the sound of keys and the banging open and shut of the transom on the door.

They brought me hot water in a tin mug, a piece of sugar, and some tea leaves wrapped in paper in the form of a "dog's leg."[2] I throw the tea leaves into the mug, which produces a blackish kind of water, with a strong odor of tin. The warm drink pleasantly warms my insides, raising my spirits. The dim morning light is just beginning to enter through the window. I begin to get acquainted with my cell.

There were two iron squares firmly screwed to the wall, one somewhat larger, the other somewhat smaller: a table and a chair. There was a massive iron bunk with a thick, hard, canvas mattress, a small basin with a water faucet, and, in the corner, a huge seat for your natural needs. What attracted me most was the window. What did it look out on? What could be seen from it? Perhaps I could manage to glance at freedom, if only through a peephole! I try to estimate the distance. The window is high, the windowsill is sloped, so even if I managed to climb up I could never keep my footing. Then I notice a thick iron hook on the upper windowframe. Hurrah! Taking a strong, linen, government-issue towel, I stand on the toilet seat and throw the towel on the hook. Then I pull myself up to the window and eagerly survey the interior of an enormous prison courtyard with a multitude of grated cell-windows overlooking it.

"Away from the window, on the double!"—I heard the harsh cry of the guard behind me. I was so enthralled by the view from the window that I hadn't heard the sound of the keys or the banging of the falling transom.

Turning around, I saw the guard's protruding whiskers and his two angry eyes in the transom.

"If I catch you again it'll be the punishment cell for you," was his stern warning as he angrily slammed shut the transom.

By now I have the feeling that my every move is being watched, but I can't figure out how or from where the guard can see me. However, I soon discovered a tiny round pane of glass in the door: from time to time there appeared a human eye, to which the entire interior of the cell was visible.

Sometimes I got the urge to annoy the guard. I would stand in the corner nearest the door and wait for him to make his rounds. The guard on duty would softly steal up to the door and look through the "peephole," but, because I was standing outside his field of vision, he couldn't see anyone in the cell. I could sense the agitation of the guard on the other side of the door, so frightened by my disappearance; I felt the rotation and rattling of the cover that concealed the little observation window. I heard people whispering and running about and then, all of a sudden, the cell door noisily opened wide and two confused and alarmed guards, obviously convinced that I had either escaped or killed myself, burst in on me. Pleased with my successful joke, I emerged from my hideaway to meet them. The senior guard addressed me in a rough and angry tone:

"It's forbidden to stand near the door! One more time and it's the punishment cell for you."

Again the monotonous, wearisome hours dragged on. Again my spirit was crushed by the callous walls of the cell, the dead graveyard silence, and the dense semidarkness, dispersed only briefly by the daylight, as it fell through the grated window.

Once a day they would take me for a walk to the well in the prison yard. In the middle was an enormous circle, divided into twenty oblong cages by high wooden fences. High above the cages, in the center, was a circular terrace, where, one after the other in single file, walked three guards, revolvers in their holsters, closely watching twenty prisoners, penned in their twenty bestial cages. How dreadful and offensive it was for a human being! To encounter a comrade during these walks was almost impossible. Unless, as occasionally happened, the guards got confused about their watches. Then we would run into each other, shake hands, rapidly throw some fragmentary sentences at one another as we walked by. This would calm the soul. But then the perplexed guards would hurriedly shove us into the nearest empty cell, slam the door, and hold us there until they had let all the others walk by.

Once every two weeks we were taken to the baths. But even there we were kept in strict isolation. Once I tried to go to the prison church, hoping to meet one of my comrades there. But even here disappointment awaited me. For the entire duration of the service they locked me up in a small cage,[3] where I could neither sit nor lie, but could only stand and contemplate the long-haired priest who, dressed in his chasuble, conducted the morning service, speaking boringly through his nose.

The endless, monotonous days stretched into weeks, then months. I was losing count. I grew desperate at the thought I would have to stay in this cursed isolation for half a year. And then what? Exile, unemployment, want, starvation. . . . And how many of us conscious people are there? Dozens? Hundreds?

Thousands? And all the rest of the masses continue to sleep their perpetual sleep. Is life really worthwhile? My eyes began to look for a hook or a sturdy nail. My enfeebled will no longer resisted. My crushed consciousness sought out arguments to justify a pessimistic ending.

I had recently read an article in the journal *God's World* in which Chelpanov, the author, explained the teachings of Schopenhauer.[4] In this world, Schopenhauer said, pain outweighs pleasure. Indeed, pleasure itself was nothing more than the absence of pain. And when pleasure was prolonged, it became boring and it too was transformed into pain. Animals are less sensitive to pain than are people. And the more intellectually developed a person is, the greater his pain. Eventually people will become aware that life is pain, and will therefore escape it by means of self-destruction. . . . However, I was too healthy, both physically and psychologically, to allow myself to be seriously dominated by that kind of mood for very long. All I had to do was read the familiar name of a comrade on some wall during one of my walks and I'd no longer feel "lonely and abandoned." The awareness that alongside me in the big slammer were dozens, perhaps even hundreds who, just like me, were suffering for a just cause, immediately raised my spirits. I felt myself an advanced fighter for the cause of the working class, which was sending more and more new warriors to assist us with each passing year; I now felt ashamed of my momentary cowardice.

"The most terrible thing in the world is death," I reasoned, "but I'm not afraid of it. I'm prepared to die for the revolutionary cause at any time, without even blinking an eye. But to die simply because I was weary and bored would be both cowardly and stupid! . . ."

Using my intuition, I would try to guess which were the good books in the catalog of the prison library and would enter their names on the request sheets. Prior to my imprisonment, I had known about many of the better writers only by hearsay, or at most I had read one or two of their works. There in the prison I was able to read Turgenev, Uspensky, Dostoevsky, Spielhagen (*Between the Hammer and the Anvil*), Shchedrin, and others.[5] It was Shchedrin who made the greatest impression on me; from that moment on he was my favorite writer for life. When I read his "Letters to Auntie," I laughed so hard that the guard repeatedly opened the transom and stared at my face, evidently wondering if I'd lost my mind.[6]

Cases of insanity were not infrequent at the preliminary detention prison, what with its horrible regime of isolation. And it was the workers, people accustomed to physical labor, who fell victim to mental illness most of all. The experience of complete idleness and their unfamiliarity with intellectual activity had such a murderous effect on the workers' nervous systems that many young workers were transferred to the Hospital of Nicholas the Wonderworker and thence to the cemetery.[7]

My mental state, weakened by solitary confinement, was greatly fortified and comforted by reading books about struggle and suffering. Two short biographies, one of Pisarev, the other of Lassalle, happened to fall into my hands.[8] The biography of Pisarev corresponded very closely to my mood. "Here's a man imprisoned in a fortress for nearly four years," I thought, "under the worst possible conditions, yet he didn't lose heart!" I was also captivated and very impressed by the boldness, profundity, and simplicity of Belinsky's correspondence with friends.[9] You read that work over again, then you stop and think: "What a simple yet profound idea! How come I never thought of it myself?!"

Describing some personal failure or terrible grief to one of his friends, Belinsky wrote:

"When I look around and view the sea of human sufferings, and see that so many people are a thousand times unhappier than me, then my unhappiness seems petty and insignificant compared to theirs and I become ashamed of my faint-heartedness."[10]

I cannot recall when or to whom Belinsky wrote this letter, and I cannot even guarantee its accuracy, but that was the basic idea of the letter. Many years later, whenever I had to live through even more terrible times, I would automatically recall that letter and my usual cheerful, joyful mood would come back to me.

Once or sometimes twice a week I would have a genuine holiday. It seems that on Thursdays, at about two o'clock, the guard would unlock the door and drop a whole pile of little packages on my table. A quarter pound of butter, cheese, coffee, a lemon, sometimes a piece of sausage. Once a month I would receive a yellowish receipt for three or five rubles "from Elskaya." For a long time I puzzled over the identity of this fairy godmother named Elskaya. It was only after my release from prison that it was explained to me that these had been deliveries from the Revolutionary Red Cross.[11]

Materially, we workers were generally better off in prison than we were in our regular lives, when we worked in factories. And yet I have never encountered a single worker who was capable of recalling his first solitary confinement without trembling. (Though it's true that later, when I had turned into a more seasoned inmate of prisons, I began to feel much better in solitary than I did in a group cell, even among very good friends.)

One day, during my walk in the cage, I noticed the inscription "Langeld"; and another time I saw the name "Tolmachev." This meant they too had been arrested! On my next walk I found a piece of paper on which was written the prisoners' alphabet for tapping on walls. I committed it to memory and began to tap with a pencil. A couple of times I was caught by the guard, which nearly landed me in the punishment cell. Thereafter, educated by bitter experience, I began to tap more cautiously, choosing a time when the guard was busy passing out hot water, bread, or dinner.

I was able to make contact this way with Shendrikov,[12] who was held two floors below me. From him I learned that our entire Nevsky region group had been arrested. I asked him to recommend a book on psychology. Shendrikov recommended James.[13] I began to read it but understood nothing.

About three months of prison life had passed for me. With great effort I had begun to get used to my isolation and my monotonous, tedious, vegetative life. I was tortured by uncertainty about my future. What will they do with me? Where will they send me?

Finally, they summoned me for interrogation, which I had long awaited with such trepidation. It was not so much the gendarmes' rudeness or shouting I feared; I was much more afraid of their flattery, cunning, and politeness. I didn't want to be interrogated by Piramidov,* the head of the gendarme administrative office, of whom it was said both in the illegal press and in intelligentsia circles that he could "see seven feet into the ground."[14]

Despite my expectations, however, nothing terrible happened. On the contrary, the ride in the "dark coach"—just thinking

---

* Piramidov was accidentally killed in 1901 by a beam that fell on him while his boat was being launched. (Author's note.)

about it had long since filled me with fear—with "two gendarmes at my side" actually brought me a certain amount of satisfaction.[15] Seated between the enormous mustachioed gendarmes, I felt like a hero; involuntarily, I drew myself tall and tried to affect the serious, somber look found on heroes on the way to their executions, though I was actually dying to laugh, to chatter, and, more than anything else, I wished to be seen in this condition by my friends. But when I attempted to look at the street through the opening in the carriage window, the strict gendarme drew the curtain tighter.

I did not have to await my turn very long. The gendarmes led me to a spacious, brightly lit office where a tall young gendarme officer was seated at his desk; to his right was a pleasant-looking heavyset man in civilian clothes, a horn-rimmed pince-nez on his nose. The gendarme gestured me to a chair and asked me to sit down, after which he very gallantly offered me the traditional cigarette. I was on guard and refused the cigarette. "It's beginning," I said to myself, "they want to worm their way into my heart with kindness."

"You are to testify in the presence of the deputy prosecutor," the gendarme said, pointing to the pleasant-looking gentleman seated nearby.

This was followed by some routine questions—my date of birth, relatives, citizenship, travel abroad, etc. Then I was shown several photographs of students and workers, some familiar, some unknown to me. The gendarme named several familiar names and asked me if I knew them. To all these questions I responded decisively and firmly, looking straight into the gendarme's eyes: I don't know, I'm not acquainted with him. After repeating his questions two or three times the gendarme, apparently convinced of my obstinacy, declared that he had no further questions. I actually experienced a certain disappointment: I had expected a jesuitical interrogation, but the affair ended in mere formalities. Evidently I was not a very big criminal.

The same two gendarmes who had brought me there then put me back in the coach and returned me to the prison. The stretch of gray, monotonous days resumed. But by this time I had begun to adjust somewhat to my solitude and I tried to work on myself more systematically. I ordered textbooks on arithmetic and grammar. Each day at certain set hours I would sit at my table with a notebook and begin to cram. Zelinsky's textbook, which was particularly adaptable to self-education, served me very well.[16]

To relieve my boredom I tried my hand at writing. I attempted somehow to write a story about workers' life. Much hard labor and effort went into it, but nothing came of it. Even the assistant director of the prison seemed to disapprove of my work when he came around for inspection. He scrutinized my notebook attentively and at length, smiled condescendingly, and silently put it down on the table. I was disappointed and hurt. I had read all kinds of literature about the gentry, about government officials, about merchants, and even about simple peasants, yet no one had ever written anything about workers, just as if they didn't exist. So much fuss is made about the workers, they are looked after with such tender care, they are called the true creators of all material wealth, and yet no one wants to write about how the workers live and think.[17]

One day among my packages I found a small volume of the works of Gorky. I found it so absorbing that I didn't so much read it as swallow it in one gulp! True, there was nothing said in it about workers as such, but the ideas, the words, were so familiar, so truthful, appropriate and authentic! As I read it, I felt as if I was being transported from the face of the earth, rising high above the vulgarity and injustice of human existence. I wished to rush at once into battle with our mortal enemy, the autocracy, to arouse the sleeping mass of workers and summon them to combat! I wished they all would recognize at once the greatness of the force and power that lay within them!

> *Intrepid falcon, even though you die,*
> *Yet in the song of the bold and firm in spirit,*
> *You'll always live as an example,*
> *A still proud summons—to freedom and to light!*

These words from "The Song of the Falcon" resounded in my ears like a clarion call. They braced my spirits, excited me, summoned me to battle and great deeds.[18]

Every evening, while the guards were busy making deliveries, I would assume my pose in the middle of the cell and loudly begin to declaim "The Song of the Falcon." It was pleasant to hear my own voice, which I hadn't heard for so long. I dreamed about how, once I was free, I would recite the song to comrades at our evening gatherings. How it raised my spirits! My austere, uninviting cell was transformed into a bright, cosy room. I longed to study, to improve myself, so that later, when I was released, I could return to the factory and share my knowledge with my comrades.

Thus, little by little, I grew accustomed to my situation; I studied, I worked, and, with pride and enthusiasm, I dreamed of the day when, enriched by experience and knowledge, I would again return to my own element. I was no longer frightened by long solitary confinement.

I do not remember how many months had gone by since the day of my arrest. I received no letters and had no visitors. Then one fine day, when I returned from my walk, I found a letter on my table. The letter was crisscrossed with yellow strips of chemical reagent. This had been done by the gendarmes in order to discover whether the letter contained anything written in invisible ink. The handwriting seemed familiar, much like the poor handwriting of my father. The letter was from my brother. This had to mean something had gone wrong at home! . . . I began to read with agitation and alarm. The letter began with conventional words of greeting and respect.

". . . And I also enform you," my brother wrote, "that last week the soul of our papa, Ivan Egorych, was delivered to God, and he died suddenly, and we buried him in the village cemetery next to mama and arranged a forty-days' requiem. . . ." [19]

The lines of the letter began to jump, to flow together. Sobs mounted to my throat and choked me. I tried to restrain myself with an effort of will. In vain! With sobs I threw myself on the cot and, burying my face in the pillow, gave vent to the flood of tears I had been holding back. The depth of my grief was immeasurable! For the first time I felt how deeply I had loved my father. Past injuries were effaced and disappeared. With my father's death the last thread that had tied me to my home, to my village, was torn away. At first this filled me with a feeling of melancholy and loneliness. But in the depth of my soul another feeling was simmering and growing—a feeling of freedom and proud independence. While my father was alive, dimly, unconsciously, but stirring within me nonetheless had been some kind of vague feeling of "obligation," "responsibility." Now all this was torn away and vanished forever. Of all the feelings I experienced, the most painful was the sense that I was now alone, with myself, with my thoughts, feelings, and doubts.

One day, on a Thursday (visiting day), the guard came up to me and said:

"Get ready for a visit, please."

In a state of joyful agitation I quickly get dressed. I walk rapidly through the long prison corridors. I'm at my wit's end, trying to guess who it might be. I have no kinfolk here; friends and distant relatives are not permitted. . . . Perhaps my brother has come from the village? The guard leads me to a cupboard-shaped booth with wire grating and locks me in. I sit there and wait with trepidation. From the opposite side of the room they lead a woman, wrapped in a gray shawl, to the booth. After examining her very closely I cry out with joy:

"Avdotya Petrovna!"

"How's your health, little nephew?" I heard her say in her kind, tender voice.

Why "nephew"? In the past she had always called me "Seniushka"! Oh, I get it! She said she was my aunt so as to get the gendarmes to let her visit me! Through the screen I see her take out a white handkerchief and, from time to time, dry her tears and blow her nose. A few scattered phrases are audible through her sobbing:

"They all feel sorry for you. . . . Some ladies came to ask about you. . . ."

"Aha! That means Olga Nikolaevna and Anna Nikolaevna have still not been arrested," I reason.

"And your fellow with the long hair come by too. Papa[20] and me don't like him—what's his name, Tarakanov or something?"

"Mukhin," I correct her.[21]

"He keeps asking questions about you and your comrades— how are you, where are you. . . . By then father was real sore. He grabbed him and kicked him out."

"He did the right thing!"

"'Come back here,' says he, 'and you'll lose a leg!' He gave the guy so much hell that we haven't seen hide nor hair of him since!"

Avdotya paused for a moment, wiped away her tears with her handkerchief, glanced apprehensively at the gendarme, and then said with a sigh:

"I completely forgot to tell you that our little Misha has been ill for two months."

The gendarme pricked up his ears, but there was nothing he could find fault with. But I grasped her meaning: they had arrested Mikhail Orlov, the metalworker who also lived at the Bykovs, and whom Avdotya Petrovna meant by "little Misha."

"The visit is over," the gendarme announced.

With a feeling of deep gratitude, I took leave of Avdotya Petrovna and returned to my cell.

I felt joy and light entering my heart. My cell no longer appeared so gloomy. I wanted to sing, declaim, jump up and down, cry out! The visit of this simple, illiterate woman, who surmounted so many obstacles in order to obtain her meeting with me—what better proof of the justice of our cause than when the masses, dimly and unconsciously, begin to show their sympathy!

Later, when I was released from prison and had briefly returned to the Nevsky Gate region, it became even clearer that I enjoyed enormous sympathy from both workers who knew me and those who didn't. Spotting me from a distance on the street, even my former enemies would rush up to me, warmly squeeze my hand, and question me at length about my health and about the prison, while speaking with disdain about gendarmes, spies, and the oppressive and arbitrary conduct of factory administrators.

Winter and spring went by and summer came. Now the prison was really stifling, both literally and figuratively. No one summoned me anywhere and, so it seemed, no one had any interest in me. On the wall of my cell hung a sheet of white paper—it had turned almost yellow during the time of my imprisonment—which said: "Prisoner so-and-so, born 1879, registered with the St. Petersburg provincial office of gendarmes. . . ." No further remarks had been entered on the sheet. Was it possible they had forgotten me?

One bright summer morning, on a day when the prison walls seemed particularly depressing and stifling, I heard the jingling of the keys. The door opened and the guard stood at the threshold and said:

"Get your things together and go to the office."

At first I didn't understand.

"What things?"

"Your belongings; you're being released," he repeated.

With my head spinning from joy and happiness, I spread one of my sheets on the floor and start to pile up all my things — my pillow, the teakettle, a glass, my books and notebooks, and the tooth powder that I had begun to use to clean my teeth for the first time while in the prison. I tie it all up in a knot and rush through the dark corridors, following the guard. In the office a stern-faced gendarme was seated at a table; he read to me from a piece of paper, from which all I understood was that I was to be returned to my native village under police guard. This didn't scare me, but it didn't particularly please me. Then the gendarme began to shove some papers at me for my signature. My hand was shaking so much that the pen jumped around the paper, splattering ink all over it. I was able to scrawl out my name only with the greatest effort. The gendarme concluded by adding that I must leave Piter in three days and should get my documents at the municipal governor's office on Gorokhova Street.[22] I cannot remember what other formalities I had to complete or my actual departure from the prison.

I returned to my senses only when I found myself on the noisy sunlit street. I grabbed the first cab and drove to the Nikolaev station to catch a steam train to the Nevsky Gate region.

The first to meet me in the Bykov courtyard were their children, who threw themselves at me and embraced me with cries of joy. Avdotya Petrovna was so overjoyed she completely lost her head; she laughed, cried, wiped her tears with her apron, blew her nose . . . :

"I never expected such joy! And how happy papa will be! We thought they'd never let you go. The kids were just saying that everyone's being driven off to Siberia these days. . . . Did you figure out what I meant at the prison when I mentioned little Misha?"

And without even waiting for my answer she began to describe how the gendarmes had questioned her about me, how she had played the fool and lied to the gendarmes.

Bykov and the other inhabitants of our apartment soon arrived. They gathered around me and, full of curiosity and sympathy for me, they questioned me about my prison life, about the food, my interrogations, and so on. They were all especially struck by my account of the strict regimen of solitary confinement with which the autocratic government drove people to madness.

"What sons of bitches, to treat a man so spitefully!"—was the angry reaction of even the usually taciturn Mikhailo, the boiler-maker with whom I once had shared a cot and who had never before been well disposed toward me. Half deaf, he stood there with the other residents, his hand held to his left ear like a mega-phone, and listened attentively. With a menacing gesture, he raised his huge fist, blackened by grease and soot, grated his teeth, and said:

"One of these days the workers' patience will run out! And then what a thrashing we'll give them!"

To my surprise, I was visited on that very day by Langeld and Tolmachev who, as it turned out, had been released from prison at the same time I was. Our joy was unbounded. Interrupting one another, not even hearing each other, we recounted our experi-ences, spoke of our fleeting encounters with comrades and of our pending exile; we laughed and chattered, chattered endlessly, making up for our half year of prison silence.

That evening we got together a few of our worker friends and all took a boat trip to the Strelka.[23] We wanted for this one last time to spend the evening among close friends, to bid good-bye to our home city, our beloved Piter, before we went our different ways, chosen for us by the gendarmes, perhaps never to meet again. Well past midnight, having enjoyed the beauty of the sea-shore and breathed the fresh and bracing air, we returned home, in a pleasant state of physical exhaustion.

In the morning I awakened to the siren and headed for the fac-tory to pick up my old tools at the workshop. Again there were encounters, questions, conversations with old friends and ene-mies. Most of the pattern-makers were warm and sympathetic. My old friend Vasily Evdokimovich squeezed my hand with feel-ing and, visibly proud of me, said in a paternal and didactic voice:

"Well done, Semën! You have taken the right path. Go forth and never stray from it. But be careful, beware of evil people! Where are they exiling you?"

"Back home to my village."

"Doesn't that mean we'll never see each other again?"

"How can you even say that, Vasily Evdokimovich? The revolution may be almost upon us!"

"Well you're still young, Semën, you young fellows can expect to see it, but as for me. . . ." He swayed his old gray head and added sadly: "I'm too old, I'll never live to see it. . . ."

We embraced very warmly and, indeed, we parted forever.

"Hey there, big mouth, you got what was coming, eh?" Maliciously and meanly, the old worker Andrey Petrovich Riabtsov stopped me as I passed his workbench on my way out. "Say, you've turned out to be quite a 'shtudent,' haven't you! Why he don't even know how to wipe off his snot yet and he's already going against the tsar. . . . Let 'em thrash you one, 25 hot whacks! Then you won't badmouth the tsar no more."

I could hardly hold back my rage. "Listen, Andrey Petrovich," I said angrily, "the days when you could have your own way are over. Your hands are tied now. Just wait, you old sponger, before long you and I will be talking to each other differently!"

One of the pattern-makers who overheard our skirmish came up behind me and tried to push me gently toward the door, apparently afraid that the quarrel might culminate in something more serious. At the door he slipped a ten-ruble note into my hand, saying:

"Take it, Semën, we took up a collection in the shop. It'll come in handy in the village."

I firmly pressed my comrade's hand, picked up my heavy toolbox, and left the Semiannikov factory forever.

On the following day, after bidding good-bye to my friends and dear ones, I departed for the village.

Part Three

My First Exile

19
Departure

I DEPARTED for my village with a heavy heart.[1] How am I going to make a living? What will I do there? I was completely cut off from my brother's family, which could only view me as a burden, another mouth to feed. They'll imagine that I want to arrange a division of the family property.[2] There's hardly any work to be found in the village. There are no factories in the region. . . . But then again maybe I could be hired somewhere as a carpenter or joiner. . . . No, they'd probably be scared to take on someone who's been designated "unreliable."[3] These were the somber thoughts that pursued me relentlessly when I left Piter. My railroad car was spacious. The sun was shining brightly. The countryside rushed past my window. The marshy green plains, the forests, the gray wooden huts of the villages, the telegraph posts, the herds of lean red cows.

My comrades—Kostya Langeld and Aleksandr Tolmachev—rode with me as far as the Klin station. They too were being exiled to their native regions, the former to Saratov, the latter to Tambov.[4] But they had wandered off somewhere, leaving me alone with my weighty thoughts.

They were gone for a long time. When they returned they were merry and animated. They laughingly grabbed their little suitcases and pulled me after them.

"Stop feeling so melancholy, Senka. No matter what happens, you can only die once," Langeld said to me in a hearty voice as we moved along. "We're going to a car that's full of students. Just think, the whole Saratov student organization is aboard—plenty of friends."[5]

The car was indeed overflowing with students. Some sat in groups on the benches and argued; others lay in their berths, their shaggy heads dangling to one side, while they exchanged witticisms with their neighbors, smoked, and laughed. And in the middle of the car, enveloped in a blue cloud of smoke, a large group was singing revolutionary and student songs.

An engineering student in a close-fitting jacket kept time with his right hand while he led the singing in his baritone:

> *Our Russian system is no good—*
> *Reminds us of a savage wood.*

Then the chorus joined in, singing in one voice:

> *Black is the jackdaw, clear is the meadow—*

And so on, and so forth.

> *They talk of Catherine the Second now*
> *As if that Catherine was a cow,*

the baritone continued to sing, fiercely rolling his eyes. They all sang with spirit, enthusiasm, and skill. When they sang out the words—

> *Along the dusty road there goes a coach,*
> *And in that coach two gendarmes sit on either side—*

words from a song I'd never heard before, I was even moved to tears, for they sang with so much feeling and the song was so in tune with our mood.[6]

Near the doors of the car, picturesquely arranged in natural poses, a group of students was crowded together, almost filling an entire compartment. At times silence prevailed among them, but it would suddenly be interrupted by a friendly, infectious outburst of laughter, which went on for quite a while.

I timidly approached this group. Constantly interrupting one another, they told various anecdotes "with a tendency."

"Now listen while I tell you how Tsar Alexander III went to heaven," hastily began a heavyset brown-haired student in an unbuttoned university jacket, worn over a black shirt, clasped by a broad leather belt. "The tsar goes up to the gates of paradise and knocks.

"'What strange forest creature comes to us so early in the morning?' asks Peter-the-Apostle from behind the gates.

"'It is I, His Imperial Highness, Emperor of all the Russias, King of Poland, Grand Duke of Finland, etc., etc.'

"'We don't accept such a big herd of people all at once. Come back one at a time, and make it a little later, when the heavenly powers have had their tea,' Peter-the-Apostle angrily replies.

"There is nothing he can do. So the tsar-peacemaker walks away, sits himself down, and begins to cry bitter tears. Then a smuggler comes up to him and asks:

"'Why are you crying, Sasha?'

"'They won't let me into heaven.'

"'Well, tell you what,' says the smuggler, 'if you promise not to be stingy with me, I'll help put an end to your misery.'[7]

"So they reached an understanding.

"Now just at that time who should step up to the gates of paradise but some kind of foreigner. He knocks. The keys jingle and again the grumbling voice of Peter asks:

"'Who's there?'

"'It's me, Carnot, President of the Republic of France.'[8]

"Again the jingling of the keys. This time the gates open wide. Now the smuggler takes a sack and says to the tsar: 'Climb into it.' At first Alexander III refuses, pointing out his origins and his services to the Russian people, whose benefactor he'd so recently been, having provided them with land captains and village policemen and having restored the birchrod to the peasants, who longed for it so much, by permitting them to be flogged in the township administrative offices.[9]

"However, even these indisputable services failed to move the unrelenting smuggler:

"'Then you'll go to the devil's furnace, no more no less, if you won't climb into the sack. Just remember, you too wanted to maintain a high moral tone. But I'm sure when you were drunk like a pig you lolled around under the table and didn't observe all the . . . ,' the smuggler declared forcefully.

"After hearing such convincing arguments, the tsar climbed into the sack. The smuggler slowly strapped it up, bent his knee to the ground, and, having barely managed to hoist it to his shoulder, carried it to the gates of paradise.

"'Who's there?' Peter asks, once again.

"'It's President Carnot's baggage.'

"The gates opened wide and the smuggler was allowed into paradise."

The story was constantly accompanied by bursts of laughter,

but they didn't disturb the storyteller. With a smile, he would change the intonation of his voice and the expression on his face, but he didn't allow himself to be distracted by the infectious laughter. And you could tell by his face that this self-restraint did not come easy to him.

"Well, there's also the story of Alexander II—that's an old one too—about the time when he climbed up the stairway to the kingdom of heaven." Thus began a tall blond fellow with a round, ruddy face, as he bit his lips and stuck out his eyes to stifle his inner laughter. "As we all know, Alexander II was bald. Well it seems that when his bald spot came into view as his head entered the heavenly aperture, Peter-the-Apostle quickly covered it with the palm of his hand.

"'What's with you!' says Peter, 'You don't climb into the kingdom of heaven rear end first!'"

Again a big burst of laughter.

Meanwhile, in the center of the car, the same sonorous, elastic baritone could still be heard:

> *Since time immemorial our Russian throne*
> *Has been mounted by swine after swine.*
> *Well, my friends, let's take up a cudgel*
> *And drive the swine from the throne.*[10]

I moved timidly from one group of students to another, observing these rather unfamiliar people with curiosity, and rejoiced in my heart that it was not only we isolated, anonymous, simple workers who were fighting against the tsarist yoke and for the revolutionary cause, but that fighting together with us were these intelligent, educated, brave, and daring students.[11]

"Look how fired up our little students have become," Kostya Langeld said as he sat down beside me, poking me in the side as he ironically nodded his head in the direction of the singing students.

"What's wrong?" I retorted sharply. "Do you think they're just playing games?"

"No, why should they play games. . . . But I still don't believe in their radicalism; it won't last very long. As long as you're a student, you sing forbidden songs, tell funny anecdotes about the royal family, put on high boots, and go around unkempt, with long hair. But once he finishes the university and gets a good position, that student will become a hard taskmaster or a tsarist flunky, the kind who sits on our necks just like the ones we're fighting now."

"Comrade, you shouldn't jump to such conclusions. Not all students will be like that. . . . Our intelligentsia, in the person of our students, has had its share of martyrs to the cause of the people," said a long-haired student with a light-colored beard who was seated opposite us, obviously hurt.

"I'm not saying *all* of them. . . . But the fact remains that only a certain number of individuals will stick with the people, whereas the majority will settle down and play it safe."

"Comrade, your view of our student youth is much too gloomy; the truth is that they're the only revolutionary force with any life in it," the student admonished Langeld with gravity.

"Perhaps, but what can that force accomplish without the workers? Sing a little, scream a little, even rebel a little . . . and after that? Not a thing. . . . Once the police and gendarmes are after them, they settle down in a jiffy."

"And where are these workers of yours? They're sound asleep! . . . All progressive society is in a state of excitement and indignation; it protests against the tsarist government's repressive measures, while your workers remain silent."[12]

"Have no fear, the workers' turn to say their piece is coming soon. . . . But they're going to speak in their own way, the worker's way. . . . And if you people try to act without the workers, why nothing will come of it. . . ."

"But the workers can't get by without the intelligentsia either," Tolmachev intervened in a firm voice, having said nothing up to this point.

"Well, have I said anything to the contrary?" Langeld responded with excitement. "All I'm saying is not to put too much faith in the intelligentsia—it will deceive you. . . . Just like the French Revolution: the workers fought on the barricades, but the bourgeoisie got the profits. . . . So we don't have to act like fools."

"You shouldn't confuse the intelligentsia with the bourgeoisie. Our intelligentsia has nothing in common with the bourgeoisie. Ours is a working intelligentsia," the student replied nervously, shaking his thick head of hair. "It's exploited by the bourgeoisie, just like the workers."

Soon other students began to join the argument with Langeld. Most argued against his position. Only a few remarks could be heard in Langeld's defense. With all these debates, songs, and conversations, the day slipped by imperceptibly. With a warm and melancholy feeling, I soon bid farewell to my friends. Would it be for long? Perhaps forever. This was the year I was supposed to be taken into the army.[13]

20
The Meeting

I WAS MET at the station by my brother. He was overjoyed. All the way home he asked me questions about the mysterious "students" and about prison. It had even surprised him to learn I had survived and had not been ground into dust at the Peter-and-Paul Fortress.[1] He recounted at length all the rumors about me that had been circulating in the village.

We arrived in the village on a bright July afternoon. Almost half the village was gathered at our home, eager to see "the one who'd been resurrected from the dead," as they described me. More women arrived, some very old, both close and distant kinfolk of my father and mother. They all expressed their sympathy to me, sighed, cried, wiped their noses with their aprons and skirts. Whenever someone mentioned my father's sudden death, they'd cross themselves, wish him the "kingdom of heaven," express sorrow over my "orphanhood," and so on.

That evening our closest relatives came to our cottage for tea. Among others, there was Aunt Marya, my mother's sister, stout and healthy, a very kind woman, an Old Believer,[2] 25 years a widow, who still ran a modest one-horse farmstead by herself; Gramma Natalya, a talkative, lively old woman, a midwife, who knew everything about anything; Uncle Andrey, a simpleminded peasant who could barely make ends meet but remained an incorrigible optimist and braggart; and "Godfather" Kuzma, a commercial butcher, a miserly, sober peasant, trying with some success to become a kulak.[3]

They drank tea through pieces of sugar, slurped from the saucer, and talked about the peasant's problems; they spoke of the land shortage, of excessive rents, and of the new village elder, who was playing up to the land captain and refused to be indulgent toward the peasants.

Aunt Marya complained about her son Matvey, from whom there hadn't been any news for over two years and who was sending no tax money back to her.[4]

Uncle Andrey was boasting about his latest purchase—a cow:

"I'm telling you, she's some cow! You never seen one like that before. She got horns like a buffalo. And her udder? The biggest basket wouldn't cover it!"

"That's enough out of you, you old braggart! If the cow was so good you wouldn't have gone all winter without milk," Gramma Natalya interrupted Andrey.

"You don't understand a thing," said Uncle Andrey, refusing to give in. "She was dry in the winter, and now she's off having some fun."

"It's sure gotten hard to live. There's nothing to brag about anymore. My sons who have gone away don't send any money; I've got nothing to pay the taxes with," lamented our neighbor Emelyan, whose children were rapidly getting the better of him.

"Well you shouldn't have slept with your wife so much; you should have prayed to God more and kept the fast days," my "Godfather" Kuzma reproached him.

"Listen, Kuzma Fedrych," Emelyan replied. "You work and toil your whole life long without knowing any happiness. Why the only consolation a poor fellow has is to sleep a little with his wife. God wouldn't punish you for that."

"God is pleased when you do it, Uncle Kuzma, because the Bible says: 'Be fruitful and multiply, as the sand of the seas,'" came the wisecrack of the joker and mocker Ivan Kulagin, who worked as a journeyman in the shoemaking shop of the village rich man, Petr Lipatov.

"You can see how true is the saying: the rich man has a calf, the poor man has a child," Gramma Natalya threw in.

"You're a rich man by the grace of God, you're a good man by dint of patience," said Kuzma to edify us.

Emelyan objected: "Patience is for the man with money in his purse. He's the one the village elder collects from last. It's the poorest who's always the first to pay up. As it is we never have enough, but then on top of that we're the first to pay the dues. There's not much justice left in this world, that's why we all live so badly."

"It's not about justice at all; it's about who gets to enjoy what. This one has good fortune, the other one does not," Uncle Andrey joined in. "I'll give you an example. Here's what happened once in our regiment. There was this medic serving with us named Trushkin. This happened during his last year in the army. One day he's called to the quarters of Major General Laptev, who says to him real severely:

"'Trushkin,' he says, 'the most brilliant doctors have been unable to cure me of my shortness of wind. I've wasted piles of money on those sons of bitches without results. Now I want you to heal me. If you can cure me, I'll get you discharged from the army, but if you can't, I'll have you put in the punishment battalion.'

"And what do you suppose happened? The medic cured him, he did! It worked like magic, within two months. And he used the simplest of cures: every day, twice a day, he brought fallow soil from under the cow dung for the general to inhale. May God be my witness, I'm telling no lie." To convince us of this Uncle Andrey crossed himself.

The young people roared with laughter, while the old folks shook their heads reproachfully.

After tea everyone spread out on the benches and, with curiosity, quietly waited for me to begin my story.

Naumovna, my brother's wife, was fussing about, clearing the table, rattling the cups. I had been seated far back in the corner, behind the table. Since I was the last to get up from the table, everyone noticed that I didn't cross myself.[5]

"Semën Ivanovich! It looks like you've completely forgotten God!" said Gramma Natalya in an accusatory tone.

"Why should I remember Him when He's forgotten me! First they stuck me in a prison for no reason at all, now they've exiled me to your village. If God is just, how can He permit such injustices?" I replied. Trying hard to be restrained, I chose appropriate expressions, words that were accessible to the people around me, so as not to violate their religious sensibility and not to set them against me by speaking too pointedly.

"Our Father, the Lord Jesus Christ, was patient and commanded us to be patient too. For then, in the other world, our patience will be returned a hundredfold," Kuzma replied with humility in his voice.

"Isn't it true that all the priests preach humility and patience to the poor? But I'm sure they don't say that to the rich. Let's just suppose you didn't pay your taxes to the elder and your rent to the landlord; then let's hear the priest say to them: 'Be patient, God commanded patience. . . .'"

The stern faces began to break into smiles and the young people laughed resoundingly, but Kuzma and Gramma Natalya shook their heads reproachfully.

To the question of God's existence I tried to respond evasively. I had no wish to frighten anyone by speaking harshly.

The conversation turned to more earthly themes, closer to their lives. In the course of his agitational activity, Lassalle had once had to prove to the German workers that they lived in misery. But in my conversations with my co-villagers this wasn't necessary, since nine-tenths of them were extremely dissatisfied with their difficult situation; it was just that they didn't know how to find a way out.

I must confess that I too had only a foggy notion of the "way out." I tried to talk to them about the socialist society of the future, about how wonderful life would then become. But my stories did not succeed. Sober, practical, crushed by need, distrustful of anything new, the peasants listened to me with interest, but they treated my propaganda of socialism like an entertaining story or fairy tale, amusing to hear, but which had no relation to their somber daily lives and, of course, could never really come to pass.

They listened to my stories about the prison and my explanations of who the "students" were and how the workers were fighting "for justice" and were persecuted and flung into prison for this by tsarist police agents.[6] Then they began to ask my views on such questions as whether the tsar would reduce the peasants' taxes and when the gentry's land would be transferred to the peasants.[7]

As I have already said, most of these questions were not even clear in my own mind. One thing, however, was obvious to me: there was nothing they could expect from the tsar except the birchrod and the dungeon. I answered their questions in that spirit.

My answers, of course, failed to satisfy them. Yet it was clear from the disturbing questions with which they increasingly came to me for clarification that to some extent I had awakened their consciousness that it was impossible to live this way any longer.

Our gathering ended late in the evening.

21
Summer and Fall

THE COTTAGE was stuffy and crowded; it smelled of baking bread and children's swaddling clothes. There were hoards of cockroaches that appeared to be cast in red bronze and swarms of flies that turned white objects to gray or black, endowing them with life and movement. I preferred to settle down in the shed, on freshly mowed, aromatic hay. I took my trusty toolbox there, fashioned myself a workbench, and, during the hours I wasn't working in the fields or on rainy days, made all kinds of knickknacks. I cut some pine boards with a jack plane and evened them with a long heavy smoothing plane; the fragrant, aromatic shavings crept up from under the plane and settled lightly on my arm. I banged away with a hammer or gnawed away with a chisel, or, while leaning against my chin, I made screeching sounds with a handsaw. I was often visited by one or another of the peasants, who would watch me work or would examine my complicated tools with curiosity.[1]

In keeping with my factory habits, I arose at 6 A.M., went to the river to bathe, then drank tea with the whole family and went to work with them in the fields. Three teams of horses were there for haymaking time. Then I would get up before sunrise, as early as two o'clock. Until seven o'clock the entire village would mow the dewy grass. The hay would be dried during the day. Toward evening it was taken to the shed, while the part that had not dried out was stacked up. We slept for five or six hours. At first I was exceptionally tired, but it became easier with time. We reaped the rye, mowed the oats, pulled up the flax, dug up the potatoes, gathered the garden vegetables, chopped the cabbage, spread out the flax, threshed the rye with our flails, and so on.

On Sundays and major religious holidays everyone went to

mass at the church in the neighboring village, about two miles away.[2] I would either remain home and read or stroll to the river along the mown hayfield.

Some three weeks later, on one of those Sundays when I was sitting in my shed and reading, I was visited by the village elder, Vasily, a sedate and sober old peasant of average means. His visit struck me as odd. Up until this time he had never said a word to me and, so it seemed, had been blatantly avoiding me. And now he suddenly shows up. . . ; something must be on his mind. Stooped, holding the long knotty stick with which he usually knocked on the shutters of the huts when summoning the men to the village meetings or collecting their tax payments, the elder shook my hand in a manner that seemed unusually "polite" for him and stood there for a while, silently shifting his weight from one foot to the other. Understanding that he needed something from me, I asked:

"Do you need something from me, Vasily Ignatevich?"

"A gendarmer has come from town. He's sitting at Petr Lipatov's drinking tea. He called for me and sent me after you. Semën Ivanych, please come along with me to see him, without delay," he said, in a voice that asked forgiveness.

"You just go to your gendarme and say to him: I have no need for him, and if he needs me, then he can come to me himself," I said with deliberate rudeness, to make it clear that I wasn't afraid of any authorities.

Taken aback, the elder stood there in a state of confusion:

"Well, uh, now what should I say to him?"

"Tell him just what I told you: I refuse to go!" I repeated with persistence and determination.

The elder left. But half an hour later he reappeared, this time in the company of a tall gendarme.

"Greetings, Mr. Kanatchikov."

"Greetings."

"Here are your belongings; I need you to sign this receipt," said the gendarme politely, as he handed me a package.

Amazed, I unpacked the package and discovered three or four shabby books that had been taken from me when I was arrested.

"Will you be making any statement?"

"No, no statement."

The gendarme saluted very politely and clanged his spurs. His broad back could be seen for a long time as he walked down the middle of the street. He was followed at a respectable distance by the elder, who, his long stick in his hands, could barely keep up with him. I could see the gendarme climb up to the high porch of Petr Lipatov's two-story house, and I could hear the rumble of the gate as it slammed shut.

Soon after the gendarme's departure, I learned from some of the peasants that he had been very disturbed by my disobedience; he had scolded the elder and given him very strict orders to watch me and report my every step.

The gendarme began to show up every week to make some kind of "inquiries" about me, but not once did he attempt to summon me to his quarters.

He behaved rudely with the peasants, yelled at them and cursed. My independent conduct and the unqualified rebuff I rendered the gendarme astonished everyone and soon filled them with admiration.

The downtrodden, intimidated peasants cowered and trembled in the presence of any authority figures, beginning with the district scribe and the village policeman.

Not very long before my arrival in the village, the district land captain, while driving by the village, had decided to summon a village meeting.[3] The entire population of the village attended the meeting. The land captain spoke on and on, teaching the peasants about rational behavior: about the need to pay their taxes on time and to meet their various obligations in kind. He spoke of the solicitude shown by the tsar and his officials toward the peasants. The peasants stood in silence, their heads bare, and listened. Suddenly the land captain cuts himself short and cries out:

"How dare you stand before an official with your hat on, you son of a bitch?"

Spiridon, who was absent-mindedly standing there with his head covered, immediately pulled off his cap.

"Place him under arrest!"

Spiridon was arrested. Though it was the height of the harvest season and he was the sole able-bodied worker in his family, they kept him in jail for seven days.

Grigory Aleksandrovich, the peasant who recounted this incident to me, finished his story with these words: "What's a poor peasant to a gentleman? Why he's worse than a dog. . . . At least a dog can bite, but the peasant is meek and humble and tolerates everything."

"But why tolerate it! The whole village should have submitted a complaint against him," I said, feigning naiveté.

"Very funny! That's just what he said: submit a complaint," Grigory mimicked me with bitter irony. "And to whom would you submit this complaint? To those same gentlemen? Does a raven ever peck out the eye of another raven? They'll always say that you're the guilty one."

After the incident when I stood up to the gendarme, Grigory Aleksandrovich began to come by my shack more often to see me. A tall, thin, round-shouldered man, with long arms and an enormous hooked nose, he stood out sharply from the other peasants. His farmstead was on a very shaky footing; no matter how hard he struggled, it was constantly near the dividing line between poor and middling.[4] The slightest misfortune—like the death of some cattle or a bad harvest—and he could suddenly find himself in the weakest group of households, from which it was very hard to escape. He was well aware of this situation and, of course, he refused to submit to it. He would come to me, sit down on the thick birch stump on which I usually cut slabs, stakes, and boards with my axe, wave his huge arms as if they were the blades of a windmill, and say:

"You, Semën, are a wise man; you know shtudents; you've suffered for the people. Tell me, then, if there's any hope that things will get better for the peasants."

"No, even more enslavement may be in store; improvement is impossible as long as you yourselves remain quiet and continue to hope."

"And the tsar? You don't think he could take our part? Intercede for the poor peasant?"

"How can the tsar go against the landlords when he's a landlord himself?" I rejoined.

"But Alexander II did it, our little father, the tsar-liberator! He gave the peasants fleedom," said Grigory, refusing to give up.[5]

"Yes, but he didn't free them out of the kindness of his heart; he did it for his own benefit and that of the landlords. The peasants were beginning to rebel more and more. The tsar himself told the gentry: either you quickly free the peasants from above, or you wait for the peasants to free themselves from below. And then they'll take all the land away from you."[6]

Grigory scratched the back of his head in silence, while he thought about something.

Using my handsaw, I continued to saw some studs for a chest, fixing my gaze attentively on the barely discernible line that had been traced with the tip of an awl while I tried to catch the middle of the line with the saw blade. I could not see Grigory's face, but I could sense from the way he sighed and the way he crumpled and worried his goatee that he was straining very hard over his thoughts.

"Then it would seem that the district chief and elder are also appointed by the tsar? . . ." Grigory continued to pursue his thought without raising his head, either asking himself the question or asking me.

"Well, uh . . . not directly by the tsar himself, but by his trusted officials," I affirmed.

The land captain and the district elder were the mortal enemies of the inhabitants of the entire district, with the exception of a small group of well-to-do. The people despised them and cursed them, but also feared them. They wrote complaints against them to the provincial governor, they sent messengers on foot with complaints to Moscow, but nothing helped. The land captain simply increased his repressive measures.

About seven years earlier three peasants, Grigory Aleksandrovich among them, had submitted a written declaration to a gendarme cavalry officer who happened to be passing through. In this declaration they wrote that there were witnesses to the fact that the land captain had abused and insulted the name of Tsar Alexander II for having liberated the serfs. The case was handled in accordance with legal procedures. With smoldering hope, the peasants expected the mysterious "black coach" to arrive and whirl the land captain away to distant, unknown parts.[7] But days turned into weeks and weeks into months, and still the land captain continued to administer justice to the peasants in the same old manner.

Finally, one fine day the originators of the complaint were summoned to the city. No one knew what they were questioned about there or what had been done with them.

About three days later they returned from the city all gloomy, dejected, and taciturn. They responded morosely to all the questions posed by the other villagers: "We have been sworn to silence." All kinds of rumors swept the village. Some said that they'd been tortured, others that they'd simply been flogged for submitting a false report.

Grigory Aleksandrovich himself did not like to recall that incident, and I preferred not to question him. So I remained in the dark about whether the land captain had really insulted the tsar or whether the peasants had made up the accusation in order to ruin an official whom they loathed. Grigory Aleksandrovich was probably the most advanced and thoughtful peasant in the entire village. Nevertheless, he either could not or would not grasp the connection between the tsar up above and the village officials close at hand. To be sure, according to the law, the elder was supposed to be elected, but somehow there was no one left who knew or remembered about that.

On a quiet summer evening, when the sonorous songs of the village girls could no longer be heard, when the Livna[8] accordion of Egorka, the irrepressible shoemaker, had grown silent, when the barking of the dogs had ceased, when everything in the village was covered by a deep, hard sleep, I would quietly ease open the folding doors of my shack and go for a stroll along the mowed, dewy meadow. The grasshoppers chirped, the crickets sang and sang. The fog hung over the river, barely visible in the darkness. My thoughts—sad, happy, somber—rushed through my head in a rapid torrent. . . . Thoughts about my newly discovered world of struggle and suffering for a better fate, thoughts of my various friends, scattered one by one in remote places where they were drowning all alone in a sea of darkness, ignorance, and the benighted aspirations of the working people. I thought of the difficulties of the struggle that lay ahead. The struggle wasn't frightening, the suffering wasn't frightening, even death itself wasn't frightening. Does it really make any difference whether you die ten years sooner or ten years later? Not if you die with pride in yourself for having lived a life that was not in vain. . . . What is really frightening is the opposite; what is frightening is to live in solitude, surrounded by dull indifference, even to be content with this animal, beastly existence. . . . No, better death, better suffering than such a dull, gray, benighted life.

But I was frightened of the military service that awaited me. Four years of subjugation to the harsh barrack regime of the petty officers, drill sergeants, and company commanders; four years of repeating, day after day, their idiotic and meaningless liturgy, deprived of the opportunity to read any newspapers or books or to engage in rational conversation with your comrades! Oh . . . how frightening!

How I wished to be closer to my comrades, to share my thoughts and experiences with them, to struggle, live, and die together. . . . I would sit for a long time on the bank of the river, staring at its dark, smooth surface, covered by the light haze of the fog.

"What if I went for a swim?" I went up to the water and touched it with my hand. It was warm, like steamed milk.

Overcoming my fear, I slip into the water. I try to swim to the middle of the river, but an incomprehensible animal fear drives me back toward the riverbank. Why? I certainly don't believe in demons, wood nymphs, or water sprites. Then, irrepressibly, Uncle Andrey's story slips into my mind:

Not very far away, in a tiny village close to the course of our river, an enormous catfish dwelt in a pond. On a warm summer day a calf came up to this pond to drink. Suddenly, without any warning, the catfish flew up from the depths of the pond like an arrow, seized the calf and carried it away.

"As God is my witness, I'm telling no lie!" Uncle Andrey swore. "I heard it from the very same peasant whose calf was taken by the catfish."

Implausible nonsense. There aren't even any pike left in our river. And yet I felt I might be grabbed by the leg by a catfish.

My swim was brief. Refreshed and stimulated, I walked along the meadow to the point of exhaustion. When the curtain of night began to fall and the dim white horizon, slightly reddish, grew visible, I went to sleep.

These nocturnal swims continued until the end of the summer. The peasants listened to me talk and continued to be amazed by my "fearlessness"; the girls and the older women would shake their heads: "what a desperate life this man has had—what filth he's had to deal with!"

One day it occurred to me to build a boat. I climbed all around the courtyard, the shack, and the storehouse, collected dirty, rotten boards, got some oakum and, in lieu of pitch, some shoemaker's tar, and began to perform.

More than a week went by: I planed, carved with my axe, sawed, and hammered. Every free minute I would run to the shack and work. My materials for the boat were very inadequate. I was forced to do things not the way I wanted to but the way the materials allowed. What emerged was a flat-bottomed boat that looked like an oblong box with a pointed nose. I carved the oars from boards—they were straight and unsuitable. My peasant friends, when they'd heard of my venture, came by every day to follow the progress of my work with interest.

"Hey, Semën, you gotta caulk those grooves through and through; you never know what might happen, water could run in," Grigory coached me. He had lived in Moscow and had seen boats on the Moscow River.

I would knock the oakum into the grooves with my chisel even more firmly and then pour the tar over them.

Every once in a while I was visited in my shack by Iashka-the-Priest, the son of my "godfather" Kuzma. He was a ruffian, not very bright, about a year my junior. He had been studying for the priesthood, "for a priest," as the peasants said of him, in a clerical seminary. Kuzma had done everything in his power to make his son into someone "proper."[9]

Before sending his son in the clerical direction, Kuzma had long pondered the question: where is it best for him?

"Suppose, for example, I sends him to study to be a military ufficer? It takes a long time and costs lots of money, and what's the benefit? You're not allowed to marry when you want. First you have to put away five thou in the bank, in cash; then you can marry. And where will I get their five thou? Give birth to it or something?! Or maybe just wait 'til a rich bride comes to him and puts five thou in the bank for him. Not everybody can count on that kind of luck," Kuzma reasoned carefully, while scratching his long red hair with his enormous fingers.

"And what kinda life does an ufficer have?" he continued. "One that's nothing but trouble: every day whatever the weather, hot or wet, he drives his soldiers on the field and teaches them to jump over pits and ravines full of water. And if it comes to war—he has to go ahead of his regiment, to be an example of heroism. . . . No, it's not fit for our peasant-brethren, not that kinda life. We need something simpler!" Kuzma concluded. "Now what if you send your son to learn to be a government clerk? It still don't mean he's got a very good trade in his pocket. He goes to the office every day, writes all sorts of papers, lights up like a candle when his bosses are around, and all he has to show for it when he's old is tuberculosis."

Kuzma rejected quite a few other ways of life for his child before he finally alighted on the "clerical."

"I'll have Iashka study to be a priest, and nothing else! First of all, it's the most carefree and peaceful business, and the most pleasing to the Lord God. As soon as the boy finishes his studies, he takes on his duties right away. He'll find himself a good healthy wife from a priestly family. Priests are fertile people, so there's as many priests' daughters around as you like, maidens waiting for a bridegroom. And he'll find one who already has a property, so he'll get some land, a farmstead, some shacks, storehouses, horses, cows, and all kinds of other animals. . . . You can put aside your worries and cares, and just thank the Lord God for His mercy and patience with us sinners. And as for the work, well what kinda work does a priest do anyway? Why, the easiest work in the world. Once you've held the Sunday Mass and morning service, you can curl up on your side all week with your wife and take it easy."

Iashka, as the worthy child of his pious parent, obediently accepted the news of the lifetime career that had been picked for him and, within the limits of his meager capacities, began to advance toward his bright future.

"Stop reading all those books, Semën," Iashka says to me when he sees me with a book. "Doesn't it bore you to tears? At the seminary the only time I read is when I have to do it so I won't fail in class, but I'd prefer if there weren't any books at all. Why don't we go find some girls instead, or else let's go to Iaropol[10] and beat up some bums there and maybe eat some sausages."

"Everyone to his own taste; as they say, some like the priest, some like the priest's wife, and some prefer his daughter," I answered Iashka, in his own joking style.

"For me there's no question—the daughter; but so long as

she's not too old, I won't say no to the priest's wife, either. Anyway, stop confusing me with your smart talk; just send your books to the devil's mother and let's get a move on."

Sometimes Iashka was actually persuasive, and off we went to have some fun.

On several occasions I tried to propagandize Iashka; I'd tell him about the workers' revolutionary struggle, about the brave deeds of various outstanding revolutionaries; I'd teach him to sing revolutionary songs, and so on. But nothing really came of all this.

It's true that he was happy to sing the songs and that he would gladly tell "blasphemous" anecdotes about priests, but he did all this mainly for mischief's sake.

"What do you want—that they put me in prison too? And kick me out of the seminary? No thanks, we humbly thank you," he'd retort.

"Have no fear, they don't put fools in prison."

"You think I'm a fool?"

"I didn't say *you*. I was just talking about what kind of people they don't put in prison."

Iashka was neither proud nor in touch with his own human worth, so he soon calmed down. But there were a couple of times when we had more serious clashes, which turned into fistfights. To my surprise, in these bouts I turned out to be stronger than Iashka; when I decorated his face with a big black eye he ran from me, feeling disgraced in the presence of girls. When he was out of reach he hurled a rock at me, but missed. Inspired by my success, I caught up with Iashka and knocked him off his feet with one punch. Nor did I stop hitting him when he was down, for even my elevated consciousness was incapable of preventing me from piously observing the tradition of beating your opponent all over his face.

After that incident it was a long time before Iashka would show himself in public places—either he was ashamed of his defeat or he didn't want to be seen with his shiners. This was my last decisive clash with Iashka. Thereafter he avoided sharp conflicts with me and silently acknowledged my "moral" authority.

It goes without saying that the entire village had learned of this event before the day was over. Iashka's authority in the village was significantly weakened. He understood this and was unable to adjust to it for a long time to come.

By the end of the summer my boat was ready. Its launching was viewed as a major event by all the villagers. Not only women and children gathered at the riverbank, but even staid and hearty peasant fellows came there as well. Fortunately, the launching was relatively successful. True, the boat was not very fast, but it floated down the river without serious mishap, much to the surprise of the solid peasants and to the joy of the village lads. I went sailing in my boat until late in the fall, when the early frosts appeared and the river was covered with ice.

When the season for field work was over the time for military recruitment finally arrived. The village lads, together with the new recruits, moved in crowds from village to village; they played their accordions, sang outlandish songs in their strained voices, shouted, danced their village dances, drank vodka, acted rowdy, and fought over girls with the boys of other villages. This bravado and drunken revelry was their way of drowning the dread they felt in anticipation of their coming departure from their dear ones for many long years of soldiering, harsh barracks life, and perhaps even war. Not one of them would have joined the army voluntarily. To the very last day, every recruit was hoping to avoid his military service by some means or another. Some were counting on exemptions, others dreamed of "drawing the long straw," still others hoped to be found unhealthy, and so on. Some of them went to see the "wise old women" and "healers," who fed them all kinds of formulas to ruin their health and often made them into cripples for life. The wealthier ones—the sons of kulaks—bribed the doctors and the military authorities.

Since I had nobody and nothing to count on, I firmly resolved to meet my fate head on—whatever shall be shall be. I would still fight on to the end for my great ideas.

> *And if indeed you perish*
> *In mines or prisons damp,*
> *Your cause will always echo*
> *For generations of the living.*[11]

This, more or less, was my state of mind—naked, exposed, trembling from cold one moment, from the extremely hostile environment another moment—when I approached the table where the district military authorities were seated, wearing their shiny golden shoulder-straps, buttons, sword-belts, sabers, and medals.

The army doctor touched me and tapped me with his cold fingers, listened to my chest through a pipe, knocked about with a little hammer, and said very coldly:

"Fit for service."

However, when he noticed that I was wearing glasses he asked:

"Why are you wearing glasses?" [12]

"I have bad eyesight."

"Well, then, take them off!" he commanded.

I removed my glasses and carefully placed them on the window-sill.

The doctor—a stout, phlegmatic man—slowly examined my eyes, had me look at a cardboard square with several letters on it from a distance, and, after a whispered exchange with the district police chief and the military commander, said:

"Take him to the Moscow military hospital."

22
At the Moscow Military Hospital

O<small>N THE EVENING</small> of the very same day, in the office of the military commander, I was handed an official letter dispatching me to Moscow by horsedrawn cart.[1] In those days, that is, in the year 1900, there was still no railroad linking Volokolamsk to Moscow. So I made the 65-mile trip in a simple cart, together with a load of goods, riding for three whole days on the uncomfortable, bumpy highway. We stopped each evening at an inn, where we spent the night and fed the horses.

On the morning of the fourth day I finally arrived at the military hospital in the Lefortovo district of Moscow.[2] I was tired, worn, and hungry.

When they had washed me, dressed me in government-issue linens, and fed me, I felt so exhausted that I could barely make it into bed. They were unable to wake me up for lunch or supper. I slept until the following morning, when I was awakened by a noise. I looked all around, but for a long time I could not figure out where I was. Sitting next to me on the bunk and reading a book was a thin, spectacled man with a small, reddish, wedge-shaped beard. On the shelf beneath his table stood two piles of books in beautiful, dark bindings.

I was irresistibly drawn toward the books. I longed to read them, to find out the contents of these beautiful dark volumes.

"Please permit me to look at your books; I am dying of boredom, I haven't read anything for ages," I said.

"Please, go right ahead. . . . But first allow me to introduce myself. After all, we're neighbors, aren't we?" he said, offering his narrow, fragile, feminine hand. "I'm Gvozdev, a student at Moscow University."

I introduced myself. We immediately began an animated conversation. We began cautiously, groping for common ground. While we were talking I was examining two of his books, one after the other.

"Are all of these Chekhov?"

"Yes, Chekhov. Why, don't you like him?"

"Well, it's hard to explain. He writes very well, entertainingly, but his characters are so sluggish, such whiners, and he provides no solutions," I answered cautiously.

"You're wrong. Why those are just the things I like so much about him: his tender, soft sadness and his—how should I put it?—his reconciling pessimism."

"Well I don't like the kind of writers who drive you to despair. I read Chekhov when I was in the preliminary detention prison— pure boredom. But not if you read Shchedrin, Gleb Uspensky, or Nekrasov. Reading them raises your spirits, and you clench your fists. . . ."

"Sh-h-h . . . . Be careful, not so loud; you don't know who could be listening here," Gvozdev interrupted me. "What were you in prison for?"

"For belonging to a circle in the Nevsky region."

"Are you Marxist?"

"A Marxist, yes."

"From the university or the technical institute?"[3]

"I'm not a student, I'm a worker, a pattern-maker, from the Semiannikov factory," I said.

Gvozdev looked at me in bewilderment, then grabbed my hand and pressed it firmly in his.

"I never believed that worker-intelligentsia types like you existed, even when my colleagues told me about them. But now I'm convinced, I've seen it with my own eyes."

"You know . . . , well really, in our circle there were workers even more intellectually developed than me," I said with embarrassment. "But that's not really the point; the point is to stir up the masses, to lead them to consciousness."

"I'm a Marxist myself, but I have lots of doubts about the accuracy of some of Marx's ideas. It seems to me that he penetrates very deeply to the heart of things but he ignores human individuality. One feels no soul in his teachings; they're too dry."

"Perhaps, but he certainly studied the soul of the working masses, and he sure knows where surplus value comes from, and he's shown us the road to socialism," I retorted passionately, as if I had actually read Marx myself.

"You talk about socialism," Gvozdev said, lowering his voice, "but just what is socialism? Marx has nothing to say about that, does he!"

Although I had never read Marx, there was no way I could admit that Marx didn't say anything about socialism, so I began to argue impassionedly with Gvozdev.

In this way, we continued arguing right up until lunchtime. After lunch Gvozdev was called to the visiting room to see his wife. He returned with an armful of little packages and boxes.

Because he had a poor appetite, Gvozdev didn't know what to do with all the food his wife had brought. Food that had been brought earlier still was lying under his table, where it had grown rotten and dry and was no longer fit for consumption.

However, when I arrived at the hospital I rescued him from this embarrassing situation and did him a comradely service: I devoured to the very last one—all his sausages, cutlets, chickens, dumplings, etc.

Gvozdev watched with envy as I speedily coped with my task—the annihilation of the stale provisions—and he praised me for my appetite.

While I was at the hospital I was summoned once a day to the doctor, who would do various kinds of tests of my eyesight every time I came. He was evidently looking for malingerers.

We were poorly fed, our walks in the courtyard were short, and we spent our days loafing about aimlessly in the long narrow corridor.

At that time I managed to read several books by Mamin-Sibiryak,[4] which had been brought to Gvozdev by his visitors. They pleased me so much I couldn't put them down.

During my first days there I had heated arguments with Gvozdev. He was a very questionable "Marxist." He was much closer in spirit to Bernstein,[5] whose ideas I first encountered through Gvozdev. I could only argue with him "intuitively," relying on material from his own statements.

What upset me the most in Bernstein, and in Gvozdev as well, was the gradualism, the rejection of violence and class struggle.

"Nature is governed by the law of evolution, it knows no catastrophes; it follows that there can be no catastrophes in the development of the social organism either," he tried to persuade me.

"False, your Bernstein is lying. And the great French Revolution, and the Revolution of 1848—what were they, in your opinion? Not catastrophic shifts? Not times of violence?" I boiled over with excitement, turning to the attack.

It was only now that I began to appreciate the enormous value of my earlier participation in the propaganda circle. Except for some popularizations, I had read no books on the French Revolution, but I had heard a great deal of talk about it at our circle meetings. And that exposure greatly facilitated my argumentation, despite the fact that I didn't know many foreign words, words that Gvozdev could manipulate so easily.

"You see, that was a very different historical conjuncture; since then, given the progress of technology, capitalist development has entered the path of evolution and of the smoothing of class contradictions. In this way, in maybe five hundred or a thousand years, we'll achieve socialism imperceptibly, without catastrophes and revolutions," Gvozdev would say calmly and confidently, his golden eyeglasses sparkling as he stretched his arm forward, as if to point out the peaceful road of evolutionary progress.

"No, the workers will not wait that long for your peaceful road to socialism—we don't have the patience for that. Don't you know that in a thousand years the capitalists will have driven us all to the grave, we'll all die out or degenerate. Why the facts themselves speak against Bernstein. Every economic crisis is deeper than the last one, unemployment increases. How can you fail to see that, to feel it!" I said with ardor. "The workers of all countries are awakening to consciousness, organizing, preparing themselves for the overthrow of the capitalist yoke, while you're saying that things are moving toward the slackening of the class struggle. And the arbitrary conduct of our autocracy, the raiding and plundering by tsarist officials and by manufacturers—do you call that slackening?"

"Our country is a special case: if the government doesn't start thinking clearly, of course it could end in revolution," Gvozdev agreed. "But you still cannot violate the laws of nature," he added obstinately. Gvozdev was a natural scientist and a passionate supporter of Darwin. When he gave his clear, simplified explanations of Darwin's theory I would listen to him with delight, but when he mechanically transferred that theory to the development of society I'd feel an anger stirring inside me that I was incapable of expressing in words.

"And just what are these laws of nature? Who invented them? If they're anything like our tsarist laws, then they're not worth a brass farthing; they were invented by the rich so that we'd sit more quietly on our backsides. When the day comes when we can invent our own laws, then we'll believe in them, but for now we believe only facts and deeds, and they speak in our favor."

Gvozdev could not maintain his calm tone much longer; he soon grew tired, became increasingly nervous and angry, and then turned silent. At this point he would lower his head and let his whiskers hang down. Then, for a long time we would wander through the corridors in silence, shuffling along the asphalt floor in our hospital slippers until it was time for some hospital "activity."

We remained in the hospital, in "good health," for fourteen days. Then I was again handed an official letter, which I was to take back to the military commander in Volokolamsk.

Before my departure Gvozdev invited me to visit him at his home. I promised to do so.

I must admit that I went to him with very little enthusiasm. I probably went because he'd promised to give me books to take back to the village.

He lived with his wife and mother-in-law, either on Pliushchikha or on Polikha,[6] in a very comfortable, nicely furnished apartment.

I was received cordially. Several guests had apparently been invited to join us: about three male students, some kind of gentleman dressed in civilian clothes, and a female student with close-cropped hair.

They looked me over as if I was some kind of fossil. They asked me if I read Marx, if I liked Turgenev, if I thought that workers would struggle for a constitution, and so on. Although I did not feel very comfortable in this company, I couldn't figure out how to escape with dispatch. The hostess, a young student who had recently become a mother, tried to start a general discussion, but without any success.

To make matters worse, I committed a serious blunder at the table. When thin little pancakes were served on a platter, no one wanted to be the first to take them. The hostess proposed that, as a new guest, I be the one to begin, but I too refused, since this was an entirely new dish for me and I had no idea how to handle it. The hostess insisted. Then, collecting my courage, I took a fork—which I wielded very ineptly—and poked it into the pile of pancakes right down to the bottom of the platter. But then, since I had made no effort to shake the pancakes off the fork, nothing remained on the platter; instead, I managed to put the entire pile on my own plate, leaving the astonished guests without any pancakes. However, the kind hostess quickly came to the rescue by bringing a second pile of pancakes from the kitchen. I was extremely embarrassed. The other guests pretended not to have noticed. By now my mood was definitely ruined. After drinking a glass of tea out of politeness, I made haste to depart. While I was taking leave of Gvozdev, he thrust two books into my hands, one of which, I recall, was Smails,[7] and then we parted.

23
Working for a Tradesman

I WAS EXEMPTED from military service forever. I do not know if
the reason was my poor eyesight or if my political unreliability
played a role here, but I was free. Once again the monotonous
days of my vegetation under official surveillance droned on, occasionally interrupted by the visits of a gendarme.

In the autumn, on a certain Friday, I was visiting the bazaar in
Iaropolets. While walking along the flour and fish rows of the
market, I encountered my kinsman Kiselev. A tall, broad-
shouldered man with brown hair and a small blond beard, wearing a tanned sheepskin coat trimmed with seal and a high lamb-
skin hat, he seemed more like a boyar of ancient Russia than like
a tradesman.[1] This illusion was spoiled, however, by his screwed-
up little eyes and his big dark teeth, which looked like the tusks
of a boar.

"Hey, come over here," he called to me. "You must have become rich if you can't even recognize your relatives." And without
even waiting for my answer he broke into merry laughter.

"Well," he continued, "How is it going, student? They didn't
take you into the army? But you should have gone to serve the
tsar, our little father. A smart nation needs soldiers."

"They'll manage without me, and besides, I'm not a trustworthy servant of the tsar," I replied.

"I guess that means you got an outright deferment. . . . So. . . .
Well what do you plan to do next?"

"I'll try to get the gendarmes to let me go to some city or other."

Customers began to approach Kiselev's stall. They touched the
flour, tested the groats and peas with their teeth, poked the moldy
pickles in the herring barrels with their fingers, crumpled the un-

derbellies of the herrings to ascertain whether they contained milk or roe.

Kiselev, his wife, and their workers were barely able to take care of all the customers.

"Listen, Semën Ivanovich, this evening, when there won't be all these customers, you come back here. We'll go to the tavern, drink some tea, have a bite of fish," Kiselev cried out to me when I began to move on.

"Apparently Kiselev needs me for something," I thought to myself. "He's not one of those stingy old peasants, but he is calculating; he doesn't give anyone tea and cake without a reason. And here he is getting ready to treat me to fish!"

In the evening, after strolling around the bazaar for a while, I returned to Kiselev's. When he saw me he cut off a thick piece of sturgeon, wrapped it in paper, and handing it to me said:

"You go to Pishchikov's, order us each a couple of teas, and have the waiter scald the sturgeon with boiling water. As soon as I've tied my wares into the carts, I'll come join you."

Kiselev wasted no time. I had no sooner managed to carve up the cooked sturgeon than the imposing figure of Kiselev appeared in the doorway of the tavern. Amid all the uproar he stopped at the threshold and began to seek me out with his eyes. When I caught sight of him I motioned to him with my hand, and Kiselev, after removing his hat, came over to my table. He took two little granular rolls from his coat pocket and placed them on the table.

"Would you like to drink a little vodka?" he asked. "It's on me."

"I don't drink."

"You mean people of your status aren't supposed to drink?"

"That's right, a socialist shouldn't drink vodka," I replied firmly.

"And in your opinion, is it wrong to appropriate someone else's property?" he asked, slyly screwing up his left eye as he looked askance at me.

"Why 'in your opinion'? I do believe that stealing is forbidden according to all 'opinions'!"

"Well, of course, if. . . . But forbidding something is one thing, and life is something else. . . . If someone is hanging around near someone else's property or money, he's bound to take a certain amount and conceal it. . . . You can't keep watch over everything, even if the fellow's your close relative. It's clear: an in-law is an in-law and a brother is a brother, but money is nobody's kinsman."

While he was saying this Kiselev was banging me on the shoulder, staring into my eyes, and rapidly, hungrily devouring bite after bite of sturgeon, which he chewed up with a roll. I wasn't far behind him. The waiter brought us at least two more kettles of boiling water for the tea. Kiselev kept pouring it into the flat, wide cups. It would have taken a long time for the tea to cool off in the cups, so we poured it into our saucers, blew on it noisily, and, making loud sounds, sipped it up.

"Semën Ivanovich, you have nothing to do now, right?"

"Nothing. Why do you ask?"

"Come spend the winter with me. It'll be more peaceful for you at my place, and you won't have to eat at your poor brother's; every morsel counts for him. . . . I'm no stranger to you, right? And since you have nothing else to do you can help me sell fish at the markets."

My situation really was difficult. The season for field work was over. My brother had gone off for the winter to a nearby textile factory, where he worked as a warper. I was idling away, day after day, with nothing to do, dying of boredom. Looking after the cattle—bringing them the hay and the straw from the spring grain—didn't take much time.

I had finished reading all my books. The young men had left for wage-earning jobs. There was little hope that the gendarmes would give me permission to leave. Kiselev's proposition, though it didn't strike me as all that generous, still seemed to me—I was, after all, very young—to be sincere. Besides, I had no other solution, so I accepted.

Three days later I was already with Kiselev busily selling his beluga, sturgeon, herring, smelts, fish heads, and other goods. We traded at bazaars in the larger villages on Fridays, Thursdays, Wednesdays, and Sundays. We would wake up when it was still dark, around 4 A.M. We loaded the wares on our sleighs, using two or three carts, depending on the distance and size of the bazaar. It was a little over 25 miles to the farthest bazaar and about seven to the closest. We'd return home from the bazaar when it had again grown dark, in snowstorms, blizzards, and terrible frosts. . . . My clothing was of poor quality, so it was difficult for me to sit in the cart very long. My feet would grow numb, and I was pierced to the bone by the frost and wind. I'd frequently jump

from the sleigh, lag a little behind the horse, and then start running to catch up. When I had warmed up a bit I would tumble
back into the sleigh and keep sitting there until I began to freeze
again.

Sometimes Kiselev, all wrapped up in his warm sheepskin coat,
would happen to turn around and, when he saw me "warming
up" behind my sleigh, he'd strike his horse with his whip. His
well-fed red front horse ran off with the sleigh while my poor
little horse dashed after her, leaving me far behind. I trotted on
foot for a couple of miles, short-winded, on the difficult snow-
bound road, catching up with my horse.

We'd arrive at the bazaar early in the morning, unpack our
carts, and begin to lay out our goods. We worked for a long time
on an empty stomach, for Kiselev considered it a bad sign to
drink tea purchased with money that hadn't been earned at the
same bazaar.

I handled the simpler goods: groats, flour, hops, malt, fish
heads. I often had to plunge my naked hand deep into the brine
to fish out the herrings that were in there. My fingers grew numb
and ached terribly.

As for Kiselev, he would stand near a large table and handle the
more expensive kinds of fish, while overseeing the whole trading
procedure. His wife stood at the cash box and settled accounts
with the customers. On the big bazaar days, when trade was particularly brisk, he would hire two helpers—a male and a female.

I was able to handle the goods—to set them out and wrap
them—in short order, but I often spent too much time fussing
over the large rusty scales, with their thick dirty plates, since it
took so long for them to settle into equilibrium. Kiselev noticed
this and would often look askance at me.

"Hey there, 'student' (he often called me that as a joke), you
sure spend a lot of time fussing about the scales. Why do you wait
for the plates to even out? That's not how to weigh things. If you
just toss the item on with a quick throw, your plate will move
down quickly and shift the weight; then you immediately take the
item off the board without waiting for the two plates to even out.
That way we profit and the customer thinks he's been given the
full weight," Kiselev would instruct me.

"But that would mean the customer is being cheated out of two
or three pounds per forty," I said.

"When you're in business you have to do it—it's the risk! Here you lose a pound, here you find one; a kopeck more, a kopeck less. Why just last week the brine leaked out of my barrel; the salt just stood there in a dry spot and dried up. Now who's going to cover the loss for me?"

Kiselev was plainly exaggerating the costs of his business. I knew his "commercial secrets" in precise detail. I knew that he added water to the dried salt and that he often sprinkled the hops with a little water; so when that salt dried out, he not only sustained no losses, he actually profited.

"And the customer, what's it to him? So he gets nine pounds instead of ten—he eats it and doesn't even notice," Kiselev went on, trying to convince me. "In our business it's the only way you can possibly begin to make ends meet; and like they say, if you're not a sinner in the eyes of God, then you're innocent before the tsar."

"You can argue as cleverly as you like, I refuse to cheat with the scales!" I declared firmly.

Kiselev clenched his teeth, looked askance at me, and said in an even voice:

"Well then, just stand by the cash box—you'll handle the customer's payment. . . . Hey, Aksenya," he turned to his wife, "give Semën the change purse and you take over the scales."

After Aksenya and I had exchanged roles we continued our sales. This new arrangement apparently suited Kiselev even more. He distrusted his wife, who was a quiet, frightened woman. He knew that she was secretly aiding her daughter, who, following the dictates of her heart, had married a poor peasant lad without the blessing of her parents. He often caught her concealing money or household items for the daughter; he would scold her and beat her for this, but he still wasn't certain that Aksenya wasn't pocketing money for the daughter. But the old swindler and cheat had no doubt whatever about my honesty and reliability. When he had questioned me so carefully about whether our "sect," as he put it, appropriated other people's money, he knew just what he was doing. And in our transactions he had plenty of occasions to grow confident in my honesty. That is why it was so easy for him to accept what was for him a major shift. Of course it goes without saying that Kiselev paid me no money for that difficult work; he evidently thought that in this way he was fulfilling the role of "benefactor" to his kin.

We continued working right up to "Nicholas Day," that is, until

December 6.[2] In our village Nicholas Day was considered a saint's day celebration, and for this reason all the local tradesmen and kulaks—except the ones Kiselev was on bad terms with—all the clergymen of the local church, the village police inspector, and the steward from the nearby estate gathered at Kiselev's home. Even the "gentleman" who owned the estate was expected, but for some reason he failed to appear.[3]

The priest and the sexton were regular guests at Kiselev's. They ate large amounts, until they were belching, they drank vodka and sweet wine, and, in the evening, they played cards with their host.[4]

I too was drawn to all these luxurious feasts. To be sure, I attempted to keep aloof from this "company," but I did not always succeed. Kiselev, who treated me in a slightly patronizing manner, while at the same time fearing me somewhat, liked to "set me against" the priest, as he put it.

When the subject of God or the church came up, Kiselev would turn to the priest and say:

"It seems, Father, that this young man says that God didn't create man but that man appeared by himself, from the monkey; is that true or not?"

The priest throws a lightning-swift, crushing glance my way and says solemnly:

"That's a blasphemous, sacrilegious lie, invented by that sinful philosopher Darwin."

"Not just Darwin, but other outstanding scholars also support that view," I retort.

"They too are apostates from God. You show me, young man, where to find the line between a human being and a horse. Let your blasphemous scholars tell me the answer. You're not going to find such a line, because the Lord God didn't create one. In the eyes of the Supreme Creator every creature is equal and serves to praise the wisdom of His deeds," says the priest, prophetically and with inspiration while shaking his reddish mane.

"I think you're taking the wrong tack now, Father," Kiselev says to him provocatively. "To this very day scientists cannot demonstrate how a man can come from a monkey, for it's nothing but a huge lie."

"They have already proved it by means of examples, comparisons, and experiments on other animals," I counter. And with

great passion I begin to draw the picture of the process of evolution in the animal kingdom that I had rather recently heard described by the student Gvozdev.

"That's not proof either—that's speculation. Can you show me
a place where a monkey gave birth to a man?" says the priest with
fervor.

"You can't ask for that kind of ridiculous proof. Only completely illiterate, ignorant people could put the question that way,
either ignorant people or professional frauds," I answer harshly,
losing my patience before the insolence and obtuseness of this
Orthodox priest.

"How dare you insult me! Such impertinence!" The priest ex-
plodes; he stands up at the table while raising his fists in the air.
Kiselev and the other guests make haste to calm the infuriated,
intoxicated priest.

"I'll call the police inspector! How dare you! . . . da-dah, da-
dah, da-dah. . . . I'll show you! You little urchin! You rebel! . . . "
I hear these words of the enraged servant of the altar as he runs
down the stairs.

On the next day, early in the morning, I gathered my belongings and left for my home in the village.

But a week later I received a written order from the gendarmes
to travel to Saratov under police surveillance.

Part Four

Saratov

Introduction

T HE CITY to which fate now delivered me appears in my imagination today in the form of a blacksmith's shop where an enormous variety of weapons for the impending political and class wars were sharpened and forged.[1] Everyone there could feel that these battles would soon be upon us. But neither the master craftsmen nor the journeymen, and least of all the apprentices, had a really clear picture of how this or that weapon would be used to smite the enemy when the time for action came.

Our weakness lay in the fact that there had never been a revolution in Russia; as a consequence, we also had no revolutionary traditions of organized class struggle.

To be sure, in the remote historical past there had been peasant insurrections—the Stenka Razin "rebellion," the "rebellion" of Emelyan Pugachev.[2] But that epoch in our national history was already too far in the past. It was the time of the struggle of an oppressed, enserfed peasantry against its oppressors—the gentry, the boyars and landowners. This unquestionably heroic struggle took place mainly in the countryside, far away from our urban commercial and industrial centers. It was an epoch with very different features from the period of relatively developed capitalism.[3] Hence there was nothing to learn from that epoch, and in any case the authentic archival records of those events were deeply buried in the hidden recesses of the tsarist autocracy. It was therefore natural that our gaze turned to the West. There we could see the Great French Revolution, the Revolutions of 1848, the Paris Commune; there we could find the brave Jacobins, who had severed the heads of countless aristocrats; there were the barricades, the skirmishes of the toiling masses with royal troops and guards from bourgeois families.[4]

Young Russian Marxists returned from their sojourns abroad filled with enthusiasm and admiration for the unbelievable victories of the German Social Democratic Party and for the great achievements of the English Trade Unionists and the Labour Party, which had just recently made its appearance in Parliament.[5] The brilliant, talented leader of the German workers, August Bebel, a turner by trade, and the Member of Parliament Keir Hardie, an English coal miner—these were our kinfolk, tied to us by class and common struggle.[6]

But alas, there were still very few of us who understood "what was what." With the autocracy pressing down mercilessly with its mighty apparatus, and the capitalists, those greedy beasts of prey, sucking the workers' blood, the workers' class instinct searched for an advanced theory capable of illuminating the road to revolution; with caution and uncertainty, the workers picked and tested reliable and steadfast leaders in the course of revolutionary struggle.

The great and very difficult mission of solving all these essential problems was taken on by *Iskra*, inspired and headed by its young and fearless leader, V. Lenin.[7] However, like every new idea, it could not win over supporters and friends all at once, not without a struggle, and not without encountering resistance even in those circles that were closest to it in mood and spirit.

The name of the city of which I speak was Saratov. In 1901–2 it contained many artisan shops, a few factories, and a total of about 10,000 workers. Saratov also had several secondary-level educational institutions—a school for medical assistants, a technical school, a secondary school based on modern language instruction, and a classical gymnasium.[8] The city was also inhabited by representatives of both the secular and the spiritual authorities, in the person of the governor, the bishop, a gendarme colonel, and all their usual entourage.

In the center of town, on the city square, stood the temple of worship—the cathedral. There were also many taverns and many churches. At the edge of town was a prison.

The government authorities, who considered Saratov a remote, out-of-the-way city, had turned it into a place of exile for political criminals and unreliable elements of every kind. Representatives of the free professions were also drawn to Saratov, which had a liberal zemstvo,[9] a municipal council, and two newspapers.

These institutions made it easier to find employment. Hence Saratov became a gathering point for a very large number of people of revolutionary bent, people with nothing to lose in their lives. Workers were exiled to Saratov who were still at the "beginners'" stage of untrustworthiness, whereas workers burdened with greater degrees of criminality were exiled by the gendarmes to Siberia and to the extreme north.

From the point of view of the "wise" autocracy, Saratov was obviously seen as a kind of correctional colony for prisoners, to which were sent people who had only recently joined the ranks of the unreliable or people who had already undergone severe punishment in Siberia.

According to the "pedagogical" logic of the state security police, it was evidently assumed that the transgressor, having tasted imprisonment or exile to a remote corner of the country, would have to acknowledge the error of his ways. Saratov would give such a person the opportunity to strengthen definitively his devotion to the "true" faith, to enter the path of virtue, to begin to live by God's commandments and the instructions of the authorities.

However, the "pedagogical" theory of the security police was too far removed from real life, so that its application frequently had the opposite results: "it sowed the wind, but reaped the whirlwind!"

Workers who were politically undeveloped were put into prison to correct their ways, but for them the prison was transformed into a university; it strengthened their character and turned them into steadfast revolutionaries. Workers were exiled to their native regions, to their villages, and were transformed there into agitators and leaders of the oppressed peasantry in their struggle against the landlords. The practice of exiling people to the peripheries of Russia turned those regions into sources of contagion of revolutionary struggle. A sort of natural selection of revolutionaries took place there—those who were weak of spirit abandoned the revolution, often abandoning life itself, whereas the strong and steadfast hardened themselves for future battles.

25

"To Unknown Shores" (Under Special Police Surveillance)

I DEPARTED from my "native" region with raised spirits. The immense snow-covered plains, the telegraph poles, the wretched gray huts, pressed toward the earth, of the villages where dark ignorance, endless need, and the peasant's unbearable grief built their solid nests—all these things sped off into the distance. The high belfries of the gentry's country homes and the squat houses of the kulaks, the wealthy, and the innkeepers thrust themselves insistently before your eyes. Its wheels knocking and rattling, the train carried me farther and farther away. Where to? It was all the same to me, just as long as it was farther from my "native" region.

The words of an old song came to my mind: "abandon not your native fields or you encounter wicked folk." But these words aren't meant for me. I have no "native fields." I do not wish to be manure or fertilizer for the people who erect these belfries, inns, and taverns and place heavy candles before icons. I wish to be free, like a bird; I want to live, work, and die in combat!

Finding myself once again on the streets of a big city, I was immediately drawn into the whirlpool of local life. And the ever thoughtful authorities, in the person of a gendarme lieutenant colonel, lost no time in taking note of my new situation; he hastened secretly to inform the Moscow office of gendarmes that "on January 30 the peasant Semën Ivanov Kanatchikov, currently under special police surveillance, arrived in the city of Saratov, where the above-mentioned surveillance over him has been established."[1]

Thus was I passed from hand to hand!

I immediately moved in with my friend Konstantin Langeld and began to look for work. His apartment was located on one of those sleepy streets with a religious name and consisted of two rooms and an entrance hall. One of the rooms was inhabited by Langeld and a friend of his, a tall fellow with a dark beard and eyeglasses, who wore a blue wide-belted shirt, which he would constantly adjust from behind, apparently wishing to conceal the defects—the patches and holes—of his trousers. In the other, smaller room lived a tall, skinny young blond woman. Langeld put the hall at my disposal.

The man with the dark beard was called Uncle Misha. He earned his bread either by doing office work or by teaching, and he had very radical ideas. The skinny girl was called either Aleksandra Mikhailovna or Aleksandra Vasilevna—I don't remember which. She had recently graduated from the school for medical assistants, worked in the municipal hospital, and had no "ideas" at all, but she was very eager to attach herself to anyone who did, especially if it was someone with real "information." But all in all she was a very quiet and sympathetic creature.

Konstantin Langeld did not have a steady job, but made his living from repair work: he either repaired the water pipes in the hospital or he installed electrical bells in the offices of the zemstvo governing board. The investigation of his Petersburg case was supposed to be completed soon, and he expected notification from the Department of Police of his exile to one of the northern provinces at any moment.[2]

In the evening and on holidays my friends' apartment would be transformed into a veritable passage area. I deliberately say "passage" rather than "lodging" because it was so narrow. People would begin to appear around 7 P.M. Uncle Misha would usually come and unlock the door when the bell rang. He would let in two or three male or female visitors, who were almost always conversing noisily, then calm himself down and, apparently assuming that these were the last of the guests, take a book and lie down on the couch. But then the doorbell would keep ringing. Uncle Misha would put down his book and quietly open the door, saying good-naturedly: "A guest has arrived."

The "guest" usually asked for "Kostya" or for "Konstantin Fedorovich," depending on his degree of friendship with Langeld. However, the lively, sociable, merry Kostya did not like to stay at home; he preferred to go visit other people although, with his characteristic carelessness, he invited everyone else to visit him.

Thus the task of receiving and entertaining the guests fell to the lot of Uncle Misha, the stay-at-home, and then to me as well. Aleksandra Mikhailovna would join the guests only in two situations: when she wished to learn some new piece of political information, or when she began to get tired of hearing the doorbell and the loud conversation. In the latter case she would thrust her narrow, foxlike physiognomy through the door of her room and make some biting remark.

Before long I had made the acquaintance of all of Langeld's guests. This was no burden to me, since most of the guests were young, cheerful, interesting girls—students from the special courses, medical assistants, and midwives.[3] At first I was embarrassed and avoided the conversations. But I very quickly adjusted to the situation and would even engage with them in various political arguments.

26
The Non-Resister

FROM TIME TO TIME a local follower of Tolstoy by the name of Sergey Gerasimovich Nalimov came to visit Langeld.[1] He was a graying man, of average height, who moved about in an agitated and troubled manner.

Nalimov would eat no meat or fish. Instead of shoes, all year long he wore rubber galoshes, which he wore over foot-cloths that were tied with cords. He was an eternal student at the Forestry Institute.[2] He had suffered for his convictions on more than one occasion, was privy to the "eternal truth"—"to love one's neighbor"—and at present preached the doctrine of nonviolent resistance to evil. He was also something of an inventor and could boast some fairly significant successes in that area: he had constructed a wire apparatus for heating children's milk with a kerosene lamp and he had already printed a wall grammar, which hung from the walls of all his good friends. In our apartment the grammar could be seen in all its glory above Uncle Misha's couch.

One day Serezha Nalimov, as we called him familiarly, stayed with us longer than usual; at the beginning he was waiting for Konstantin to come home, but then he began to chatter about current events. We discussed the student riots and the demonstrations; we talked about constitutions, revolution, and related topics.[3]

"Oh my," Serezha Nalimov sighed, "I feel very sorry for you, my dear friends, but there's nothing can be done to help you."

"Your pity is of little use. What we need is not your pity, but your help in our struggle," Uncle Misha retorted.

Serezha jumped up and began to dart about the room.

"One mustn't defile the spirit with violence, for nothing good has ever come from violence, only evil. Life must be organized according to the truths of the Gospels. Love, love, and love alone can save humanity!" Serezha repeated, standing in the middle of the room waving his arms. "That is the eternal, unchanging truth. It alone can bring you victory!"

Uncle Misha stirred his tea with his spoon, glanced mockingly in the direction of Serezha, and said in a grave tone:

"It's time you put an end to your fairy tales, Serezha; we're not little children. Just tell us, if you please, where and when loving your neighbor has ever triumphed in this world?"

"It has to triumph!" Serezha interjected with passion.

"But it's been nearly 2,000 years since Christ began to preach love. And what have been the results? People fight one another like dogs. The strong offend the weak. Not peace, but the sword rules the earth!" exclaimed Uncle Misha in a stentorian voice.

"Now that's a lie, old boy!" Konstantin broke in. "It's not the sword, it's the coin. . . ." Konstantin leaped up from his chair and, striking a pose, began to sing:

Only one sacred idol rules the world. . . .

Konstantin's voice wasn't very strong, but it was pleasant, and he really knew how to control it. Later I would have more than one occasion to hear him sing Tchaikovsky romances in Auntie's "salon,"[4] accompanied on the piano.

Aleksandra Mikhailovna brought in a huge smoking frying pan full of eggs and put it down on the table.

"Now that's something I understand! That's a woman for you! Kind, provident, and to the point. . . . I don't know about the rest of you, but I'm as hungry as a wolf," said Konstantin.

"As the Scriptures say: a man without a woman is like a steer without a tail," Uncle Misha could not resist adding.

Armed with forks, everyone began to eat straight from the frying pan, which was sizzling with fat, whetting our appetites.

Serezha Nalimov hesitated at first, but not for long: he soon grabbed a fork and began to eat greedily. He would not eat anything that had been slaughtered, that is, neither fish nor meat, because, as he put it, it was wrong to take the life of living creatures that man himself could not create. And it was dangerous to the human organism to devour the corpses of animals. He would eat eggs only as a kind of compromise, under very exceptional circumstances. Having satisfied his hunger, Serezha seemed to regret very much that he had yielded to temptation.

"Were those eggs fried in oil?" he asked.

"We're not capitalists. We usually cook with lard," Uncle Misha responded severely.

"This is already the second month we haven't seen any cooking oil. God only knows how low our wages are," Aleksandra Mikhailovna confirmed.

Serezha Nalimov changed his expression. "Ladies and gentlemen, it is important to respect the convictions of one's fellow human beings," he pronounced his words coldly and sternly.

"Look, Mr. Fellow-Human-Being, you should have asked what the food was fried in before you ate it," Uncle Misha parried.

We laughed merrily. I would later have many occasions to witness "misunderstandings" of this kind with Serezha Nalimov. There was no way we could ever take his Tolstoyism seriously. I doubt if he even took it seriously himself. But circumstances determine your obligations: as they say, if he calls himself a mushroom, then put him in the mushroom box!

27
The Liberal

SHORTLY THEREAFTER Uncle Misha found me temporary work through one of his friends.

"There's a certain liberal whose furniture needs to be repaired," he told me joyfully, seeing how heavily the burden of unemployment weighed upon me. "And he's a remarkable individual! He's really very radical, extremely so! He gives money to the SRs, for terror," Uncle Misha explained, in praise of the man.

"I don't care a fig for his radicalism, so long as he gives me work," I said.

"Wait a second; that's not right, you know. It's always nicer to work for your own kind!"

The liberal occupied a private residence not far from the banks of the Volga. When I came to examine the furniture and ascertain the nature of the repairs, the maid announced my arrival to the lady of the house and conducted me to the kitchen. Soon a young woman emerged, languid, dark-haired, resembling one of those women one saw in the decadent drawings of that period. She moved all around, bent this way and that, and put on all kinds of airs, just as if she had been on springs. And while she was putting on her airs, every now and then her thin, knotty extremities would appear through the slits of her loose silk dressing gown.

"She must be a wicked one!" I thought.

The woman stopped at the threshold of the kitchen, stared at me attentively through her tortoiseshell lorgnette, and said through her nose: "Are you the one that Ivan Ermolaich sent to us? This is charming, just charming!"

Although I didn't know who this Ivan Ermolaich was, I responded affirmatively.

"Are you a student? I'm terribly fond of students; they're such charming men!"

"No, I'm a worker," I replied.

"Well it makes no difference at all! You both rebel against the government together. . . . Charming! Glafira," she said, turning to her maid, "you will show him the broken furniture in the garret, and he shall repair it." And with this she disappeared, leaving behind her the aroma of delicate perfume.

I carried the dusty, dirty furniture from the garret to the room next to the kitchen, returned home to get my tools, bought some varnish, polish, and glass paper, and set to work.

Because the lady of the house slept late in the mornings and I might have disturbed her rest with my noise, I was not permitted to come to work before 11 A.M. But often she would lie around in bed past twelve. On those days—and this was only after my most persistent demands—the maid would allow me to work surreptitiously, but she strictly forbade me to make any noise.

For some reason or other the bell in the lady's bedroom was often out of order. At such times I could hear her desperate cry resounding throughout the apartment:

"Glafirka! You tra-a-sh, you goo-oo-d-for-nothing! Where have you disappeared to?"

Glafirka rushed from the kitchen to the bedroom as if she were on fire. When the lady had left the house, Glafirka pleaded with me to repair the bell. I told her that I wasn't a mechanic and didn't know how to fix bells, but she kept after me:

"Never in my life have I heard of a good craftsman like you who couldn't fix a bell!"

I gave in. I went to the bedroom, where I inspected the wiring. Using my awl and my screwdriver, I tinkered with the "pear," with the white button that was hanging over the back of the bed. To my surprise, the bell began to ring. Glafira was delighted. She led me to the kitchen and ordered the cook to feed me in her "top style."

A few days later I was confronted by the "extremely radical" liberal himself. He was a middle-aged man who wore rings on his chubby fingers, which were as soft as the nipples of a hill-country cow. He shook hands with me in a careless manner and began to examine my work. The freshly polished card table shined brightly and emitted the pleasant aroma of the varnish. The Viennese chairs and the hand-carved armchair, which I had washed with liquid ammonia and polished with emery cloth, looked almost brand-new.

"Well, it turns out that you're a true master of your trade! And to think I was on the verge of throwing out this old junk," the liberal said condescendingly.

"I am a master, but not of this trade. I'm a pattern-maker by specialization, but I'm working as a joiner now because there's no work available in my own trade."

"Well I guess you have to try everything in life, especially under our lousy government. Things are tough for everyone these days," the liberal declared with a sigh of sympathy.

Under his legs a floppy-eared reddish dog fidgeted around, sniffed at things, and thrust about with his muzzle. "He must be a hunter," I thought.

"Please forgive me. I'm leaving my dog here with you," said the liberal, turning toward me unexpectedly. "This is her room. I took her hunting with me; she's tired and needs to rest."

I didn't object. He politely took his leave and went out. The dog turned out to be an agitated creature. My jars and bottles of varnish, lacquer, and pumice all came flying off the table. A brown puddle of spilled varnish took shape on the floor. At first I tried to appeal to the dog by peaceful means, but this proved useless. She just kept on bustling about the room and interrupting my work, while responding to my admonitions by snarling. Then I picked up a narrow piece of sawed-off board and struck the agitated dog lightly on the back. The dog let out a squeal, bolted toward the exit, and raced through the wide-open doorway. Barking and squealing, she tore like a bomb through the corridors and passages, knocking over everything that happened to cross her path. Their faces filled with terror, the cook and the maid came running up and, combining their efforts, tried to catch the dog. Hearing the uproar, the lady of the house dashed in and began to revile the maid and the cook: how dare they let the dog go free! Realizing that the outcome of my struggle with the dog boded ill, I quietly changed clothes and vanished inconspicuously.

On the following day I returned to work on the assumption that yesterday's canine passions had abated. However Glafira, the maid, came to the kitchen with my tools and five rubles and said:

"My lord and lady say you're not to come in!"

I was surprised and indignant: according to my own calculations they owed me twice that sum for my work.

28
"Auntie Marseillaise"

Let's go, Semën, there's a certain place I'd like to take you to meet some people. That way you'll at least have some connections when I'm sent away from this town," Konstantin proposed one evening.

This "certain place" was located on Krapivnaya Street, on the second floor of a rather small stone house. We took off our coats in the hallway and entered a spacious room. To the right of the entrance stood a large, ancient piano; to the left, a leather sofa; and, along the entire length of the front wall, a table covered by a white oilcloth. On the table a copper samovar of imposing dimensions was bubbling away. Also on the table were big platters filled with large loaves of coarse bread, fat little rings of wheat bread, and butter. Seated at the table pouring tea was a stout, short-haired woman in a wide cotton-print blouse. Groups of three or four people were scattered in each of the corners of the enormous room, almost lost from sight. We approached the table and began by presenting ourselves to the stout woman. Konstantin told her my last name.

"It would be better if you told me your first name and patronymic; I already know your last name, since Kostya has told me about you," she said loudly and crossly, staring right at me with her huge black eyes.

At first I thought something was upsetting her and that she was cross with everyone who spoke with her. But later I realized that this was her usual manner when she engaged in conversation. She gave the impression she was scolding everyone.

I told her my first name and patronymic.

"Well, that's just fine. And that's what I shall call you. You are welcome here any time you like. Take a seat, relax, and make yourself at home. The people who come to me are simple, unpretentious; if you say something improper, they won't be offended," she said in the same scolding voice, but by this time I could already feel its warmth and tenderness.

She poured a glass of tea, offered some bread, butter, and sugar, and then continued either to darn children's socks or to read.

She was the very same "Auntie Marseillaise" of whom I'd already heard so much from Langeld and whose name I often heard from our "guests."

Elizaveta Adrianovna Diakova—Auntie's real name—was one of the oldest Social Democrats of the region. Either in 1894 or in 1896 she and some other Social Democrats had formed a Social Democratic group that began to conduct propaganda among the intelligentsia and students. In order to print their proclamations and leaflets they set up an illegal printing press on the Diakov family estate, in Tambov province,[1] but it subsequently went under. Diakova was imprisoned twice for her revolutionary activity, and on several occasions she was subjected to searches. At the time I met her she was an active participant in Social Democratic circles and was involved in the dissemination of illegal literature. But above all she was famous as the hospitable hostess of the "SD salon." Calling Auntie's democratic apartment a "salon" was hardly appropriate, since the word has too much of a pretentious, aristocratic quality. A more precise and simpler designation for it would be "staff headquarters." But since the word "salon" has stuck to it historically, we'll call it that too, albeit in quotation marks.[2]

In Auntie's apartment, every day, from early evening until long past midnight, there was a veritable Babylonian clamor. Some people were arriving, others were leaving, some were making business appointments, others had rushed over after the theater or after the sessions of their revolutionary circles just to rest a bit, drink some tea, argue, chat about the burning political issues of the day, sing revolutionary songs, or listen to piano music—Auntie herself could play very well, when she was in good form.

It appeared to some that access to Auntie's "salon" was extremely easy. People claimed that anyone could wander in from the street. But this was only an illusion; the reality was very different. Let's just begin with the fact that even in those days the town was pretty small. The native, core population rarely changed, and the intelligentsia could be counted on one's fingers.

Those people involved in revolutionary activity, those people who were free-thinking to any extent, knew one another by reputation, if not by sight. How then, could an outsider or a suspicious person wind up in Auntie's apartment? He would have to be brought there by someone already well-known. Moreover, Auntie kept a pretty sharp eye on any new people. It happened often enough that she would summon one of the comrades and insistently advise him not to bring along some little-known person who had aroused her suspicion. Among those who frequented Auntie's apartment were many contemporaries of her grown-up daughters—including senior students, male and female, from classical high schools, seminary students, and students from technical schools; they would gather in separate rooms to read and study the writings of Dobroliubov, Pisarev, Belinsky.[3] But these were people of the younger generation, and they had no relations with us.[4]

These, then, are the reasons that, among the frequenters of Auntie's salon, there were never any informers or provocateurs, as has now become clear from the archives of the gendarme office.[5]

The most that any spies might have hoped for was to eavesdrop on the conversations and careless chatter of particular visitors at the "salon" and to listen by the windows to the spirited and loud singing of revolutionary songs and the mighty sounds of "the Marseillaise," which Auntie played on the piano with great vitality. That was how she acquired the nickname "Auntie Marseillaise."

Auntie's apartment was not simply a place for innocent radical chitchat and pedestrian tea-drinking. On the contrary, it was more like a political club, and of a clearly defined social democratic coloration. It was frequented by all the prominent *Iskra*-ites of that period: M. N. Liadov, the late N. N. Mandelshtam (whenever he came to Saratov), S. M. Baramzin, Fofanov, the late Gorin-Galkin, A. I. Rykov, A. A. Bogdanov, Bogdanova, P. A. Lebedev, and many of us workers.[6]

The Socialist Revolutionaries had their own "salon," at the apartment of Elena Ivanovna Averkievaya. It was apparently maintained by her brother-in-law, the rich and prominent SR Zot Sazonov, brother of the famous Egor Sazonov, who later threw the bomb that killed Minister von Plehve.[7]

Averkievaya's "salon" was frequented mainly by the SR "generals"—L. P. Bulanov, P. P. Kraft, N. I. Rakitnikov, Kocherovsky, and others. Her "salon" was also visited by Breshko-Breshkovskaya, the "little grandmother," during one of her agitational trips to Saratov.[8]

Among the rank and file, at that time, there were still no clear political boundaries dividing us from the Socialist Revolutionaries, but basically, and especially among the higher leadership, the watershed was absolute, the boundaries clear and definitive. That is why the higher SR leadership never made an appearance at our "salon," just as we never appeared at theirs. Among the intelligentsia youth, however, there were several who, having not yet defined their positions, went to both "salons." This probably explains why it was that I used to encounter the late Stepan Balmashev at Auntie's "salon."[9]

My first visit to Auntie's apartment was a delightful, heartening experience for me. It was the first time I had met so many people who were not only conscious, but also clearly defined themselves as revolutionary Marxists in orientation. They were vying with each other to question me about the Petersburg workers, about my imprisonment, about my village, about the mood of the peasantry, and things of that sort.

I now heard arguments among living and breathing people about the vital issues of the revolutionary movement, about agitation and propaganda, about the role and value to the working class of organization, about the importance of demonstrations. I would sit and listen openmouthed, for many of the subtleties were barely comprehensible to me. It seemed to me that some of the questions that closely affected the workers were being approached incorrectly. But I was not prepared to join in debate with members of the intelligentsia, whose command of the gift of speech was greater than mine.

It was at Auntie's that I made the acquaintance of Vasily Abramovich Fominykh (now deceased), who played a prominent role in the Saratov organization.[10] He was a very gifted person, very dedicated to the revolution. He had completed his university studies in the natural sciences, and then enrolled in the Technological Institute.[11] Half a year before he was to graduate, he was arrested for conducting propaganda among workers. After serving some time in prison, he was banished to Saratov, where he earned his livelihood giving lessons. However, he spent the lion's share of these meager earnings on various experiments aimed at discovering the most convenient and accessible method for printing proclamations and leaflets. Tall, slender, with a light-colored, wedge-shaped beard, he coughed a lot and often complained about his chest. Yet he never abandoned his cheerful, always self-mocking mood. He was one of the most frequent visitors at Auntie's "salon," and later even married one of her numerous daughters.

On the very first evening I visited there, Auntie, evidently wishing to put an end to some excessively heated and prolonged arguments, sat down at the piano and played a barcarole, followed by a song called "Mountain Tops." The arguments were soon snuffed out. Everyone began to listen to the music.

At the time I neither understood nor enjoyed serious music— the gay sounds of an accordion were much closer to my heart— but for politeness' sake I found a place on the sofa and sat quietly. I do not know what she was playing or for how long; nor do I know what I was thinking about; but I dissolved so deeply into my dreams, I drifted so far into endless space, that I didn't even notice when Auntie finished playing and the guests began to disperse. . . . A nudge in my side brought me back to reality.

"You've grown soft, my friend, let's go home. . . . A proletarian is not supposed to dream; that's the business of the intelligentsia," Konstantin said to me.

This joke struck me as out of place, and offensive to those around us. "Konstantin is a good fellow," I said to myself, "and a splendid comrade, but I just can't get used to the prickly, suspicious way he speaks about the intelligentsia."

As a farewell act, Auntie played "the Marseillaise," and everyone joined in the singing.

On our way home, we exchanged impressions of the evening and spoke about Auntie:

"Elizaveta Adrianovna comes from a family of impoverished landowning gentry," Konstantin explained. "She was educated at the Institute for Noble Girls.[12] She was a real beauty, and she caught the eye of a brilliant aristocrat, to whom she was given in marriage at the age of sixteen. Her husband turned out to be a spendthrift, very dissipated; he loved horses, beautiful women, cards, and, most passionately of all, horse races. In the end, he lost his entire fortune, damaged his health, and resettled on his one remaining property, a small country estate called 'Krasivka,'[13] in Tambov province, where, fortunately, he passed away. After his death, Elizaveta Adrianovna was left with five or six children to care for. Worse than that, it was soon discovered that her deceased husband had been maintaining a second family right on the premises. He had been living simultaneously with the housekeeper and had had four children by her.

"Elizaveta Adrianovna took all four children from the house-keeper—with her permission, of course—and henceforth raised them together with her own. She assigned a plot of land to the housekeeper and built her a home right there on the Krasivka estate. This is how it came about that Auntie has such a large gaggle of children!

"While her husband was still alive, Elizaveta Adrianovna began to meet various revolutionaries. At first she became a follower of the "People's Will," but she later became a Marxist. I won't go into how and when this came about. She was imprisoned twice. One of the times, she served nine months under extremely harsh conditions: for six entire months the gendarmes would not even allow her to be visited by her children. . . .

"About six years ago she was remarried, this time to a Social Democrat, by whom she has two marvelous little boys. They were asleep during our visit, but you'll get to see them another time. Her husband, Nikolay Ivanovich Solovev, works in Samara as a statistician and rarely comes to Saratov.[14] In Samara he's involved in revolutionary work. He's been in prison a number of times. . . .

"Well, that's the story. What more can I tell you about her? . . . Oh yes, about the country estate: it has remained extremely small. Elizaveta Adrianovna gave it all away to her children, and, inasmuch as she has maintained good relations with them, she goes there to spend her summers. The estate is run by her oldest son, Adrian, a big dreamer and visionary, but basically a good fellow. He graduated from the School of Agronomy and then began organizing some kind of socialistic experiments on his land. He managed to organize a cooperative among his reliable peasants, whom he'd indoctrinated, and he transferred his land to them on a contractual basis. But either he neglected to read the fine print in the contract or he placed too much trust in the leaders. For it seems that even right on his own property he isn't permitted to organize a cooperative. So he has to do it in a way that evades the law. But then, one fine day, it turns out that the very same peasants in whose name the contract had been drawn up come up to him and declare: you go to the devil, this land is ours, we bought it from you! . . . So instead of a cooperative, he ends up with some kulak-parasites. Now he's on the bit of land that remains to him, trying to figure things out. . . . He's the kind who can't keep still!"[15]

Later, I would make the acquaintance of Adrian Aleksandrovich Diakov. He turned out to be a genuine man of the steppe, very bushy-looking, dark-haired, tall, and muscular. On the surface he seemed soft-spoken; he talked slowly, almost as if he were stammering. And yet there was an irrespressible energy seething within him: he was always worked up over some new projects, which he'd attempt to implement right away.

After the 1905 Revolution, I thought I'd lost sight of this interesting family forever. When February 1917 came along, we completely gave ourselves over to our revolutionary work, in preparation for the seizure of power.[16] Then came the October Revolution, which placed an even greater burden of concern and responsibility on us. The Civil War began.[17] I started to spin around in the whirlwind of events, and it seemed as if these grandiose class conflicts and upheavals would bury forever my memories of the earlier little sources of this titanic struggle, while effacing from my memory all recollection of the people who had begun that struggle.

Then, in 1919, I was put in charge of the VTsIK's courses for agitation, from which Sverdlovsk University would later be formed.[18] Despite their brevity (only two or three months each), not one of these courses was ever completed by anyone. Too many fresh reinforcements of Communist agitators were needed at the Civil War front.

Apart from my purely administrative work as director of the courses, I also gave lectures on the history of the Party.

One day, having finished my lecture, I was returning home, walking through the endless dark corridors of the Merchants' Club,[19] where Sverdlovsk University was first housed, when I was accosted by a tall, ungainly man in a military overcoat.

"Don't you recognize me, Semën Ivanovich?"

I stopped and began to peer at him.

"N-no . . . ," I drawled, after some hesitation.

"It's me, Adrian Diakov. . . . Don't you remember 'Auntie Marseillaise'?"

"Why, is it really you?! Who could have recognized you!" I exclaimed with joy, and I dragged Adrian to my quarters to drink some carrot tea with raisins.

"Where's Auntie? What's with her? Is she alive? . . . How's Nikolay Ivanovich? And the boys?" I bombarded him with questions.

Adrian did not answer right away. I attributed this to his slow manner of speaking. He looked at me, sighed, and said very quietly: "Mama. . . ." Here he stumbled, no doubt remembering that it wasn't proper for a grown man like him to call her "Mama." He corrected himself: "I mean Elizaveta Adrianovna—we buried her about three months ago, here in Moscow. She died a Bolshevik; she remained true to her convictions to the very end," he added with pride. "Nikolay Ivanovich Solovev is also in Moscow—he's in charge of coal distribution. Iurka—the oldest son[20]—is a Red commander, serving at the front. As for me, I still live in the same place, out in Krasivka. I helped the peasants confiscate the land from the landlords, and I've been fighting against the SRs since the February Revolution. Our province, Tambov, is an old nest of the SRs. You remember that, don't you?"[21]

"How could I forget it! Viktor Chernov himself, I think, was born in Tambov," I confirmed.[22]

"And now our Party cell has sent me to take your course for agitators. I'll study here a little, and then I'll get to work."

As usually happened, he was mobilized even before the course was over. I never saw Adrian again.

Later, in 1921, when a kulak uprising under the command of the notorious bandit Antonov was under way in Tambov province, rumors reached me to the effect that Adrian—who as chairman of the local Party executive committee headed the forces that defended Soviet power, i.e., the poor peasants—was conducting a successful struggle against Antonov's bands, and that Antonov himself had promised a big reward to anyone who would bring him the head of Adrian Diakov.[23]

It was a difficult struggle. Adrian managed to hide from the bandits who were pursuing him. He spent his nights in the chill, damp cold of the forest, and concealed himself in the swamps in his light, tattered clothes. He contracted pneumonia and died. Where he died, I never learned.

29
At the Volga Steel Mill

A MONG the "guests" who occasionally frequented our apartment was Mikhail Ivanov, a metal-fitter from Kolpino.[1] He too had been exiled to Saratov administratively for political unreliability. He was a short and stocky man, with a pimply face and straight dark hair combed back on his head. He worked in the railroad repair shops and had good connections among the local workers. During one of his visits he informed me with great joy that the Volga steel mill was looking for a pattern-maker.[2]

"The only problem is that the foreman won't hire a stranger, an outsider," he warned me.

"Oh well, I guess we'll have to look for some good connections," I said with disappointment.

"Just don't get upset, I've got the connections. Hurry up and get dressed and we'll go off to the 'Ochkin' area. A comrade of ours lives there. His name is Fisher—he's also from Petersburg, under surveillance here.[3] Now he's working at the Gantke factory as a turner, but before that he worked at the steel mill, and he still has connections there. Only hurry; first we'll go to Fisher, and then he'll introduce you to his friend, who will recommend you to the foreman of the pattern shop."

All this business seemed rather complicated to me, and not very promising. But I was sick and tired of idling about without any work, and there were no other options. So I made no objections, hurriedly put on my clothes, and off we went.

We were greeted by a broad-shouldered, dark-haired man of medium height, with a big forehead that protruded over his intelligent, calm, sparkling black eyes. It was Fisher. After we exchanged greetings, he asked me what I'd been imprisoned for and whether I was exiled to Saratov for a long period. It turned out that we had common acquaintances in Piter. Then we turned to the matter that concerned me.

"Does it really make any sense?" I asked, expressing my doubts.

"It should work out, provided he doesn't lose heart. I've managed to pull it off myself," he said with confidence. "But you've already been in town nearly a month without coming here," he added, looking at me reproachfully from under his forehead. "Could those light-minded triflers have mixed you up that much?"

I didn't understand the last sentence and wasn't even sure whether it was addressed to Ivanov or to me. I looked at Fisher with puzzlement.

Ivanov resolved my perplexity: "That's his way of casting aspersions on the intelligentsia. He just can't stand them."

"And why should I like them?!"

Fisher offered me some tea. I turned it down.

"Well, it's true. You have to strike while the iron is hot. Or else he'll keep refusing!"

He put on his coat and we went out. He guided me along the sleepy, snow-covered streets, back alleys, and wastelands, none of which had ever been illuminated. This is where the workers lived, and there clearly was no one concerned with the quality of their living conditions. It was all right to exploit them, to squeeze the most exorbitant rents from them; but to see to their comfort and well-being—that was an unnecessary, dangerous luxury. The houses here were wooden and uncomfortable. They all belonged to the same proprietor, Ochkin, and the neighborhood was known by the same name. Every three years, if not more often, the entire neighborhood would burn to the ground, and with it all the workers' goods and chattels. The owner would collect the insurance and build new houses, and the workers would then pay higher rents.

The name of the pattern-maker to whom Fisher brought me was Ivan Nikolaevich Gordeev. He greeted us rather cordially. His wife put on the samovar, hurriedly heated up some fritters, and began to regale us. Nor did we decline. We attacked the fritters ravenously. Soon a general conversation began to unfold about conditions at the mill, prices, the administration, and things like that. We spent quite a long time at Gordeev's. The following plan was devised: he would speak to the foreman of the pattern shop

about me tomorrow, and on the following day I would go directly
to the factory gate and meet Gordeev there, and he would take
me to the foreman.

It all turned out very well. The foreman asked me where I had
worked, but made no other inquiries. As to the fact that I was
there as an exile, under political surveillance, either he wasn't interested—they needed a pattern-maker so badly—or he already
knew everything from Gordeev.

Three days after the meeting just described I was working at
the steel mill. The test they gave me was a very simple one—to
cut the pattern either for a bearing or for a pipe-bend with
flanges. I finished it quickly and neatly, for I had a powerful
yearning to return to work.

The pattern shop was large and spacious; it was obviously designed for a large number of workers, though there were only ten
or so pattern-makers in all. I immediately began to look for safe
ground for making new connections, but this did not pan out.
This particular contingent of workers was most inappropriate,
sluggish, conservative; they were middle-aged men, burdened
with families, and had numerous ties to the little townspeople.
You can't cut through them, as the saying goes, with the dull side
of the knife—these men had taken root in the soil of the factory,
had grown accustomed to the sights and smells of all the outrages
perpetrated by the factory administration.

But it's a very sorry agitator who retreats before the first obstacles. So I began to act.

The first duty of anyone who sets about to do propaganda work
is to study and understand the object you're preparing to influence. I acquired this fundamental rule from practical experience.
There is no such thing as a worker who is satisfied with absolutely everything. What is needed is to locate his weak spot. Then
beat on it, keep pecking away at that one point—and he will give
in. The ways of approaching a worker may be very varied. Some
workers like to sound off on religious themes, others like to complain about the disarray of their lives, others like to listen to tales
about all kinds of strange happenings in foreign lands, still others
like to talk about their household and domestic problems, and
so on.

You begin by going up to them. At first you are very indulgent
with them, you echo their sentiments, you sometimes even con-
sent to things you couldn't possibly really agree with; but there's

no harm in that. Ideological and principled purity doesn't emerge right away. Later, when you have propagandized the worker and won his trust, all this can be rectified. Above all, especially at the outset, do not reveal yourself, do not disclose yourself to the person you are cultivating before the time has come—be like everyone else. Sometimes you'll even have to play the ignorant simpleton. But at the same time you must occasionally give him the feeling that you know something important. That way you'll arouse his interest, you'll "intrigue" him, though in the best sense of the word, of course. Then, he will constantly be drawn to you when he's looking for explanations and information.

Let us suppose that even your single-handed propaganda activity fails to achieve the desired results—that is, you fail to turn the worker into a Social Democrat and an active revolutionary. You are still likely to make him into a sympathizer, or, at the very least, into a "doubter" about the validity of certain ancient truths. And doubt is the mother of all negation.

You usually begin your propaganda activity in a factory with the workers who are working next to you or not far away. It is impossible to walk around the factory, or even the workshop, with impunity for any length of time without attracting suspicion. For this reason, your neighbors are, so to speak, your natural terrain for propaganda. Of course, the original boundaries of this terrain are not immovable. Widening them depends on the persistence, the skill, and the personal initiative of the agitator.

At the steel mill my workbench neighbors were, in front of me, a middle-aged, taciturn, diligent pattern-maker named Kvasnikov, and, behind me, a young, fit-looking fellow named Kubichek, who spoke with an accent. I did my work rather well; I was good at reading designs, and, having passed through a vast—though not a long—education at several different factories, I was able to adjust quickly to whatever new work came my way. The foreman assigned me a wage of something like one and a half rubles a day. For Saratov in those days this was considered high pay. Taken together, all these circumstances immediately endowed me with professional authority in the eyes of the other pattern-makers. And this, in turn, had great significance for our cause. Professional authority was usually indirectly transferred to other areas. A highly qualified worker, one who really knew his business, was always listened to very willingly, was trusted more than others. That is why we always tried so persistently to agitate a worker who really knew his craft. This was hard work, but the results were great. Moreover, the highly skilled worker, even if he was particularly untrustworthy in the eyes of the gendarmes, was likely to maintain a longer connection with his factory. Because of our country's general ignorance and backwardness, factory administrators were always in need of highly qualified workers; hence it was always easier for such workers to find work.

I began with my neighbor, Kvasnikov. I had some meaningless exchanges with him, then I advanced to more serious themes. I began to give him books to read—legal ones at first. But then, when I was convinced that he was a person of basic honesty— that is to say, that he wouldn't inform on you just because he disagreed with something—I began to provide him with illegal books and proclamations. However, I soon became convinced that nothing much would come of all this. He was a quiet, subdued, rather primitive man, not even very successful in his own craft, despite his prolonged experience. In his heart he was sympathetic to us, but he was afraid to act; all he could do was join with the majority. He actually put it to me this way: "Now if everyone rose up and turned against the tsar and the bosses, then I would do it too."

So I left him to his own devices and turned my attention to my other neighbor. Rudolf Kubichek—or simply Rudolf, as we all called him—was a Czech by nationality, and like all Czechs in those days, being oppressed by Austria, he was an ardent nationalist.[4] He had no understanding of the Russian revolutionary movement, which he looked upon with complete indifference. His only real enemies were Germans, whom he absolutely despised, loathed.

Rudolf was honest and straightforward, and, in the manner of a knight of old, he perceived any social injustice or insult as a personal offense: he would get excited, wax indignant, and was always prepared to "avenge." We soon became friends and decided to take a room together. At first we argued a great deal and at great length. I was incapable of comprehending his nationalism, and he couldn't understand the class struggle. I remember how one day I gave him a legal book to read—Ezh's novel *At Dawn*, where the author describes the Bulgarian independence struggle against Turkey.[5] When he finished this book Rudolf was in an indescribable state of delight. From then on he began to call the gendarmes "zapties," from the Bulgarian word used by the author of the novel to refer to the Turkish gendarmes. I didn't bring Rudolf into the small propaganda circle that had been formed at the steel works. Nevertheless, he soon became a highly energetic and resourceful disseminator of proclamations and various other kinds of illegal literature.

Soon after I began working at the factory, the Saratov radical intelligentsia decided to organize a demonstration at a theater, in protest against the presentation there of an anti-Semitic play called "The Smugglers."[6] The workers offered to lend support to the demonstration. The demonstration was to take the following form: during the play someone was to throw hydrosulfuric acid on the stage; this would give off a stench, and we would begin to whistle; then we would all get up and leave the theater, singing "the Marseillaise." I gave the theater tickets to Rudolf and entrusted him with the organization of the event. But the organization of this kind of demonstration was still something new, and the organizers were not very skillful.

Here's how it turned out: the chemical intervention began too early, the whistling was very feeble, and the police burst into the loges and removed the hecklers almost effortlessly. Rudolf had brought along a whole gang of his comrades, ready for anything, and my people were there too, but it was already too late. So the show went on, though we didn't see anything really anti-Semitic in the play. Apparently the most odious parts had been prudently eliminated or altered. The smell of the hydrosulfuric acid continued to waft lightly from the stage.

To begin the demonstration all over again, when our reserves arrived, no longer made any sense. So we dispersed to our homes feeling dissatisfied, cursing the intelligentsia.

Work at the steel mill was very trying. Although the workday was not very long for those times (ten to ten and a half hours a day), in practice it often turned into twelve or thirteen hours. We lived some four or five miles from the factory, and since the trains were often not on schedule, we had to get up at five in the morning and rush like mad to the train that took us to the mill.

I endured this torment until the month of May. With Rudolf's assistance, I spread large quantities of May Day proclamations throughout the factory for that occasion; shortly thereafter, without any explanation, I was fired by the director himself, with two weeks' severance pay.

30
The Workers' Group

THE GROUP was formed without any preconceived plan or intent. Banished under police surveillance to a strange, unfamiliar city, a conscious worker, even if his ideas were still quite amorphous, would always begin by seeking close contact with people who were similar to him in class, in living standards, and in cultural habits and style of life. In that milieu he would look for moral and material support, and that is where he could confide his doubts and confusion, for these were the people who really understood him, and responded most quickly and attentively to his needs and requests. It was also the milieu where it was easiest for him to find the more steadfast and trustworthy comrades in arms for the revolutionary struggle.

The headquarters of our workers' group was the apartment of Semën Voronin, a weaver from Ivanovo-Voznesensk, a Bolshevik, and later a member of the Third State Duma.[1] It consisted of two rooms and a kitchen, located in a small wooden house on Astrakhan Street, if I remember correctly. The mistress of the household was Voronin's wife Katya. She too was an Ivanovo-Voznesensk weaver who'd been banished under police surveillance. Her brother, Makruev, also under surveillance, lived with them.

The rather fluctuating membership of the workers' group consisted of M. A. Fisher, P. I. Denisov, A. E. Efimov, S. P. Shepelev, A. Morozov, S. I. Kanatchikov, M. Ivanov, A. N. Grigoreva, A. Retling, the mistress of the household, plus two members of the intelligentsia—V. A. Fominykh and S. M. Fofanov—who were honored with our trust; later there was also E. N. Popova.[2] I don't even place the name—workers' group—in quotation marks, because, though that is what we called it among ourselves, the title was never formally registered anywhere.[3] With a few minor exceptions, we were all people of the same age, and we all had long periods of revolutionary service behind us.

Fierce struggles and passionate arguments, the repeated defining and division of boundaries, took place within the workers' group. There were arguments over questions such as the relation between the political and economic struggles, between the worker and the peasant, between the intelligentsia and the worker, and our attitude toward terrorism.[4] Because of these disagreements, Mikhail Ivanov (from Kolpino) stopped coming to our meetings and openly switched to the Socialist Revolutionaries, whereas A. N. Grigoreva declared that, although in favor of terrorism, she was a worker, and wished to stick with us workers, with whom she agreed on all other questions.[5] All the others were convinced Social Democrats. We kept Grigoreva in the workers' group because she served as a link between us and the intelligentsia and she had access to money to help meet our needs. I also believe that the SRs had deliberately planted her in our midst in order to cultivate an SR tendency among us and to use our group as a link with the factory workers.

Within our group there was a rather strong anti-intelligentsia orientation. On this question I held a conciliatory position, and I had to listen to repeated recriminations for my frequent visits to Auntie's "salon." Later, however, many of our workers began to go there themselves.

As to the question of the relation between the political and economic struggles, we all stood for a conciliatory position. We formulated our views approximately like this: as a practical matter, a worker who is not yet conscious needs to be initially approached around those questions that touch him most closely, that is, economic questions; but, at the same time, one must explain political issues to him as well. In practice, however, several of us would sometimes lean in the direction of the "Workers' Cause" position.[6] We were pushed toward that position by the negative attitude of many prominent Social Democrats toward economic questions, and their inclination toward "pure politics."[7]

"First let's overthrow the autocracy," they would say, "let's win our political freedom, and then we can see to your petty, material interests."[8]

This negative and contemptuous attitude toward the workers' economic struggle offended us. We would then shift the disagreement to the arena of the relations between the workers and the intelligentsia, and we would attack the intelligentsia with harsh words. One worker distinguished by his particularly irreconcilable position was the passionate, sharp-tongued A. Efimov, known as "The Artist."

"For you the revolution is an amusement, a sport, which you take up in your youth," he would say, "but for us, the workers, the revolution is our element, like a fish must have water or a bird air. You look down on our struggle for our 'petty' material interests because you yourselves can live off your papas and mamas. The workers are forced to work not only to earn their own livelihoods, but also to produce the surplus value that makes your lives so plentiful.[9] You make a lot of noise, yell, mouth radical phrases when you're young, but then you finish your educations, obtain nice little positions, get married, and become the same kind of exploiters and hard-driving masters as your papas."

At the time we still didn't know what "fellow traveler of the revolution" meant. But that is precisely what The Artist was talking about.[10]

Later, when the Socialist Revolutionaries and the Social Democrats of Saratov merged into a unified group, this circumstance reconfirmed the correctness of our evaluation of the advocates of "pure politics," whose negative attitude toward the workers' economic struggle had brought about the union with the SRs. This also explains why it was that all the workers' strikes of that period were led exclusively by our workers' group.[11]

The newspaper *Iskra*, which had begun to be published abroad, reached us rather late.[12] Our workers' group greeted its first issues rather coolly. We saw—once again—an excessive tendency to favor a purely political struggle. However, it wasn't long before *Iskra* won our sympathy and confidence. Articles began to appear in it about our workers' group and the paper we were publishing, *The Workers' Newspaper*.[13] The tone of these columns was serious, calm, and very convincing. The columns seemed to converse with us, as if we were comrades of equal standing; they neither patronized nor slighted us, but persuaded, explained, and demonstrated. They demanded that we take re-

sponsibility for our actions and opinions. We began to correspond with *Iskra*, first via M. P. Golubeva, and then via M. N.
Liadov.

Before long *Iskra* had won an indisputable authority in our
eyes. In its pages we were able to find answers to the problems
that beset our practical activity; in its pages we found support and
argumentation for our struggle with our current and potential
enemies.

Again and again there were attempts by various different
groups that were hostile to *Iskra* to attract us to their side, but
they were unsuccessful. I can now recall one such incident:

One evening, apparently wishing to take advantage of our anti-
intelligentsia state of mind, N. A. Arkhangelskaya invited Fisher
and me to talk about "our affairs." I cannot recall if the meeting
took place at Beliakov's apartment or merely at an apartment he
had located for the occasion. Present at this "colloquy," in addition to us, were Beliakov, Fominykh, and, I believe, V. M. Obukhov and his wife. When we had taken our places at the table, a
young man emerged from a side room; he had reddish whiskers
and, so it seemed to me, was irreproachably attired. Beliakov introduced him to us as a representative of the "Workers' Cause"
group, who wished to "talk a bit" about the disagreements between the "*Iskra*-ites" and the "Workers' Cause" supporters. The
young man delivered a detailed report, I recall, in which he made
a long, drawn-out attack on *Iskra*'s "crudeness" in its treatment of
subordinates, the unscrupulousness and harshness of its polemics, its takeovers of local committees, and the unfair, one-sided
manner in which it explained all the disagreements to the
workers.[14]

The bearing of the representative of the "Workers' Cause" was
haughty; his responses to questions were slipshod and arrogant,
as if he was doing us a favor. His extremely polished figure, his
gentlemanly appearance, the way he spoke in a drawl, through
his nose—all these things disturbed us. However, when someone
whispered to him that we were workers, he immediately changed
his tone, drew back, and became mawkishly polite. We were now
drinking tea, and while we were drinking the representative
would talk more and more. At the conclusion of our "discussion"
he asked us to sign a piece of paper containing a protest from the
workers of Saratov. We categorically refused. But when he began

to press us and appealed to our "honor" as representatives of the working class, we said: "We'll talk it over in our workers' group." So he left empty-handed.

It was especially pleasant and flattering to us to read the report from Saratov that appeared in the sixth issue of *Iskra*, which said, in part:

> About two weeks ago, copies of *The Workers' Newspaper* reached us. Two issues had appeared (by now numbers three and four have also appeared). Everything, down to the very last line, is written by workers, and in general the intelligentsia has not yet taken any part in its publication.
>
> It is interesting that, beginning with its very first issue, the paper has been speaking about *socialism and the political struggle*.[15]

So flattering an assessment of our *Workers' Newspaper* by *Iskra* cheered us up tremendously and reinforced our belief in the correctness of our position.

Before I began working at the Bering factory, I had already made some connections with some of the workers from that plant. A circle was formed among them, and I began to conduct systematic classes there. Whatever I already knew, I would relate orally; I would read still other things from a book and then explain them in my own words. I read them Dikshtein's *Who Lives from What?* and Schramm's *Political Economy*.[16] Occasionally I invited V. A. Fominykh to the circle to guide it through the more complicated readings. The circle included the following members: Polikarp Ivanovich Lalov, a pattern-maker from the Bering factory; Nester Grigorevich Kalashnikov (now deceased), a turner from the same factory; Dmitry Bochkov, a joiner who later became an SR and, after the Revolution, became a Communist again (now deceased); and a couple of men from the steel mill.

Fisher had connections at the Gantke factory, where he was now working as a turner, as well as in the railroad shops; Semën Petrovich Shepelev had connections at the Chirikhinaya factory, where he also worked. We had connections at other factories as well. Ponty Denisov was close to workers at a flour mill, where he had briefly worked as a repairman. Thus at the main enterprises of the region, our workers' group was virtually the only group at that time with real connections.

At first the workers' group was mainly engaged in printing proclamations on a hectograph[17] and distributing them. But this proved to be inadequate. Life itself and the process of struggle required the expansion of our methods of influencing the masses. In the circles, as well as in the "salons," arguments raged about whether or not it was time to shift from circle work to broader agitation,[18] but for all practical purposes our workers' group had already resolved this problem.

How *The Workers' Newspaper* first arose and at whose initiative is a question hardly worthy of attention. The paper was published by the workers' group, which also served as its collective editor, and the members of the same group were its correspondents and collaborators. The first issue of *The Workers' Newspaper* appeared in April 1901, when I was employed at the steel mill. That issue contained my first "literary" work. I would now like to cite a short passage from it, particularly since it conveys a certain sense of the hard life experienced by workers in those times:

The Volga steel mill.

The past year, 1900, brought great mishap and misfortune to the workers of the Volga steel mill.[19] As a consequence of the fall in production, the administration fired several hundred men.

Thrown out on the street in the most inhumane manner, these workers were forced to go hungry, and to experience every possible kind of deprivation. Nor did those who retained their jobs have it any better. The systematic reduction of wages was a common occurrence in all the workshops.

. . . The length of the workday was increased by one-half hour thanks to the arrival of a new factory director, who, hoping to cling to his position, decided that breakfasts were a superfluous luxury for the worker, and therefore ordered that they be terminated.

. . . Moreover, the Volga steel mill, as we all know, is located some four miles from the city, and it is extremely difficult to find living quarters near the plant. Hence most of the workers live in town. Previously, the workers were at least transported to and from work on a special train, at the factory's expense. Today there is no question of doing this; today the worker pays for all this himself. In order to go to the factory by train, the worker must arise before five in the morning, for the train departs very unpunctually: there are times when it leaves as early as five, there are times when it leaves as late as six, so that you sometimes have to shiver in the freezing weather for a whole hour while waiting for the train. Comrades! The time has come for our patience to run out. When will we finally start thinking about our lot and searching for ways to fight for our rights—not to starve and not to suffer?

The entire issue of *The Workers' Newspaper* was composed in a spirit of broad popular appeal adapted to the stratum of workers that still had very little consciousness, which was the dominant group even in Saratov's metal industry.

There were extended arguments within our group over what to name the future newspaper. We were determined at all costs to underline our self-sufficiency and independence as workers, even in our choice of a name. Someone proposed that the paper be called *The Saratov Worker*, but we knew that another group was already using that title, and we didn't want to be confused with that group. Moreover, affixing the word "Saratov" to the paper's title would have made it sound too local, whereas we dreamed of extending its reach beyond the limits of Saratov, since we were all linked to Saratov only by virtue of the gendarmes' coercion.

So we decided simply to call it *The Workers' Newspaper.*

The Workers' Newspaper began to appear before we started to receive *Iskra*. With the first few issues of *The Workers' Newspaper* we encountered lots of problems getting the paper printed: how and where to have it printed? —we hadn't even thought of this question when we began our venture.

31
Chizhik

ONE DAY I went to the home of an acquaintance who had promised to get me a copy of Chernyshevsky's novel *What Is to Be Done?*[1] He didn't have the book, but we began to talk about political questions. This fellow had either graduated or been expelled from technical school; he survived by tutoring people for a few kopecks, he was an SR sympathizer, and he of course looked with favor on heroic acts of terror. He refused to be satisfied with anything less than the murder of the tsar. He even reproached the SRs for the tsar's continued survival.

His outward appearance was menacing. He had long, dark hair, kept his hat pulled over his eyes in a sinister manner, wore very large eyeglasses, and held a thick, knotty walking stick in his hands. He moved very rapidly, taking large strides and brandishing his cane. Yet deep inside he was a gentle soul, even timid. Indeed, he was so timid that he was even afraid of his landlady, although, to be sure, he had his own special reasons for this. He was also distinguished by his great sociability and liveliness, and was talkative to the point of verbosity. He was capable of talking ceaselessly for six straight hours, and about any conceivable topic. It must have been for all these qualities that people nicknamed him "Chizhik"—"The Finch." I was aware that the SRs often made use of his technical knowledge in printing their proclamations. He had nothing to do with his time—either he'd rush headlong through the city, frightening the townspeople with his appearance, or he'd dash off copies of proclamations on the hectograph.

On the day I went to see him, a thought suddenly flashed in my mind: "Why not ask Chizhik to print *The Workers' Newspaper* for us?" Upon further reflection I decided it was best not to get that involved with him. But then Chizhik, as if he were reading my mind, said to me:

"You know, comrade, I think the time has come for us to have an illegal newspaper! There used to be one here, you know. . . ."

The demand for such a paper had been building up for a long time. I had heard that the SRs were also thinking about this problem. "Perhaps Chizhik has heard something about that too," I thought. I responded agreeably:

"Of course, that would be good. . . . But where would we do the printing?"

"Don't worry about that—it'll be a cinch! I can arrange for a hectograph in no time at all."

"Let's give it some thought; we'll talk it over with our comrades and keep it in mind," I replied.

I returned to my comrades and told them of Chizhik's proposal.

"Let's not get involved with him, it's just not worth it. He'll blab, he'll shoot his mouth off, and the whole business will fall through," said Fisher, dismissing the idea. He had a skeptical attitude toward all measures that emanated from the intelligentsia.

"But why not give it a try? Doesn't he already print all kinds of nonsense for the SRs? And on the other hand, don't forget what happened the last time we printed our own leaflet—the only thing you could see were the blue streaks, the ink was running all over the place, and you couldn't even read it with a magnifying glass. When the workers saw it they swore at us more than at the autocracy," said Morozov, a supporter of Chizhik's proposal, who became passionately involved in this affair.

We wanted the printing to be of high quality. We didn't want to see our newspaper go under with its very first issue. This argument of Morozov's won the day. I returned to Chizhik's place and we worked out an agreement on all the details. I gave him the material and awaited the results. I was especially eager to see my own first work in print. With excitement and trepidation, I awaited the time that had been fixed for the appearance of the paper.

Then, about two days later, in the evening after work, when Rudolf and I were sitting around drinking tea, Chizhik suddenly bursts in like a bomb, greets us, and without removing his hat begins to run around the room.

"Comrade," he says to me, placing his walking stick in a corner in a state of great agitation, "I've got to speak with you about an extremely important matter."

Rudolf, having finished his tea, quickly left the room. He was a very tactful person, and was never offended if I preferred not to speak in his presence. I had taught him never to question me about anything, and in general to show less interest in what I did, where I went, and who came to see me. At first he seemed to resent me for this, but I pretended not to notice, and in due course he made his peace with the situation.

I turned on Chizhik: "What's going on? Why did you come here? Didn't we agree that I was always supposed to come to you, or to send someone in my place?"

"There's been a calamity, comrade, a great misfortune!"

And he began to pace the room again, while pulling on his sparse little beard.

"Have we gone under? Was there a police search?" I asked with alarm.

Chizhik stepped up to the door, fastened the hook for some reason, listened carefully for a moment, and then whispered mysteriously:

"A dog ate up all the gelatin!"

"What gelatin?"—the words escaped from me automatically.

"The gelatin for the hectograph. . . . Believe me, the wretched creature devoured the entire panful, even licked it clean! What a good-for-nothing cur! I asked the landlady to get rid of it long ago. . . . And now see what the damned thing has done!"

"What do we do now?"

"We have to concoct a new mix. . . . We'll need to buy some gelatin, some glycerin. . . . And I don't have any money."

I gave Chizhik some money and he departed, apparently satisfied.

Within a week or so we actually had the first issue of *The Workers' Newspaper*. It was written by hand in printed letters. The print came out clear. Only a few of the final copies came out faded. Chizhik had apparently been too lazy to wash the hectograph again. Unless my memory betrays me, the first issue of *The Workers' Newspaper* was printed in 900 copies. That was the normal capacity of the hectograph.

Our delight and our pride knew no bounds. We felt as if reborn. But my own satisfaction was greater than anyone's. All my close friends didn't just guess but knew definitely that the article on the steel mill was written by me, and me alone. Apparently, this was also guessed by the factory administration, for it later served as one of the reasons for my dismissal.

The authority of the workers' group now grew significantly, for everyone knew we were the editors of *The Workers' Newspaper.* The Socialist Revolutionaries began to woo us; they asked us to their meetings or simply invited us to their individual homes as guests for "a spot of tea."

It was around that time, it seems, that the SRs were intensifying the publication of their illegal literature on hectograph and mimeograph machines. They printed the tale of "Tsar Akhreyan."[2] They put out a copybook version of the journal *The Intransigent,*[3] as well as other publications. They had more money than we did and easier access to printing facilities, so their printed works were of higher quality and looked neater.

The first issue of *The Workers' Newspaper* was discussed at the factories and in the "salons." The workers were pleased with it; they read it inside and out, praised it for the simplicity and accessibility of its language and the skill with which it revealed the needs and aspirations of workers. A large segment of the intelligentsia reviled and condemned it: the SRs because it didn't propagate the idea of individual terror, and the SDs because it had so little to say about political questions. But in general its appearance was welcomed by everyone.

There was some truth to the accusation that the paper was excessively narrow in its illumination of political questions. We sensed this, and in the following issues we decided to devote more attention to politics. In practice we had already shifted to broad agitation, but in our debates with the intelligentsia some of us preached gradualism, arguing that noisy but fruitless chatter only hurts the cause. Still others among us were convinced that broad agitation and circle work do not get in each other's way, but actually complement each other.

Our second, May issue also occasioned a dispute. We had entrusted all our dealings and relations with Chizhik concerning the printing to Morozov. When we had gathered all the material, Fominykh made the necessary corrections and annotations and turned everything over to Morozov. The exact process whereby we edited *The Workers' Newspaper* is hard for me to remember. But

I believe that we entrusted most of that work to the more literate people. However, each of us edited his own columns. In any case, two or three weeks went by while we waited impatiently for the appearance of the second issue. Then, one day, Morozov shows up in a state of great agitation and rage:

"It's Chizhik—everything has come unglued. We're going to have to find someone else to do our printing."

"Why? What's going on? What happened?"—we jumped all over Morozov.

"What an idiot! What a good-for-nothing! It would be one thing if the old hag had a good-looking ensemble, but she's got the face of a cow, and with a whole brood to boot—two kids!"

"Can't you just tell us what's going on! You can vent your anger after you tell us!"

"Don't you understand? The bastard's gotten married! Well?"

We were still puzzled: what could be the connection between Chizhik's marriage and his refusal to print the newspaper?

"For you it's funny, but for me his marriage has meant nothing but trouble!" Morozov continued, tapping on the back of his neck. "So I say to Chizhik: 'Just think, so you're four months behind in your rent! So what? We could collect the money among ourselves and pay it off in installments. . . . Why let yourself slip into bondage?!'"

We were becoming even more perplexed, but it was hard to get Morozov to make any sense when he was this angry and agitated. Finally, he calmed down and was able to explain what had happened. It seems that Chizhik had gone into debt for his apartment and, in order to cover the debt, had decided on a desperate measure: he had married his landlady, who was twice his age and had two children. Then, when the landlady began to feel her power over him, she simply announced that henceforth she would not allow him to participate in any more conspiratorial activities, since she had two little children. And Chizhik had submitted. . . .

"I even think that the old witch sicced the dog on the gelatin that time," Morozov concluded his sad tale.

We now had to look for new printers. The task was taken on by Albert Retling, a member of our group who was a photographer by trade. I believe he was assisted by Anisya Aleksandrovna Chubarevskaya, a medical assistant, and E. N. Popova. Soon *The Workers' Newspaper* was appearing on schedule.

From a conspiratorial standpoint, the printing and publication of *The Workers' Newspaper* were so well organized that, when many of us were later arrested, and the gendarmes charged some of us with direct or indirect participation in putting out the newspaper, they were incapable of proving anything. And today, when we find ourselves in possession of the archives of the gendarme office, we can see how little was revealed there about the identities of the paper's organizers and collaborators.

Of course I am speaking of the initial period of *The Workers' Newspaper's* existence. Later—in the first quarter of 1902, I believe, when the Saratov Social Democratic Committee (basically composed of the same workers' group) was formed—the publication of the newspaper passed completely into the hands of that committee. But I cannot recall with what issue that shift began. All told, ten issues of *The Workers' Newspaper* were published.

32
"The Artist"

THE GENERATION of worker-Bolsheviks dating from the *Iskra* period has not only departed from the historical field of combat, it has, with some minor exceptions, actually died out.[1] Even their names, in many cases, have managed to drift away from our memory. And yet that generation, together with Lenin, achieved enormous successes in the building of a party and the organization of the working masses. Their skills, their methods of combating the class enemy, their moral principles forged in the heat of severe and painful struggle, their complete dedication to the interests of the revolution—all this has been passed on from generation to generation in the form of ready, effective "norms."

Many of these workers did not survive to see the happy day when the cause for which they had struggled and to which they had dedicated their brilliant lives finally emerged triumphant.

I would now like to recount the story of one such worker.

Aleksandr Egorovich Efimov—that was his real name. Here are the words of a short report about him, taken from the files of the Saratov provincial gendarme administration for 1902:

Efimov, Aleksandr Egorovich, townsman registered in city of Kronstadt, born 20 February 1869 in St. Petersburg.[2] In 1899, one of several persons summoned to St. Petersburg gendarme office for preliminary investigation regarding charges of membership in an antigovernment workers' circle and criminal acts of propaganda among workers. Outcome of investigation, in accordance with Imperial order of 25 December 1900, was via administrative means:[3] Efimov was sentenced to public surveillance by police for a three-year period. To serve this term he was exiled [after ten months in jail—S. K.] to city of Nizhny-Novgorod[4] and then transferred to city of Saratov, where he arrived 23 June 1901. At request of the chief of the Nizhny-Novgorod provincial gendarme office, doc. No. 3048 dated 26 November 1901, Efimov was searched and ordered to appear at an inquiry then being conducted at that office, accused of violation of art. 318 of the Criminal Code.[5] In order to bring the case to a speedy conclusion, he was placed in a special category of police surveillance.

Another part of the file contains a supplement to this report:

. . . In November 1902 Efimov was ordered to appear at an inquiry concerning a Social Democratic workers' group, then being conducted by the Saratov provincial gendarme office; investigation is still in progress.*

I first met Efimov in 1899, in Petersburg. We literally "met," without really getting to know each other; I didn't even learn his family name or his nickname at the time. He came to see me one evening after work—a bearded man of medium height, wearing a gray suit; he said the password, handed me a packet containing illegal literature, and vanished as if he had sunk through the earth. I can still remember his big blue eyes: so spirited, sprightly, and bold. He came to me a second time and vanished just as quietly and hastily.

The third time we met was in Saratov, where we both were exiles. We recognized each other right away. We recalled our first meeting and talked about our common acquaintances. He soon joined our workers' group and became one of its most active members. Before long he found work. Efimov was a woodcarver by trade, and, as was common, he had undergone a long and agonizing apprenticeship in a small artisanal workshop owned by a subcontractor in Petersburg, in the Okhta region, where he had some relatives—his mother, I believe. He went through a long period as a journeyman there, and then became a talented master craftsman, or, as we jokingly called him, a "skillman."[6] He rented himself a little room somewhere on the outskirts of the city, installed a workbench there, and began to work at home.[7] He kept his own tools and he always found customers. "Show me a neck and I'll find you a collar"—that was his favorite saying. Work in this field was tightly held in the hands of subcontractors and contractors, who callously exploited their journeymen and apprentices, so that the self-employed worker was paid very little. In order to earn barely enough to make ends meet, Efimov would work from morning to night.

To be sure, working "at home" did have the advantage of not tying Efimov down to any predetermined hours: he could stop

---

* This file is now located in the Saratov regional archive. (Author's note.)

working whenever it suited him, and he could go wherever he pleased. And for our revolutionary brother, this was "a real treasure." First, it made it easier to "unleash the revolution," and second, you were not dependent on the gendarmes: whether or not they thought you reliable, you still had your own work, whereas the factories and workshops had completely stopped hiring workers who were under surveillance. In short, we all envied Efimov.

No matter where he lived, Efimov's little workshop-apartment was always transformed into a club. There were two things that attracted us there: first, the gay, joyful, quick-witted, clever host, whose spirits never fell; and second, the unusual appearance of his room. It was like a small museum, or, if you will, an antique store. Hanging from the walls, scattered in artistic disarray, were pictures that had been made by Efimov and by others. These were mainly sketches, either in pencil or in India ink, of Roman emperors, patricians, and slaves with low foreheads and muscular, powerful bodies. There were also handsome female heads, in various poses and aspects of Venus, as well as portraits of Efimov's friends, and so on. The room also contained statuettes, figures, and heads modeled in clay or plaster or carved out of wood. Scattered around, on the floor, on the workbench, and on the windowsills were stockpiles of wood for carving, splendid finished woodcarvings to be used for the backs of seats and armchairs, some cornices for cupboards, and the like. As a matter of principle, Efimov refused to do any icons or woodcarving for churches.

But Efimov was not only a skilled woodcarver, there was also a talented painter buried somewhere inside him. He was attracted to the art of painting all his life. He sensed and understood perfectly well that natural talent and "originality" by themselves will not take you very far, and he would often say:

"Alas, if only I'd been able to study a little longer, I'd have been more than a match for Raphael himself!"

And wherever the winds of fate happened to blow him, he would always try to enroll in some art or drawing school. In Piter he attended Baron Shtiglits' School of Painting and Sculpture.[8] And in Saratov as well, he got involved in some kind of painting classes. He read and purchased many books on art. Hence the origin of his nickname — "The Artist."

But above all Efimov was a revolutionary, and he devoted all his energy to the goal of revolution. A remarkable propagandist-psychologist, was he also an able orator? Hardly. No skills and talents can develop unless the appropriate conditions are present. In those days, when the police prohibited the "gathering together" of more than two people at a time, what kind of conditions were there for the development and flowering of oratorical skill?

In this regard, the intelligentsia found itself in a more favorable position: the very nature of their professions—and this was especially true of lawyers and teachers—gave them ample opportunity to deliver orations. This is why orators and agitators from the workers' milieu were so rare in those days—they were like white crows in nature, and were worth their weight in gold to us.

On the other hand, the art and skill of "cultivating" and "propagandizing" workers individually or in small circles was flourishing. The Artist was a propagandist of just this type. No one was his equal in this art. "He could convert a corpse with his propaganda," we used to say of him in our group.

We would send The Artist on missions to the most dubious and dangerous places, where it was impossible to accomplish anything with our usual resources. He would never refuse and he almost always vindicated our confidence in him. In all the most difficult situations, he would display an amazing resourcefulness, a real understanding of people and life, and—most important—the ability to "hide his colors," to dissemble, to mimic the characters of the most varied kinds of people.

One such incident comes to mind: At a certain factory there is a capable metalworker who is wavering in his attitude toward us. He stops frequenting our circle, he avoids encounters with his comrades, and finally he completely disappears from our field of vision. Thus our only contact with that factory is broken. We do everything we can to recapture him in our net. In vain! Then we get the idea of entrusting this task to The Artist. We tell him what it's all about, and explain how crucial it is to remain in contact with that factory. He takes on the job with enthusiasm. Then he disappears and is not to be seen for a couple of weeks.

"Well, you sure gave me one hell of a job!" he declares, looking gay and content when he finally appears at our headquarters.

"What happened? Did you win him over?"

"Let's say not only him, but his wife and his mother-in-law as well!"

And he begins to tell us the story:

"I began by trying to find out where he lives, who his kinfolk are, does he maintain a homestead in the country, and to which church his mother-in-law goes to pray to God. . . ."

"Why in the world did you have to drag it out like that? We sent you to propagandize Filatov, not to pray with his mother-in-law!" I said impatiently.

"Just cool off! . . . You should have gone yourself," he snapped. "Don't interrupt me. . . . So the next thing I do is show up at his apartment one afternoon disguised as a country bumpkin. He's still not home from work. I can see his mother-in-law standing in the entrance hall, steaming a little barrel under some cucumbers, with a measure of cucumbers lying nearby. They are stocking up for the winter.

"'God be with you, Granny,' I say to her. 'Pickling the cucumbers, are you?'

"'Thank you, my good man. . . . And who might you be? What do you want?' And she stares at me without batting an eye.

"'Who I am and why I'm here—I'll be telling you later, only listen, Granny, don't be steaming the barrel like that. My mother, may she rest in peace'—here I crossed myself—'why back in our village, she would pour in some water, burn three cobblestones 'til they were red-hot, and then throw them into the barrel. Then, when the water started boiling, she'd cover it with a blanket and throw on some juniper or ashberry—the grass you're using is no good. The barrel would just stand there for a little while; then when it's all steamed through it has the aroma of juniper. Then Mother would begin to pickle the cucumbers. And she'd add some chick-pea or blackberry leaves and some oakwood to them. . . . Do that and the cucumbers will turn out like sugar. They can last until next year's cucumbers are ready while staying as fresh as if they were right from the garden.'

"'And where do you think you can find this juniper of yours? It's too much of a bother, the things you're saying.'

"'Don't worry, Granny, no bother at all. . . . I'll help you myself. . . . Tomorrow I'll bring you either some juniper or some other grass.'

"'May Christ save you, my good man. Thank you, little Father!'

"Now I can see that she's beginning to bite. The old woman's starting to take to me.

"'Listen, my good man, you're not one of them stubents, are you?,' she suddenly cut at me, like a sickle slicing into a naked back.

"'How can you say such a thing, Granny! Christ be with you! I'm a good Orthodox Christian, a craftsman, I am, a woodcarver. Why, not long ago I did a woodcarving at the church for the icon of the prophet Elijah, and I've just fixed up the hubs and spokes in the wheels of the holy prophet Elijah's fiery chariot.[9] They had come apart.'

"'Now there, now there, my good man, one can see right away that you're no featherbrain. . . . You see, not long ago those stubents had taken to idling about with our Mikita Ivanych. There was no getting rid of them. And even Mikita Ivanych himself began to sneak out of the house and disappear somewhere. So Katerina—that's my daughter—Katerina and I went after him. Can sin be far away? . . . Only one provider, and he'll end up in prison! . . . But what about you, my good man, did you work somewhere with Mikita Ivanych?'

"'Yes, Granny,' I say to her, 'Yes I did. I've come here to look him up.'

"Well, in a word, I got the old woman to the point where she put on the samovar and served me some tea. I wasted no time on the next day; I brought her an armful of juniper. In short, I had her so thoroughly propagandized that I became a welcome guest at her place anytime I wanted. And even Filatov has begun to follow me wherever I like."

"Well, what about his wife?" I inquired with growing interest.

"His wife! Why, his wife listens to her mother. Believe me, I didn't spend two whole weeks with them just to kill time. I went there almost every day."

And so it was that from that time forth, in The Artist's room, you could often encounter a tall, thin, somewhat older worker from an engineering factory—Filatov. The Artist would talk with him for hours about all kinds of subjects, serve him tea, and occasionally visit Filatov at his own home.

In those cases where we had no connections at a factory, but wished to distribute our proclamations there, The Artist would not hesitate to go to the local beer hall, get to know the workers over a bottle of beer, and use them to disseminate the proclamations.

When the gendarmes conducted searches—and they did this to us quite frequently—they would always begin with The Artist, and then go after the others. But as a rule, they would find absolutely nothing on him.

Rumors of searches always began to circulate in advance, and all "unreliable" workers, all those that were "under surveillance," would prick up their ears, "clean themselves up," and "put their houses in order." We would learn about these impending general searches roughly as follows: first, some gendarme would blurt it out to some trustworthy functionary, who would then tell it as a secret to some untrustworthy relative, who in turn would pass on the information to others. Sometimes there was a particularly dramatic political event, which would be followed without fail by a series of searches. Thus, for example, when Minister of Internal Affairs Sipiagin was assassinated by Stepan Balmashev at the beginning of April 1902,[10] they immediately began to conduct searches in Saratov, even among Social Democrats, who rejected acts of individual terror as a matter of principle. This was because Balmashev came from Saratov, where he still had relatives, friends, and acquaintances. In those cases when no event likely to incite a search had taken place, and when no one had forewarned us, we were still prepared for the searches simply because there hadn't been any for a long time. There could be no doubt about the regularity of these searches, as predictable as the regularity of solar and lunar eclipses.

When the gendarmes called on him, The Artist was always mockingly polite with them:

"Oh, greetings, greetings! Welcome, welcome! I've already been waiting for you for three days. . . ."

The angry cavalry captain would shout his command: "Begin the search!"

The gendarmes would furiously throw themselves on The Artist, turning out his pockets and rummaging in both appropriate and inappropriate places.

"Wait, wait, gentlemen, wait: there's no need for you to go to all that trouble," The Artist would assure them, and he'd begin to turn out his pockets himself, shaking out their contents.

Nervously, the gendarmes would turn the furniture upside down, rummage in the dirty linen, and tap on the walls, the floor, and the ceiling, but they still couldn't find anything. Meanwhile, The Artist—as he liked to put it himself—would circle around them like a wheel and redouble his "politeness."

"Over here, gentlemen, take a look, you might find something here," and he'd cautiously open the soot-covered vent of the stove. A gendarme would angrily roll up the sleeves of his uniform and thrust in his arm all the way up to his shoulder. After rummaging around inside the vent, the gendarme, repressing his rage, would pull back his empty hand, now covered with gobs of soot. The Artist, enjoying his triumph and barely containing his laughter, would then suggest that they check into some other dubious spot.

"This time it seems you called on me at the end of your rounds," he'd continue, feigning a naive tone.

"How could you possibly know that?" the captain would ask angrily.

"I have a really good sense of smell for you people."

The Artist knew from experience that these jokes at the expense of the gendarmes would cost him dearly: though their search yielded nothing, they would still hold him in jail for two or three weeks. Therefore, when the search was over, without awaiting the orders of the captain or colonel in charge, he would collect his things—his blanket, his pillow, his books—and prepare to go to jail.

"Where do you think you're going, Efimov?" a puzzled gendarme would ask.

"Dare I hope, based on the example of previous years, that you won't refuse to take me with you?"

Usually, the gendarmes would "comply" with his request and take him to the prison. They simply could not forgive him his mockery.

The Artist's feeling of comradeship was developed to an extreme. He was always ready to lay down his life for a comrade.

Very neat, tidy, and thrifty, Efimov always carried along a big basket of odds and ends—trousers of various cuts, waistcoats, old hats, peaked and visored caps, shabby, threadbare neckties, detachable shirt fronts, and other items of that kind. Despite their dilapidated character and the awkwardness of carrying them around, all these things were cleaned, pressed, and care-

fully darned. He also kept a stiff box, in which he stored all manner of buttons, needles, pins, hooks, studs, and feathers. Whenever we were in need, we went to The Artist. If one of us had to
make an appearance "in society," somewhere where tattered
breeches wouldn't do, or if for conspiratorial purposes someone
needed to don a nice hat and a tie and collar, we would always
turn to The Artist. He would usually take a very active part in the
selection of an outfit appropriate to the occasion. Removing very
shabby pairs of trousers—shiny from wear at the seat and at the
knees—from his basket, one after another, he would merrily
sing:

> These trousers are a lovely sight,
> Yet I never put them on.
> That's because they're much too tight,
> And I'm too weak such pants to don.

And, in fact, these pants of his were very old-fashioned, narrow, elegant, and so close-fitting that, when you wore them, all
the prominent parts of your body would be visible to the public,
and, when you walked, you looked as if you didn't have on any
pants at all. But by far the most difficult, most agonizing task was
to take them off. Somehow or other you could manage to get
them on all by yourself, but to take them off without any help was
simply impossible. A client who'd been utilizing the trouser part
of The Artist's wardrobe would dash into his room, lie down on
the couch, and raise his legs, whereupon The Artist would begin
the extremely painful operation of pulling off the trousers.

By his habits, customs, and nomadic way of life, Efimov was a
typical, confirmed old bachelor, and he looked very askance at
those workers who approached girls too closely and devoted a lot
of attention to courting them.

"Now is not the time for our brother, the proletarian, to be getting married. Once a man has married, he's as good as done for.
A wife, children, a family, himself a beast—it means he's gone
from the ranks. Wait until the revolution has come, then you can
marry, as many as you like!" he loved to repeat.

But, as we know, everyone is liable to go astray at one time or
another. The Artist, too, would meet with this fate. He was a jolly
fellow, very lively, and not at all bad-looking. His big blue eyes
were particularly splendid. Everything was contained in them:
the audacity and courage of youth, great tenacity, and yet at the

same time, barely perceptible to the outside observer, a certain sadness and warmth shined through, which he was careful to mask and conceal from the outsider's unsolicited gaze.

He was well aware of the value of his eyes and he would say in jest:

"I am like the fantastic hero of a Russian folk tale: he slays all his foes with a single blow—I have but to show my muscles and flash my eyes and a mountain of female bodies lies before me. But I will proudly step over them and move onward."

About two months after his arrival in Saratov, I dragged him along to Auntie's "salon." Despite the fact that, like many of us, he was anti-intelligentsia in orientation, he liked what he found there: the simple, natural surroundings, the somewhat cross but generally cordial tone of the hostess, the somewhat disorderly but generally nice, unaffected guests. To be sure, he also encountered people there who struck him as supercilious and arrogant, but he paid them no heed. On his free evenings, The Artist now began to go there and sit around drinking tea and arguing about "higher matters."

The Artist was an interesting debater: witty, resourceful, a man of great experience, well versed in the life and ways of workers, and fairly well-read. He could say many foolish things, many funny little concoctions of his own. But when you argued with him, even about questions on which you strongly disagreed, you could always feel how much knowledge he had, and you would learn all kinds of facts and details from him that you had never before imagined, whose existence you hadn't even suspected. Somehow he knew how to touch the most vibrant strings. He disliked discussions that were lifeless, scholastic, "arguments for argument's sake," which our intelligentsia loved so dearly. He would scornfully refer to such arguments as "an argument about the influence of the moon on cabinet-making" or "about the influence of the sense of smell on foul odors."

Among the regular guests at Auntie's "salon" was a young lady, a graduate of the special university courses for women. She was quiet, modest, lacking in any particularly distinctive characteristics, and as a young woman, perhaps even overripe. She had had some unsuccessful romances, which she secretly grieved and mourned over. She especially liked to lament them in the presence of music. The hostess would begin to play something very sentimental on the piano, and Mashenka—as we all called her—would sit in a corner, her chin in her hand, lost in reverie, and listen. Long after the hostess stops playing, while she's off intervening in some argument, Mashenka is still sitting there and dreaming, until someone finally approaches and begins to speak to her.

"She is dreaming of castles in the air," The Artist would say of her.

The daughter of a councillor of state,[11] Mashenka had graduated from a diocesan school, and her parents had already prepared her a career as wife of a priest in some wealthy parish. To their misfortune, however, she became acquainted with a radical student who led her away from the straight and narrow path. In defiance of her parents' will, she went off to the special women's courses, and she returned from there an SD.

Whether or not she was placed under police surveillance I am unable to say. She broke with her parents, took separate quarters, and earned a living as a private tutor. But when things got tough, she would secretly rush back to her parents' home, to her mother, who, behind the father's back, provided her with everything she needed.

Mashenka was a sensitive soul; she disliked passionate political arguments, sharp polemics, and satirical books just as she disliked pepper in her soup. She liked the "theoretical" workers because SDs were supposed to like them, just as SRs were supposed to like the peasants.

Well, it came to pass that The Artist made the acquaintance of this very same Mashenka. At first he treated her with indifference, and didn't even notice her presence, just as one often fails to notice many of the objects in an apartment until one stumbles on them or knocks one's arm or leg against them.

The affair began late one evening when, the rest of the guests having already departed from Auntie's, Mashenka asked The Artist to escort her to her home. The Artist was a good comrade, nor was he lacking in chivalrous feelings. So he gladly agreed to see Mashenka to her door. On the road she held him by the arm, which took him somewhat by surprise, since he had very deliberately refrained from offering his arm to her.

"Here's another girl growing warm with tender feelings," he thought, "and soon she'll be talking of the moon, sighing, while

I have to get up early in the morning and complete a job. I should never have stayed at Auntie's so long today."

Yet when she took him by the arm, he did not object. They walked silently in this manner until they reached her apartment. He bid her good night and quickly dashed home.

The next time, the very same story repeated itself, with only one difference: Mashenka asked him to escort her home without even waiting until the end of the evening. Also, instead of going home, they walked to the banks of the Volga, where navigation was already ending for the day and the last of the steamships were departing. The pier was brightly lit. A cluster of gray clouds was hanging over the Volga, and the cold autumn wind was driving them toward the immense trans-Volga steppes. A departing steamship gave off a prolonged whistle. The wind joined it in song and carried the hollow peal of the whistle to the same trans-Volga steppes.

"It's cold and windy here. Why don't we go down the embankment?"—Mashenka's tender, delicate voice resounded in The Artist's ear.

They descended, sat down on a bench in a little booth, and the wind seemed to abate. For a long time they gazed quietly at the seething surface of the water and the cold, silvery lights reflected in it. Mashenka shuddered from the cold and pressed closer to The Artist.

"Warm up my hands a little," she asked him in a soft voice, thrusting her hands into the sleeves of his coat.

The Artist could feel her narrow, froglike hands, with their long, sticky fingers, in his large, rough hands. . . . For a moment they even felt unpleasant to him. They sat this way for a long time, without exchanging a word, gazing at the cold autumn surface of the water.

From that moment on, The Artist was often lost in some unknown space. His mood was constantly in flux. Sometimes he came to us with his head held high, his eyes radiant and open wide, in a merry, contented mood, and he began to laugh infectiously, to crack jokes, to be playful, as if he had become "godfather to the king, friend to the minister"—to use his own expression. But at other times he appeared in a minor key: his eyes would be filled with sadness, which then turned into an inconsolable grief, a condition that he normally disliked, but which he now was neither able nor willing to conceal. At such moments he would begin to wax philosophical. He spoke about Diogenes-the-Cynic, who supposedly used a sugar vat for shelter, was satisfied with everything in the world the way it was, and was not even afraid to ask Alexander the Great to move aside so as not to block his sunlight.[12] Or he spoke of the wisdom and firmness of Socrates, who drank the hemlock without even knitting his brows.

"The way Xanthippe tortured your Socrates with her nagging every day, no wonder he'd turn to drink and do himself in with a bottle,"[13] said Aleksandr Morozov, mockingly. We liked to call Morozov "Mephistopheles," because of his wicked tongue and Mephistophelian beard.

Mephistopheles hit The Artist right where it hurt the most: "You haven't settled in with a Xanthippe of your own now, have you? Look, my friend, in our climate you won't be able to live with her in any sugar vat."

"And was there any sugar then?" someone else commented.

They were beginning to get malicious with him, while The Artist held his tongue.

Sometimes he would show up feeling sullen and morose. He would hurl a tool at something, break some of his wood supply or even a finished carving. At times like this he'd be rude and disagreeable to all the other guests. He would inveigh against the intelligentsia for its unreliability and inconsistency, as if he had just discovered these traits in it for the first time. However, The Artist would not remain in this condition very long.

One evening, when I was returning home on the late side, I saw from the street that there was a light in my window.

"The gendarmes," I thought, "they've come for another search. What should I do? Spend the night at home or stay away? Everything inside should be clean. True, there's some illegal literature, but it's hidden in a safe spot."

I was extremely tired, and had neither the strength nor the will to go looking for a place to spend the night at that late hour.

"Whatever happens will happen. I'll go home. Does it really matter if they arrest me a day earlier or a day later!" And I resolutely marched to my home.

What a pleasant disappointment it turned out to be when The Artist obligingly opened the door to my room for me.

"I've been waiting for you here for a whole hour. . . . I was thinking about spending the night at your place."

"Well, sure, that's fine! I'll ask Grigorevna to put on the samovar for us."

"I took care of that in your absence. Grigorevna has already thrown in the coals twice while we were waiting for you."

Grigorevna was my landlady. An old woman, she was completely her own person, and even helped us hide our illegal literature. She knew all my friends and acquaintances, and she knew whom she could allow into my room and whom she could not. Hence I was not really surprised that The Artist had settled down in my place and taken over, making himself at home.

While I washed, went to the kitchen, and busied myself with the food, The Artist was rushing about the room, pulling wildly on his hair, cracking his knuckles; his general appearance was that of someone who had just done something important, felt burdened by his secret, and was now looking for the opportunity to tell somebody about it.

"Well, enough of this, no more! It's high time to get down to business." He cut through the air with the palm of his hand.

I made no effort to hold back my thoughts, for I immediately understood what it was he wished to bring up; so I said to him in an agreeable tone:

"It was high time quite a while ago. . . . I just knew the affair would end like this."

"And how did you find out?" he suddenly took note.

"I haven't found out, I'm just guessing. . . . I know you very well. . . ."

"But it never occurred to me that it would all turn out so stupidly, and worst of all, that I'd end up looking like a fool. Oh, what an idiot I am, what a ninny!"

He began rushing about the room and pulling on his hair again:

"And who the hell is she! It would be one thing if she were attractive, but she is base and vile, with the mind of a hen! And what's even worse—fool that I am!—I had already seen it all and knew it. . . . And yet, suddenly, I fell for her. For shame! To hell with it! I've been possessed by the devil!"

"Just don't get so agitated. Sit down, drink some tea, and begin from the beginning."

I sat him down on a chair, made him drink some tea; after he'd
calmed down somewhat, he recounted rather incoherently everything that I described above.

"If I were a student," he said, "or a teacher, or even some kind
of pockmarked little medical assistant or government clerk with
the soul of a pen-pusher, why then she wouldn't hesitate to throw
herself into my arms. But I'm just another worker, and under police surveillance to boot! What kind of future can she expect from
someone like that? . . ."

"She actually said that to you?" I asked with amazement.

"Why would she want to say it so directly? When it comes to
serious matters, she has the mind of a hen, but when it comes to
all kinds of women's tricks and subterfuges, why she's more than
a match for the cleverest man. . . . First she began by questioning
me, trying to worm out of me just how I planned to organize my
future life. Wasn't I planning to study? Didn't I intend to be employed some day in one of the intellectual professions? And
when, in response to all these overtures, I answered directly—'I
am a revolutionary and will remain one to my dying day; I've no
intention to look for easy money and I'll never abandon my
fellow-workers'—she immediately looked discouraged. . . . So I
said to myself: when all is said and done, what in the world am I
going to do, just hang around her?! This business has got to be
faced squarely. Then she said something to me that made me
really want to cut her down to size. . . . It was extremely difficult,
but I managed to restrain myself."

At this point The Artist again leaped up from his chair and
started running around the room.

"What was that 'something' she said to you?" I inquired with
curiosity.

"'Friends,' she says to me, 'let's stay friends.' . . . Ha, ha, ha—
'friends'! 'I already have plenty of friends,' says I, 'as many as you
please. And real friends, too, the kind that would brave fire and
water for me.' And on this note we parted company."

On the following day The Artist arose early, and, without even
waiting for his tea, disappeared somewhere. He did not reappear
for a whole week. Some of us would run into him near the factories with some other workers, and sometimes he'd turn up at
the tearoom in the marketplace, where there were many unemployed workers, or at the beer hall.

"Where have you vanished?" we asked him.

"I've made some new connections. I've discovered some re-markable fellows. They're longing for battle! We've been stewing in our own juices too long. It's time to raise new layers of workers."

"You'd better cultivate the old ones first," Mephistopheles re-marked with skepticism.

"The one doesn't prevent the other. I like to work on the new ones, and you can work on the old."

After the episode I described, The Artist became unusually ac-tive, as if he were hurrying to make up for what he had lost, or perhaps he simply wished to lose himself in his work, to efface, to eradicate from his memory everything that had happened, the quicker the better.

Just about on the eve of the May Day demonstration of 1902, he and I were arrested together, for the last time. First he was kept in the Saratov prison, then he was transferred to the Samara prison,[14] where as a protest he staged a seven-day hunger strike. The Artist was held in the Samara prison for about two years. After that his trail disappears, though I did hear rumors that, during the "days of freedom" of the 1905 Revolution, he was one of the organizers of the woodworkers' union in St. Petersburg.[15]

I did meet him again, however, in Piter, in 1908, in the course of our Party work during the darkest period of reaction. For a brief time, I was the organizer of the city's Moscow district, while he was working in the Vyborg district, on the Okhta.[16] I remem-ber that we both appeared as speakers a couple of times at some kind of protest meeting against the "recallists," who were then carrying out their anti-Party activity with considerable success.[17] The Artist enjoyed enormous authority among the workers of his district, and he was able to drive out the recallists without any difficulty.

He was just as cheerful as ever, just as gay and full of faith in our victory, in the coming revolution. No matter what transpired, I never saw him in a mood of despondency, a state to which, un-fortunately, even the most prominent of our Party workers aban-doned themselves in those times.

During our conversations, at a time when I had to move in with him for lack of money, we often recalled Saratov, and talked at length about our former and present comrades. He continued to ply his woodcarver's trade. As in the old days, his room was crammed and adorned with drawings, statuettes, sketches, Venuses, and other female heads modeled in clay. As in the old days, he was attending some institute of fine arts, where he was making progress learning how to paint portraits and representations of various types of workers and artisans. And as in the old days, when he spoke about art his big blue eyes would burn with joy and tenacity.

Soon thereafter, under instructions from the Party Central Committee, we decided to publish our own Bolshevik central organ to guide the workers' trade-union movement and to serve as a counterweight to the Menshevik journal *Professional Herald.* According to our plan, the journal was supposed to appear biweekly at first, and then weekly. We called it *Herald of the Professional Movement.* The editorial board consisted of G. Zinoviev, N. Rozhkov (who later became a Menshevik), Efimov (The Artist), myself, and someone else. We made Efimov the editor-in-chief.[18]

With the appearance of the second issue, the journal was confiscated by the police and Aleksandr Efimov, the editor, was brought to trial. I believe he was sentenced to two years in prison. But he managed to escape and became a fugitive from justice. After this, under the instructions of the Party Central Committee, I shifted to trade-union work and served as secretary of the woodworkers' union right up to my arrest in 1910. During that entire period I managed to stay in personal contact with The Artist.

Early in 1910 I was arrested. A period of imprisonment and deportation to Siberia began for me, and I completely lost sight of The Artist. Where was he? What had become of him? There were rumors that he'd died somewhere. But where?—no one knew. We were living under the cursed conditions of the barbaric yoke imposed by the tsarist autocracy. Our best Party workers frequently perished in prison or at hard labor, often disappearing without a trace. . . . So there was nothing surprising in the notion that the same fate had befallen The Artist.

It was only in April 1917, while working in a Siberian town, that I received a detailed letter from Petrograd, from one of my old comrades, in which he included, among other items of news:

"The Artist, a man who is not unknown to you, died a heroic death in the February days while driving a pack of policemen from his garret. . . ."[19]

33

At the Bering Factory, "Collaborator" (The Strike)

A FTER I WAS discharged from the Volga steel mill I didn't remain without work for very long.[1] I had good connections at the Bering machine works,[2] especially in the pattern shop, where P. I. Lalov and F. N. Ivanov worked at the time. I can't remember whether one of them asked the foreman to hire me or, following their advice, I went to the factory gate myself just when a pattern-maker was needed. Be that as it may, I joined the factory shortly thereafter.

The workshop turned out to be the worst by far of all the shops I have ever worked in. It was located on the second floor, right above another shop. Its windows looked out on the courtyard and directly adjoined the lavatory. It was dirty, crowded, and rather dark. There were piles of wood shavings, sawdust, pieces of board, and old, dirt-encrusted patterns all over the shop. The screeching sounds of the belt saw and ring saw never ceased. Two lathes were also in operation. Dust would pile up from the wood all day long, making it difficult to breathe. In the summertime the effect of these unsanitary conditions would be multiplied by the incredible heat. The sun would scorch the iron roof and brick walls of the shop, making it unbearably stuffy. The workers were sweating from every pore, and they were constantly drinking the unboiled water, which added to the flow of sweat. The workday was fixed at eleven hours, but the wily employer contrived to lengthen it by half an hour by "adjusting" the factory siren.

I passed the test without any difficulty, and my daily wage was set at either one ruble or one and a quarter.

After a day's work under these conditions, I was always in a state of complete exhaustion, and when I returned home I'd have no desire left except to lie down and sleep. There was only one day a week—Sunday, together with Saturday evening—that I could devote to meetings with comrades and to the revolutionary cause. Even a healthy young man had difficulty enduring such a brutish existence for a prolonged period.

The basic contingent of workers at the Bering factory was rather "gray," worn down, and passive. But even they had trouble putting up with such a heavy burden. Frequently their discontent would burst forth into the open. Still, there was an enormous distance between the usual grumbling over and discontent with arrangements at the factory and a really organized demonstration. They needed to be organized, agitated, prepared. But where to do this? And how? Certainly it wasn't possible to gather together all these workers at a single meeting. That stage of development of the workers' movement was still a thing of the future. In the meantime, then, what was needed was to carry out our work on an individual basis, to propagandize and cultivate each of the workers separately. But that would have taken much too long— you cannot cultivate the workers of an entire factory one by one. Instead, we needed to cultivate and recruit the most advanced and active of the workers and then to influence the larger mass through them. This was the main activity of our circle at the Bering factory. We recruited and cultivated workers individually.

Even the most ordinary strike, with purely economic goals, was something new and unprecedented for the mass of workers in Saratov. Most workers there looked upon a strike as an act of rebellion. I can remember my effort to propagandize a certain turner. He was a middle-aged man, married, fairly well paid; he had done a little reading—for his own pleasure, of course—but was very much afraid to share what he had read with others. And he of course looked down on those "others." "Personally, I have no problem with a strike, myself," he would say, "But what about 'them'? Do you really think they would go on strike? They're gray, they're not even conscious—they still need to be taught for a long, long time!"

He used this perspective in order to justify his own unwillingness to do anything. Yet in his own shop—and not only there— he was considered an authority, a good worker, and a "conscious" one. But what was the value of his "consciousness"? He feared everything. But he didn't mind chattering and prattling at the tea table in the company of clever people, for it enhanced his authority in the eyes of others.

I devoted a good deal of time to him. I visited his apartment, joined him for tea, and, when the weather was hot, I lay around on the floor of his cool room with him, which was sheltered from the sun. His wife would bring us some cold kvass,[3] which she prepared herself, and we would lie there and talk about higher matters and about the well-organized socialist order to come. But whenever I brought him back down to this wicked world and asked him to consider distributing our proclamations in his workshop, he would shrug his shoulders and say something like this:

It wouldn't do any good, only harm. As soon as the proclamations turned up in the shop, they'd ask: well, who put them there? I'd be the first one they suspected, since they know I'm conscious. . . . I'd be dismissed on the spot. . . . That would cut off our last connection. . . . And just when I've begun to pick out some promising fellows there.

Meanwhile, however, things were getting even worse at the factory. The owner had apparently decided to take advantage of the period of economic crisis by squeezing the juices out of the workers even more. My turner now began to move "leftward." He not only agreed to distribute the proclamations, he even began to incite me to strike. He also brought me some new workers and introduced them to me as "conscious."

I described the situation of the Bering workers at the time in an article in the May issue of *The Workers' Newspaper*. I will cite some excerpts:

The situation at our factory, or, better still, the "disorder" at our factory, is truly scandalous. Bering, the owner, is the most predatory and merciless exploiter that walks the face of the earth. You need only look at the way he prowls through the workshops looking like a dog that has broken loose from his chain. You wait—then suddenly he hurls himself at a terrified worker; and the poor fellow is really in for it now.

In complete disregard for the law, this bloodsucker has stuck little children all over the factory, and he exploits them in the most inhumane way, paying them a few measly coins for an eleven-hour workday. Thanks to this excessive use of child labor, the situation of the adult workers is slightly better. Nevertheless, wages have fallen terribly, and the workers are enslaved to such an extent that the owners can do whatever they want with them. In order to get their hard-earned kopecks, the workers must humiliate themselves a great deal and act as if they were asking for a favor. . . . With the aid of various fraudulent devices, they are compelled to work two extra hours a week.

In order to deceive the workers, the owners are not too squeamish to stoop to such methods as setting back the hands of the clock. An announcement was recently posted declaring that the workday was to be calculated as beginning at 6 A.M. and ending at 6 P.M., with a one-hour break for lunch. Prior to the announcement, according to factory regulations, there had always been an hour and a half for lunch and an additional half hour for breakfast. In other words, they want to rob us of one whole hour of the time we need to revitalize our powers. Because of the restless mood of the workers, the new regulation has still not been implemented. . . . Well, brothers, let us support our oppressors in their fear of us! Let us not allow this flagrant outrage to occur! We, of course, are never consulted, and there is even reason to doubt that they consider us human beings, given the impossible conditions in which they make us work. . . .

Comrades, the time has come to start using our heads and put an end to all these outrages. . . .

Our wages must be raised. We must be paid, in full and on time, twice each month. The siren must sound on time and our full lunch and breakfast hours must not be taken away. The abolition of the new regulations, the reduction of the workday, the improvement of hygienic conditions—these are all goals that we must take upon ourselves. There is no one else to look after our needs, no one except our brother—the workingman!

As the reader can see, this article aimed for the preparation of a strike. In essence, it formulated all the workers' demands on their employer, Bering. However, to go on strike at this point would have been premature. Although Bering was threatening to implement the new regulations, he was still frightened, vacillating, afraid to miscalculate. And the workers, it seemed, were not prepared to respond to a call to strike:

"It really doesn't matter what new regulations the owner wants to introduce! He may not go through with them, he may be too scared. . . . This is not the right moment for 'rebellion.'"

Nor were we, the organizers, prepared yet either. It was important to select the leaders from among workers at the factory, and not outsiders. We still had to distribute proclamations, engage in agitation, and inspire the masses with faith not only in the justice of our cause, but also in the certainty of victory. It is only at such times that a burning fever begins to be felt.

Most of the work fell on my shoulders. This was understandable enough: my revolutionary past was no secret, I had good connections with the intelligentsia, and I was a hard worker. I endeavored to maintain the leadership group in such a way that its head didn't stick out too high from the ground. We met, we made decisions while on the move—in the nooks and crannies of the workshop, out in the courtyard, in the lavatory, at the factory exit.

At last everything is ready—all the demands have been formulated. Our workers' group has approved all the preparations. It is already in a triumphant mood, since we have recently scored some brilliant and virtually bloodless victories in the railroad workshops, where we won our strike. We have stressed that fact at every opportunity in our agitation at the Bering factory.

Then, on June 15, 1901, an announcement was posted at the factory gate proclaiming the introduction of the new regulations. For about three days we had already been showing up at the gate earlier than everyone else, in order to see if the announcement had appeared. Now they had thrown down the gauntlet: the announcement that working conditions were about to deteriorate had been made. It was time to begin the struggle.

One after another, the workers gather at the gate and read the announcement. Shouts of rage and indignation, threatening noises resound in the air:

"Bloodsucker! Thief! Tormenter! The rascal should be carted out in a wheelbarrow! We should beat the hell out of him."[4]

Our ringleaders were scattered through the crowd and agitating for a strike. Little groups of workers gathered around each agitator and began to argue, with everyone hurling insults at the owner. Not one person spoke against our position. We could sense the mood of unanimity. . . . The siren roared, once, twice, and then, at greater length, a third time, after which the gate was normally locked. But no one budged, and the gate remained open. The siren sounded once again.

"Let it screech or not screech! Either way, we're not going back to work. . . . That's enough, that's all the work we're going to do!"—voices resounded. "Now let's see the boss do a little work himself!"

Someone had spread the rumor that a group of workers had slipped into the factory and was working there alongside the foremen. . . . Volunteers were found to go in and get them. But others urged:

"No, no one should be let into the factory; they'll stay there and work! They want to work!"

Cautiously, not very sure of myself, I support the view that no one should be allowed into the factory; it seems like a rational suggestion to me. . . . I notice that people are listening to my opinions. I begin to act more boldly and decisively.

Our meetings continue for several hours. Wherever you look,

you can see my comrades agitating other workers. I move around from group to group, trying to hear what's being said. They're all saying the same kinds of things, but with less and less spirit. The men are growing tired, exhausted; they're all shifting restlessly from one foot to another, waiting for something to happen. They're afraid to leave the area of the gate, lest others return to work in their absence. I exchange a few hurried words with members of our group and then address the crowd in a loud voice:

"Comrades, let's all go back to our homes! . . . We'll meet here again tomorrow morning, when the siren sounds!"

Little by little, cautiously, the people disperse, the crowd melts away. The turner and I head for his apartment. Several men start off with us, but they disappear along the way. The turner is in a joyful, confident mood:

"The strike must continue, the owner is sure to give in!"

We spent the rest of the day and the evening at discussions and meetings. We formulated demands and drafted a proclamation, which was to be ready for the following morning.

I spend the night away from home somewhere. I arise early in the morning. It is stuffy in the room. Out in the street there's a sort of yellowish dry fog, a dust suspended in the air, completely blocking off the sun. I dress hurriedly and rush off to a designated place for the proclamations. But, for some unknown reason, it turns out that they haven't been printed. I am seized by feelings of malice and despair. Thanks to the slovenliness of the intelligentsia, a strike that began so nicely may now miscarry! I run to Fominykh's apartment. He's a resourceful fellow—together we'll come up with something. . . . I get him out of bed and tell him of our unfortunate situation. Fominykh rubs his forehead, then his hands, pulls at his goatee, and finally says:

"There's only one solution: to write a new proclamation and duplicate it by hand on copying paper. I already have some carbon paper, so let's sit down and start writing!"

"That's impossible," I object. "We have something like an hour till the siren, and we'll need at least two hundred copies of the proclamation."

"Two hundred would of course be out of the question, but we can do a hundred, I promise you," he says calmly. "The paper is thin, the pencil will do ten copies at a time. I'm certain we can do a hundred in an hour."

We sit at the table, arm ourselves with pencils, and, writing in print, we begin to produce one printed sheet after another.

The proclamation is a very short one, consisting almost entirely of a list of demands, and our work goes very well. Only the last couple of sheets come out rather blurred, but even these are legible.

Finally, after we have written the last copy, I put the whole batch right under my shirt, button up my jacket so my stomach won't stick out, and run full speed to the factory.

Arriving just before the siren, I thrust a bundle of proclamations into the hands of each ringleader. The proclamations soon passed rapidly from hand to hand, rustling in the crowd and glimmering whitely in the sun. The workers read them completely openly—singly and in groups, to themselves and aloud. This raised everyone's spirits. There were no police in the area, just some suspicious characters walking about at a distance, unwilling to risk coming closer. We all knew one another here, and the appearance of an outsider in our midst would have been noticed right away.

We were growing tired of hanging out by the gate and holding meetings. We began to discuss our next move. We decided it was time to announce our demands to the owner, so he would know what we wanted and why we were striking.

But someone else explained:

"The owner has known all our demands for a long time, and they're already stated in the proclamation."

A rumor spread that the factory inspector had arrived at the factory.[5]

"Let him come out to us! He can come here! Why is he whispering with the owner before he's even seen us? The owner means more to him!"—voices resounded everywhere.

Someone from the administrative staff appeared in the courtyard and proposed that we send representatives of the workers to negotiate with the inspector.[6] The crowd grew noisy and agitated. Some saw the offer as a sign of our enemy's weakness.

"Let's not send a deputation! They'll arrest it! Let him come to us himself!"

"Let him speak with all of us! Bring on the inspector! Bring him out here!"

Our group supported this attitude.

After a while the factory inspector appeared in the doorway to the courtyard in person. He was a tall, heavyset man with a graying beard, and his hat bore an official insignia. His body filled the entire doorway.

His self-satisfied appearance and government insignia did not inspire confidence; they were provocative. He tried to establish an informal atmosphere with the workers.

"I have come to you, my brothers, to speak openly and candidly, from the heart," he began in an ingratiating voice.

"Sure, but first you went to the owner, not to us! You've already made a deal with the owner!"

"Go ahead, say what you want to say! Stop interrupting him! Let him say his piece!"

The crowd was noisy and agitated. The inspector began to wave his arms:

"I can't speak with all of you at once! Just select one of your more sensible men, my brothers, and I'll speak with him. There must be people here you trust!"

"Sure there are! But you'll just arrest them, won't you? . . . Let him speak with everyone!" the crowd resumed its jeering.

"Just send me someone. No one will lay a finger on him!" says the inspector. "I promise you that, my brothers. No one! My word of honor!"

I stood in the rear and watched. I didn't want to expose myself to the authorities prematurely, not unless it was really necessary. But everyone's eyes were fixed on me.

"Go ahead, Kanatchikov! Talk with him, Kanatchikov, Kanatchikov! Kanatchikov!"—their shouts could be heard.

I had barely managed to exchange glances with my comrades when I was pushed forward and found myself face to face with the inspector. He looked me over from top to bottom and said:

"Well, tell me, what is it you want from me? Only be frank!"

At first I was extremely nervous. But when I saw the inspector's fat, self-satisfied figure, I felt such a flood of hatred and anger well up in me that, barely suppressing a shout, I said to him:

"We didn't call you here. We know perfectly well that you'll support the owner no matter what! . . ."

"Not true! I am a guardian of the law. I uphold the law, and I will oppose anyone who violates it," the inspector broke in angrily.

"The law here is like the draft bar on a team of horses—which-

ever way you turn it, it always follows! How come you don't prevent the owner from exploiting children?"

The inspector turned purple, but he evidently restrained himself and didn't respond to my question. By letting the word "exploiting" slip out, I gave myself away. The inspector understood
that he wasn't dealing with a run-of-the-mill, gray worker, whom
he could play with and treat like a fool.

"You've known our demands for a long time. . . . You should
have convinced the owner to satisfy them."

From behind, somebody slips me a copy of the proclamation. I
take it to the inspector and hand it to him:

"Here are our demands. They are all summarized here."

The inspector took the proclamation, looked at it very hurriedly, and tucked it in his pocket.

"I see from your leaflet that you're demanding a reduction in
the length of your workday, but is it really all that long? No, some
ill-intentioned outsiders have obviously put these ideas in your
heads. Stop listening to them!" he said, casting a malicious, dev-
astating glance in my direction. I understood where he was heading. "Why, I work a good sixteen hours a day myself, sometimes
even more. . . ."

Laughter could be heard coming from the crowd. The inspector suddenly realized that he had gone too far, and he began to
talk some lighthearted nonsense, obviously hoping to neutralize
the bad impression he had made. I took advantage of the
situation:

"Mister inspector! Just look at all of us—just see how emaciated we are, how thin and pale." I turned toward the workers
and made the appropriate gesture with my hand. "And we work
only eleven hours! Judging by your appearance, it's impossible to
believe that you could be working sixteen hours!"

In the crowd, more laughter and shouting:

"That's right! Let him come work at the factory for a day or so!
Let him be in our skin for a while!"

The inspector turned more purple than ever. His thick neck
filled with blood. He got ready to leave, declaring:

"My mediation is over. I wished you well, but you are listening
to all kinds of troublemakers. . . . Go back to work! I say to you
one more time: if you don't want to listen, then you have no one
to blame but yourselves!"

He turns around and leaves. I yell after him:

"You're the boss's lackey! You toady!"

Again the workers begin to gather and talk in groups. Words drift from the crowd:

"The bribe taker! He's sold out! The Judas! The seller of Christ!"

But here and there some discontented, skeptical voices have already begun bursting through. We tried to stifle them, to maintain the confident, high spirits of the crowd, which was scattering into smaller groups and arguing about the situation. We clearly sensed that the workers' spirits had begun to fall. The number of skeptics was growing rapidly. The workers were growing tired and tense. And yet, despite all this, no one wanted to pursue the factory administration's invitation to return to work.

It was hardest of all for us: we had left the factory gate later than all the others and we had returned to the factory before the morning siren. We hadn't left the strikers for a single minute; we tried to stick with them wherever they were, to help maintain their confidence and high spirits.

The factory administration acted as if nothing had happened: in the morning, at lunch time, and in the evening, the siren sounded at the usual times, the gates were opened and closed, and the noise of the operating motors and the steam engine could be heard from the depths of the factory courtyard. Sometimes one heard the metallic sound of the sledge hammer banging against the anvil in the forge. . . .

However, this kind of staging of the "normal course of work" didn't deceive any of the strikers. We all knew perfectly well that there weren't any real workers inside the factory and that the people participating in this dramatization were all foremen, technical employees, and possibly some of the unskilled laborers. Still, these contrivances of the administration did have some effect once the spirits of the strikers had begun to fall. Each peal of the siren, every sound of a hammer blow in some workshop gave rise to all conceivable kinds of rumors to the effect that someone or other, somewhere or other, had returned to work. It took enormous efforts to dissuade and disabuse people of all this. . . . What it all boiled down to, quite obviously, was that the number of workers who didn't believe in the successful outcome of the strike was becoming larger and larger, and they were seeking a pretext to return to the factory.

My friend the turner had somehow disappeared completely from my field of vision in the course of the past day. He was obviously trying to avoid me. And when, by chance, our eyes would happen to meet, he'd try to turn away. He was gloomy and sullen, and he walked with his head bent and shoulders stooped.

"Yes . . . our people is lacking in consciousness. . . . Is there anything to be done with people like that? I've always said that nothing will come from our people," said the turner, sighing and waving his hand in a gesture of despair, when I encountered him face to face.

"What are you yelping about, my friend? Aren't you the one who was trying to convince me to begin the strike earlier?" I interrupted him.

"And why did you have to listen to me! . . . One can say almost anything in a fit of passion."

And he disappeared, losing himself in the crowd.

This kind of desperate talk was no longer exceptional. I began to rage indignantly against the inconstancy of human nature, and especially against the cowardice, confusion, and panic of people who still had nothing to lose. But I soon calmed down and awaited the inevitable outcome. It came on the third day of the strike.

As was to be expected, the police intervened in the affair. Their self-restraint did not last very long. Every time there was a conflict between workers and entrepreneur the police would openly take the side of the entrepreneur, which demonstrated the unity between employer and police better than any possible agitation. The economic struggle was transformed into a political struggle. And we would translate that cordial unity into our own revolutionary language—"Down with the autocracy!"[7]

On June 17, a quite unambiguous announcement by the Saratov provincial governor was posted at the entryway to the factory: "If the workers of the Bering factory fail to return to work on the morning of June 18, they will all be dismissed."

However, this extremely firm statement from a very zealous administrator had no effect. On the morning of that day, as was now our wont, we arrived at the factory gate. But, notwithstanding the repeated invitations of the siren, no one went to work. Seeing that it had failed, the administration then asked us to settle our financial accounts and accept dismissal. But we refused to do this as well. The workers continued to hang about near the gate and hold their meetings.

Soon a detachment of city policemen, led by an inspector, appeared on the scene. They surrounded us on all sides and drove us along to the police station. This procession took place in the daytime, on populated streets, and it attracted a great deal of public attention. At the station they herded us all into one dirty, narrow room, where they held us until evening, at which time they sorted out the "instigators" and took them off to prison.[8]

Thus did the Bering factory's first economic strike end in failure. But it taught the workers an enormous political lesson. Simultaneously, there had also been an unsuccessful strike at the Makarov engineering works, also led by a member of our workers' group, comrade S. P. Shepelev.[9]

On June 20, the chief of Saratov gendarmes reported the "happy" results of his victories to the Department of Police.[10]

As a supplement to my communication of 11 June . . . I have the honor to report that the workers of the Riazan-Ural railroad shops have now returned to work and order has been fully restored.[11] But at the Bering steel foundry, with 400 workers, and the Makarov ironworks, with 100 workers, a strike took place on 15 June as a result of the introduction of new regulations requiring workers to be at work from 6 A.M. to 6 P.M., with a total of only one hour of rest for lunch and breakfast. According to information provided by our agents, the strike at the Bering factory was led by one Semën Ivanov Kanatchikov, currently under official surveillance, reputed to be extremely unreliable and noted for his close connections with people like Arkhangelskaya, Vasily Fominykh, both under official surveillance, Aleksandr Arkhangelsky, now under special surveillance, and others of the same category. The strikers at the Makarov factory were led by one Semën Shepelev, who is under secret surveillance, and the workers Ivan Shchukin, Aleksandr Kalmykov, and Andrey Cherviakov. The workers are asking for the abolition of the new regulations and the reestablishment of the old ones, which allowed them two hours for lunch and breakfast. The workers have not engaged in any riotous behavior and have been conducting themselves calmly. A leaflet was found at the Bering factory, a copy of which is attached herewith. Since the Bering workers would not agree to return to work, but also refused to accept severance, 23 persons were arrested by the police on 18 June by order of the acting governor and there are plans to arrest fifteen persons on the 19th. The workers at the Makarov factory have returned to work, and no arrests have been made. Work has also resumed at the Bering factory.

(Signature.)

Having reestablished order and calm at the factories, the gendarme colonel proceeded to set the stage for bringing the "instigators" and the disturbers of public tranquility to justice, and he also hastened to report this to his superiors in the Department of Police:

SECRET.

As a supplement to my report of 20 June . . . I have the honor to report to the Department of Police that, at the Bering factory, in the city of Saratov, there have recently appeared various kinds of proclamations and a leaflet containing an appeal called "To All Saratov Workers," in which the workers are invited to go on strike. As a consequence, and in accordance with the oral proposal of the procurator of the Saratov court of justice, a preliminary investigation of this matter was launched under my jurisdiction, following the procedures set forth in art. 1035 of the Criminal Code, resulting in the indictment of Semën Ivanov Kanatchikov, a peasant from the village of Gusevo, Volokolamsk district, Moscow province, currently under official police surveillance and now confined under guard in the Saratov provincial prison, on charges of having been the principal inciter of the workers to go on strike.

Colonel (signature).

Imprisoned together with me were P. I. Lalov, Ivanov, Kalashnikov, and several others. As a dangerous instigator, I was placed in the isolation section, where they held me for nearly a month and a half. But my comrades were soon released.

This unprecedented wave of strikes at several large enterprises produced a powerful impression not only on workers, but also on the entire so-called public opinion. For the backward mass of workers the strikes were an object lesson in how it comes about that an economic struggle transforms itself into a political struggle; the workers were shown by experience that, standing behind the employer, the capitalist, there are always the policeman, the gendarme, the governor, and that a successful struggle to improve their material situation requires, above all, that the autocracy first be overthrown. And, of course, the mass participation of workers in the May Day demonstration of the following year, 1902, would not have been possible if the Saratov workers had not passed through this preliminary school of struggle.[12]

34

"A Prison to Some, But to Me— A Home"

EXPERIENCE, habit, the ability to adapt yourself to circumstances with the goal of mastering them, the ability to orient yourself to new surroundings very quickly—all these qualities are necessary, it turns out, not only in any new business, undertaking, or profession, but also in the business of serving time in prison. This kind of prison "adaptability" eventually becomes one of the inalienable qualities of every professional revolutionary. What was necessary was to take prison, exile, and even hard labor, and change them from a means for the repression of the revolution, which is what they were in the hands of the enemy, into a weapon to be used in our struggle against that enemy. This was difficult, but we did achieve it in many instances—not without struggle, not without losses, not without suffering, but we achieved it nonetheless.

Even the prison administrations learned how to divine intuitively whether it was a "casual" guest or an experienced prisoner, a professional revolutionary, who had fallen into their clutches. In each individual case the administration would make the appropriate "arrangement."

Having landed in prison for the second time, I felt myself "at home." I even recalled the contemptuous proverb I had heard in the country: "To some it's a prison, but to him it's home." This proverb referred to the "destitute paupers," the "homeless vagabonds," with nowhere to go and nothing to lose.

Just two years earlier that saying would have really injured my self-respect. But now I entered the prison with my head held high, with a proud awareness of the fact that I was a prisoner of the autocracy only temporarily, a prisoner captured from the advanced detachment of an attacking army, one that had not yet begun to deploy its reserves and put them into combat. The enemy is still powerful, but he feels that his end is near. He despises us, but he fears us; he has no confidence in the triumph of his cause.

When the heavy door of my cell slammed shut behind me, it did not destroy my will, it did not cut me off from my friends and comrades, who were carrying on the struggle with our foe. I still remained with them, reliving all the ups and downs of their struggle in my mind, gladdened by their successes, saddened by their failures. . . .

Having crossed the threshold of the prison, I began to prepare myself for a long sojourn there. I had plenty of grounds for that assumption.

In the turmoil of the revolutionary struggle, in the process of coping with the long, exhausting workday, there is no time to work on yourself, no time to fill the gaps in your theoretical knowledge. Now, however, a great opportunity stood before me. I sketched out a study plan in my head; huge quantities of wisdom-filled books rushed by in my mind, books that I would master with great delight and that would vastly expand the limits of my horizons. They would teach me to grasp all the mysteries of life; they would provide support and a broad foundation to my sacred socialist goals and my dreams about the reconstruction of human existence; they would arm me with arguments for use in the struggle with my opponents and enemies. And when the foe released me from the captivity of prison, I would bring my knowledge to those who dwelt in the capitalist inferno and were forced to endure the agonizing chains of a humiliating slavery. I would open their eyes and inflame their hearts with hatred for their oppressors; I would show them the path and the means leading to their emancipation.

Such were my thoughts, such were my dreams, while I dwelt in my prison cell.

The cell was large, gloomy, and uncomfortable, with cold, thick walls; it was filled with a foul human odor and was populated by innumerable bedbugs, those fellow travelers of the tsarist autocracy, who turned people's lives into an agonizing torture.

Before my arrival, the cell had evidently held some fifteen or twenty convicts, but by now there had been orders to turn it into an "isolation cell," in order to tie down an "important" political criminal. Up to now, "politicals" had only rarely been "guests" between these walls.

After a sleepless bedbug-ridden night, I demanded that the cell be cleaned up and the bedbugs eliminated. The deputy warden responded to my call very sternly:

"This is a prison, not a hotel."

"In that case I'm going to bang, smash the glass, and break the stools!"

"Then we'll put you in a straitjacket."

"Just try it!"

The foppish deputy turned on his heels, brandished his sword angrily, and left my cell. An hour later two guards arrived carrying enormous, steaming kettles and began to pour boiling water over my plank bed.

Thereafter, I would carry out this kind of "disinfection" procedure by myself, about twice a week.

About three days after my arrest and the extermination of the bedbugs, I slept soundly, without awakening, through the day and the night—I was so exhausted and worn down. My prison life gradually began to enter the usual routine.

The food in the prison was bad, but my comrades soon began to take care of me. Someone began to bring me very good dinners. They also provided me with money, and, of particular importance to my prison life, they brought me interesting and useful books.

This kind of organized comradely assistance always had a cheering effect on me and on workers in general. It quickly extended an invisible thread between freedom and confinement. Hence a person didn't feel himself isolated, abandoned, superfluous; instead, one's desire to act, to struggle, to hate one's enemies grew stronger.

Here, in prison, one could feel with special acuteness the difference between our class origins and those of our comrades in struggle—the intelligentsia. Rare indeed were the occasions when a member of the intelligentsia completely broke his ties with his bourgeois or petty-bourgeois family, burned all his bridges, completely and unequivocally came over to the point of view of the working class, and struggled in its ranks with total dedication, without looking back at his own past. What usually happened was that even after expelling the recalcitrant child from the family hearth, the kind-hearted relatives would soften, be filled with pity for the imprisoned martyr, and manifest more and more concern for him. They would visit him in prison, provide him with necessities, petition the authorities, request that his situation be mollified, and so on.

There were some who acted this way without any selfish motives, not hoping for any future advantage. But the large majority of them were strengthening their kinship bonds and secretly cherished the hope of returning their errant child to the path of family virtue and making him tread in their footsteps.

The worker's story is very different: he has no bonds, he has no "hearth," and he has no connections in the camp of his oppressors. And if a worker who has a family of his own happens to be arrested, then not only will his family be unable to help him, it will fall into dire need itself.

This is why for the worker a comradely milieu, an organization, and eventually a party become his family home and hearth, and his comrades in struggle take the place of his brothers, sisters, father, and mother. And it is then that the distinctions between him and those who came from another class but have burned all their bridges behind them are effaced.

One day I was summoned to the prison office to see a visitor. This call both surprised and cheered me: surprised me because I had no relatives in the area, and pleased me because I was anxious to receive any news at all from the outside and to see live human beings.

I was led to the office through the dark, damp, arched prison corridors. There I saw, seated at the table, a young girl who looked only slightly familiar to me. When I stood close to her, however, I recognized Faina Ivanovna Rykova (the sister of A. I. Rykov[1]). We both rejoiced and rushed to embrace each other. She managed to whisper to me that she was pretending to be my fiancée, and we began to conduct ourselves accordingly. However, we were immediately pulled apart and seated at opposite sides of the table, while the deputy warden sat between us.

At the time I did not know F. I. Rykova very well. I had met her only a couple of times, at Auntie's. But this in no way prevented us from having a free and easy conversation; there were many points of contact between us. Finally the deputy warden seemed tired of listening to us; he got up from his seat several times and then disappeared somewhere, leaving us alone together. Thus Faina Ivanovna was able to tell me about the unfortunate consequences of the strike, the attendant arrests and dismissals of comrades. She also told me that the latest issue of *The Workers' Newspaper* had appeared. She asked what books I wanted and whether or not I needed anything else. The visit ended and we took leave of each other.

When I returned to my cell I felt very happy. I was infinitely moved and touched by the concern for me displayed by my comrades who lived in freedom. It was pleasant to think that they held me in such esteem, thought about me, and cared about me. It meant that my life on this earth was not useless!

I would sit at my books all day long; I read a great deal and with great pleasure. Unhappily, I had lost so much time in the past, time when circumstances had derailed me and deprived me of the opportunity to read. Now I was provided with enough books to last me a whole year! The selection had not been made very systematically, but that really didn't matter; I wanted to know everything there was that could aid the cause of the revolution, whether directly or indirectly. And the selection did have a definite character. I recall that my collection included Lippert's *History of Primitive Culture*, Kliuchevsky's lectures on Russian history, Timiriazev's *Popular Exposition of Darwin's Theory*, Zheleznov's *Political Economy*, and V. Ilin's *The Development of Capitalism in Russia*.[2] At that time, I still didn't know that Ilin was the pseudonym of Lenin. Among works of fiction, I recall Erckmann-Chatrian's *The Peasant*.[3]

One night, some two weeks after my incarceration, I heard a suspicious rustling sound in the neighboring cell. I listened carefully. It seemed as if a giant rat was scraping away and gnawing at a rotten brick behind the wall. I knocked, and was answered in turn by a tapping noise. Using the prison alphabet, I tried to tap out the word "Who?" as well as my last name. . . . There was no reply. "It's probably a common criminal," I thought, and I resumed my reading. After a short interval the rustling sound resumed, followed by some very quiet, short taps, as if a woodpecker was knocking on dry wood with its beak. I paid no attention, but continued to read, and I soon stopped noticing altogether the mysterious sounds from the other side of the wall.

But then, completely unexpectedly, I heard a sort of compressed, restrained voice close by. I gave a start, pricked up my ears, and began to look around the cell. I saw nothing suspicious. Everything was in its proper place. . . .

"Is it possible I've begun to hallucinate?"

Recalling the stories of comrades who had been pursued by hallucinations while in solitary confinement, I grew frightened. Suddenly, I heard the voice again, and I distinctly heard it call me by name. . . . There was no doubt that this was a living, human voice, but such a subdued and inaudible voice as comes from a person who is covered by a mountain of pillows or a stack of hay.

"Senka, what the devil! Climb under the bed!"—the voice is now completely clear, and is coming from somewhere below me.

I throw myself under the bed. There are pieces of lime, plaster, on the floor, and a big hole in the wall. I lie down on the floor and place my ear against it.

"It's me, Sisenkov. I'm serving a three-month prison term. . . ."

Our joy was indescribable. Endless conversation poured out. . . . Sisenkov gave me heaps of news and spoke at particularly great length and in great detail of his own case.

I had known Sisenkov almost from the very first day of my sojourn in Saratov. He was a blue-eyed, jolly fellow, still very young, who loved to put on airs of darkness and mystery. He was brave, daring, bold, and unreasonable. He was always rushing about with some "frightening" terrorist plans, of which barely a single one was ever carried out. We weren't that easy to astound with boldness and daring, and his terrorist plans always served as the object of merry amusement and witticisms among us. Sisenkov was a metal-fitter by trade and an anarchist by conviction. Why he was an anarchist he could not explain very clearly himself.

"I'll never be an SD because they are cowards: they don't recognize the value of terror," he would say when he came to our headquarters.

"In that case, why aren't you an SR?" Morozov would torment him.

"The SRs are cowards too: they like to use others to kill ministers, but they never touch the smaller reptiles. We must exterminate all the bosses, anyone who sits on the worker's neck!"

As a matter of principle, Sisenkov would join no organization, for, as he saw it, all organizations destroy your free will and tie down your initiative. But he would gladly participate in the distribution of any kind of literature—be it SD, SR, or even Tolstoyan.

He had worked in a municipal hospital as a handyman in charge of repairs. The "case" for which he was serving time in prison consisted of the following.

While working at the hospital, he had begun to disseminate illegal literature among the hospital workers and staff. This was soon reported to the senior physician. This zealous administrator—a petty tyrant and a big ruffian who liked to dub his subordinates with the names of domestic animals such as donkey, cow, and pig—decided to get even with the impertinent worker. He summoned Sisenkov to his office, where lines of patients were waiting to be seen, began to scour him with some choice vulgar obscenities, and ordered him to "get out of his sight."

Sisenkov did not respond to this incredible outrage by "exterminating the reptile," as was required by his theory, but he did pull himself together and land a most powerful blow smack on the face of the "reptile-physician." The terrified administrator covered his head with his hands and, with an agility not often found in men of his rank and calling, dived under a table and let out an incredible scream.

"So then they came running, seized me, took me off and had me arrested," Sisenkov said very hurriedly, carried away with his words.

However, Sisenkov's "case" soon took a completely new turn: he was charged with assault and battery on a physician during the performance of his official duties. And had it not been for the intervention of local liberal public opinion, then, according to law, the court would have had to "stick" him with three years in prison, and, after his release, a permanent entry in his passport describing him as politically dangerous. Because this zealous administrator—the doctor—enjoyed a terrible reputation in local liberal society, the best lawyer in town agreed to take on Sisenkov's defense.

At the trial Sisenkov presented himself as an enlightened liberal, one who taught workers how to read and write and, for practice, would give them the official publications of the "Committee for Diffusion of Literacy" to read.[4] And the obscurantist senior physician was presented as having placed all kinds of obstacles before these worthy efforts on the part of the government.

As a result of the pleadings, Sisenkov managed to get off with only a three-month prison sentence.

Our "telephone" conversations often had to be delayed. The authorities were bound to notice what was happening. Our "connection" was soon revealed; a guard arrived with a hammer and two wooden plugs and blocked up the hole from both sides.

I was summoned to the prison office for interrogation. My interrogator was Captain Semiganovsky, whom I already knew from the numerous times he had searched me on the outside. He was an enormous man with the appearance of a Turk, rather handsome, a courageous old veteran, a careerist—dull and self-satisfied. Instead of Semiganovsky, we called him Semi*pogan*sky.[5] He was very friendly during the interrogation and he put into motion the usual, hackneyed gendarme tricks: he offered me tea and cigarettes and asked me if everything was all right for me in prison.

I came close to suggesting that he serve a little time himself, but I didn't wish to enter into amicable banter with him so I held back.

The questions that he asked me had already been written down on a piece of paper. He was not even capable of formulating them properly. By now I no longer remember whether I absolutely refused to testify or whether I responded to his questions very stingily, but our "conversation" did not go on very long. He came close to trying to break my resistance by resorting to threats, promising to send me some kind of scorpions. I then declared that in that case I would no longer talk with him, and he could go ahead and do what he pleased. On this note we parted company.

Later, this dull-witted gendarme still managed to have a successful career, even attaining the rank of general, I believe. During the Revolution of 1905 his name would flare up in the newspapers, where he appeared in the capacity of one of the most savage butchers of the revolution. The finale of this "brilliant" life went like this: after a "successful" raid on a certain conspiratorial apartment, the gendarme was "fortunate" enough to capture an entire storehouse of bombs, after which the bombs were dis-

armed, rendered harmless, either by him personally or by someone else in his presence. As a result of a careless, or perhaps even
a clumsy gesture, one of the bombs exploded, and this worthy
man ceased to burden the face of the earth.

The large, lattice-shaped window of my cell looked out on a
thick little garden, overgrown with poplars and limes, so that the
cell remained in semidarkness all day long. But on the other
hand, when I opened the window the green freshness of the fragrant trees wafted through the air, the chirping of the grasshoppers burst into the cell, and in the nighttime I could hear the
singing of the crickets. Sometimes in the evening I would sit on
the windowsill and, without turning on the light in my cell, peer
into the thick darkness of the calm summer's night and let myself
be transported in my imagination far beyond the high, thick walls
of the prison out to the vast green fields, sparkling in the rays of
the sun, and to the meadows, with their fragrant smell of clover
and chamomile, near the village I had abandoned so long ago. I
seemed to hear the songs of the skylarks, and the carefree sounds
of the accordian playing "Shall I Go Down to the Rivulet?" and
the clear voices of the village lads and lasses as they sang. . . .

Never—neither before nor since—have I served my time in
prison with such a feeling of well-being and, with respect to my
self-education, so fruitfully, as I did then.

However, I was not fated to relish my peaceful prison life for
very long. One fine evening, when the daily routine of prison life
had come to a halt, a guard came to my cell and ordered me to
gather my belongings. . . . Needless to say I was overjoyed at the
thought that I would at last be free once more, that I would be
with my friends and comrades again; nevertheless, I regretted
that I would not be able to complete the program of self-
education I had planned for myself.

35
Unemployed

Aᴼᴛᴇʀ ᴛʜᴇ ᴀʀʀᴇsᴛs it was impossible for me and my comrades to find employment in local factories, or even in small artisanal workshops. The gendarmes had advised employers not to hire "unreliables," and their advice was followed to the letter. No matter how many times we knocked on the factory doors, no matter how much we argued with the foremen or stood in the thresholds of the little workshops, we invariably came up against the connivance of the owners and the police.

Our material situation was deteriorating with each passing day. For a while we were able to survive on the miserable remnants of our wages from our last jobs, but soon these too were exhausted.

Hunger and want drew us together, and we huddled against one another like a pack of hungry wolves. In the fall, when there were plenty of vegetables in the market, life was still tolerable. On rare occasions one of us would come up with a 20-kopeck piece and we would buy a big watermelon for seven or eight kopecks, a couple of dozen tomatoes, and a loaf of coarse brown bread at one and a half or two kopecks a pound and eat our fill, but after that kind of food we'd soon be ready to eat again.

Our communal meals were exceptionally merry events. We would laugh, tell jokes at our own expense, inveigh against our worst enemies—the gendarmes—and curse the entire capitalist order.

The "scourge" of our consumers' cooperative was Panteleimon Ivanovich Denisov, or, more simply, Ponty. All of us possessed excellent appetites, which provided abundant material for The Artist's witticisms. He would often turn to V. A. Fominykh, The Chemist, with a written request that he prepare an appetite-reducing potion for our artel. Such a potion, he believed, would significantly relieve the pain of our lives during our unemployment.

But Ponty's appetite could not even be compared to ours: he ate enough for three men. Later, when I had the occasion to dine with him during better times, he would usually order two whole meals for himself. The waitress would set three places, bring a third chair to the table, and keep glancing at the door to see if our companion was coming. We would finish the meal, but still no sign of our third party.

However, Ponty's appearance was not as imposing as his appetite. True, he was broad-shouldered, lean, and, in general, powerfully hewn, but because he was only a little taller than average and was so skinny, The Artist used to call him one of the Pharaoh's lean kine. Ponty had an enormous, almost reddish head of hair and dreamy blue eyes. By turn of character he was self-possessed, calm, circumspect, and—when it came to everyday matters—practical even down to the smallest details. Now and then his practical bent would turn into stinginess. At the same time, he was also a sentimental type. He loved to sing old, traditional Russian songs; he had a strong but soft tenor voice. He adored nature, was captivated by adventure stories, and was able to write excellent, extremely sensitive proclamations and articles for *The Workers' Newspaper*.

Unfortunately, we have been unable to preserve any of his writings, except for a speech he delivered at a trial, which was published in *Iskra*.[1]

Ponty's proclamations, which were imbued with a passionate love for the oppressed and a burning hatred for the oppressors, made an enormous impression on us. They were veritable prose poems. And he really didn't write, he "created." Sometimes he would read and reread them aloud to one of us or to all of us together, then correct them, add something new, and then rewrite them yet another time.

Ponty had another valuable quality, one which none of us possessed at the time and which all of us envied: he was capable of speaking fluently for a good half hour before a large gathering of people whom he barely knew or didn't know at all. He would always speak and debate self-confidently, with aplomb, even about things he didn't know or knew very slightly. He considered himself infallible and was never eager to acknowledge his errors.

Later, when I had experienced more revolutionary practice, I was convinced that this was characteristic of a large number of orators.

We usually gathered at the apartment of S. P. Shepelev. He was about six years older than us; he had a wife and two small children. He too was unemployed, and life was harder for him, of course, than for the bachelors. Yet he never fell into despair. On the contrary, he was an incorrigible optimist. He was always excited about some plan or project: he would dream up some new way to store our illegal literature or to print proclamations; he would invent a neatly proportioned gun that was easy to conceal from the police; he would devise a new scheme for making bombs that were easy to carry in one's bosom. But inasmuch as we needed neither bombs nor guns at that time, and because he himself was a Social Democrat, an enemy of terror by conviction, he liked to inveigh against the SRs for their lack of skill in the use of terror.

"If I were an SR," he would say, shaking his fists, "I would have long since killed not only the tsar, but all his ministers and all the grand dukes as well."

"Yeah, you're such a well-known hard-hearted monster," Mephistopheles would dampen Shepelev's ardor, "you probably wouldn't leave anyone alive to continue the human race."

Mephistopheles—Morozov—was a skeptic by nature: he had doubts about everything and subjected everything to criticism. In our discussions, when someone let himself get carried too high "into the clouds," Morozov would bring everything back down to earth, to reality.

"You know, boys, we've got to come up with an idea, otherwise we'll all die of hunger," Shepelev would say after one of our meager meals.

"We've got to get work," Ponty remarks, gloomily but authoritatively.

"Work! That's easy enough to say! But who is going to hire you?" Mephistopheles retorts.

"But what is work on the scale of eternity? Indeed, what is our life itself? . . . A mirage, a smoldering . . . ," The Artist philosophizes.

"A man cannot live by bread alone," Mephistopheles echoes approvingly.

"True enough. . . . But don't imagine that it was Christ who said that. It was said by the great Greek sages well before him, only they used different words," The Artist—who considers himself an expert on antiquity—continues. "Human passions and sentiments are nothing more than our subjective experiences. Love, hunger, cold—they are nothing but appearances."

"Well, I really don't know who said that, but I do know that those ancient words of wisdom are preached by our priests from the altar on every holiday," Mephistopheles remarks bitingly.

"And you don't believe them? . . . All right then, here's an example: when you go to the baths and you undress in the dressing room, then you feel cold there, but when you come out of the hot bathhouse and go back into the very same dressing room, then it seems hot to you. Isn't that a fact? And here's another example: when you are ill, honey tastes bitter, but when you are healthy, it tastes sweet. Right?"

"Boys, it sure would be nice to eat a good morsel of honey right now, so grainy and fragrant. . . . Oh, to spread it on a hunk of bread, and drink some tea with it! . . ." Mephistopheles fantasizes.

"But you just finished eating, you glutton!"

"There's always room for a good morsel. Do you remember the time the governor pushed his way into the church where there were so many people? . . . Besides, we didn't eat anything sweet today. . . ."

"Yesterday I was reading Schopenhauer," says The Artist. "He's a good philosopher. There's only one thing I can't understand— how is it possible for someone to suffer from too much satisfaction?"[2]

"You shouldn't read him. With your appetite, you couldn't possibly get it! For you, Nietzsche makes more sense. Place yourself beyond good and evil. Just push the man who is down out of your way and follow your own instincts."[3]

"Well, well, now haven't they begun to philosophize! This really passes all understanding. And where are we supposed to get money for tomorrow's meals? No one has even thought about that!" Shepelev remarks.

"God provides the day, God will also provide the food!"

"All joking aside, boys, let's try to think of something. It would be good if we could get a hold of some money from some liberal, so we could use it to rent a good plot of land where we could grow watermelons, pumpkins, cucumbers, and tomatoes! . . . There'd be enough for everyone, and even enough left over to sell," Shepelev says dreamily.

"Your project, dear Horatio, is sublime.[4] Except that melons, if I'm not mistaken, do not grow in the winter, whereas we, in all probability, will want to eat tomorrow."

"I'm talking about next year. As for tomorrow, I still think we'll get hold of half a ruble from someone or other. If worst comes to worst, I'll bring a nicely carved box to the market—a good one just came out, it took me three days to finish. It sure would be a pity to have to sell it!"

"Praise it all you want—we still won't be able to buy anything!"

"If we could only get about a hundred rubles from someone! Then we could open our own workshop. We would all have work. We could get orders from the factories. And we could probably get orders for carpentry work from the liberals in the zemstvo, too.[5] We could make them desks, tables, and blackboards for the classrooms. . . . They aren't indifferent about who they give work to. I even believe they'd prefer to give work to conscious workers like us," Shepelev continues.

"Oh sure, sure, that's it—now all we have to do is take care of some mere trifles. Like say, money," Mephistopheles sighs.

"I believe the SRs would even give us the money for that kind of undertaking. They are rich people. And they are believers in associations. Semën Ivanych could go to them," Shepelev says, nodding in my direction. "Bait the hook. Just drop the word when you talk with them. An 'artel,' as they say, we'd like to organize an artel. . . ."

Shepelev repeated his idea about opening our own joiner's workshop more and more frequently and insistently. Occasionally he would switch from vague, general desires to concrete calculations: how many tools we'd need and of what quality, how much it would cost, what kind of material we'd buy and where we'd buy it, and so on. This notion did not seem completely unrealistic to the others, but we always ran up against the very same obstacle— money.

Shepelev would grow angry: "Damn it—should we start doing it or should we rob somebody?!"

When we have exhausted all possible and impossible themes for discussion, we disperse. Some go to the homes of friends, others to their own. Not infrequently, of an evening, the whole noisy gang heads for Auntie's. We lay waste to the table and drink endless quantities of tea. From time to time the generous hostess adds some butter and some bread loaves and bread rings, while she laughingly encourages us to indulge our huge appetites.

Auntie has important connections in Petersburg, Moscow, and in the south of Russia. Everyone who travels to or through Saratov considers it his duty to visit the "salon." There the latest political news is gathered, malicious anecdotes about tsarist satraps are recounted, and the latest proclamations from the central leadership or the latest issues of *Iskra* or *Zarya* are passed from hand to hand.[6] Occasionally a letter appears there from some "emboldened" liberal.

I still recall the enormous pleasure we received from the reading of Amfiteatrov's serialized story "Messrs. Obmanov," which was printed in the newspaper *Russia*, and for which the paper was closed down and the editor and the author were exiled to the north, charged with having insulted the tsar and his entire family tree.[7] That issue of the paper was brought to Auntie by an acquaintance from Piter. Some liberals had advanced a great deal of money to assure that it was read. We made many copies of the story on our hectograph; it enjoyed great success among the workers.

Prison and unemployment were our scourges, but they still made important contributions to our revolutionary self-education. When you work an eleven- or twelve-hour day at a factory, you can't accomplish much. The indomitable fatigue, the preoccupation with food and sleep would drive away all our thoughts.

I remember one occasion when I was summoned to a meeting that was attended by five or six people. We spoke about the political struggle and about agitation. Until about 10 P.M. I still held firm and managed to understand some of the things that were being said in the circle. But once it was past ten, I was literally falling off my feet. I tried to keep myself awake: I walked around the room, I pinched myself, I drank strong tea—but all in vain. No sooner would I lean against anything solid, than I immediately fell asleep. So I left the meeting without even waiting for it to end.

I remember yet another occasion: one of my intelligentsia comrades invited me to go to the opera after work. (I was working at the steel mill at the time.) I agreed, particularly since I had yet to attend an opera in my life. *A Bride for the Tsar* was playing. I was able to listen to the first act, not so much with interest as with curiosity, but by the end of the second I could no longer resist, and I fell into such a deep sleep that my comrades, who were sitting in the loge with me, had to poke at me rather harshly.

Now the situation was entirely different. We had no idea what to do with our free time. Those in our group who had never developed a passion for intellectual pastimes suffered the most from the inactivity. In the winter and fall some of us attended the Maleev evening courses.[8] These courses were organized by a liberal educator, and they were very jealously guarded from anything that was even remotely suggestive of politics. The classes included mathematics, physics, chemistry, psychology, and other subjects considered "useful for the bourgeoisie." There were also lectures on mnemonics, which produced all kinds of sarcasms and witticisms in our group. We even nicknamed our comrade Mikhail Karev—a joiner who was a great idolizer of the Maleev courses—"The Mnemonic."

Occasionally we managed to attend some discussions that were sanctioned by the authorities. These meetings were organized by different groups of liberal social reformers under the auspices of various legally authorized institutions that were not very accessible to our working-class brothers. The speakers in these societies would sometimes include legal Marxists such as P. P. Maslov (on the agrarian question) or V. S. Golubev (giving the statistical results of some investigation).[9] There were also presentations by representatives of the populists: Kocharovsky (on the Russian land commune), Rakitnikov, and others.[10]

We got very little that was useful from the speeches. As a rule, they were long, boring, and hard to follow. They were also studded with "scholarly" words—"differentiation," "intensification," and so on.

I have a clearer memory of a report delivered by some literary scholar about a newly published collection of stories by Leonid

Andreev, still a beginning writer at the time; for some reason, special attention was devoted to a story called "The Story of Sergey Petrovich."[11] It is the story of a rather unattractive, shy young student, a reader of Nietzsche, who wanted to be strong, daring, and ruthless. But when he came up against real life he became timid, frightened, and spineless. Finally he ended his life by suicide, with Nietzsche's aphorism on his lips: "Know then this, that if your life has been a failure, your death shall be a success!"[12]

Here is how we interpreted this symbolic story: Sergey Petrovich represents the average, ordinary person of our times, who is crushed by the yoke of the existing political order, which prevents him from living. In our times, it is the daring, strong personalities who are successful, people who seize their positions in life by force. The era of people like Sergey Petrovich will come only when the turbulent waves of the revolutionary storm will have rolled away and life will have entered the peaceful shore. That is how it happened in France, at the time of the Great Revolution. There, the rule of people of ordinary abilities—that is, of the Sergey Petrovichs—came only when the Marats, Dantons, Robespierres, and Saint-Justs had exited from the historical stage.[13] We spoke warmly of Sergey Petrovich, and we looked forward to the days that would follow the storm with eager anticipation and passionate longing.

It was rather obvious that our liberal men of honor were quite frightened of these storms, for the revolution had barely arrived and they were already looking forward to Thermidor.[14] It goes without saying that for the dull-witted Sergey Petrovichs, workers and peasants were not even part of their field of vision.

Next we got to attend a reading and analysis of an article by N. Berdiaev, "The Struggle for Idealism," published in the 1901 volume of the journal *God's World*.[15] This was apparently a circle of SR or SR-oriented youths. I am judging by the fact that I had met many of them in the company of prominent SRs, and some of them even referred to themselves openly as Socialist Revolutionaries. We had lots of trouble understanding the article, for it was written in an incomprehensible, abstract language, embellished with a multitude of foreign words, such as we rarely encountered in ordinary speech. The article repeatedly employed such words as, for example, "positivism," "eudaemonism," "naturalism," and the like.

But there was one thing that was clear to us—that the author was criticizing Marxism. He was criticizing it gently, cautiously, under the guise of someone who cares for Marxism and is favorably disposed toward it, but he was criticizing it nonetheless. True, the article seduced us in that Berdiaev was constantly attacking the bourgeois spirit, narrow-mindedness, and philistine vulgarity, while summoning the reader toward some higher ideals and goals. But occasionally a malicious, anti-Marxist phrase would escape him: that Marxism blindly adhered to the doctrine of social catastrophe, that Lassalle's view of the world was broader and deeper than Marx's, that Bernstein had something new and important to say, and so on and so forth.[16] When the discussion began, people again directed their comments against the "narrowness" of the Marxist view of the world. But when someone remarked that Berdiaev's idealism smacked of mysticism and reaction, people attacked the doubter and began to accuse him of not having understood the article and of oversimplification. This was the worst accusation imaginable in a milieu with pretentions to being the true bearer of progress.

The only part of Berdiaev's article that met with general disapproval was the place where he condemned the call to "give one's life for the sake of one's comrades." But even here he had defenders, who explained that Berdiaev had no objection to sacrificing one's body for others, just one's soul. This was followed by arguments about the moral ideal, about the value of life, about the perfectibility of the human spirit, which is foreign to any bourgeois values, about the struggle for art and for eternal beauty, not created by human hands, a beauty that Marxism "debases and profanes with its narrow focus on practice, materialism, and bourgeois values."

"The vulgarization of the spirit is the worst of all moral crimes," thundered a young student named Sokolov, quoting Berdiaev almost verbatim. "Social utilitarianism, which encroaches upon Faustian aspirations and destroys the human spirit, is a reactionary tendency in human thought."

It was evident that the ubiquitous and omniscient Kholodov was present at this circle meeting in the capacity of consultant. Kholodov was a somewhat older man with a big, spade-shaped beard and a leonine mane, thrown back on his head. From a distance he resembled the famous theoretician of populism, N. K.

Mikhailovsky.[17] Apparently Kholodov himself placed great value on that resemblance: he even imitated the manner in which Mikhailovsky proudly threw back his head. Kholodov had a stentorian, thunderous voice, and he was given to long fits of self-satisfied laughter.

One had only to hear his laugh to conclude that this was a man who possessed an enormous appetite and a splendid digestion, a man whose metabolism would satisfy the strictest requirements of the most captious physiologist. And should the theory of eugenics ever start to be applied in our country, then he'd surely be one of the first to be used for breeding.

Kholodov threw back his mane with a bold, theatrical gesture and, interrupting the disconcerted young student, began to speak:

"This article, gentlemen, like the sound of a tocsin ringing in the night, summons us to struggle with that lifeless theory, so deadly to the human intellect and to the desire for creativity, for reaching upward"—here Kholodov raised his hand toward the ceiling, while his listeners involuntarily turned their eyes in the same direction—"with that theory of quietism that calls itself Marxism!

"No," he continued, "our sense of the sublime and the magnificent, our creative intuition, whose inspiration comes upon us from unearthly sources—we shall not permit these to be destroyed. Suppose that only the world of appearances were accessible to us. Wouldn't that destroy the value, the immediacy of our experiences? We shall not permit those spoilers of the human race to use their syllogism to destroy the joy of the joyful, the love of the loving. We shall not permit them, through the deadly analysis of cold reason, to deprive humanity of life's joys, to drag humanity down to the level of a soulless, weak-willed creature, thrown about by the elements, like a grain of sand, in the world's eternal and infinite expanse. The eternal depths of the starry skies will always beckon to us with their mysteries. The vault of heaven will always encircle us with its dense grandeur, and the silent mass of the mountaintops will catch the eye of mortals, whose lives, in the long run, are but an instant! . . ."

Kholodov possessed an amazing capacity to talk about any subject at any time, and always with great inspiration. His voice would thunder, like the trombone of a large orchestra, the one that Alexander III, our monarch of blessed memory, liked to practice on in his leisure hours.[18] Once he had begun to talk, it was rare that Kholodov could stop talking in a timely manner, a circumstance that almost always ruined the impression made by his speech. And that is what happened in this case as well. His audience grew so weary that all it took was the slightest outside intervention for everyone to stop listening to the inspired orator.

It was The Artist who, noisily addressing himself to the leader of the circle, instead of saying, "Permit me to speak," hurriedly pronounced the words: "Permit me to express myself."

An infectious, youthful laughter resounded in the room. Kholodov stopped speaking, looked at the people all around him, waved his arms with dissatisfaction, and sat down.

The Artist began to speak. The audience knew him and expected him to come up with some amusing routine:

"Well, Kholodov has certainly dwelt at length on the unfading beauty of the mountaintops, which the evil Marxist intriguers want to destroy. But, dear gentlemen, what about those people who have never seen any beautiful mountains above their bell towers and their factory chimneys, and who will never see such mountains for the rest of their lives?! Does it follow that we Marxists are planning to take away their beauty as well?"

The room grew noisy. Some of the people liked The Artist's playful act and laughed with pleasure; others were indignant, taking exception to the way he had "debased" or "vulgarized" such an elevated discussion. . . . So it was that we dispersed, animatedly discussing not so much Berdiaev's article as The Artist's prank.

Sometimes we would gather together with some young SD sympathizers at one of our apartments, where we'd discuss and debate every conceivable question. We had long understood that economics lay at the foundation of everything else, for it was existence that determined consciousness. This had always been repeated to us by our propagandist-mentors. Just what it meant we grasped only very dimly, but the practice of life and the experience of struggle repeatedly confirmed this axiom of Marxism to us. It is therefore only natural that our self-education always began with the study of economic questions.

At that time we were hearing a good deal about the Utopian socialists—Robert Owen, Fourier, Louis Blanc, and others—

and some of us had even read something about them.[19] We had grasped with great clarity the fundamental truth that inspiration and "intuitive" understanding were inadequate to the task of remaking the capitalist world, the site of our penal servitude. It was also in the light of these judgments that we approached our quarrel with the Socialist Revolutionaries.

The lone heroes, the creators of disembodied ideas who wished to take command of the ignorant, senseless crowd, failed to captivate us with their feats. We rejected the kind of history that leaps from the person of one monarch or hero to the next; we wished both to learn and to make the history of the mass movement.

I still recall the delight and admiration with which we read and discussed Plekhanov's letter to the editor of the journal *Russian Thought*, V. Goltsev, on the role of the individual in history.[20] We still had only a weak grasp of philosophical questions, but we felt instinctively that the SR "direction," as we would now say, contained much that was obscure, mysterious, and "subjective." I remember one occasion when we read aloud an article by Viktor Chernov that appeared in a collection dedicated to N. K. Mikhailovsky called *On Honorable Duty*; the article was entitled "The Worker and Peasant as Economic Categories" and was written with the boldness of expression that characterized that writer.[21] In it he tried to demonstrate that there was no essential difference between the peasant and the worker. Both were subjected to exploitation, both lived by their labor, both were "poor"; hence they constituted a single, oppressed class.

It was hard for us to combat Chernov, but it is always better to argue with a living opponent than with a dead book. The SR sympathizers spoke out in defense of his point of view, and attempted to prove that there was no difference between the peasant and the worker and that each was equally receptive to socialist ideas.

They usually invoked what was then a very widely used argument against us:

"Take the tailor," they would say, "who has only his needle and his thimble; is he too nothing but a lousy bourgeois, as you see it?"

To this we boldly replied:

"Yes, a petty bourgeois."

"But doesn't he earn less than the salary of a good worker?"

"That doesn't prove a thing. The worker doesn't own any implements of production, whereas your tailor does." [22]

A second example that the Socialist Revolutionaries would use against us was the factory director:

"According to you, by Marxist standards," they would say, "it follows that the director of some giant factory who earns 15,000 rubles a year is a proletarian too, since he lives from the sale of his own labor power, right? And the poor tailor is a bourgeois?"

This example was harder for us to handle. Of course we did not hesitate to include the director among the bourgeoisie. But beyond that, we had to prove and substantiate our point by using economic categories. And this is where endless scholastic debates would begin. It was usually one of our intelligentsia—a Fominykh or a Fofanov—who, having read their Marx and having learned how to approach a question dialectically, extricated us from this embarrassing situation.

In sum, our SR opponents were incapable of grasping the difference between a "poor" person and a worker-proletarian.

In our circles, as I mentioned earlier, there were often arguments between "Economists" and *Iskra*-ites—were workers capable of coming to the idea of socialism on their own or not? These debates continued until the appearance of Lenin's booklet *What Is to Be Done?* [23] The Economists maintained that the working class itself, by dint of its economic situation alone, could arrive at a socialist consciousness. We too were ready to grant that possibility. But for that to happen, we argued, too many victims and too much time would be required. Marx's role had consisted in just this: that he generalized and formulated those notions that had been dimly fermenting in the workers' minds, and he thereby shortened the road to socialism.

In the summer, we often sailed along the Volga as a party of young people. At such times, our free, defiant, and melancholy youthful songs would carry across the entire width of Mother Volga, frightening the peaceful populace and attracting the attention of spies. And when evening fell we would light a campfire on the opposite shore, make some tea, eat something, sing more revolutionary songs, argue about the same old problems of Russia's cursed existence, devise plans for a better life, and thirst after struggle and daring exploits; we were ready to turn the whole world inside out.

36

The Socialist Revolutionaries

ALL THE GREAT WHALES of the SR Party were gathered in Saratov: some were exiled there by the gendarmes against their will, others picked the city "voluntarily," to be their abode after they had served time in prison or in Siberia. Most of these people were highly cultured and well educated, with a long tenure in the revolutionary movement; they were honorable people, with numerous connections to liberal zemstvo deputies, government functionaries, lawyers, and even merchants. Comfortably well-off materially, they possessed ample leisure time, and were able to devote themselves to their dreams, to art, and to science, while piously clinging to the "People's Will" tradition of heroes and martyrs and glowing beneath the halo of their glory.

By this time the Socialist Revolutionaries had already formed into a party, enjoyed the support of large cadres of leading activists, and had put together the basic features of their party program.[1]

Viktor Chernov, the leader of the SR Party, says in his recollections of the creation of that program:

We took as our fundamental principle a mass popular movement, based on the close, organic union of the urban industrial proletariat with the working peasantry of the villages. For the future we also proposed, among other things, the application of terror, using the methods of the People's Will, the one difference being that, for the People's Will, whether intentionally or unintentionally, terror was sufficient unto itself, whereas we conceived of it as the revolutionary "song" of soloists, whose presence was needed, so that the refrain would immediately be joined by the chorus, that is, by the mass movement, which, in mutual interaction with terror, would be regenerated as a true insurrection. The circles of the revolutionary intelligentsia would act, as it were, as the pioneers. The proletariat would be allotted the role of vanguard, the peasantry— the role of the basic, main army: "aroused, the cavalry moves swiftly; the infantry advances behind it and, with its weighty power, strengthens the cavalry's resolve."

Memoirs of a Socialist Revolutionary, Viktor Chernov.[2]

In short, Viktor Chernov pictured the SR Party of the future in the form of the episcopal chorus of a cathedral choir, with a "first singer"-archdeacon at its head, and he imagined the revolutionary struggle with autocracy in the form of Pushkin's "Battle of Poltava."

But what was good in poetry turned out to be unsuitable to a political program, and the SR Party would be subjected to the cruel punishment of extinction for this confusion of its purposes, while its "first singers" turned into bootlickers.[3] However, though all of this would become clear to the broad masses by the time of the October Revolution, it was far from being clear to them at this time. Only *Iskra*, under the guidance of Lenin, was able to unmask the treacherous bourgeois nature of the SRs, assessing the SR Party as a bourgeois-democratic faction.[4] But all of this happened later. Our own struggle with the SRs had to be waged at our own peril and our own risk.

It is true that at the time of my arrival in Saratov relations between the SRs and SDs there were completely neighborly. We were not especially close, and each side kept mainly to itself, but we all knew one another and from time to time we would meet somewhere on neutral ground. Typically the neutral ground took the form of an occasional evening party or an organized debate. These parties would usually include dancing (including folk dancing), the singing of revolutionary songs, joint radical speeches against the autocracy, and the recounting of antigovernment anecdotes. In the corners of the rooms there were sometimes heated clashes between Marxists and SRs.

I remember one time when a prominent Marxist named Ivanov arrived from Astrakhan.[5] A gathering was organized for him somewhere beyond the city limits, and the SRs were invited to join us. A fairly large contingent from each sect assembled there. Ivanov delivered a rather thorough report on the prospects of the revolution. The SRs were then invited to speak, but apparently the young SRs in attendance didn't dare to take the floor while their leaders were absent from the debate.

The meeting had begun in the "salon" of Serafima Georgievna Klitchoglu.[6] She was a beautiful young woman, quite modest, well educated, who had the same pleasant smile for everyone. She was the daughter of a rich, liberal member of educated society, and had been raised in a bourgeois family in the south. After graduating from a classical secondary school and completing the Bestuzhev courses, she enrolled in the Institute of Medicine,[7] which is where she became an SR. Then she was arrested and banished to Saratov, where she rented the wing of a small building on one of the city's quiet streets and lived together with her sister and a servant. Her home was tidy and cosy, always replete with flowers and sweets.

On the upper floor of the same building lived Anisya Aleksandrovna Chubarovskaya, our SD woman. She was stern and taciturn, but she was also a very sociable, unusually considerate and unselfish comrade, completely devoted to the revolution. We would often visit her apartment in the evening; we would light up the stove, put on a big teakettle, buy some bread loaves, eggs, or tea sausages, and sit there for hours on end, debating and discussing the burning political issues of the day until we were hoarse. In the summertime we would all go to the Volga together, where we went out in a rowboat, sang songs, and had ourselves a good time. We would return home exhausted, late at night.

At the home of Serafima Georgievna Klitchoglu we frequently encountered P. P. Kraft, a prominent SR who often belonged to their Central Committee.[8] He was a very proper, well-bred, and—as we saw it—gentle person. He was particularly polite and courteous with us. The conversations in Serafima Klitchoglu's "salon" dealt with general themes, subjects that did not provoke major disagreements. And if, occasionally, someone there chanced to touch on the subject of Marxism and Marxists, then the response was always favorable, or, at worst, jocular. The people there tried very hard to woo the workers—we could feel that ourselves.

Once one of the younger, more zealous SRs brought Kheruvimov, a worker whom we knew well, to Serafima Georgievna's apartment. Kheruvimov was a long-haired fellow with a gloomy, conspiratorial appearance; he liked to call himself an anarchist, since that was a title that didn't oblige him to belong to any organization, and it gave him the freedom to talk like a revolutionary without having to do anything.

Visibly delighted by his new connection with a "conscious"

worker, the ardent SR marched triumphantly in front of Kheruvimov and proclaimed to each of the guests:

"Allow me to present—the worker Kheruvimov."

When the happy SR brought him to us and introduced him in that way, we burst out laughing, to the great embarrassment of Kheruvimov.

At Klitchoglu's "salon" one could often encounter L. P. Bulanov.[9] He was a tall, thin man of some 45 years, completely gray, always gloomy, a man of few words, who seemed to have a permanent bellyache. He had recently finished serving time—either plain exile or exile with hard labor—in connection with the People's Will cases, and now he was busy creating direct links between the Socialist Revolutionary Party and the traditions of the People's Will. Bulanov spoke constantly of the heroic deeds of the members of the People's Will; he referred to them all by their first names, like good friends of whom he had only recently taken leave.

Another frequent visitor at Klitchoglu's was the then famous student of Russian landownership, Kocharovsky, author of a sensational book on the land commune that contained the theoretical foundations of the SR views on the commune.[10] A man of medium height, thin, with a fair beard, always elegantly dressed, agitated, supercilious, he gave the impression of a dandy.

Notwithstanding the SRs obvious interest in us, Kocharovsky never condescended to engage us in conversation. That task was undertaken by the hostess and by P. P. Kraft. The hostess, too, spoke very often and at great length of the members of the People's Will, but mainly about the women. She would speak about them with an unfailing pathos and with the kind of enthusiasm found among graduates of the women's institutes. She referred to Sofya Perovskaya as Sonya, and to Vera Figner simply as Vera. We used to say that Klitchoglu wished to play the role of Sofya Perovskaya.[11]

I recall one occasion when the discussion centered on the Decembrists.[12] Ponty Denisov was describing how, in his circle, some of the workers had asked him why the Decembrist uprising had ended in defeat.

"I explained to them that, when all was said and done, the Decembrists were still men of the landowning class, who feared to provoke a peasant upheaval," Ponty recounted.[13]

"Oh, no, no, no! That's all wrong! . . . How could you speak that way about the Decembrists!" Klitchoglu said reproachfully, shaking her head. "Why, they are sacred people! They sacrificed themselves for a great and pure idea, they offered up what was nearest and dearest to them on the altar of freedom, and you say that they were still men of their class!"

"So what! There's no contradiction. They still had to consider the question of whether or not the peasants should be freed, and with or without land. . . ."

"True, but those were just tactical questions, weren't they? The Decembrists weren't thinking about themselves, they simply feared that radical demands would drive away the progressive landlords, whom they hoped to convert to their views later on. There was no class interest involved in this," Kraft remarked very gently.

"But why did they have to hobnob with the landlords? They would have been better off arousing the peasants against the system of serfdom. Yes, and the soldiers would have followed them. . . . Why had Napoleon's troops won so easily wherever they went? Because they always freed the peasants from serfdom.[14] And these were facts that the Decembrists must have known," Ponty interjected sharply.

"You have to understand, comrades, that the Decembrists were the earliest originators of the liberation movement. And just because they were unable to foresee everything, you accuse them of class egoism. Believe me, not only did they have no class interests, they stood above all classes. Those were fighters for the pure ideal of liberty, which they brought back from France when they were at war with Napoleon."

Now the atmosphere was heating up. The debate grew sharper. Klitchoglu, who prided herself on her ability to combine good manners with revolutionary commitment, managed to extinguish the inflamed passions very tactfully and gently before it was too late. She quickly arose from her seat and politely asked Kraft to fetch the boiling samovar from the kitchen. Kraft, equally politely, excused himself and left the room. By the time he returned, the hostess had adroitly guided the conversation into the tranquil channel of everyday trifles.

"And why must we lose our tempers like that? What is it that divides us? We have a common enemy—the autocracy—and a single goal—socialism. Only we're taking different paths. And that's all right too, I believe. . . . How boring it would be to live in a world where everyone thought and acted in exactly the same way!" That is what Klitchoglu would say whenever she wished to extinguish the smoldering flames of an argument.

We expected "Simochka"[15] to repeat her usual "refrain," as we called it, on this occasion as well. But evidently she was occupied with something, or else she was out of sorts, for she tried to send us packing.

Later, when we were sitting in Anisya Aleksandrovna's apartment, we could see through the window how, one after another, Bulanov, Kocharovsky, and Zot Sazonov[16] showed up at Klitchoglu's apartment.

"It's obvious that the SRs are holding some kind of council," Ponty said, looking out the window.

"That's why 'Simochka' tried to send you packing," Anisya Aleksandrovna interjected.

Somehow, I didn't visit Klitchoglu's for a long time. And then I suddenly get an invitation via Grigoreva to go see Serafima Georgievna about a very important matter. Since there had never been any particularly important matters between me and "Simochka," I took this invitation for a routine act of courtesy and made no haste to call on her. The invitation was soon repeated.

When we finally met, Klitchoglu was reproachful:

"Could it be that I have insulted you in some way?" she asked, smiling pleasantly.

I assured her that there had been no insult, that I simply hadn't had the time.

"Do you know why I wish to talk with you?"

"No, I don't."

"Would you be willing to go away to 'work'?"

I understood the question literally, so I answered:

"But I'm under police surveillance, see? I'd go, but only with permission from the gendarmes."

"You don't understand what I'm saying. I mean *revolutionary* work," she emphasized.

I was not prepared for this kind of proposition. For several minutes I stood there silently, pondering the question. This was just at one of those times when I was unemployed. The temptation was great. I was attracted by the secrecy, the mystery, the chance to move to another city. I understood perfectly well that I would have to become an "illegal." But, then, I was a Social Democrat, wasn't I!

"The fact that you're a Social Democrat is of no consequence," she pronounced, as if she had read my thoughts. "You will go to Penza or Samara, as you prefer."[17]

"Yes," I interrupted her, "but for me it is of consequence."

"And why is it of consequence to you? You won't have to change your convictions. Stick with your SD convictions and views, and conduct your propaganda any way you like. We demand nothing of you. Don't think we're such dogmatists. What's important to us is practical work. With such an enormous shortage of people to send to the countryside, we're not about to argue with you over some trivial differences that not even workers, let alone peasants, would comprehend. . . . Look, when we've overthrown the autocracy, that's when we can argue about these things, not now. The unfortunate peasant-victim doesn't even know how to read or write, and you're going to creep up to him with theory? . . . So, do you accept? I'll give you addresses and the necessary papers, and I'll provide you with money. . . . Everything will be wonderful!"

"It seems to me that you take me for a newborn child, Serafima Georgievna, to whom you can tell nursery tales," I said very stridently, enraged by her unprincipled and unceremonious approach.

"My, aren't you harsh! . . . But where are these nursery tales?" Klitchoglu replied in an injured tone. "I was being completely sincere in offering you a real chance at revolutionary activity."

"We already have our own."

"Well, if you're satisfied, that's your business! I'm not going to force you," she said coldly.

In taking leave of me, she earnestly requested that I not repeat our conversation to anyone. I promised.

However, I did not feel that I had the right to conceal this conversation from my comrades, and I believe it was on the very next day that I talked about it to The Artist.

He literally jumped in the air.

"Now that's a clever woman! How shrewdly she has tried to confuse us! Why, she even made the same proposal to me and

Ponty; she approached each of us separately and made each of us promise to keep the conversation a secret. What an unscrupulous swindler!"

Ponty turned out to be more perceptive than we were. When we all got together, he said:

"Do you really think she thought it all up by herself? Nothing of the sort: she was simply assigned the task of converting us to their faith by their generals! They would have sent us off somewhere in the countryside. We would have lost contact with our own people. We would have stopped studying. . . . Well, enough of that! . . ."

We felt instinctively that we'd been subjected to a dirty trick, but we had no way of proving or substantiating this. However, when *Iskra* began to publish articles about "revolutionary adventurism" and correspondents' reports unmasking the SRs, everything became clear to us. At the time, the Socialist Revolutionaries were engaged in intensive work among the peasants of the Volga region.[18] They were really very short of workers, and they tried to recruit them anywhere and by any means they could. Just what kind of peasant organizations were these? Of whom did they consist? Very little has been written about this in our literature. But here is what Viktor Chernov himself has to say about the peasant organizations in his memoirs. He had "gone to the people" in Tambov province a little earlier.[19]

Popov appeared before the leaders of the peasant organization and started to ask them to accept him in their midst.[20] This proved to be a real task for them. For a long time they carried on their weighty deliberations about what they should do with him. Finally, they decided to subject him to a serious experiment: they proposed to him that, in order to prove that he had abandoned his past, he destroy all the promissory notes from peasants that were still in his possession. Popov thought very hard, stopped his drinking, and kept out of everyone's sight for about ten days while he probed his own soul—(thus does Chernov write in a tragic mode about the sufferings of this superparasitic kulak!)[21]

Finally, Popov appeared before Shcherbinin[22] with a packet of promissory notes amounting, as it turned out, to 10,000 rubles—a grandiose sum for those times. All the members of the organization gathered together for the triumphal burning of the notes, and, together with the notes, of the Ivan Trofimovich Popov of old. Thereafter, his entire past was forgotten. Popov was welcomed with open, outstretched arms and initiated in all the plans of the group. A new life was beginning for him. . . .[23]

Thus did a superparasitic kulak grow into a member of the SR Party; he swore an oath never to plunder openly, and in return he was able to retain the property he had stolen earlier. Yet, in the words of the very same Chernov, he had plundered his neighbors "mercilessly," and "all his remarkable strength of character was spent on that activity."

Other members of the group were characterized by Viktor Chernov as follows: "All seven of the village 'conspirators' gave the impression of being such solid and firm, indeed such outstanding people, that you couldn't talk with them without your heart swelling with joy."

When I read this description, I involuntarily recalled "Simochka's" attempt to cast us off to the countryside, giving us leave to conduct our Social Democratic propaganda "freely." It was only natural that such a "powerful" kulak organization would try to drive all the Marxist spirit from our midst.[24]

After my conversation with Klitchoglu our relations cooled off. Nevertheless, she continued to invite us to her place with the same tender smile, though we understood full well that she was simply maintaining a proper tone.

At that time there was a very young but very capable man named Arkady Altovsky who worked for the SRs as a link with the workers. He had connections with some of the exiled workers and, through them, with some of the local workers as well. He was a clever propagandist, and he led circles of both students and workers. Altovsky endeavored to adapt the views of the SRs to the workers. In those days the workers were weak in their understanding of theoretical nuances, so they listened eagerly to his demagogic speeches. I remember one occasion when we reached an agreement with the SRs to hold a debate in which each side would explain its program to the workers. The SRs were to be represented at the debate by Altovsky, and our side was represented by Ponty and me. Aleksey Rykov,[25] who was rather close to the SRs at the time, was also supposed to be there. But the police got wind of the meeting, and our debate did not take place.

In the winter Breshko-Breshkovskaya, "The Little Grandmother," arrived in Saratov.[26] She was apparently there illegally, although everywhere I happened to go people were talking and arguing about her. Among the student youth, her name was pronounced with great enthusiasm and adulation, especially among the girls. There was a great deal of talk about her at Auntie's.

An old member of the People's Will,[27] when still only a young woman she had left her rich landowning family to go to the people. As someone who had been a defendant in the "Trial of the 193" and had served time in Kara performing hard labor,[28] Breshko-Breshkovskaya made a stunning and overwhelming impression on the green youths. A veritable pilgrimage to The Grandmother—as she was already called at the time—was established, and the authority of the SR Party began to grow not only by the day, but by the hour. The radical student youths flocked to the Party in droves and vied with each other in offering their services for activities such as printing, seeking out conspiratorial quarters, collecting money, and hawking and storing literature.

Needless to say, joining the Party in those days was not the same as we conceive of it today, what with our forms and records, our membership cards, and items like that. In most cases you simply announced your adherence to the Party and agreed to take on a specific line of Party work, if they trusted you sufficiently. And the SRs did it even more simply than we did.

Our workers' group adopted a very restrained and even cold attitude toward the arrival of Breshko-Breshkovskaya. And more generally, The Little Grandmother's presence in Saratov found little resonance in working-class circles, notwithstanding all the efforts of the SRs to popularize that name in the workers' milieu.

I remember that one of my SR friends proposed on several occasions that I go pay homage to The Grandmother. But I rejected the proposal every time, and not for reasons of principle, but simply because I was proud, and didn't want to imitate the herd.

One day, however, I was unable to restrain myself from going. The encounter took place in one of the SR "salons," probably Averkieva's.

The SR "Mother of God"—as I called her in my mind—was seated in an armchair talking about something. Young people were piled all around her in a thick circle, some standing, some sitting on the floor and on chairs. Girls predominated. The Little Grandmother looked like a real prophetess, with her high forehead, her gray head thrown back, her thick braid, and her inspired countenance. She spoke of the long-suffering Russian people, crucified by the tsarist autocracy, and summoned us to go and serve the unfortunate martyr-people, to open its eyes to its life and needs. She heaped curses on the evil autocracy and its heartless servitors and *oprichniki*.[29] All this angry rhetoric ended in a call for the erection of the universal temple of socialism.

She spoke with conviction, with a tone of authority that permitted neither doubts nor objections. Listening to her deeply moving speech, I could not help but be infected by the solemn mood of the people all around me. In my eyes, The Little Grandmother grew into a mighty, formidable figure, a personification of our revolution and, especially, of its heroic past.

And yet, strangely, there was something that bothered me in her pompous, solemn, and sometimes condescendingly patronizing speech. At times, something unpleasant, something false, penetrated my ears. I began to catch and to ponder some of her individual words and phrases: "The people is a suffering Christ," "Socialist paradise." . . . Educated in a spirit of hatred for religion, for Christianity, indeed for everything that even remotely reminded me of religion, I never liked to hear any talk about the marriage of Christianity with Socialism, the kind of talk one sometimes heard in SR circles. And here all of a sudden we were listening to such strange evangelical comparisons and images. And from whose lips? From the self-sacrificing representative of the heroic and fearless "People's Will," which once had shaken the very foundations of the tsarist autocracy. . . . Is it possible she believes in God? Incomprehensible! . . .

True, I had often heard that the SRs had quite a few sympathizers and even followers not only among seminary students but also among priests. In fact, only recently I had seen the most genuine priest-SR at Auntie's "salon." One of Auntie's daughters had brought him there as a curiosity. And there was indeed good reason to be surprised: a revolutionary priest! We looked at him with our mouths and eyes wide open. To be sure, he was a pretty shabby little priest; he was small and emaciated, with long chestnut hair, a wedge-shaped beard, and a glossy woolen cassock that reached his heels and was draped on his body as if on a stake. He too sat quietly, gazing at us and smoking. Then, suddenly, someone asked him: did he believe in God? The priest shook his head negatively and answered in the young bass voice of a seminarian:

"This was never foreseen by the code governing Christ's church. It is the parishioners who carry this burden. . . ."

When The Little Grandmother had finished, people began, very timidly, to ask her questions. Mainly they questioned her about the theme that was stirring everyone up at the time: the significance of terror in the struggle with the autocracy. She responded in the same imperious tone:

The administrative machinery of the Russian tsar is the greatest hindrance, the main force, that prevents the replacement of the old order by the new; for this reason, as our first order of business we must punish and destroy all representatives of the authorities whenever they commit a crime against the people. It is the Socialist Revolutionary's duty to come to the aid of the people when needed and to help it again and again to avenge itself against the tsarist *oprichniki* who dare to tyrannize the people. The people still lacks the strength to stand on its own, so our own sacrifices are needed to defend it. We are carrying forth the work of Christ, who preached the idea of peace and paradise on earth, and offered himself as a sacrifice for the sake of the suffering people. Every socialist should be prepared to sacrifice himself with joy. Perhaps we shall not live to see the bright future, but will it not be joyful to us when, as a result of our sufferings, our graves will be covered by the brilliant and luxuriant colors of the blossoming happiness of mankind and the children of the people will suffer no longer? . . .

To illustrate her point, The Grandmother provided examples and illustrations from the experience of the terrorist struggle of the People's Will. Everyone listened with the same attentiveness and deep respect, without allowing the slightest cough or other involuntary sound to escape. Youthful eyes were shining, fists were clenched. Many of those present longed to undertake great deeds and swore to sacrifice their lives for the weary, suffering people. An atmosphere of sacrifice and impending doom was being created. And what emerged as the most understandable, consistent, and accessible outlet for the mounting youthful energies was—terror: to lay down your life for your fellow man. It became instantly clear to me how and from where this kind of atmosphere of mysticism and religiosity appears.

A young woman, a favorite and confidante of The Little Grandmother's, exchanged a few whispers with her and began to take leave of her. The Grandmother arose from her armchair, kissed the girl on the forehead, and, to my amazement, made the sign of the cross over her with maternal tenderness:

"May God be with you! May the Lord send you good fortune!"
she said as the girl departed.

It was as if I'd been cured of all my fascination for the Grandmother with a single touch. I had no reason to stay here any
longer, and I hastened to depart.

I told this story to my friends down to the last detail. Thereafter, an anecdote about me continued to circulate for a long
time, according to which I had gone to The Little Grandmother
to receive her blessing.[30]

It was still in the autumn of 1901 that I made the acquaintance
of A. I. Rykov, who had just been released from the Kazan
Prison.[31] He was good-natured, small, animated, and witty, wore
an everyday student coat that he kept unbuttoned, and made a
very positive impression on me. But there was a heated argument
between us at our very first encounter. At that time he had a very
harsh attitude toward any economic struggle for "small change"
and advocated a purely political struggle. It was apparently this
predilection for pure politics that had led him to his close ties
with the Socialist Revolutionaries, and then to the formation with
them of a unified group of Social Democrats and SRs. True, this
unified group of SDs and SRs did not exist very long; it soon
broke down into its constituent parts. Nevertheless, the SRs were
able to exploit it in their struggle with *Iskra* and the *Iskra*-ites.[32]

Later, our negative attitude toward the Socialist Revolutionaries found approval in *Iskra*'s report to the Second, 1903 Congress of the RSDLP.[33]

Here (in Saratov—*S.K.*)—writes the *Iskra* correspondent—there are
both Socialist Revolutionaries and Social Democrats, and there is terrible enmity between the two groups. At present there is a rather respectable number of Social Democrats here, more than the Socialist Revolutionaries. The Social Democrats are now grouped close to *The Workers'
Newspaper*. It must be said that this is the most active element. The Socialist Revolutionaries, by contrast, engage in a good deal of idle chatter
and accomplish very little.

This report was written by N. K. Krupskaya and edited by V. I.
Lenin.[34]

One day a student came to the home of one of Auntie's adult
daughters—Varvara Aleksandrovna (she later took part in the
Saratov demonstration,[35] was put in prison and, after about two
years, died of tuberculosis). The student was a tall young man,

blond, with an honest face, shy, awkward, and embarrassed by his great height. He wore a very tight student uniform from one of the higher educational institutions. When he met us, he pronounced his family name indistinctly, and none of us caught it; indeed, in accordance with our conspiratorial habits, it didn't even concern us.

Auntie treated him like a good friend, and called him "Stepa." [36] None of us paid much attention to him, since many students passed through Auntie's and there was nothing that distinguished him from the others.

Toward the end of the evening an argument broke out between Ponty Denisov and this unknown student. The argument was over the role and significance of the individual in history in general and in the revolutionary movement in particular.

"It's the masses who make history, not some individual heroes," Ponty said calmly, smiling condescendingly while bending his shaggy head forward as if preparing to knock it against his opponent's chest. "The tsars, the heroes of history and of the ancient Russian epics—these men were powerful and formidable only when the masses followed them, supported them, and actively joined in the struggle with their foes. A hero without the masses is nothing!"

"That's not true! A hero can do a great deal for the masses. I don't deny the significance of the masses either. But first those masses have to be awakened, extricated from their passive, inert condition. And who will be capable of doing that? Separate individuals who have initiative," said the impassioned student, waving his arms.

"A single individual cannot awaken the masses, no matter how mighty and powerful he may be. You won't awaken the masses with a bomb or a shot from a revolver. You'll just put them back to sleep—they'll put their trust in others. They'll think that a hero will win their freedom for them. To arouse the masses against the autocracy you need to conduct propaganda and agitation among them, which will get them to rise up themselves and march against the autocracy," Ponty continued.

People began to listen to their debate; a small group was gathering around them. It was rare indeed to hear anyone at Auntie's defend the use of terror as openly and directly as this student was doing.

"And in ancient history, weren't there occasions when a quarrel between tribes or nations, who were prepared to drown each other in torrents of blood, was settled in single combat between two military commanders or leaders? Didn't these leaders save many, many of the masses' lives? Individuals and heroes with initiative, locked in single combat with the autocracy, will win freedom for the masses long before the masses begin to bestir themselves and awaken from their timeless hibernation," said the student, embracing his entire audience with his inspired look.

"All that has already been tried, comrade! Was the People's Will so bad at organizing terror? Did they have any fewer heroes and daredevils? And what came of it? After the assassination of Alexander II, Alexander III came to the throne, which marked the beginning of two decades of cruel reaction," said The Artist, who now entered the argument, interrupting the slow Ponty. "You cannot destroy the autocracy by the individual assassinations of tsarist officials, even of the tsar himself. For every scoundrel that you kill, dozens more will be found. We want to destroy the entire autocratic system, not its individual representatives. And that can be done only through the organized power of the working masses, and no one else!"

"But I'm not against actions by the masses," the student objected passionately. "All these acts can be combined: the individual will perform his task, and the masses will be active as well. This will only make the blows against autocracy that much stronger. . . ."

"But to do that you have to go to the masses yourself, arouse and enlighten them, whereas you squander your best forces on terror," The Artist broke in.

"You shouldn't think of me that way. I carry out that kind of work myself. But I just wanted to clarify the issue," said the offended student. "Is it really impossible to combine terror with a mass movement?"

"It is possible. . . . But only when the revolution has already begun. Then you'll see how we rip them to pieces. . . . Do you really think we're such softies?"

"Comrade, I think no ill of you."

"Maybe *you* don't, but the SRs think we reject terror out of cowardice."

"Well, you should understand that I don't answer for the SRs.

I don't even consider myself to be one. But I do stand up for terror."

It was evident that Ponty had gladly yielded his place in the debate to The Artist: he sat down at the table, strained himself some tea from the no-longer-lighted samovar, and, heartily but not hastily, began to devour fat chunks of thickly buttered coarse bread.

Midnight was already approaching, and little by little the guests were creeping away. The Artist and the student remained alone and continued to converse, more calmly, until Auntie took the samovar and the dishes to the kitchen, thereby notifying the seated guests that they had exceeded their welcome.

The Artist and the student departed Auntie's apartment together and strolled for a long time along the empty streets, continuing their discussion of the questions they had been addressing. They had evidently become good friends. Occasionally we would encounter the student—now in civilian clothes—at The Artist's place. They were deliberating about something or other in a conspiratorial manner, and the two of them would soon disappear somewhere.

When we'd meet The Artist, he would never say anything about the student, and—in accordance with our conspiratorial habits—we would never inquire. And, it must be acknowledged, the student didn't arouse much interest among us. Each of us already had acquaintances who were students at universities or the women's courses, people whom we visited or who came—very cautiously, so as not to arouse the suspicions of neighbors and not to land in the field of vision of spies and gendarmes—to visit us.

Thus, when it came to pass that the student completely disappeared from view, we simply failed to notice it, and we soon forgot all about him. Only The Artist resumed his complaints about the inconstancy of the intelligentsia, who are so easily inflamed by love for the workers, and then cool off just as easily, abandon their propaganda activity in their workers' circle because of some personal business, and depart.

At that time The Artist, together with another group of comrades, was intensely involved in the piecing together of Social Democratic circles among the most backward sector of Saratov's artisanal workers. This was hard work, demanding attention, persistence, and sensible people. The circles often fell apart, ties would be broken. And most of the time this was the fault of the leaders and organizers.

At times like this The Artist would come home petulant and irritable, and would start to heap vulgar and abusive insults upon everyone and everything on earth. . . .

By the beginning of April 1902, when we learned of the assassination of Minister of Internal Affairs Sipiagin,[37] and when searches and arrests had begun, we had already managed to forget the little-known student completely. It was only when the gendarmes began to accuse our arrested comrades of participation in Sipiagin's assassination and to show them pictures of a certain student that it became clear to us that the student who had been involved with The Artist was none other than Stepan Balmashev.[38]

Later, when we were familiar with the proclamation issued by the SRs on the subject of Sipiagin's assassination, and with the articles on the same subject in the SRs' party organ, *Revolutionary Russia*,[39] we perceived their great similarity to the argumentation employed in defense of the individual with "initiative," that is, in defense of this kind of act of terror, by Stepan Balmashev at Auntie's. Obviously, these views were already widespread in SR circles at that time, and Stepan Balmashev, who associated with the SRs in his quest for a theory that would unite individual terror and the labor movement, could not have been unaware of this.

One thing remained unclear—had Balmashev been a convinced partisan of individual terror from the very outset? Or had he been vacillating and, by forming links with artisanal workers through The Artist, had he then wished to test more "peaceful" means of struggle against the autocracy, only opting for terror after having become convinced that "peaceful" socialist activity, as he declared at the inquest, was impossible?

The Artist, to whom we turned for clarification of these questions, added somewhat to what we already knew:

"Balmashev is a good fellow, but he's still intelligentsia." The Artist always used that word in awkward situations, when he could not or would not explain the conduct of a particular individual. "How hard I tried to get him to clear his head of that terrorist nonsense! But he just wouldn't listen. What a pity! He really was a good propagandist. The workers took to him right away. He could have been valuable. . . . But the SRs shouldn't be whirling around him the way they are. He really had no sympathy for them!"

As we know, the Socialist Revolutionaries began to profit enormously from the death of S. V. Balmashev, claiming that his assassination of Minister Sipiagin had been carried out entirely under the orders of the SR Combat Organization. But, in a series of issues, *Iskra* definitively exposed this SR trick and, with the help of a whole series of letters from Social Democratic organizations in which he had worked, established that Stepan Valerianovich Balmashev had committed his terrorist act on his own. The SR Combat Organization, however, tried to claim credit for it. This for example is what we can read in the letter to *Iskra* from the Kiev committee of the SDs, published in issue No. 34, 1903.[40] The Kiev comrades wrote:

To the extent that we were able to get to know this heroic, self-sacrificing young man, the elucidation of his personality presented in *Revolutionary Russia* strikes us as completely improbable, as does the enormous significance that journal ascribes to the "Combat Organization" in the affair of 2 April. The overall impression produced by its articles is that the central figure in the affair of 2 April is not Balmashev at all, but the "Combat Organization" itself: it had decided on Sipiagin's assassination as early as September 1901; one of its members had yielded "his martyr's crown to Stepan Balmashev," for a time; it had chosen the moment for the assassination; it had designed Balmashev's plan down to the tiniest details; its participation had guaranteed the success of the attempt on Sipiagin's life. . . . Balmashev, on the other hand, is presented as some kind of pawn in the hands of the "Combat Organization." . . . But the truth is, beyond any doubt, that the central figure in this entire affair was S. V. Balmashev, whose entire life up to that time, and whose years of struggle as a Russian university student, had led with psychological inevitability to the decision that he carried out. It is true, of course, that he could not have managed without outside assistance, and Balmashev—a man of strength and deep conviction—had quickly attracted a congenial entourage of terror-oriented people, who provided him with money and assisted him with advice and moral support. . . .

Thus did *Iskra* expose the fabrications of the SRs.

37

Our Literature and Propaganda

AFTER THE STRIKES conducted at the factories of Saratov by the workers' group in the summer of 1901, the workers there were aroused, and even the more backward workers showed an intensified interest in politics. The influence of the workers' group grew stronger, and *The Workers' Newspaper* was read far and wide.

Left without work for a long time after the strikes, we carried out widespread agitation and propaganda even at those enterprises where our links had been weak before the strikes. Now not a single political event, whether large or small, went by without a response on our part. Either we would issue a proclamation about the event, or we'd write about it in *The Workers' Newspaper*, or else we'd organize a workers' meeting where we explained the meaning and significance of this or that incident. At the same time we were also putting out all kinds of propaganda literature, which was not particularly distinguished by its caution and self-restraint.

The best answer to the question of what kind of literature we used for our agitation and propaganda among the workers may be found, in part, in the report of a Saratov colonel in the Department of Police regarding the searches conducted among us in April 1902. The gendarmes were particularly fortunate in their search of a certain worker who was a novice. Here is a list of what they found:

"How the Minister Took Care of the Workers"; "Explanation of the Law on Fines" (by Lenin); "The Russian Political System and the Workers"; some issues of the revolutionary newspaper *Iskra* for the year 1901; an offprint from the revolutionary journal *The Workers' Cause*, containing the article "What is Autocracy?"; thirteen copies of a proclamation entitled "A New Atrocity by the Tsarist Government"; "The Execution of Sipiagin" (two copies); "To All Russian Workers" (one copy); "Address to the Soldiers" (one copy); and three sheets of paper on which were lithographed the revolutionary poems "The Marseillaise," "Varshavianka," and "Into Bloody Battle."[1]

And here is another list, recording the literature found by the gendarmes in the courtyard where we lived. These particular works were not typical of our group; they were not the kind of thing we printed ourselves. But we were not unwilling to disseminate them:

"Vankovsky's Reform"; "The Demolished Pier"; "On Crimes Against the Property of Private Parties"; "Conversations About Land"; a work by Count Leo Tolstoy called "On the Subject of My Excommunication" (two hectographed copies); "Letter to a Weeping Female Student"; four hectographed drawings depicting the sovereign Emperor and his ministers in caricature; and an excerpt from an antigovernment article.[2]

And finally, there were various revolutionary pictures:

Two photographs, one of which ("The Pyramid") represents an allegorical portrayal of government in Russia in the form of a human pyramid, with portraits of the Imperial family on the top, and the other of which ("Finland") depicts a young woman, out of whose hands a two-headed eagle is ripping a book with an inscription (a constitution—*S.K.*); and two photographic negatives of snapshots of Count Muravev (The Hangman—*S.K.*) on a heap of skulls, and of the writer Melshin (in shackles—*S.K.*).[3] ... *

But this is by no means a complete list of the items we distributed. In addition, we issued proclamations on the burning political issues of the day. These proclamations were written by Comrades Ponty Denisov (I have already mentioned them), Petr Aleksandrovich Lebedev, Aleksandr Alekseevich Bogdanov, Vasily Semenovich Golubev, and others.[4]

Bogdanov's proclamations were very good. They were really poetry in prose. Sometimes he even inserted his own verse. But because V. S. Golubev's proclamations usually came out somewhat dry, occasionally we even rejected them.

Once we ordered a proclamation from our man of letters,[5] but it didn't come out right. Then we asked the other one,[6] but it came out rather dry again. Then we took an illegal brochure by

* The originals of these files are held in the Saratov regional archive. (Author's note.)

L. Tolstoy, *Must It Really Be Like This?*, and reshaped it in our own manner. We retained the part of the text where Tolstoy vividly and colorfully describes class contradictions, the luxuries and pleasures of the rich, and the sufferings of the workers, how they toil as if in penal servitude; but we got rid of the Tolstoyan, nonresistance ending, and replaced it with our own social democratic conclusion. The result was a very nice proclamation.[7]

The printing and reprinting of our literature were in the hands of Albert Retling and E. N. Popova. They achieved great success in the arts of hectographing and mimeographing. Retling, who was a photographer, was also able to make excellent photographic copies of illegal pictures and caricatures.

In addition to illegal literature, an auxiliary role was played in our work by legal and semilegal literature. Here is a sample list: Chernyshevsky's *What Is to Be Done?*; Omulevsky's *Step by Step*; Zola's *Germinal*; Franzos' *A Struggle for Justice*; Schweitzer's *Emma*; Ezh's *At Dawn*; N. Rubakin's *Little Sparks*; Melshin's *In a World of Outcasts*; Faresov's *In Solitary Confinement*; the poetry of Nekrasov; and the works of Gleb Uspensky and of Petropavlovsky-Karonin.[8]

Most of these books were rare editions. We obtained them from the well-known "Enlighteners" of those times: N. A. Rubakin and A. V. Panov.[9] Rubakin's permanent residence was in Piter, and only rarely did he visit Saratov. But he had people there who functioned as his agents, and these people would also provide us with books with—as we said in those days—"revolutionary tendencies." Aleksandr Vasilevich Panov had a splendid library, and he was delighted to let us use it.

In our party, not only then but even much later, propaganda was one of our weakest points. Not elementary propaganda, but propaganda of the higher sort, which requires that the leader of a workers' circle not only be a man of deep, many-sided learning, but also one of great revolutionary experience, broad knowledge of people and of life, and, above all, theoretical firmness. To find a propagandist who embodied all these qualities at that primitive stage, when our Party work was still so undifferentiated, and when every party worker was still a jack-of-all-trades, was a very difficult business. Yet the need for such a division of labor within the Party was sorely felt.

When we did manage to find a broadly educated propagandist,

he frequently turned out to be a poor revolutionary and conducted his circle in a strictly academic manner, out of touch with our revolutionary practice. Still other propagandists failed to satisfy the varied demands of the workers' circle. In addition, there was a great shortage of the requisite literature and textbooks.

Later, when the Saratov Social Democratic Committee was organized, a group of more specialized propagandists emerged from our midst, including Fofanov, Fominykh, P. A. Lebedev, A. A. Arkhangelskaya, M. N. Liadov, and others.[10] Ponty Denisov and I also conducted propaganda.

True, this higher sort of circle rarely completed its assigned program, not even later, when we had already formed a completely centralized Party organization, with a division of labor according to categories of work. Successful completion of the program was prevented by our frequent loss of Party workers, the shadowing of our people by police spies, and arrests.

By what principles were we guided in the conduct of our propaganda? Basically, by the same ones that *Iskra* was endeavoring to implant in its "local" organizations and that it subsequently elucidated in one of its articles:[11]

... What, exactly, do we want to turn our listeners into?—*Iskra* asked. Revolutionary Social Democrats—was its reply. We have the right to demand that a revolutionary Social Democrat have a correct understanding of the aims of the Party and, beyond that, that he be capable of putting those aims into practice and of fighting for them as if he were a member of a military unit. Remember the words of the worker who wrote: "Teach us how to go to battle!" The worker who, despite all the danger, comes to our circles is above all a warrior, one whose blood is already boiling, and our task is to release the powers and talents of that warrior, to place the sharply honed weapon of revolutionary socialism into his hands and teach him to use it.

Consider the state of mind of the worker when he joins a circle for the first time. It's something like this: He has long since felt all the futility of his situation. Now and then, despair and dejection over having to live the dark and gloomy life of a slave of capital has crept into his soul; he was unable to reconcile himself to his lot, and, perhaps for quite some time, he has been carefully seeking a way out. This wish soon turned into a passion. . . . He would hear what was sometimes truth, sometimes legend about the revolutionaries of old, about their heroic struggle, about the existence of certain circles, and so on. Revolutionary activity is pictured by him as something mysterious and as something so elevated, so fascinating, so captivating, that it will readily allow him to forget all the torments of his life. . . . So here he is, at last, in your circle; he anticipates your words with great excitement.

You should begin with the part he expects—the history of our struggle. Page by page, you should reveal to your listener the blood-soaked history of our struggle, a history that demands revenge. Over a period of generations, two hostile forces have stood before the listener: the autocratic government and the revolutionaries—two worlds, two mortal enemies. The further your story progresses, the brighter will the flame of hatred toward our cursed mother country burn in the audience: the act of reliving the struggle of the revolutionaries in their imaginations will attach them more closely to the revolutionary family. How many hopes and dreams, how much suffering is placed before the circle! Your story should be accompanied by the reading of excerpts from illegal literature. Events that your listeners thought of as semilegendary now turn out to be reality.

Here it is, then, the world of which the worker has been dreaming! He will quickly ally himself with this world. Images of genuine, hardened revolutionaries will pass before him; he will see examples of revolutionary firmness during interrogations, at trials, and so on. . . . The very atmosphere of this life will harden the character of the listeners. . . .

. . . But then comes March 1, 1881, followed by the swift destruction of the People's Will Party.[12] A party that had once seemed so powerful, with its outstanding group of self-sacrificing warriors, is routed by the government. The government celebrates triumphantly, holding a wild bacchanalia over the corpse of its fallen foe.

At this point in the story the audience is transfixed. It has relived the beginnings of the struggle, and it is awaiting the conclusion of that struggle, hoping with all its heart for victory . . . but now its heroes are led to their execution. . . . "But why, then, why were they defeated? Won't we be defeated too?!"—you can read the question in the eyes of the listeners. Here you reveal the reasons for the failures of previous revolutionaries; you illuminate particular moments in their struggle and demonstrate the logical inevitability of this kind of outcome. . . . Then, you point out that it is necessary for a revolutionary socialist party to base itself on the masses, on a broad mass movement.

Then you need to shift to the history and teachings of Social Democracy. In discussing the history, you should underline the struggle with economism and other nonsocialist tendencies, and so on. After this you give a detailed exposition of the doctrine of scientific socialism. . . .[13] Explicating the role of our party as the most advanced detachment of the working class, you must not forget that our party is a fighting army, and not a debating society. Having explained the purpose of the struggle, you should show in detail how the struggle is to be carried out.

Next, you have to examine the weapons of struggle: the newspaper, the leaflet, the strike, the demonstration, and others. It would be best to illustrate all this with examples from the activities of your committee and of the Party in general, right up to the moment of the popular armed uprising, for whose possible occurence we should be preparing the workers right now. . . .

. . . In connection with the study plan outlined above, the circle should also engage in systematic reading of the newspaper (the reference is, of course, to *Iskra*). . . .

Such, more or less, were the plan and methods of conducting propaganda that our party set forth as its basic principle and that we strove to realize in our daily routine of practical work.

The tempo of the development of revolutionary activity among the Saratov workers was accelerating significantly in this period. New connections were being formed, and we were meeting and getting to know many of the workers who had previously been in a state of perpetual slumber. We were becoming "dangerously" popular people, and our popularity was beginning to interfere with our work. We began to be pursued, shadowed, by awkward, sluggish spies who were not even capable of concealing their presence. Annoying like autumn flies, they persistently intruded in our lives, arousing our anger and animosity.

Occasionally, when in the presence of a spy, one of us would quicken his pace. The spy would start pursuing him. The person being followed would turn into some isolated side street, while the spy continued to follow on his heels. Then the person being followed would conceal himself around a corner and wait. The spy, having lost sight of his prey, continued running. Then the "prey" would jump out from behind the corner and beat the spy to a pulp. After that, the spy would disappear for a while. But a new one always took his place, and the same kind of pursuit would resume.

There is no doubt that the police had some vague notion, based on rumors, of the accelerated tempo of our work, but, apart from what could be observed from the outside, they possessed no factual material or evidence. At that time there were no provocateurs or informers in our midst.

But to the police, the "danger" posed by our presence was beyond any doubt. For this reason, at the end of 1901 the Saratov chief of police brought a request for our exile before the governor.

The Saratov governor, apparently not convinced that there was sufficient ground for the request, addressed the following inquiry to the office of gendarmes:

The Saratov chief of police has petitioned for the administrative exile from Saratov of the peasant Semën Ivanov Kanatchikov, who is here under public and special police supervision, and of the peasant Semën Petrov Shepelev, here under public police supervision, on the ground that they are exercising a dangerous influence on the local workers. Because of this, I would like to request your Excellency to provide me with as much detailed information as possible about the aforementioned Kanatchikov and Shepelev, as well as your own opinion regarding the question of their banishment from Saratov.*

Apparently, no incriminating information on us was found at the office of gendarmes, and perhaps there were other reasons as well, but they decided not to banish us from Saratov at this time.

* The original document is held in the Saratov regional archive. (Author's note.)

38
The Cooperative Workshop

OUR UNEMPLOYMENT dragged on. All of our resources were exhausted. Everything that might have been sold or hocked had already been spent and consumed. And there were no real prospects before us. . . . There was only one possible solution—to run away to some industrial center, to assume the status of fugitives and find work there. But it would have been pitiful to adopt the position of a fugitive before the law just for the sake of a piece of bread. As a rule, revolutionaries endeavored to remain on legal ground as long as possible, shifting to an illegal position only in extreme situations.

A couple of times, when I met Zot Sazonov at Klitchoglu's, I tried to raise the question of procuring money for the organization of an artel workshop.[1] Finally, one evening when we were leaving Klitchoglu's together, I screwed up my courage and told him the heart of the matter, actually naming the sum that we needed—100 rubles. To my amazement, Sazonov quietly reached for his purse, rummaged around, and handed me a 100-ruble note. I put on an air of indifference and pocketed the note. But no sooner had I taken leave of Sazonov than I rushed off to Shepelev's. That very evening, our entire brotherhood of the unemployed gathered together and discussed in detail an organizational plan for an artel workshop. We dispersed late at night, full of hope and confidence.

On the very next day, Shepelev began to develop an incredible energy. Somewhere or other he managed to purchase, at a low price, five joiner's benches and some tools; he also managed to buy some lumber at a lumberyard and to locate a secondhand lathe that was in need of relatively little repair. We found a suitable little apartment, and before long our workshop was ready to begin.

Because of my more extensive connections with the intelligentsia, I was assigned the task of looking for orders. In the beginning, the basic nucleus of our joiners' artel consisted of the following comrades: S. P. Shepelev, M. Karev, P. I. Lalov, Dmitry Bochkov, S. I. Kanatchikov, and The Artist. Later, the composition changed somewhat. We accepted a young fellow named Vasily Gromov as an apprentice, and shortly thereafter added a joiner from an artisanal workshop by the name of Vasily Alekseevich—I've forgotten his last name—a very good worker, but a malicious and bitter man who hated the intelligentsia.

With the exception of Bochkov and Vasily Alekseevich, we were all Marxists, and therefore were negatively disposed, from a theoretical standpoint, to producers' cooperatives. We knew that under conditions of capitalism, a producers' cooperative inevitably either would degenerate into a stock company, or would fall into the hands of some cunning worker who would transform his former comrades into his employees, or else would simply fall through. As to the prospects of our own artel, we were not in the least bit deceived, and we had no fear that it would degenerate into a stock company; we assumed that it would simply go down the drain. Nevertheless, we set to work with enthusiasm.

With the help of my connections, I got us a big order from the book warehouse of the local zemstvo to make blackboards for its schools. The liberal zemstvo members squeezed us plenty, taking advantage of our need; they set very low prices for our work. So as not to go under, we established a ten-hour workday and worked with enormous effort, never leaving our workbenches. During the first month we would earn either one ruble ten kopecks or one ruble twenty kopecks per person a day. This wasn't much, but it was still more than we would have gotten from an employer. Shepelev even got us an order from some factory to do some pattern-making work.

In the course of its existence, we had to change the location of our workshop twice, since our landlords did not consider us very agreeable tenants: the police were simply paying much too much attention to us.

From the very first month of operation we were faced with the problem that we did not have an adequate supply of liquid capital. We were unable to accept big, profitable orders, since the purchase of materials required more money than we had. Nor were we able to acquire wood and other materials in advance, at lower prices, and keep them in storage. In short, we ran up against many of the same constraints that a private enterprise must face, and we felt the laws of the market, the law of supply and demand, through real experience. At first this was quite unpleasant, but, as the saying goes, necessity knows no laws— when there is no razor, you shave with an awl. And so we reconciled ourselves, began to change, to adapt. . . .

Except for The Artist, we all lived in private quarters and came to work at the designated hour. At our first location there was one free room, and The Artist moved into it with all his goods and chattels, including his art supplies. As usual, he had many different kinds of visitors, so that our shop soon turned into a center of revolutionary life.

In addition to our normal work for our customers, we began to provide services to revolutionaries. The SRs would order equipment for their underground printing operations: type cases, frames, rolling cylinders, and presses. And the indefatigable Shepelev invented a whole series of contrivances in which to conceal illegal literature while maintaining an ordinary household routine.

The most widely distributed of his many inventions was a small round table with one leg (or column). The column was hollow, and a plug was inserted in its bottom section, terminating in a small decoration in the form of a little ball or mushroom. The little table was carefully finished and varnished and it had an elegant appearance. It was small and light. It could easily be used as a night table; you would simply turn it upside down, pull out the plug, hide your illegal literature (which you rolled up in a tube inside it), and put it back in place. It took very little effort to make such a table, since the entire object could be turned on a lathe.

We sold them for only three rubles. At that price the conspiratorial tables sold like hotcakes. We also made conspiratorial cupboards, with double walls and other adaptations. But we made them available only to our steadiest customers, so they were not widely distributed. Our conspiratorial contrivances withstood many gendarme raids, without once being uncovered.

True, there was one occasion when our patented products came

very close to failing us. One evening the gendarmes, accompanied by the deputy public prosecutor, came to The Artist's quarters to do a routine search. At the time, we were working on a
rush order. I had remained in the workshop for the evening and
was at the lathe, cutting little beads for a vertical schoolroom
abacus. The pack of gendarmes and regular police, their spurs
clanging and swords clanking,[2] filed past me to The Artist's room.

"Well," I thought, noticing a man in civilian clothes behind the
cavalry captain, "this means it will go badly for The Artist today."

As usual, The Artist was mockingly polite. Rushing ahead
courteously, he showed them everything, opened everything, and
turned everything inside out, thereby demonstrating his "purity"
and "innocence." On top of a basket near the wall, with its column
turned upward, lay a big conspiratorial table, made by us on special order for The Artist. The column was of imposing dimensions, recalling a roadside curbstone, and inside it was a large
quantity of the most diverse kinds of illegal literature: newspapers, brochures, proclamations, and even books. It was really a
special kind of warehouse.

Whenever anyone came to The Artist for literature, he would
lead the visitor to his room, lock the door, turn the table over on
the basket with its column facing upward, and, grabbing the polished head of the plug—which was the size of the head of a year-
old child—he would begin to shake it. After removing the plug,
he would pull out the contents, give his client what he needed,
and, always observing all precautions, dismiss him. As a consequence, The Artist's conspiratorial table became famous far beyond the limits of our workshop. Still, we didn't go under, the reason being that there was no provocateur among us at that time.

But then, somehow, The Artist's table began to "limp": one of
the three brackets that supported it had been broken, and the
table could no longer stand up. Several times I offered to fix it,
but The Artist would gesture casually—there's no hurry!

The door to The Artist's room was now ajar. Tearing myself
away from my work and cautiously looking around, I could see
the backs of the gendarmes as they rummaged in his old things,
The Artist as he rushed from one end of the room to another, and
the conspiratorial table, stuffed with literature, as it lay there de-
fiantly with its column sticking up in the air. Now the gendarmes

want to get in the basket, but the table is lying on top of its lid, so, to remove the lid, they first have to remove the table. . . . With a natural movement of his hand, a gendarme grabs the head of the column and . . . it just stays there in his hand. The astonished gendarmes let go some indistinct sounds of joy and triumph. Does The Artist understand what's happening? . . .

I could feel the shivers going up and down my spine and my hair beginning to stand on end. The search was coming to an end. The minutes passed with agonizing slowness. I pressed more vigorously on the footpedal of my workbench, straining to suppress an insufferable feeling of apprehension as the outcome drew near. . . . The chuck turned more forcefully, and the odorous shavings gleamed in the air. Suddenly I hear a noise, a bustle, behind my back. My spirits fall. This means that we're finished. Our "tables" have done us in.

Without ceasing to rotate the foot-drive of the lathe, I turn my head and what do I see! The Artist, having seized the top of the table with one hand, and carefully holding the end of the column, as if it were a sick child, with the other, brings the table into the workshop and delicately puts it down on the floor in one of the corners.

"This way, gentlemen, you'll be able to search my room more comfortably. Why let this thing get in your way? My room is small, and you still might find something there," he said anxiously, waving his arms in puzzlement, as if no one could imagine how sorry he was that the gendarmes had been unable to find anything.

A weight was lifted from my heart. The search was just about over. The cavalry captain had sat down to draft his report. I kept working hard at cutting on some blocks of wood, trying to look as if nothing that had happened concerned me in any way, and I would only turn around stealthily to see what was happening behind my back. With a sad look on his face, The Artist sat there, casually leaning his elbows on the edge of the table, while the man in civilian clothes sat on the other side. Finally, the whole disreputable crew, with lots of noise and the clatter of heavy boots, filed past behind my back, while I, just as soon as the door was locked, tore myself from the lathe and caught sight of The Artist grinning from ear to ear.

"Well, the danger has passed! This time they didn't even take me away with them," he said merrily.

I jumped all over him and began to scold him for his carelessness, pointing to the table.

"All right, all right, lay off me; I understand that myself. . . ."

"And who was the man in civilian clothes?" I asked.

"He introduced himself to me as the deputy public prosecutor. I am here, he says, to assure that legality is observed. And he's the one who saved me. The cavalry captain was completely prepared to drag me off to prison, but the prosecutor says that would be illegal, since the search came up with nothing."

"Let this be a lesson to you! You almost ruined all our conspiratorial work!" I said angrily.

"That'll do, that's enough! I'll fix everything tomorrow; I realize I let myself get carried away. . . . Only please don't tell the others," he asked.

On the next day the lame table was repaired. The Artist pulled himself together and we all began to conduct ourselves very strictly. Everyone had been frightened by the unexpected gendarme raid. However, it was hard to remain in such a state of alert very long. As soon as we felt we were out of danger, we became less disciplined again. Almost all day long our workshop was frequented by the most varied kinds of people.

But then there began to be problems in our relations with our landlord, and we had to look for a new location for the workshop. There turned out to be an extra room in our new quarters. Almost all of us were in difficult financial straits, especially because so few orders had been coming our way recently. Driven by need, Lalov, Retling, and I moved into the workshop to live. The number of visitors to the shop increased. For their benefit, we hung revolutionary caricatures and photographs along the walls— "The Pyramid," Muravev-the-Hangman atop a heap of skulls with a rope in his hand, and others.[3] On the other side of these pictures were portraits of the tsar and tsaritsa. During the day, when visitors came to us, they saw the pictures with revolutionary content, but in the evening, when the gendarmes were more likely to show up, we would turn the pictures around. So carelessly had we begun to conduct ourselves that Albert Retling stored the tin sheets for the hectograph and negatives of our revolutionary photos in his room, while I placed a type case under my head, turning it upside down to use as a pillow.

These type cases had been ordered from us by some of the SRs, but they never came for them; their underground printing operation had apparently come unglued. So the cases were scattered about our shop.

What happened to us was evidently the same thing that happens to carp when they swim in a pond without any pike: when they feel safe, they begin to degenerate.

There began to be clashes between members of the artel in the workshop itself. As a consequence of the reduction in our orders and our earnings, some workers who did not belong to the artel began to grumble.[4] They placed the blame on Shepelev and me, accusing us of putting too little energy into finding orders and devoting too much time to politics, at the expense of "business." Vasily Alekseevich was particularly unhappy with us. A small, ill-tempered, bitter man, he taunted us, called us insulting names, and sometimes, simply refusing to talk, he threatened to leave the artel. We had no objection to his leaving. Mikhail Karev encouraged him in this attitude; he too seemed disturbed by the excessive use of our workshop for political activity. Dmitry Bochkov generally kept quiet, but on the basis of some of his remarks we felt that he too was displeased. After work, we would often start talking about other subjects, but Vasily Alekseevich always led the conversation back to our internal defects.

"What a shame that there's no one to crack the whip on loafers like us!" he'd say, addressing no one in particular.

"We don't think of ourselves as loafers," the honest and straightforward Lalov would retort.

"Well, I think you're a loafer. . . . And do you know why? I'll tell you right now. If you were working for a boss, he'd know how to tell you off in no uncertain terms and he'd beat you without mercy. . . . Look at this table! You've been dragging it out for three days, but if you had a boss you'd have finished it in one. . . . And you know why? Because there you're working for yourself, but who am I working for here? For the intelligentsia, that's who!"

"Don't reproach me with this table, Vasily Alekseevich, I could finish it in a day here too. But then what do I do tomorrow? There just isn't any work," the normally calm, even-tempered Lalov would say, losing his patience.

"There's no point blowing smoke in our eyes; just admit the truth—you miss the boss's whip, don't you? Well, get out of here! No one is keeping you here."

"I'm going!" Vasily Alekseevich would say in a stubborn tone, and he soon left us.

This kind of dialogue took place more and more frequently as we received fewer and fewer orders. As our workshop neared the end of its existence, almost no orders were coming in at all. Hence the gendarme was not very far from the truth when he reported to the Department of Police:

As to the way of life of Kanatchikov, Efimov, Retling, and Lalov, our interrogations of Darya Smirnova, Andrey and Varvara Artemev, who reside in the same house as the aforementioned persons, revealed that a great number of people visited Kanatchikov and his comrades, but that they kept no servants and would not even allow the woman who delivered their water to enter their apartment. According to the testimony of these witnesses, although Kanatchikov and his roommates maintained a joiner's workshop, only once was some lumber delivered to their place and only once did they see a set of shelves being carried out of the apartment; moreover, the witnesses never saw any wood shavings or other scraps normally found in a joiner's shop being removed from the premises.*

This report, not devoid of a ponderous kind of policeman's humor, contained its share of truth, but not at all in those places where the sharp eye of the gendarme wished to see it. Without any rational basis, the zealous gendarme was evidently trying to throw dust in the eyes of his superiors by constructing the following hypothesis: these people, he was suggesting, simply had a conspiratorial apartment, and the joiner's shop, as he saw it, was only a cover. To serve his own purposes, the gendarme had focused on the moment of the workshop's demise. But there was a time when our workshop had flowered, when we brought in lots of lumber and delivered many articles that we made there. As to the shavings, the reason we didn't remove them from the premises is that we used them as fuel for our stove. We also had no servant for reasons of economy. How could we keep a servant there when we had nothing to eat ourselves!

* From the files of the Saratov regional archive. (Author's note.)

This is not to say that, in organizing a cooperative workshop, we rejected its utilization for revolutionary goals as well. Not one of us would have entertained such an idea, for we were all revolutionaries. Even Vasily Alekseevich had no such intention when he joined the artel. On the contrary, in organizing a cooperative workshop as an escape from unemployment, we also set ourselves the goal of using it for revolutionary purposes, a goal we carried out successfully.

39
The Saratov Social Democratic Committee

It is impossible to state the precise date of the formation of the committee; neither direct nor indirect evidence on that question has been preserved. But as a rough approximation, we can fix the end of 1901 as the time it was formed[1]; that was the time when the wave of strikes that swept through in the summer had aroused the mass of workers and forced the Social Democrats to confront the question of how best to assume the systematic leadership of the workers' movement. The same questions were already being raised at the nationwide level in *Iskra*, which we were beginning to receive in Saratov on a regular basis. *Iskra* was waging a violent war against amateurism and localism, and was urging local groups to form organizations that would be subordinated to the authority of a single central leadership.[2]

Our Saratov workers' group had neither the structure nor the political scope required for this purpose. It represented a stage that was already behind us. Having served its purpose, the workers' group now had to make way for a more structured, formally delineated organization, with a more complex division of functions.

Nevertheless, the new committee was formed mainly from our same workers' group. Its members included S. M. Fofanov, V. A. Fominykh, P. I. Denisov, A. E. Efimov (The Artist), S. I. Kanatchikov, P. A. Lebedev, N. A. Arkhangelskaya, E. A. Diakova (Auntie). Later, the following were co-opted into the organization: M. P. Golubeva (she was the representative of *Iskra*), Baramzin, Obukhov, and M. N. Liadov.[3]

In his memoirs, published in *The Old Bolshevik*,[4] Comrade Liadov writes that as soon as he arrived in Saratov from his term of exile in Iakutsk he landed in Diakova's apartment, where the

Saratov committee was in session. During the session they co-opted him into membership on the committee. This was at the beginning of April 1902.

In spite of all its shortcomings, the Saratov committee did embark on the path of forming the kind of single, centralized, Social Democratic Party for which *Iskra* had been steadfastly working. This was already a step forward. Not very consistently, not very firmly, our committee was endeavoring nonetheless to lay the foundation for a division of labor within our organization. We already had people with technical know-how—that was handled, as before, by V. A. Fominykh and Albert Retling—and we had E. A. Diakova to store our literature, and S. M. Fofanov and Arkhangelskaya to handle propaganda. Our connections with liberal society and the procurement of money were placed in the hands of P. A. Lebedev, although finding money was certainly a permissible activity for members other than the comrade designated for that purpose. Maintaining connections with the factories and other enterprises was our responsibility, that is, the responsibility of the worker part of the committee.[5]

Our weak point was our lack of contact with the peasantry; we were frequently attacked for this by the SRs, who prided themselves on the strength and durability of their ties to the village. Just what was the nature of those ties is, of course, another question; one has only to recall the words of Viktor Chernov, cited above.[6]

At that time, our most important source of contact with the village was the Mariinskoe Agricultural School.[7] A former student at that school, Stepan Ivanovich Danilov—or "Stepochka," as we called him—was living at Auntie's. It was he who became our main contact. From time to time students from the Mariinskoe School, people who either sympathized with the Social Democrats or actually thought of themselves as SDs, would show up at Auntie's apartment. These included I. Borisov, Nikolaev, Kravchenko,* Ustiugov, and others.[9] Our committee supplied them with illegal literature for the countryside, and they disseminated it among the peasants. Later, the committee's links to the countryside would become considerably broader and stronger.

The Saratov committee's work among the peasants, carried out

---

* In 1919 Kravchenko was an outstanding leader of the Enisey partisans.[8] (Author's note.)

through the Mariinskoe Agricultural School, was destined to produce great results in 1905, when the peasants began to rise up
spontaneously. At that time, when the Socialist Revolutionary
Party was dragging itself behind the tail of the agrarian movement, calling for agrarian terror, the Social Democratic organization, led by Bolsheviks, brought systematic planning and organization to that movement.[10]

With the arrival of M. N. Liadov from his exile in Iakutsk, the
work of the Saratov committee not only became more lively, it
also took on a firmer character with respect to questions of principle. He turned out to be one of the pillars of the *Iskra* point of
view and carried out *Iskra*'s line with indomitable energy. Tall,
thin, sinewy, with blazing black eyes, daring, decisive in his actions and persistent to the point of obstinacy, he had a tremendous influence on all of us and enjoyed a well-earned authority.
Nor was this at all surprising: he had many years of revolutionary
work behind him, a great deal of experience with life, a solid education in Marxism, and many years of exile in Iakutsk, that icy
graveyard beyond the polar circle where the most irreconcilable
foes of tsarist autocracy were buried alive and from which few returned without having been morally and physically crippled.

He was the only figure among our committee members whom
we could proudly set against the conceited, inflated, empty-
headed SR generals. Unfortunately, there was a certain period of
time when the hollowness of the SR leaders was carefully concealed from outsiders by a heap of sentimental tinsel, pompous
rhetoric, and stilted speeches. Their hollowness was clearly visible to us, to our little group, but it wasn't grasped by the credu-
lous masses. It took a considerable amount of energy to tear off
all their cheap gilding and expose their petty-bourgeois hollowness to the broad masses as well. Part of the Saratov committee's
work was directed to that end, and it subsequently had some positive results.

However, the biggest and most historically valuable work of the
Saratov Social Democratic Committee at that time was the preparation and organization of the first mass demonstration against
the autocracy—the Saratov demonstration of May 5, 1902.[11]

By then the Saratov committee already represented a rather
imposing force. It had at its disposal fairly solid printing facilities,
a pretty good staff of propagandists, some wonderful mass agita-

tors from among the workers, some rather highly skilled writers, a newspaper—*The Workers' Newspaper*—that enjoyed a good reputation among and exerted a great deal of influence on the workers, and numerous solid connections among the workers of the more important factories. Moreover—and this was very important—the committee had practical disposition over a cooperative workshop, which manufactured all kinds of conspiratorial storage containers for illegal literature. Its inventiveness in this regard attained incredible proportions. In addition to the tables and cupboards already mentioned, it manufactured the following items for the concealment of literature: sofa and armchair legs with openings inside them, secret hiding places in walls, and even special logs stuffed with literature, which were carelessly scattered in kitchens and courtyards. The gendarmes were driven to a fury: the city was flooded with literature, but their searches yielded no results.

The only thing that was not carried out in a conspiratorial manner was the actual dissemination of the literature; at the time, this was not yet the specialized activity of a distinct group of people. In principle, everyone recognized the need to create such a group of "disseminators," but in practice, the dissemination of literature was carried out by almost everyone. The most ardent participants in that activity were the impassioned, inexperienced youths, who were thirsting for adventure. To glue a proclamation somewhere on a pillar on some crowded street or on the wall of a house, under the eyes of the police, to paste one at night on the back of a policeman or night watchman while he is sleeping on duty—wasn't that an interesting adventure, one to tell your comrades afterwards and split your sides laughing over? Along with their unquestionable manifestations of heroism, courage, and resourcefulness, our young comrades often allowed themselves to be seduced by the adventurous side of things, thereby endangering both themselves and the entire organization.

The Saratov committee had begun to discuss the question of an open street demonstration long before the first of May. Both the advanced workers and the radical intelligentsia felt and understood that, after all the preceding events—the mass strikes, the broad agitation and propaganda—the time had come to move on to higher forms of struggle, the time had come to teach "how to join battle." The old ways of celebrating May Day—either within the circle or at a mass meeting on the outskirts of the city, with propaganda speeches delivered in the forest—now satisfied no one.[12]

Nevertheless, there was still no one capable of clearly explaining just how the May Day celebration should unfold. This question was discussed at great length in our circles, in private conversations, and at a session of the committee itself. A majority leaned in the direction of marking the occasion by organizing a street demonstration.

A decisive moment in our preparations for the celebration of May Day was an illegal meeting in April, held on Zeleny Island on a Sunday; according to the gendarme reports, the date was April 15, 1902.

Zeleny Island was located on the upstream part of the Volga, not far from Saratov. Its numerous glades, encircled by thickets, served as regular retreats for all our more important gatherings. Surrounded with legendary tales of the Volga brigands who inhabited the Zhigulev Mountains, where, according to tradition, the self-willed Stenka Razin had hidden, Zeleny Island enticed us with its mysteriousness and aroused our youthful, freedom-loving dreams.[13] On holidays we would often gather there in a large group and conceal ourselves from the watchful eye of the police, who dared not penetrate into this refuge for a number of revolutionary generations.

On the appointed day, shortly after noon, we began to descend upon Zeleny Island by boat in a number of small parties. About a hundred people, most of them workers, were gathered there. Fominykh led the meeting. The first to speak were ardent young members of the intelligentsia. They delivered incendiary agitational speeches about the despotism of the tsarist government, about the arbitrary behavior of the police and its violence against the people, and they called for the overthrow of the "fatal yoke forever." There was near unanimity in favor of the organization of a street demonstration, and a number of radical motions were made. We argued over whether or not it was necessary to bring arms to the demonstration for self-defense against the tsarist bashibazouks.[14] Finally, Platonych, a tall, broad-shouldered, blond draftsman from Kolpino took the floor.[15] Excited, stammering slightly, he began to speak:

What a disgrace, comrades, to place our backs under the whips of the police and the Cossacks! Are we going to let them skin us alive while we stroll around "peacefully" with our red flag, singing revolutionary songs? We cannot allow such a disgrace to occur! We must answer them blow for blow. Let's let those tsarist *oprichniki* know just what they're up against. They're in for an armed rebuff. . . . Down with the autocracy! . . .

Platonych was answered by someone who spoke more calmly, reasonably: "Of course we shouldn't place our backs under their whips; we must defend ourselves by every possible means — rocks, cobblestone, sticks — in short whatever we can get our hands on. But there is one thing, comrades, we mustn't do — to start using firearms, or even to bring them along to the demonstration," the orator said, cooling the revolutionary ardor of the hotheads.

"Firing our separate revolutionary shots will be of little value," he continued, "but we'd sure be giving an excuse to the tsarist gendarmes to inflict brutal reprisals upon us. Right now we are few in number. We must conserve the forces of the advanced revolutionaries. When the day comes when the broad masses have risen up, then we shall attack the autocracy weapon in hand. And that day is not far off!"

At some distance from the orators, isolated groups of workers were gathered in crowds; they looked sullenly, mistrustfully, at the people all around them, listened attentively to what was being said, and viewed the orators' fiery speeches with considerable reserve, limiting themselves to some individual retorts and skeptical remarks. Accustomed to acting together, they weighed from a practical standpoint the degree of support that the mass of factory workers was likely to give them.

A distrustful, foolish-looking blacksmith named Akeev took the floor. He spoke excitedly, loudly, as if fearing not to be heard. Bristling all over, he strained his body as if he wanted to hurl himself on his opponent, to trample and obliterate anyone who wouldn't agree with him:

Comrades, as an honest, genuine worker I tell you that you've come up with these plans too soon! The fruit of revolution is not yet ripe, yet you want to pluck it from the tree. Before we can overthrow the autocracy, we must first enlighten the ignorant worker, we must first transform him not into a parrot, but into an honest, perceptive worker. Karl Marx has said: the liberation of the workers is an affair for their own hands.[16] That means you must help us, you must teach us, but you shouldn't organize a premature demonstration. It will harm the proletarian worker. . . . That's what I want to tell you! . . . Nothing less, nothing more!

Akeev fiercely waved his two fists and brought them down heavily, as if he were smashing the head of a hypothetical opponent with a sledgehammer.

The Artist began to object to Akeev's remarks, accusing him of "tailism" [17]:

Not everyone who says "Oh Lord, oh Lord" will enter the kingdom of heaven, says the Gospel, and, by the same token, not everyone who bangs on his chest and says he is the most genuine, honest worker is a true defender of the interests of the working class. What kind of honor can there be, Comrade Akeev, when you don't have anything to eat! How can you show another worker the way, when you lag behind yourself? It's not that the fruit of revolution hasn't ripened, it's your own brain, Comrade Akeev, that still isn't ripe! That's why you cannot even see anything. . . . Let's even suppose that our demonstration doesn't succeed, it still must be done. The time has come to teach the workers a new method of struggle. . . .

Then The Artist was followed by the calm, self-confident Ponty Denisov. Ponty spoke with authority, with aplomb, occasionally running his heavy hand along his lush head of reddish hair:

"For reasons you already know, we workers are distrustful of all your proposals"—he nodded in the direction where intelligentsia were standing. "And the reason we're so distrustful is that we have no intention of placing the workers' backs under the Cossacks' whips for nothing. . . ."

"We're not going to spare our own backs either!" came a voice from the crowd, offended.

"Yes, we're aware of that," Ponty continued, unperturbed. "But you are few in number, while we workers are many. The whip will come down on our necks first. If we're going to stick our necks out, then let's do it seriously and for a good reason. We're not afraid to fight the Cossacks and police, but let it be a fight that will aid the cause of the revolution, not one that starts frivolously just because our fingers are itching to do something. We're also for a demonstration, but a demonstration that has been carefully prepared, so that the most backward workers would know what we were fighting for, and a demonstration that would shake the tsarist autocracy to its very foundations and would serve as a prologue to revolution! . . ."

Ponty's impassioned speech aroused tremendous enthusiasm and prolonged clapping. It was followed by more speeches by intelligentsia, and the workers now began to speak up much more boldly. Toward the end of the meeting a resolution was passed unanimously—to organize a demonstration and to prepare for it very carefully.

Feeling cheerful and determined, scattered in our solitary boats, we headed home with the firm intention to engage in our first open battle with the autocracy. Our forces were unequal. We knew that we would fall, as victims in this "fateful struggle." But we were gripped by the enormous power of ideas, ideas in whose name we were prepared to give up everything we cherished and valued—our freedom, and even our lives. And, along the immense breadth of the spring beauty of the Volga, our voices carried:

> *Volga, Volga, whose waters abound in the spring,*
> *Even you don't flood the fields the way*
> *The great grief of the people*
> *Overflows our land....*[18]

After the passing of the resolution by such an authoritative and, for those times, such a heavily attended assembly, practical preparations for the demonstration began in earnest. By now there were several revolutionary organizations in the city: the Committee of the Socialist Revolutionary Party, the United Group of Social Democrats and Socialist Revolutionaries, the Social Democratic League of Artisanal Workers, and our own Saratov Social Democratic Committee.[19] The strongest of these, the one with the largest number of workers, was, of course, our committee. It enjoyed great authority among the workers, and, as a consequence, it bore the largest share of responsibility for the organization of the demonstration. Most of the other organizations, by contrast, were weak and short of members. Nevertheless, at a moment of heightened struggle one couldn't ignore even the most modest forces—all of them had to be drawn together and put to use. Our committee took the initiative in conducting negotiations for the joint participation of all these organizations in the demonstration. We drew up an agreement and even issued a proclamation with a call to the demonstration.

Of course the Socialist Revolutionaries attempted to exploit the impending demonstration for their own purposes. They wanted to peg the demonstration to the execution of Stepan Balmashev, transforming the demonstration itself into a mass protest against his execution.[20] In other words, they wished to take the notion that looked so neat and smooth on paper in commentaries to their program—that Balmashev's shot was the hero's "opening solo," and the mass demonstration was the "choir" joining in with the soloist—and turn it into a reality. However, this SR venture was unsuccessful and was soon exposed. To be sure, a black banner in memory of Stepan Balmashev was among the large banners with proletarian slogans carried at the demonstration; it bore the inscription "Balmashev has been executed, the hero's memory shall live forever." But the SRs learned of this banner only after the demonstration.

Moving somewhat ahead of my story, it should be noted that, notwithstanding all the noise and chatter produced by the SRs on the subject of the demonstration, their participation in it amounted to nothing. Eloquent testimony to this may be found in the names of the people arrested both at the demonstration itself and in connection with it. Not a single Socialist Revolutionary was to be found among the dozens of names of people arrested and brought to trial. A similar picture of the SR Party emerged from the demonstrations of the same year in Nizhny-Novgorod and Rostov-on-the-Don; they were always conspicuous by their absence.[21] Even the blind could see that the mass of workers wasn't following the SR Party. Here is what was written in a letter published in *Iskra*, No. 43, by a former member of the RSDLP's Saratov committee:[22]

The people who gave speeches at the pre–May Day agitational assemblies on Zeleny Island stand out clearly in my memory; I recall the people who prepared the banners, the people who wrote and edited the proclamations and posters, the people who drew up the campaign plan; I can also recall the ones who scattered and posted the proclamations. And yet, no matter how I strain my memory, I cannot remember a single Socialist Revolutionary among all these people. I remember the day itself, the fifth of May, I even remember the minute, when the banners suddenly flew up and the crowd that was gathered round them singing the "Varshavianka" moved toward Nemetskaya Street; I remember the demonstrators' heroic battle with the policemen and detectives, some in disguise, some not in disguise, who attacked them. And yet, once again, among those in the crowd who carried the banners, distributed the proclamations, and fought with the police, I am unable to recall a single Socialist Revolutionary, try as I may. Finally, I remember the court, I remember the speeches of the defendants and their lawyers. Both the former and the latter spoke of what had happened as a "Social Democratic" workers' demonstration, and not one of the defendants protested against this. . . .

. . . Messrs. Socialist Revolutionaries took on the difficult task of appropriating the Saratov demonstration, which was organized and carried out through the collective efforts of the Saratov Committee of the RSDLP, the Saratov Social Democratic Artisans' League, and the Social Democratic members of the United Group of SDs and SRs. They took on the difficult task *post factum*, in their periodicals and leaflets, of transmuting the Saratov workers' May Day demonstration into a Socialist Revolutionary demonstration in memory of Balmashev. But one cannot really count as participation in the organization of the demonstration the fact that, at the moment when it was really in full swing, someone handed one of the members of the SD committee a bundle of SR proclamations for distribution together with those issued by *Iskra* and the demonstration's organizers. Nor should one count as SR participation in the organization of the demonstration the fact that only after the demonstration was over did they learn about the black banner in memory of the recently executed Stepan Balmashev. . . .

The Saratov demonstration revealed the SRs' complete impotence and their petty-bourgeois, reactionary essence. Shortly thereafter, the united group of SRs and SDs broke into its component parts. Then, having left the united group, the SD component, along with the SD Artisans' League, joined the Saratov Social Democratic Committee and formed a single organization, after which the Saratov committee sent an announcement to *Iskra* in which it recognized *Iskra* as its leading Party organ.

However, we weren't the only ones preparing for the demonstration; the gendarmes were preparing for it as well. They began to step up their shadowing of our members. Day and night, the spies would never stray from our cooperative workshop; they would meet and accompany everyone who came to our place. And in the city itself arrests and searches took place one after another. We saw and felt that our days of freedom were numbered. There was no point hiding or fleeing, and besides there was nowhere to go. We intensified our revolutionary work in preparation for the demonstration.

"If we must die, at least we die for our cause!" The Artist would say.

And, in fact, early one sunny morning, on April 24, when the spring day was joyfully dawning, the sun was laughing, and everyone wished so much to live, to act, to rejoice—the entire block was suddenly flooded with police. In no time at all the building that housed our cooperative workshop was surrounded, and a mad, furious search, resembling a bandit raid, was begun. Stupid, red-nosed, with the necks of oxen, regular police, gendarmes, and some "characters" in civilian clothes broke the floors, messed up the workbenches, poked at the walls with the ends of their swords, banged on the ceiling so hard that the plaster fell down. . . . But it was all in vain. Apart from a few illegal photographs, which we had no desire to conceal, a tin sheet, a negative, and two type cases, the gendarmes, for all their trouble, found nothing.

Five passenger cabs drove up to the house. I was seated in one, Albert Retling, Lalov, The Artist, and, I believe, Bychkov were put in the others. A gendarme took a seat in each carriage next to the prisoner, and another gendarme stood facing them. In this form, the entire procession moved unhurriedly toward the familiar prison. The black jaws of the massive iron gate swallowed us into the foul belly of the prison for a long time.

40
The Demonstration

THE NUMEROUS arrests and searches, however, did not prevent the organization of the demonstration—the first in the history of the revolutionary movement.[1] In order to draw as large a crowd as possible, the Saratov Social Democratic Committee decided to move the date to the first Sunday after May 1, which was May 5.[2] The appropriate preparations were made. At noon on the appointed day small clusters of people began to gather at the upper market. The police expected the demonstration to start out at Cathedral Square, as had been indicated in our leaflet, so they concentrated their forces there. Hence there were almost no police to be seen in the market area.

At about half past twelve, a group of demonstrators suddenly broke off from the sauntering crowd, marched out on the pavement, and simultaneously raised two banners, bearing the inscriptions "Down with the autocracy!" and "Long live socialism! The eight-hour day!"

Voices resounded:

"Down with autocracy!"

The timid whistle of an isolated, frightened, hiding policeman was heard. Someone cried out:

"It's a riot!"

The crowd bolted to the sides, overturning the hawkers' trays along the road. . . .

After grabbing their baskets of goods, the tradeswomen fled from the marketplace. Panic reigned supreme.

Some people imagined they were seeing the cholera riots of 1891 again; others thought a pogrom was beginning.[3] People vacated the market square. Isolated, the group of demonstrators, still unruffled, stood its ground. However, this situation did not last very long. People moved toward the demonstrators from all directions and gathered round them. An imposing crowd was beginning to form, while the red banners hovered over their heads in the rays of the sun. Singing revolutionary songs, the demonstrators crossed Moscow Street and headed in the direction of Theater Square. The police were taken unawares and had no idea what to do next. Detectives poked about in the crowd or concealed themselves inside the houses, not daring to undertake anything. In a state of confusion, an isolated policeman was walking alongside the demonstrators. Leaflets and proclamations flew into the crowd, sparkling in the sunlight as if they were white doves. The people grabbed for them, tore them out of each other's hands, and hid them in their pockets. At Theater Square a black banner was suddenly raised above the crowd bearing the inscription in white letters: "Balmashev has been executed, the hero's memory shall live forever. Down with the butchers!"

The demonstrators successfully crossed Theater Square and passed through Aleksandrovskaya Street, singing with great animation:

"Arise, arise, ye working people!"

Two tall, stately figures could be seen in the crowd: the graceful, handsome student Kossovich, who carried a red banner, and "Platonych" (Efimov), who marched solemnly with a huge, knotty walking stick, protecting the banner. This peaceful, majestic procession of demonstrators continued for about twenty minutes. Amazed and astonished citizens stared at it from the balconies of their homes and from their windows. Here and there people waved their handkerchiefs in sympathy. Occasionally cries of "hurrah" rang out.

But then the procession reached Nemetskaya Street, the main street. No police or troops were there. However, when the demonstrators turned the corner in the direction of Cathedral Square, they were suddenly attacked by numerous previously concealed plainclothesmen, soldiers, spies, and even "volunteers" from the civilian population, who began to assault them mercilessly. A dreadful brawl ensued. The demonstrators defended themselves with sticks, stones, and even with bare fists. Kossovich and Platonych held out longer than anyone else. Using huge sticks, they beat back their attackers on all sides. And when the assailants wrested Platonych's stick from his hands, he hurled himself on a policeman, knocked him to the ground, and took away his sword. With the policeman's sword in hand, he rushed into the crowd of pogromists and continued to annihilate the foe for a long time until, battered and bloody, he was finally disarmed. About a hundred demonstrators, unable to get away, beaten and mutilated, were surrounded by police and herded into the courtyard of a nearby house. Soon regular army units and detachments of police began to show up on the street and on Theater Square. But by this time there were no longer any demonstrators. The chief of police and the governor arrived on the scene. The arrestees were taken to the police station and then, at night, were herded to the prison, where they were sorted out. The innocent bystanders were soon released. The gendarmes were looking for the standard-bearers, but they evidently had no information at all, since they accused virtually every arrestee of being one of the men who had carried a banner during the demonstration.

This, then, in general outline, is the picture of the May 5 demonstration as I learned of it while already in prison. Despite the heavy losses suffered by the Social Democratic Committee, the demonstration made a great impression on the average citizen, aroused the mass of workers, filled them with energy, and braced their spirits.

The demonstrators were kept in prison a fairly long time. Those against whom there was no real evidence were exiled administratively to the northern provinces. About twelve people were put on trial before the Special Session of the Judicial Chamber,[4] and almost all of them were sentenced to permanent resettlement in Siberia. Among them were S. M. Fofanov, N. A. Arkhangelskaya, Bochkarev, A. A. Chubarovskaya, Oshanina, P. I. Voevodin, Kossovich, V. P. Efimov (Platonych), and others.

All the defendants conducted themselves quite bravely at the trial and hurled angry repartees at their hangman-judges. The members of the court were carefully picked from among arch–Black Hundreds.[5] But apparently even this wasn't good enough for the tsarist government. The doors of the courtroom were sealed—even as big a person as the president of the circuit court was not allowed access. Frightened by the demonstration, the gendarmes worked very hard in preparation for the trial. On several occasions they conducted mass searches and arrests among

all the unreliable residents of the town; they trained and instructed well over a dozen genuine perjurers, who "saw" the defendants marching at the head of the demonstration with their
own eyes. On the day of the trial all the streets and lanes adjoining the court building were overflowing with secret and regular
police and gendarmes. The streets were deserted that day, except,
of course, for the spies and detectives, who ran about freely
everywhere.

It goes without saying that, what with all these careful preparations, not one of the defendants had any real hope for positive
results from the legal proceedings. Most of them refused to present a defense. Only one young worker, Comrade P. I. Voevodin,
managed to make a brief speech at the trial.[6] The other defendants were silenced every time they began to speak.

Voevodin spoke as follows:

Two years ago, when I was working at a foundry in Ekaterinoslav, I was
arrested for reasons that are still unknown to me, and banished under
police supervision to Saratov, a town I didn't know. There I suffered from
hunger, cold, and every kind of deprivation, tried unsuccessfully to find
work, which I was prevented from getting each time because the police
intervened, and was subjected to humiliation by ordinary policemen and
other toadies of the tsarist government; by the age of sixteen I already
understood that my misfortune was only the tiniest particle of the general grief and oppression that weigh on the entire mass of workers. Our
foes are the capitalists, who squeeze the life out of us, and the tsarist
government, which stands wholeheartedly on their side and prevents us
from conducting our struggle. Like the entire working class, I had no
choice but to take to the streets and cry out: "Down with the capitalists!
Down with the autocracy!" By participating in the demonstration, I was
only fulfilling my duty, so I demand complete acquittal!

Because of his brazen speech, Voevodin (who was eighteen at
the time) served two and a half years in prison. The tsarist government knew no mercy. The court of the landlords and capitalists showed pity neither for the aged, nor for the young, nor for
women.

The liberal lawyer Volkenshtein,[7] who delivered an impassioned speech in defense of the accused, inadvertently uttered
these prophetic words:

" . . . Here, in the defendants' dock, sit people who belong to
the party that is going to save Russia!"

And indeed, a significant number of the defendants, hardened
by revolutionary experience, later became members of the very

party that would save Russia, but not the Russia of capitalists and landowners that the liberal lawyer wished to save, but the Russia of oppressed and enslaved workers and peasants, which it would transform into a free country of soviets.[8]

The court apparently wished to demonstrate its "impartiality," and it "acquitted" three people who obviously had not taken part in the demonstration. But this circumstance did not save the "acquitted" ones from administrative punishment—exile. The "just" and "merciful" tsarist court was following the traditions of the Holy Inquisition of the Middle Ages.

In those days, when a report would reach one of those hallowed courts that a certain woman was a witch, they would seize her, tie her up, and drag her to the tribunal of the Holy Inquisition. As is well known, medieval "witches" had the temerity almost always to deny their connection with the devil, which usually incriminated them in the eyes of the "just" court. The judges always had a very simple and reliable method by which to obtain the "truth." The "witch" was bound by her hands and feet and thrown into a basin that was constructed specially for such occasions. If the "witch" suffocated and sank to the bottom, she was considered innocent, removed from the basin, and buried in a cemetery with full Christian rites. But if, in defiance of the laws of physics, she failed to sink, and remained instead on the surface, her guilt was established beyond any doubt. The "witch" was then removed from the water and delivered up for public execution "without the shedding of blood"—she was burned at the stake.

41
Ponty Denisov

A YEAR LATER a second trial took place; the defendants were accused of having participated in the preparation of the Saratov demonstration. Among the defendants were two workers, accused of having distributed the May proclamations that contained the call to the demonstration. They were P. I. Denisov and Seliverstov. Both defendants had been arrested on the street while posting and distributing proclamations on the night of May 4–5. The court sentenced P. I. Denisov to permanent exile and resettlement in Siberia, and Seliverstov to three and a half years of service in a punitive battalion.

I will not bother to describe the trial proceedings; in their crudeness and shamelessness, they differed in no way from those of other tsarist courts. The outstanding event at the trial was Denisov's speech. The old Leninist paper, *Iskra*, wrote that "Comrade Denisov delivered a remarkable speech at the trial."[1]

With a real sense of his own worth, Comrade Denisov maintained a bold and fearless posture, hurling challenges at his class enemies. He began his speech as follows:

In his indictment, the prosecutor claimed that the demonstration of May 5 was the result of events in St. Petersburg, that is, of Balmashev's execution. It is evident that the prosecutor is familiar neither with the labor movement nor with the psychology of the masses. I am a worker myself, and my attitudes toward the contemporary social order were formed under the direct influence of the environment I lived in. My sad past has emerged before my eyes in the form of distant but still vivid images, of a time when people were exchanged for dogs, a time when workers were birched at the slightest pretext. My father told me how workers were sent to the guardhouse and how they were thrashed there, whipped without mercy. There were cases of workers who were beaten to death. Sometimes the more defiant workers were made to run the gauntlet. Rare was the person who could make it across the entire green soldiers' field under the blows of the rods. The majority, covered with blood, their flesh ripped to shreds, fell at the halfway mark, fell and died.

That is how the workers lived in the "good" old days, and things are no better today. The same old oppression, the same old misery, and although they no longer beat us with birch rods, no longer murder us with their sticks, that doesn't make things any easier. The Cossack's lash and the soldier's bullet are quite capable of taking the place of the birch rod and the gauntlet. The economic situation of the toiling masses is equally gloomy. Living all over Russia—whether in Moscow or Baku—I have seen how the workers are cooped up in cellars and kennels. I have seen workers when, exhausted after a hard day's work, they returned to their living quarters. Apathetic, lifeless, they grew duller with each passing day and looked like old men by the age of fifty. Their health, their spirits, the suppleness of their muscles and their minds—all disappeared. Everything was destroyed by the long workday, everything evaporated in their gray, monotonous lives. Nothing was left of their humanity; they were nothing now but walking labor power, capable of doing nothing but work.

I have seen the children of these poor people: emaciated, dressed in miserable rags, wasting away in the stuffy atmosphere of their apartments or in the fumes of factory soot.

I have seen the unemployed, people who wished nothing more than to work, because to have no work meant to have no sustenance, to have no life. And there are thousands, tens of thousands of workers, young ones and old, women and men, who have no life, who are destined for death. And they are dying—slowly, when seen through the eyes of an outsider—as hunger almost imperceptibly drives these workers from the rut of their toil into an early grave. Yes, this is the lot of the workers, whose lives are enshrouded in clouds of darkness. This sad epic of the toiling people could not pass me by without leaving its traces: it left its mark on my world outlook; it placed me in a hostile relationship to the existing order; it made me adhere to the newly forming workers' movement; and I became a conscious fighter for the cause of the emancipation of the working class. Today the workers' movement, which had an economic character in the 1890's, has taken on a political coloration, thanks to the economic crisis, thanks in part to the repressive measures of the government, but, above all, thanks to the growing maturity of the mass of workers. The strike has been replaced by the demonstration. I felt obligated to participate in one of these demonstrations—namely the May 5 demonstration in Saratov. On the night before May 5 I distributed proclamations inviting all workers, and all people who are devoted to the interests of the proletariat, to come out and express their protest against existing conditions.

The demonstration on May 5 was also the May holiday of the workers, and the prosecutor's conclusion that Balmashev's execution was the reason for the demonstration is wrong. There were May demonstrations both before and after the execution. The demands put forth by the workers have little in common with Balmashev. The terrorist means of struggle and the program of the party from whose ranks Balmashev emerged are equally alien to the workers' movement. At the present time workers are taking to the streets not to riot, not to summon the urban population to arms, not at all! They are demonstrating, they are trying to show the ruling class that they cannot tolerate their situation any longer, that they have the right to a better life. Written on the banners carried in the demonstration of May 5 were the words: "We demand the eight-hour workday!" and "Give work to the unemployed!" For some reason, the prosecutor failed to mention these demands in his indictment, yet these demands, which express the interests of the Russian workers, mean more to me than the others.

We workers must have the eight-hour day if we are to become human beings; if we are to have time not only for work, but for self-education and the education of our children; if we are to stop becoming so exhausted at work that we turn dimwitted; if we are to preserve our strength not only to the age of thirty or forty, but for our entire lives, for their strength is the only thing of value the workers have; if the working class is to be defended from physical degeneration, since working beyond one's strength exhausts the organism. Yes, I used the word "defend," for the fact is that the right of self-defense exists and is considered a legal right among all nations, in all corners of the globe.

I hope, honorable judges, that you are not going to challenge our claim, the claim of Russian workers, to this same right.

Our other demand was: "Give work to the unemployed." If the first demand was just, then the second is even more so. The people who are nourishing the ruling classes by their toil, the people who have created and continue to create all the benefits of the culture, have a greater right to enjoy those benefits than do the people who are reaping the fruits without having sown. And yet, though having this moral right, the workers are still not using it; they are not yet saying: "All those who are reaping the fruits of our labor must go." No, they are simply declaring: "Give work to the unemployed!" Give work to the hands that have supported and continue to support the past and present governments of nobles, manufacturers, and the other nonworking strata of the contemporary state! Give work to the people who have created the wealth of others, while suffering hardships themselves!

Is it possible that you, honorable judges, will call people who are demanding work "criminals"? Is it possible you will condemn them to death by starvation? Not only would that be unjust, it would be cruel, monstrously cruel. The demand for political freedom—with the additional words "down with autocracy!"—is not only a demand of the workers. Political freedom is also needed by the middle strata of the bourgeoisie and by people of the free professions, not to mention millions of peasants.

But what might be called freedom for those people, is not necessarily freedom for the workers. For workers, political freedom is not an end in itself, but a necessary condition for the defense of their interests, for the conquest of a better future; hence an exclusively political movement cannot be the movement of the working masses.

I am a Social Democrat. Since I believe that Social Democracy, and it alone, is the true expression of the interests of the proletariat in general and the Russian workers in particular, I consider it my duty to follow its principles, to act in accordance with its program.

One of the points in that program is the demand for political freedom. This demand is not the product of any theoretical considerations. No, this demand arose from life itself. The reason for its appearance is rooted just as deeply in the working masses as are the reasons that the Russian workers are turning into Social Democrats.

The autocracy squeezes the labor movement; the autocracy uses all possible means to champion the cause of the big capitalists, so dear to its heart, in their conflicts with workers. The autocracy keeps the workers down; it offers the workers nothing but dungeons, Cossack lashes, and soldiers' bullets; it punishes them for participation in secret labor unions, for strikes, for any kind of protest activity carried out by the working masses. The autocracy exiles the best fighters for the workers' cause to Siberia, to the cold, barren tundras. The autocracy acts as an obstacle to the propaganda of socialist ideas and to the achievement by the workers of a socialist order.

In propagating socialist ideas, the Social Democrats hope that those ideas, when they have penetrated into the popular masses, will make possible the implementation of the kind of reforms that are beneficial not only to the toiling classes, but to all humanity. The introduction of social reforms requires a people's government, for reforms are possible only when the people can embody its ideas and its desires in legislation, so that the laws can then be applied to life.

One way or another, I have taken part in the struggle for the emancipation of the working class; I saw and continue to see my participation as a right, as much of a right as life itself. I believe that I also have the right to propagandize socialist ideas, to distribute brochures and proclamations, and to summon people to a demonstration. This right is founded on the rights of tens of millions of people. The endless toil of our ancestors and of our grandchildren yet to come—all this gives us the right to struggle. That is the right of starving peasants, the right of weary workers.

The right to struggle is a human right!

Comrade Denisov's speech was a generalization of the broad experience of mass revolutionary struggle; it showed which class of people was the forward detachment in this struggle and it showed the paths that had led these people to conclude that struggle was necessary.

Here is the subsequent fate of Comrade Denisov. He did not remain in exile very long. At the first opportunity, when the season of bad, slushy roads in Siberia was over, he fled abroad. There he became an active member of the Party's Bolshevik faction, and became close to Lenin. Later, he returned to Russia to engage in revolutionary work. He worked as a professional revolutionary in the Petersburg committee, but things went wrong and he was arrested. He always remembered his arrest with horror.

"That day will remain in my memory as long as I live," he said to me, soon after his release from prison. "I can remember even the minutest detail":

I was spending the night in the apartment of a certain liberal. When I woke up, a sunny morning was peeking through the window. The clock showed half past eight. I hastily threw on my outer garments and went to look for a bathroom or a wash basin. It was a fantastic, lordly apartment. I said to myself: under socialism all workers shall live in apartments like this. The endless glittering white corridor contained a multitude of doors, on the right and on the left. Which way should I go? Problems like this always confronted me when I happened to pass the night in the rich apartment of one of our liberal sympathizers. It was always simpler in the home of a worker—you didn't get confused there. I didn't like to overnight in chic apartments. The previous evening, my hospitable host—a wealthy engineer with whom I spoke about higher matters until late into the night—had pointed out the lavatory to me as we took leave of each other. Now I was pulling on the knob of the door right next to it, thinking that it led to the bathroom, when suddenly the troubled face of the maid peered through the door. "The bathroom's on the other side," she said, angrily poking her finger in the opposite direction. I opened the door and entered a spacious bathroom, where I took off my shirt and delightedly washed myself down to the waist with cold water. When I returned to my room, a glass of steaming, aromatic coffee with cream, some fresh rolls, and some marvelous tender ham were already on the table. I quickly devoured it all with great pleasure. . . . Well, you know what kind of appetite I have, don't you?

I laughingly agreed. Ponty continued his story in an excited tone:

I walked about the room, looked out the window, glanced at the clock. . . . It was too early to go to my secret meeting.

I rang the bell. A neat-looking, graceful housekeeper arrived, whose appearance had nothing in common with that of the maid I had met when I was looking for the bathroom. I screwed up my courage and asked her to bring me some more to eat. She smiled, picked up the dishes, and returned in a minute with a second, equally large portion. . . .

Cheerful, merry, in a splendid mood, I left the hospitable apartment. "Without the liberals, it would probably be very hard to prepare a revolution," was the thought that flashed through my head, as I endeavored to soften my dislike for them. At the main stairway the doorman assumed a servile posture and honored me with a deep bow. I rummaged in my pocket and carelessly thrust a 20-kopeck piece into his hand.

Out on the street, I cocked my hat on the back of my head, waved my walking stick carelessly, and slowly headed for my appointment. I walked without looking back, but I listened discreetly for footsteps and tried to let anyone who was behind me walk by. At the corner of Svechny Lane, I was supposed to turn to the left. I held up for a moment and took a quick look behind me. Seeing nothing suspicious, I walked calmly to the conspiratorial apartment. The door was opened by the very enterprising secretary of the Party's Petersburg committee—"Olga Dmitrievna." She asked me to wait, and, in a low voice, continued her interrupted conversation with a skinny, pale, blackhaired man. I sat down in the opposite corner on a soft little sofa, took the newspaper *Petersburg Sheet*[2] from the table, and began to read, starting with the next-to-the-last page, where all kinds of local news and adventure stories were printed:

"On Sredny Avenue, in the Romanov house, a male infant was left at the door of apartment No. 8, belonging to a Haymarket tradesman named Mitrokhin; it was wrapped in a thick cloth coat, baptized. . . ."

I didn't read any further. I then glanced through the stupidest article about the need to keep our cesspools in proper order. During my wanderings in and out of overnight hideaways and conspiratorial apartments, I had learned to determine the social position of the occupants by their newspapers. In this case there could be no doubt that the apartment dweller was a tradesman or an innkeeper. A typical liberal civil servant would usually get *The St. Petersburg News*, whereas dyed-in-the-wool reactionaries were sure to subscribe to *New Times*, and the intelligentsia—physicians, attorneys, engineers—would always read *The Russian News*.[3] This Olga Dmitrievna was a most valuable person! She had connections in all strata of society. . . . Now I could catch a few phrases: "To hell with him and his bulldog revolvers and Smith-Wessons. . . . you couldn't kill a fly with them. . . ." "He must belong to a workers' self-defense fighting squad," I thought, and I began to listen in.[4]

The "fighter" was insistently demanding Brownings. Olga Dmitrievna promised to get a few pieces within a week. I recalled how, at a meeting recently held at my place, the workers had also asked for weapons. "Just bring us a lousy 'bulldog.' . . . Anything is better than running around armed with nothing but sticks. At least we could scare the hell out of them," they said. I made up my mind that I too would ask Olga Dmitrievna for a few guns to protect our meetings from the Black Hundreds.

The fighter departed. I began to talk with Olga Dmitrievna. I badly needed propagandists and agitators in my district. Our workers' circles were growing and multiplying like mushrooms after a nice warm rain. At the time we were also beginning to conduct some small "flying" meetings.[5] But we had no agitators. Here and there I would take the floor myself. When our committee learned of this it strictly forbade it. They were afraid I'd be done in. Olga Dmitrievna scolded me soundly.

I briefly explained the needs of our district. Olga Dmitrievna frowned and, enunciating her words with care, said with displeasure: "I have told everyone on the committee a hundred times—there are no propagandists! You must get by with your own resources!" But after giving it some thought, she went on to say: "Then again, I guess I could send you two or three students or women from the special courses. But only under one condition: don't let them start conducting propaganda right away. First let them read a little. . . . I don't think they even know our program! They have the zeal, they have all the revolutionary passion you could possibly want, but what's in their heads?" Olga Dmitrievna sadly tapped her forehead with her finger as she spoke. "The complete absence of any presence of mind. . . . There are plenty of them around, but they absolutely should not be sent to the workers—they'll repeat every conceivable heresy. . . . Well, what other questions do you have for me?"

I describe the workers' request for "bulldogs." Olga Dmitrievna cuts me off very abruptly, before I can finish: "You should take care of your own business! Don't squander your energies! There are others to take care of the providing of weapons. A certain person will be sent to your district for that purpose."

She jokingly takes me by the shoulders and shifts her attention to the exit door. Two more people are still waiting to speak with her. I know one of them: a long, thin agitator known by the alias "Gennady." But he pretends not to know me. I walk past him and quickly run down the steep stairway. As I pass through the entrance, I look around me. All is clear. Assuming a lighthearted air, I walk to the left and cross to the other side of the street. When I reach the corner, I turn to the right. But at that moment, emerging simultaneously from behind some gates, coming from different directions, two strange characters rush up to me. One of them, the one who was farthest away, was moving faster, and almost cut me off. His stiff hat was very striking. It was of reddish color and was pulled over his eyes. His face was the color of a beet, his nose was flattened and shot through with violet; he wore a starched, upright collar and a black tie with a pin whose head resembled a small green insect. I didn't get a good look at the second character. All I remember is that he looked emaciated and feeble. His shabby gray coat was hanging on him as if on a stake. He was already very close to me. I acted as if none of this had anything to do with me, and walked on with determination. The character who was closer to me cried out "Stop!"—and he thrust out his hand so as to seize me by the scruff of the neck. I raised my arm and hit him with the back of my right hand. He landed against a wall and fell down, his feet pointing upward in a comical manner. Just at that moment the second character ran up to me. I hit him as well. He turned out to be steadier on his feet; he tumbled toward the pavement, but maintained his balance. I started running. Behind me resounded police whistles and cries of "Grab him!" People were running from every direction—janitors, policemen. "Alas," I think, "something's got to save me! It's either freedom or hard labor for me now!"

I hear the heavy stamping of boots behind me. I run, without looking back. The street is straight, wide; you can see a great distance along it. I have the feeling that the stamping and the sound of voices behind me have abated. A ray of hope. . . . But suddenly, unexpectedly from the side, a big lummox jumped out from behind a gate; I had barely caught sight of him before he knocked me off my feet and pinned me down with his whole carcass. "Farewell, freedom, and, perhaps farewell to life!"— the thought cut through me.

When I regained consciousness I was in the custody of the political police. I was beaten and exhausted. . . . Oh, how terrifying it is even to recall these events. Thank goodness it's all in the past. Yet even now I have dreams of spies pursuing me. . . . I suddenly leap up in the middle of the night in a cold sweat and tremble with fear. . . . And yet you know perfectly well that I'm no coward.

Ponty averted his face and suddenly turned silent. But then, as if he had remembered something important, he added hurriedly: "While I was in prison I suffered for a long time from hallucinations. I was afraid to sleep all alone. . . ."

After this arrest Ponty was held in confinement under investigation for about a year. Then he was once again placed on trial— before the St. Petersburg Judicial Chamber, if I'm not mistaken. The court sentenced him to three years' hard labor for unlawful flight from his place of exile. They held him for a long time in a transit prison to await relocation to one of the central prisons for hard labor. . . . But then, fortunately, the 1905 Revolution began. There was soon an amnesty for political "criminals."[6]

> *The tsar has been frightened—he's issued a manifesto:*
> *The dead shall be free, the living—arrested!*[7]

However, for a long period tsarist justice was reluctant to extend this amnesty to Denisov. It was only toward the end of 1905, when the waves of revolution had risen higher and higher, that he was finally released from prison. Cheerful, gay, full of hope and confidence, he returned to freedom and resumed his revolutionary work.

While still in prison he had begun to write a brochure entitled "The Worker in the Revolutionary Movement." He completed this brochure after his release. With great animation, Ponty later told me how he had gone to Vladimir Ilich,[8] who spoke of his work very approvingly and even wrote a preface for it. Ponty was very excited and waited impatiently for the publication of his booklet. But shortly thereafter the period of reaction set in.[9] Soon there were pogroms, searches, arrests, banishments, and firing

squads. It would seem that Denisov's brochure, together with Ilich's preface, perished in a police raid on the press where it was
being printed.

Before long, I too had to flee from Piter under duress. . . . For
many of us there now began a quiet, prolonged period of wan-
dering, prison, banishment under police escort, exile. . . . I lost
sight of Denisov.

My next, brief encounter with P. I. Denisov took place in Ekaterinburg in 1919, when, after Kolchak had been defeated,[10] the
Party Central Committee sent me, together with a group of comrades, to organize Soviet power in Siberia. I saw him between
trains. Denisov had aged, but he still was cheerful, still served in
our Party, and was preparing to reestablish the Ural industry that
had been destroyed by White bands. In the intervening years he
had lived abroad and become an engineer.

We took leave of each other with warmth and affection, hoping
to meet again soon and to have the opportunity to talk more thoroughly about our past experiences, about the present, and about
our promising future.

But, alas, our plans were not destined to be realized. A few
months later, I learned from a visiting comrade that P. I. Denisov
had come down with typhus and died. A leading revolutionary
worker had passed away, one of those who belonged to the generation of I. V. Babushkin, educated by the old *Iskra* of the Lenin
period, one of those workers without whom "the Russian people,"
as Lenin has said, "would have remained a people of slaves and
bondsmen forever. . . . With men like that the Russian people will
win its complete emancipation from all exploitation."[11]

42
In Prison Again

THE ANCIENT, ramshackle, thick-walled prison was overflowing with political prisoners. Its rancid, damp walls, still reeking from the stench of prisoners' sweat, had never heard so many free speeches and revolutionary songs. People were herded into their cells in crowds, like cattle into their stalls. Only a few of the more "important" "criminals" were placed in isolation. I apparently fell into that category, for they placed me in solitary and a guard strictly saw to it that I had no contact with anyone.

This time my cell was not as comfortable. It was located in the far corner of the yard, behind some strange projections from the wall, almost at the semibasement level. Because the cell window was set back inside the wall, the cell was dark and damp even on the brightest, sunniest days. But even that wasn't so bad. On the very first night I discovered yet another basic problem with the cell. Around midnight, as I lay quietly in the serene sleep of youth, I was suddenly awakened by a strange, unusual noise and the sounds of people romping about, and my cell was filled with an incredibly suffocating odor. I climbed onto the windowsill and began to peer into the darkness of the night. It turned out to be the handiwork of the so-called "gilders," the workers who came to clean up the lavatories. They came about three nights a week, arriving in two carts with their barrels, and, making loud noises and rumbling sounds, they spent the entire night pumping the filth out of the lavatories with their hand pumps. And the strange projection from the wall turned out to be nothing more or less than an outhouse.

I attempted to present a formal protest to the prison administration, but nothing came of it. The prison was very overcrowded.

So I remained there in a state of uncertainty for almost two weeks; I began to be seized by unpleasant thoughts and by doubts about whether the demonstration had taken place.

"This means that the gendarmes have triumphed. All the militant comrades were rearrested, and no one was left to organize it," I thought.

But one day, in the late afternoon, when I was standing sadly by the barred window, the fragmentary sounds of joyful singing drifted into my cell:

> *Let us renounce the world of old,*
> *Let us shake its dust from our feet!* . . .

The sounds grew louder, expanded, came closer and closer. I climbed on a stool and clung greedily to the window grating. Soon a motley crowd of prisoners descended on the courtyard. I could see white bandages, resembling turbans, on many of their heads, and some of them had bandaged hands. . . . Their faces looked thin, pale from the loss of blood, but also cheerful, happy, with glowing eyes. . . .

I could recognize many of them from afar. There is the tall Kossovich, there are Chubarevskaya and Elizaveta Nikolaevna Popova, who is dressed like a man, and over there, with her golden curls, tall and thin like a reed, is Varya Diakova, and behind her—Platonych, Fofanov. . . . I yell loudly and, thrusting my arm through the grating, I wave a handkerchief. Someone sees it . . . and the whole crowd rushes toward my window. They vie with one another to tell me about the demonstration, about different episodes of clashes with police, and, with great animation, they tell me the latest political news.

"Aleksey Rykov—you know? He got away. . . . When they were herding us into the yard he climbed over the fence and ran away," someone told me in a hushed voice. "It was neat! Too bad no one else was able to escape. . . ."

"Have they interrogated you?" Fofanov asks me, stammering. "We're refusing to testify. It doesn't matter. As they say, when there are seven disasters, one answer will do."

"No, they haven't," I reply, taking his statement as an indication of how I should handle myself under interrogation. But, even in isolation, I had already decided not to talk with the gendarmes.

Two guards run up to the window of my cell and "politely" prevail upon the prisoners to move away from the window and to continue their walk. For a long time I watch with longing and envy how my comrades walk around the yard in groups, talking impassionedly, laughing, clowning.

These walks around the yard and my contact with my comrades did not last very long. The prisoners were soon sorted out—some were released, some were placed in solitary confinement, and the rest, who were held in communal cells, were now kept more isolated. Once again my days dragged on cheerlessly, monotonously. I tried to organize my existence and began to study systematically. . . . There weren't many books, mainly belles lettres. But I wanted to study something serious. So I drew up a list of books on political economy and on the history of the Great French Revolution, and, on the first occasion I had, I dispatched it to my comrades who were still at liberty.

Soon I receive a big pile of books, including some I haven't even requested. Among them is volume I of Marx's *Capital*.[1] Not daring to read it, I reverently postpone doing so until such time as I have first read some other books on political economy. I begin to read Zheleznov, then Chuprov, then Tugan-Baranovsky's *Russian Factory*, and then, once again, Ilin's *Development of Capitalism in Russia*.[2]

But no sooner was I beginning to get as deeply involved as I wanted in this introductory course of studies, when they summoned me to the prison office for questioning, which immediately derailed me.

There, sitting triumphantly in the smallish office of the prison warden, was the gendarme Semiganovsky, already known to the reader.[3] He was smoking a cigar and fingering some papers in a businesslike manner. On the other side of the table sat a pleasant-looking judicial officer in a neat little uniform with bright buttons and an official decoration in his buttonhole. The judicial officer politely invited me to take a seat, indicating a chair at the end of the table with a nod of his head. Suppressing my inner turmoil, I sat down with apparent ease and warily began to await the interrogation.

"I am the deputy prosecutor; my name is. . . ." He said his name, but I didn't catch it. "I am here as a representative of the judicial authority, to see to it that the investigation is conducted properly," the official said pompously.

I kept my silence.

Semiganovsky placed a sheet of paper on the table, dipped his pen in the inkwell, and, preparing to take down my testimony, turned his well-groomed, self-satisfied face toward me. Speaking casually through his nose, he asked me:

"Your name is Kanatchikov?"

Hatred began to boil in me. Holding back my rage, I said very slowly, articulating my words very clearly:

"Before asking me any questions, you should first ask me if I want to speak with you at all."

The gendarme put down his pen and, without changing his tone, filtered his words through his teeth:

"This means you refuse to testify?"

"Yes, I refuse," I confirmed in a decisive tone.

"Well, all right, that's your right. . . . It's just that you'll have to stay locked up in prison for a long time while we're conducting the investigation. . . . If you refuse to help us. . . ."

"Helping gendarmes wouldn't even enter my mind," I broke in.

"There's no reason for you to get excited, Mr. Kanatchikov, the captain is asking you questions that are completely legal, and there is nothing in them that should offend you. He is merely doing his official duty," the judicial officer interjects gently.

"And I am doing my revolutionary duty."

It was evident that Semiganovsky did not wish to continue the interrogation in this atmosphere. Pushing the sheet of paper toward me that was to contain the inquiry protocol, he said:

"Write down that you refuse to give any testimony."

"I refuse to write or sign anything at all," I declared categorically.

The judicial officer and the captain exchanged very meaningful glances. The captain rang a bell. The senior guard entered the room and assumed a servile posture, awaiting his orders.

"Take him away!" said Semiganovsky, addressing him carelessly.

"But I still advise you to testify; it wouldn't obligate you to anything else. The investigation would end that much sooner. Go think it over." The "paternal" moralizing words of the judicial officer follow me out the door.

"I have already thought everything through and have made up my mind," I reply.

I later learned from comrades that this gallant prosecutor or deputy prosecutor was none other than the future Deputy Minister of Internal Affairs Makarov, who was to immortalize himself in the State Duma in 1912 when he responded to an inquiry into the massacre of workers at the Lena goldfields with the famous aphorism: "So it has been, so will it always be!"[4]

The dignitaries of our fatherland loved to immortalize themselves with aphorisms. Makarov's patron, former President of the Council of Ministers Stolypin, of whom Makarov was the "protégé" (they were both from Saratov), also proclaimed in the State Duma: "When a house is burning, you don't hesitate to break the windows."[5]

This was said by Stolypin-the-Hangman at the time of the suppression of the 1905 Revolution, when that suppression had engulfed many innocent victims. And still earlier, the celebrated General Trepov was able to express an entire command in one simple dictum: "Don't spare the bullets and don't fire any blanks."[6] At the beginning of his "righteous" reign, Nicholas II expressed his gratitude for the bloody punishment of the Iaroslav workers in the short aphorism: "Thank you, good lads of the Phanagorya Regiment."[7] It is true, however, that this excessive love for aphorisms on the part of our great dignitaries proved harmful to their authors, most of whom ended up badly. . . .

After the interrogation, I had barely managed to settle down and reflect on what had happened when I suddenly heard the clanking of the heavy bolts and locks of the doors to my cell and into my cell burst the small, thick figure of a gendarme, with fox-like features, dressed in a gray overcoat. Standing by the doors, he bowed politely and said:

"I am Captain Zubov."

I remained seated on the cot. The captain did not extend me his hand; he had apparently been chastened by the bitter experience of his relations with political prisoners and assumed, not without reason, that he would not receive a responsive handshake. I didn't know Zubov personally, but I had heard from comrades that he tries to play the role of an enlightened, liberal person, to whom the role of gendarme is disagreeable.

"How do you feel?" he asks, with apparent concern.

"Like a prisoner."

The guard closed the door, leaving the two of us alone.

"Yes, your cell is pretty bad," Zubov says, looking around my den.

"It couldn't be worse. . . . They've been trying to hide me here, that's all there is to it. . . ."

"Believe me, on my word of honor, I'm not here as part of this; I'm not involved in the investigation of your case."

"It makes no difference to me: you serve in the same organization."

"Even a single organization can have different kinds of people," said Zubov, pronouncing his words with great weight to let me know that he wasn't like other gendarmes. "You can believe me or not, but I serve here only in the interests of truth. Why, the gendarme bureau itself is, in principle, an extremely idealistic organization!" he said, raising his finger.

I burst into loud laughter.

"Don't laugh, young man, you've been misled about us by a deranged intelligentsia. You and they shouldn't be on the same path. You'll regret it some day. What do you have in common! Give us some time and the government itself will do everything for the people. You're still young, you have your whole life ahead of you. Why do you want to ruin it! You all say that you're fighting for the happiness of the people, but what is that happiness? No one can say. Even the Greek sages were unable to decide what happiness was. . . . Will you kindly permit me to sit down by you?" the captain asked gallantly, while lowering himself onto my creaky stool.

"And if I didn't allow you to, then what would you do?"

"You are intransigent, aren't you! . . . Please believe me, I wish you nothing but the best. It's your youth that makes me sorry for you. You are going to do yourself harm. Well, why are you so stubborn? Why not testify? All you're doing is lengthening the investigation; God knows how long you'll stay in prison, and with no benefit to yourself whatever!"

"You're wasting your time, Mr. Captain, this is getting you nowhere!"

"Well, all right. It's too bad, though. You're going to hurt yourself," Zubov said with disappointment, as he got up and pushed open the door with his foot.

The bearded figure of the guard suddenly emerged at the threshold. He had apparently been standing behind the door and listening in the whole time, lest I attempt some violence against this nobleman.

This was clearly the last attempt by the Saratov gendarmes to convince me to testify. From now until the end of my imprisonment they left me in peace.

43
The Traitor

I CAN REMEMBER how a light frost covered the brown puddles with a dull film of ice, obliterating the work of the spring sun.[1] The days grew longer. When everyone else had departed, I remained in the workshop and continued to work at my bench for a long time, without any lamplight, on the construction of a small conspiratorial table. It was very pleasant for me that no kerosene lamp was smoking under my nose, and that I didn't have to whirl and dance all around one—the way a convict dances near his wheelbarrow—while holding up my work in the path of its weak light.

Sergey Bychkov, a young, chubby, good-natured worker, entered the room. "Stop working, it's time for tea," he said cheerfully, making his way through to me between the tightly crammed workbenches. "You probably never worked this much for an employer!" he reproached me.

I took my eyes off the lathe and nodded toward Bychkov, inviting him to sit down. It was only now that I caught sight of a huge man moving quietly, like a shadow, behind Bychkov.

"I wanted you to meet; I've brought you a nice fellow from our factory."

The "nice fellow" stepped up to me, gave me his large rough hand, and said in a deep bass:

"Konstantin Tsarev."

I pressed the outstretched hand and, inconspicuously, began to conceal the traces of my conspiratorial work, having no desire whatever to initiate a new acquaintance into this affair. However, it was quite difficult to hide everything. The table was lying on the cover, and a white opening revealed the hollowness of the black table leg. At first I had the impression that the "nice fellow" wasn't paying any attention to this, but I was disturbed by the characteristic heedlessness of Sergey Bychkov, who had apparently decided to stimulate the imagination of his new convert:

"Look, Kostya, at the kind of pieces we are making here. There's no way anyone could ever guess! Why, gendarmes have come here to search and turned the whole house inside out, without finding any literature."

"Well, but where did they. . . . Why, even if I was told: 'Look around, there are proclamations here,' I still couldn't find them," Tsarev said approvingly in his bass voice, as he thrust his knotty fingers into the opening. "But what if things got stuck down there, how would you get them out?"

"They won't get stuck. The hole must be conical, wider at the lower end. Just shake and it all comes flying out," Bychkov explained in a businesslike manner.

Twilight was approaching; it was getting too dark to work. I gathered up my tools and, brushing the wood shavings and the small amount of litter off the workbench, went to the kitchen to start the samovar. I packed it all the way up with dry shavings, and it began to hoot for me like a factory chimney. In the room next to the workshop that served as our dining room and bedroom, I lit the lightning lamp and covered the table with an oilcloth. Then we sat down to drink tea. I was rather tired and had no desire to talk, so I observed my new acquaintance silently. His face, which was flat as a pancake, disturbed me from the outset. His small features, his flattened nose, his furtive, sullen glance, his watery eyes of indeterminate color, and his low, pinched-in forehead—all of these made a disagreeable impression. His small head, affixed to a broad, powerful, muscular torso, vividly reminded me of The Artist's sketches of Roman slaves.

"If you can give me lots of leaflets, I can launch a strike at my factory within a week," the fellow said. "Everyone will follow me, to a man! Whatever I say will be, and I'll tear anyone who's against us to pieces!"

Tsarev banged his fist on the table, which made the cups jump up and the samovar shake. Bychkov looked him in the face with trust and admiration and nodded his head approvingly.

"Yesterday I wanted to knock my foreman's block off," said Tsarev, "but the son of a bitch gave me the slip. . . ."

At this point he began to curse so abusively that I found it necessary to dampen his ardor.

"Stop all that foul language, Tsarev. I can follow you without it."

"I've been used to talking like this ever since I was a child, Comrade Semën. So please don't lecture me, brother. I express myself simply and plainly, like a worker. I'm no namby-pamby member of the intelligentsia. Whatever I think, I say."

"If you're a worker, does that make it all right to crap in your own pants?" asked Bychkov, trying to support me.

"You're both leaning on me. . . . All right, all right, I won't do it any more if you're going to be so proper and delicate," Tsarev responded in a conciliatory tone, pushing an empty glass in my direction.

He ate and drank hurriedly, noisily, and greedily, as if afraid that the food would be taken away from under his nose and he would be left hungry. He tore the bread, which was spongy like cotton wadding, into large tufts, crumpled it in his fist, and, instead of simply putting it into his mouth, threw it there.

"Comrade Semën, don't you have a revolver around here?" Tsarev asked me, tearing himself away from the food. "I'd like to frighten the spies. I can't seem to get rid of them."

"Where would I get a revolver? We're not SRs; we don't go in for terror."

"Well you're wrong not to. I've already said it to Sergey," he said, nodding in Bychkov's direction, "you people, you SDs, you have no fighting spirit!"

"Then why in the world have you come to us? You should have gone to the SRs."

"They've already been courting me. But I'm not very wild about them."

"Why not?"

"They don't have our working-class aroma to them. All they have are self-willed intelligentsia. . . . Well, all right, Comrade Semën, I'll come back to see you some other time. Just let me have some of your literature, and I'll be heading home. My good comrades are waiting for me there," said Tsarev, getting up from the table.

I found this degree of urgency and familiarity in someone I had just met for the first time somewhat astounding; nor was it comfortable for us to hand out illegal literature to a brand-new comrade whom we had not yet checked out. So I declared categorically to Tsarev that I didn't have any such literature at my place. He left feeling discouraged.

One other circumstance has stuck in my memory. As he was taking leave of me, Tsarev bent his face toward me; it exuded such a powerful mixture of alcoholic fumes, combined with either garlic or onion, that I no longer had any doubt about the source of his excessive familiarity.

Once we were alone together, I jumped all over Bychkov: "Why did you bring a creep like that to me? The devil knows who the hell he could be! He has some kind of hodgepodge in his head. . . . And he was drunk to boot!"

"Hey, stop scolding me, for God's sake! We had a bottle of beer together, nothing more."

"Then why do you have such a strong smell of vodka? And with garlic, too!"

"Well, maybe he dragged me into it? . . . But we didn't even get close to any garlic, though we did have some herring with onion. . . . But you're mistaken to have such a low opinion of him," Bychkov defended himself good-naturedly. "He's a conscious fellow, very well read and a fighter. He'd go to hell and back, he's fearless!"

On his next visit Tsarev made a more favorable impression on me. He talked about the routine at his factory, about the abuses perpetrated by the factory administration, about his revolutionary work, about the clever tricks and ploys he contrived in order to disseminate illegal literature at the plant. In all these adventures, in his clashes with the city police, with factory watchmen or foremen who tried to detain him or impede his dissemination of the literature, he invariably emerged victorious, whereas his enemies were made fools of or went flying head over heels into a ditch, into the mud, or into the snow, felled by a well-aimed blow of his fist.

Of course I didn't believe all the things he said, and, providing Tsarev this time with a small supply of illegal literature, I asked Bychkov to keep tabs on how well he carried out his mission.

Bychkov's response proved favorable—the literature ended up where it was supposed to. The next time, I gave him a bigger supply. Thus, little by little, Tsarev was able to gain our confidence.

Tsarev's theoretical notions were ridiculous. Providing him with Marxist brochures, talking with him, drawing him into debate, we tried to put him on the correct path. He began to visit our workshop more frequently. He made the acquaintance of almost all the comrades, and he got into discussions with them. They stopped being cautious around him, and one of them even worked on a conspiratorial cupboard, with a concealed rear wall for hiding illegal literature, right in his presence. And when the Saratov Social Democratic Committee organized a gathering on Zeleny Island to discuss plans for the forthcoming demonstration, Tsarev was one of the people I invited.

One day, completely unexpectedly, returning home to the workshop on the late side, I discovered a group of comrades there, passionately debating the fate of our revolution. In those days such debates were one of our few methods of self-education and preparation for the impending revolutionary struggle, for which each of us was striving. There was nothing on earth that we wouldn't subject to doubt, and we argued about everything. There wasn't a single truth that we were ready to leave in peace. Even the ancient axiom that a straight line was the shortest distance between two points was sometimes subjected to verification, especially by Mikhail Karev—"The Mnemonic"—who was fascinated by mathematical problems. These arguments often took place in the most unseemly places and at the most inopportune times. That is why, upon returning to my quarters, I was not really surprised by this late-evening debate and I immediately joined in. Tsarev was at the center of the group. Waving his huge arms as if they were the sails of a windmill, he spoke incoherently in his bass voice:

We must give this some thought: what would follow if we were to overthrow the autocracy prematurely? What would we replace it with in the future? The elemental masses of workers will gain nothing from the revolution. The example of the French Revolution shows us the results of the overthrow of an autocratic regime without the requisite preparation, just because the masses succumb to the mood of the moment, in a word, just because they act spontaneously. Kautsky[2] himself says: first the worker must be educated, and not just act like a parrot; but the intelligentsia doesn't want to educate us, the workers, because it's afraid we will discard them.

Tsarev droned on:

They don't allow us on their committees. They don't want a pure workers' revolution, they have to have two revolutions: first a bourgeois revolution, and then only later a workers' revolution, and just when that "later" will be, nobody knows.[3] What this means is that the workers will cast off the yoke of despotism only to take on the yoke of capitalist exploitation. The workers are baking the cake, but the biggest piece will go to their dear liberators, the intelligentsia, and their friends, the capitalists. . . .

Tsarev spewed forth this ridiculous stream of contradictory, bitter thoughts like cobblestones on a pavement; we were struck by their absurdity, their hollowness, and their political illiteracy. No one took all the things he was saying seriously. But only The Artist remarked, quite casually:

If we took seriously all the nonsense with which Comrade Tsarev has just doused us, and if he wasn't a worker, why we wouldn't even bother to argue with a man like that, we'd simply show him the door and say to him: go, we'd say, go, dear friend, and take your speech to Mr. Zubatov, the head of the internal security department.[4] You don't belong on our turf. But the real Tsarev doesn't know what he's doing. So, instead, we shall bear witness to his spiritual poverty and encourage him to read and study a little more.

Tsarev was deeply offended. He attempted to say something in his own defense, but no one would listen.

That evening we broke up rather late. When the guests had left, I removed from the secret table the latest issue of the journal *Zarya*,[5] which had been given to me by Auntie for two evenings, and began to read. It was hard to concentrate and to put yourself in the mood for serious reading after such passionate, stimulating arguments. Your attention was distracted, your thoughts rushed about hither and thither, wandered around in space, or dwelt on the excitement you'd experienced earlier in the day.

I apparently fell asleep in the middle of that unequal struggle with myself. I don't know how long I slept. I was awakened by a disturbing knock on the door. "Gendarmes! A search!"—was my first thought. The lamp was smoking, the copy of *Zarya* was lying on the floor. I grabbed it, shoved it into the secret table, and ran to the door.

"Who is there?" I asked with alarm, straining to speak in a calm voice.

"It's me, Konstantin Tsarev. Open up!"

"Shame on you! Go to hell! Scaring a person like that!" I admonished him, while letting him into the room. His voice sounded strange. When I was able to look at him in the light of the lamp, Tsarev looked like a ghost. Pale and trembling, he stood with his arms hanging down and babbled incoherently.

"What's going on?" I asked with trepidation.

"Gendarmes in my apartment," he jabbered, "a search. . . ."

"They chased you, and you escaped?"

"No. . . . I saw light in the window of my room, and some people moving about. . . ."

"Then what made you decide they were gendarmes?"

"Who else could it be! Yesterday the police were questioning the landlady about me. . . ."

I brought him a glass of water and made him drink it up. He became a little calmer. It was strange to see such a huge fellow in such an incredible fright.

He sat down on a stool and began to express his fears.

"How stupid you were," I said to him, "how foolish! Couldn't you find a better way to hide from the gendarmes than to come running to me? If there really were gendarmes at your place, do you really think they won't come here?"

Tsarev grew agitated again, grabbed his fur hat, and started to leave.

No matter how I tried to soothe him and to persuade him to stay with me overnight, he refused to listen.

"Where will you go now that night has fallen?"

"I'll just walk the streets, or else I'll go to a friend who isn't under suspicion."

And off he walked into the darkness of the night.

For a long time I was unable to fall asleep, while I listened carefully for any suspicious rustling or knocking sound.

On the evening of the following day Bychkov came to our apartment. My first question was, What was happening with Tsarev and had there been a search of his quarters?

"There was no search whatsoever. The fellow was so frightened that he imagined it. . . . He's a desperate coward! Why I didn't realize it earlier, I just can't understand," Bychkov said with disappointment.

I needed no convincing. From that moment on we decided to be more cautious with Tsarev.

Tsarev was arrested by accident. A good deal of illegal literature was found at his place, and either right away or within a couple of days he began to betray us.

This is what the Saratov gendarme colonel wrote about him in his report to the Department of Police:

Summoned to the preliminary investigation as a defendant, Tsarev testified that all the criminal literature that was confiscated from him had been obtained from the worker Semën Ivanov Kanatchikov, whom he had met through Sergey Ivanov Bychkov, a metalworker at the Terentev factory. According to Tsarev, he went to Kanatchikov's for books on several occasions, and during one of these visits Kanatchikov invited him to a gathering, to be held on the second day of Easter on Zeleny Island, which is located across from the city of Saratov. On the appointed day, he—Tsarev—in the company of Sergey Bychkov, went to Zeleny Island, where some hundred people—workers, students, and women—soon gathered. A meeting was held, at which it was decided to organize a street demonstration in Saratov on the first non-workday after May 1. According to Tsarev, none of the participants in the aforementioned gathering was known to him, with the exceptions of Bychkov and of one woman by the name of Elizaveta Nikolaevna (Popova—*S.K.*), whom he had already met in Kanatchikov's apartment.*

Evidently, Tsarev did not betray everyone right away. But once having embarked on the path of betrayal, he was unable to stop, and by frightening him the gendarmes were able to extract one admission after another. He probably said nothing about our conspiratorial tables and cupboards during his first interrogation, for the gendarmes paid no attention whatsoever to them when they searched our cooperative workshop. But sometime after our arrest they searched the workshop a second time, in the presence of those comrades who were still free, and this time they acted with greater certainty: they managed to discover the conspiratorial cupboards and tables without the slightest difficulty.

We informed all our customers of the gendarmes' "discovery." During the raids that followed, the gendarmes ended up breaking open even the most ordinary, nonconspiratorial cupboards and furniture.

In return for his "service," Tsarev was soon released, but they still sent him away under police supervision. Not one of our comrades ever laid eyes on him again.

* The original file is held in the Saratov regional archive. (Author's note.)

44
In Tsaritsyn Prison

APPARENTLY because of the shortage of space in the Saratov prison, several of the prisoners who had been condemned to long terms were transferred to the prison in Tsaritsyn.[1] Among those who were transferred were the SRs Averkieva, Kharizomenov, and Sokolov,[2] and the Social Democrats Sergey Bychkov, Gavriil Sushkin, and Kanatchikov. A little later, Ponty Denisov was also transferred there.

The Tsaritsyn prison was well equipped. All four stories consisted almost exclusively of individual cells. All the cells had asphalt floors, painted yellow and polished with wax.

From the upper cells, across the prison walls, one had a clear view of the naked, endless steppes, which looked so sad in the wintertime, when covered by a snowy shroud. And they aroused a passionate longing for freedom in the springtime, when nature awoke and the hollow echo of the steamship whistles could be heard from the Volga.

By contrast, it was dark and cold, just like a cellar, in the lower cells. The administration was able to take advantage of this to tame the "recalcitrant" prisoners: those who submitted to the will of the administration, and even the routine grumblers, were housed in Purgatory—the upper stories—whereas the "law-breakers" occupied the lower levels.

Before our transfer, the prison was packed to the rafters with common criminals. They were treated worse than cattle. Naturally enough, the prison administration was very anxious to extend the same regime to the political prisoners as well. And that is what launched our bitter struggle for our human rights, a struggle that ended in a hunger strike by all the political prisoners.

We continued the hunger strike for eight days. I kept up my courage for five days, and in the beginning I even continued to take my walks, but on the sixth day I took ill, and I remained in bed for a long time, well past the end of the hunger strike.

The most painful part of the hunger strike was the first three days. At the command of the prison administration, at the usual time, the guard would bring us the food: an aromatic meat soup, some gruel or potatoes, semiwhite bread; he placed it all on the table and left. It may well be that the prison administration deliberately arranged to prepare better food at this time, or else I simply imagined this, but the food gave off such an appetizing aroma that my mouth was filled with saliva and I experienced the torments of Tantalus.[3] But all these torments lasted only three days, after which my strength began to fade and apathy took over.

The prosecutor came to the prison a couple of times, and the prison inspector tried to persuade us to accept food. On the outside, our relatives, comrades, and friends grew agitated. The revolutionary organizations issued proclamations about our situation. It was only on the ninth day that the prison administration yielded, satisfying our basic demands.

The hunger strike had seriously damaged our health—pale, emaciated, we moved like shadows. As a result of the hunger strike, I experienced an acute anemia that lasted for many years and I suffered from headaches for a long time to come.

All this took place in the summer of 1902. By the fall I had managed to organize my studies in the prison, and I was able not only to read but even to master the first volume of Marx's *Capital.* I also read Aulard's *History of the Great French Revolution,* the Webbs' *Trade Unionism* and *History of the Labor Movement in England,* Buckle's *History of Civilization in England,* Mill's *Logic,* and a great amount of belles lettres—all of Dickens and others.[4] I began to study the French language, using Burckhardt's self-instruction manual. Unfortunately, however, during my subsequent wanderings, in the absence of any practice, all my knowledge of the French language slipped from my memory.

I attempted to write some stories from my experience of revolutionary struggle. My friends liked two of them, but all my experiments in belles lettres were later taken away in gendarme raids and buried in the gendarme archives.

In the quiet summer evenings, if the prison guard who checked

our windows was not too strict, Kharizomenov would sing for us
He had a pleasant, strong baritone voice. For the first time, .
heard the aria of the Varangian guest from the opera *Sadko*—
"Oh menacing cliffs crushed by waves. . . ." This severe, martia
song of a daring conqueror was in harmony with our mood.
Weren't we, too, daring Varangians, preparing for battle to conquer the world?![5]

He also sang with great feeling: "Who is she to me—not wife,
not sweetheart, not my own daughter. . . . Then why does her
martyred image prevent me from sleeping all night?! . . ." This
poem by Polonsky enjoyed great success among us.[6]

We were taken on our walks one at a time, accompanied by a
guard, but the windows of the cells of several of the political prisoners looked out on the courtyard, and political discussions,
sometimes even full-scale debates, often unfolded between the
exerciser and the prisoners behind bars. At first the guard would
protest, but after listening to the discussion for a while he would
begin to enjoy it himself and would calm down.

I remember the time when one of these debates was taking
place between me and M. Sokolov, an SR-leaning student from
the Mariinskoe Agricultural School. A tall, broad-shouldered
blond, at the time he was gravitating more and more toward us—
the Social Democrats, the workers. I had encountered him from
time to time at Auntie's apartment. Like many other people of his
age, he was struggling with the question of the compatibility of
individual terror with a mass labor movement. His stormy, powerful temperament, not content with the plots of the individual-
istic intelligentsia, looked for firmer support in the masses. Unable to get along with the SRs, he went over to the Maximalists.[7]
Here is the story of his subsequent fate:

In 1905, at the time of the Moscow armed uprising, he was the
leader of the workers' fighting detachments in the Presnya district.[8] Later, when the period of reaction began and Stolypin, the
tsarist minister, began his cruel punitive actions against the revolutionaries, Mikhail Sokolov (then known under the nickname
"The Bear") organized an assassination attempt (the unsuccessful explosion at Stolypin's villa on Aptekarsky Island); then he led
the expropriation on Fonarny Lane of nearly a million rubles. He
was hanged in 1906.[9]

In the summer, three new political prisoners were brought to

)ur prison. One was a young drawing teacher from the local technical school, Ivan Andreevich Kachalov; the second, also rather young, was Matvey Konstantinovich Antonov, a clerk who worked for a local merchant; and the third, somewhat older, was Aleksandr Petrovich Danilov, an office clerk. The three of them constituted a local Social Democratic group. Either they were caught in the act of printing proclamations on a hectograph or the hectograph was found in their courtyard after their landlady reported it to the police, I can't remember which.

Then an inquiry was launched. It turned out that they had connections with workers and students, and workers' circles were uncovered at the Franco-Russian factory.[10] Danilov spoke a great deal about his connections with peasant-sectarians from the settlement of Dubovka.[11] His Marxist world view contained a certain admixture of peasant sectarianism. He was a great admirer of Lev Tolstoy, and in his own strange way he managed to combine class struggle, all-forgiving love, and nonviolent resistance to evil. He was thrilled by the heroism and exploits of the Dukhobors.[12]

Kachalov and Antonov were completely solid Social Democrats. They were brought to trial and sentenced to long terms of imprisonment. In 1905 I met Kachalov and Antonov again in Moscow. Both men were Bolsheviks, and Kachalov, now a professional revolutionary, was in charge, at the time, of the Moscow committee's "technical" work.* Daring, determined, and resourceful, he was a splendid conspirator.

From the boredom of the prison, Sergey Bychkov carried on a war with God. He threw the wooden icon out of his cell several times, but every time he did it the guard would return it to its place in the front corner. Then, infuriated, Sergey decided to hang the icon upside down. The guard reported him. Soon the warden arrived, then the deputy prosecutor; they drew up an official report and arraigned Sergey on charges of blasphemy. They started dragging him to the investigating officer, then to the circuit court, and so on.

Since Sergey Bychkov was unaccustomed to the sedentary life and to intellectual activities, he now grew bright and cheerful. Day in and day out he told his neighbors, whether through the

---

* "Technical" work refers to its underground printing operations. (Author's note.)

window or during his walks, how the military convoy had conducted him to the investigator or the circuit court through the entire city; he told them whom he had seen and described his interrogations. He already knew the punishment that this "crime"
could carry according to tsarist law: he was threatened by a max-
imum of six months in prison. However, the length of his imprisonment while under investigation for his role in the demonstration could easily exceed that sentence. And, as it turned out,
whereas the court sentenced Sergey Bychkov to six months' imprisonment for blasphemy, he was held nearly a year for the
investigation.

In this way his prison time went by more quickly. Then he was
exiled somewhere administratively, and I never saw him again.
Sergey Bychkov was one of those average workers on whom our
organization relied in the factories; outside of the factory, he had
no life apart from his profession and his comradely factory circle.
Every separation from the factory had a harmful, deranging effect on him. He got no pleasure from poring over books or engaging in theoretical discussion. He was always drawn to the immediacy of life and work. I heard reports that he had died, but
where and when I never learned.

Confined in the prison, we often thought of escape—we made
plans, we indulged in fantasy. Once we even hoarded some "grap-
pling hooks." But the old common criminals, who were well
versed in the history of the Tsaritsyn prison, warned us against
this in no uncertain terms. The prison was situated in an open
field behind a railway bed; on the outside it was guarded by Cossacks, on the inside by a large contingent of convoy soldiers. For
this reason, they could hardly cite any cases of successful flight.
Besides, for many of us the town was foreign and our connections
with it were weak.

So it was that I remained in the prison through the summer
and winter. The end of the summer of 1903 was approaching.
Many of my comrades had been sent into exile, others had been
sentenced to permanent resettlement and were also sent away
under police escort. As for me, it was as if I had been forgotten.
But then one fine, sunny July day, when we were suffocating inside the burning-hot walls of our cells, they summoned me to the
office, where the warden read me a memo from the Department
of Police saying that, by order of the supreme authority, I was to

be exiled to Arkhangel province under police supervision for a period of three years.[13]

Extremely pleased, I returned to my cell and immediately passed the news on to my comrades via the nonpolitical inmates. I had grown so sick of the cheerless, monotonous, vegetative prison life that I was ready to travel to the ends of the earth in order not to remain in prison. I was beckoned by the unknown, by new surroundings, by new people; but most of all, I wanted to live and to struggle.

45
To the Far North, Under Military Escort

Together with a party of regular criminals, they took me through the dusty, stuffy town of Tsaritsyn, escorted by a detachment of soldiers, to the railroad station, where they locked me up in a special car for prisoners. It was at this point that my torment began. The convoy refused to recognize that I was a political; it discarded those of my personal things that political prisoners normally had the right to take along, it refused to accept my basket of books, and so on.

"In that case, I refuse to go! I'll make all kinds of trouble if they use any force on me or tie me up," I declared very firmly, assuming a posture of self-defense.

Apparently wishing to avoid a public scandal at the railroad station, the officer in charge of the convoy accepted my things. However, I was repeatedly faced with incidents of this kind throughout almost the entire trip, right up to Arkhangelsk, whenever a new convoy replaced the one that was escorting us and began to take charge of our party of prisoners. To be sure, it became easier for me to make my case, since the previous convoy had given in; and in the end, after some sparring back and forth, the new convoy would yield.

All this unpleasantness had been arranged for me by the prison warden, a mean-spirited and vindictive man with whom I waged a permanent war. He viewed me as a ringleader, as the instigator of all kinds of disturbances, and generally as a troublesome person, especially after he got hold of the call for a hunger strike I had written. And he decided to get even with me—he issued me an open sheet of paper without my photograph, the kind that is normally issued to common criminals when they travel under police escort. But I was always saved by the fact that I was dressed in streetclothes, and not in prison clothes.

Our journey was a long one. Our wagon would be uncoupled and pushed into some blind alley; only in the evening would we take to the road again. It was crowded and stuffy in the cart. Near one of the Cossack settlements they added three prisoners to our convoy; they were beaten, crippled, bloody, and in chains. Apparently they had somehow managed to remove their shackles and escape from the local prison. A search party had been organized and they were recaptured. The furious Cossacks had started to cut them up with their swords, and if our convoy had not arrived in time and taken them away, they would have been chopped up into little pieces.

A medical assistant arrived, cleaned them up, bandaged them, and we continued our journey.

The big, robust Cossacks who were crowded around our wagon expressed their great regret at not being allowed to finish punishing the runaways, and for a long time, until our wagon disappeared from view, they threatened us with their fists and swords.

We had a stop in the town of Orel, and we were all taken to the local prison there. I was separated from the criminals and put into a solitary cell. But the routine in this prison was not very strict, and I was able to talk with some political prisoners. I picked up some political news from them and I even read a local newspaper.

I had another conflict when we reached the Butyrskaya prison in Moscow.[1] The deputy warden, a valiant old fellow with the beard of a general on both sides of his face, questioned me at great length and was unable to make up his mind in which category of prisoners to place me—political or criminal. On paper I was a criminal, but by appearance I didn't look like one. Waving his hand at the guard, he finally ordered:

"Take him to the nobles' section!"

The nobles' cell to which they took me was a large but dirty square room with a high ceiling and yellow, soiled walls; it was furnished with wooden cots without mattresses. Housed inside it—looking just like me before my first convoy group—were about twenty of the most variegated human beings. Some were dressed in nice and even elegant suits with white, starched collars; others were dressed in incredibly filthy and tattered rags;

still others were in prison garb. For the first time, I saw yellow diamond-shaped patches sewn on the backs of some of the prisoners. These signs of "distinction" were evidently not considered badges of honor, for the prisoners did everything they could to get rid of them. But that wasn't so easy—not only were the diamond-shaped patches sewn on at the top, but, "for conscience's sake," they were sewn into the cloth itself so that, if you ripped off the diamond, a square opening was left in the garment. On the other hand, there were some specialist patchmakers around there who were able to sew a patch made out of material from the same prison clothes over the spot where the diamond-shaped patch had been, and to do it so skillfully and iron the seams so carefully that even after the closest examination it was difficult to notice it.

The entire fraternity consisted of "fallen" noblemen, some of whom had genealogical tables leading back to prominent and even illustrious families, which is why the cell was called the "nobles'"cell. Among them there were pimps, gigolos, card-sharps, blackmailers, adventurers, and runaways from Sakhalin.[2] In their common quarters, they strived to put on airs, and they didn't steal from one another. In all other respects, however, the cell was no different from an ordinary criminal cell—it was just as dirty, it contained a multitude of fleas, lice, and all kinds of other filthy things, including rats and mice, and its occupants swore, cursed, and even fought.

I was led to the cell by a prison guard, who pointed me to a free bunk and invited me to go to the bathhouse and wash myself. The invitation was tempting: I had not taken a bath since leaving Tsaritsyn prison, and my body itched. Still, I hesitated: I had various things on me—about five rubles, and, in my bundle, a pound and a half of sugar which, if I economized, was supposed to last until Arkhangelsk. If I left it here, it would be stolen, as normally happened in these prisoners' convoys; but to take it all to the bath was impossible, and in any case it could be stolen in the dressing room.

Just at that moment, a pleasant-looking little old man came up to me and, as if he had read my mind, said:

"Young man, you're probably afraid you'll be robbed while you're in the bath, right? Just don't worry, everything will be all right, just give the money to me."

This happened so suddenly, and the old fellow's appearance

and his tender, paternal tone disposed me so favorably to him, that, without any hesitation, I took out my purse and handed it to the pleasant-looking old man.

I washed myself in the bathhouse with great delight, put on a fresh set of linens, and, in a state of great emotion, returned to the cell.

"Here, young man, permit me to return this intact," the old man greeted me, handing back the purse.

And, as a matter of fact, I remained in the nobles' cell for about ten days, until our convoy resumed, without losing a single piece of sugar.

The stories of the fall of these dissipated little nobles were surprisingly uniform. The story usually began with the young little nobleman's graduation from one of the restricted educational institutions for gentry sons, and his entry onto the path of an independent career.

As a rule, having broken his chains, the young merrymaker would begin to carouse, and, failing to take proper account of his real capacities, would overestimate either the influence of his rank, or the importance of his parents, or their finances, and would enter into conflict with the existing criminal code, which he could neither step over nor circumvent. It was here that his criminal career would begin.

"You know, I graduated from the very same school," said Lieutenant Strepetov, one of the occupants of the nobles' cell, a man in prison clothes who had been slapped about by life, but who still maintained a "noble" bearing. "Well, you should understand: it was friends, companions. . . . Went to a restaurant for a good time . . . drank, ate, then went to the Gypsy women. . . . Then, spent the night with the girls. . . . Didn't get home 'til the next morning. Enjoyed it. Did it once, twice, three times—kept carousing for a whole month! A couple of times we caused scandals, broke some windows, glass, pulled out the whiskers of a maître d'hôtel, smeared the mug of a lackey with mustard. . . . The stories reached my father. He called me in, lectured me, asked me to stop. But how could I stop when friends of mine who were more distinguished and richer than me kept turning up?! Well, to make a long story short, things went from bad to worse. . . .

"I remember one incident"—Strepetov continued to recall the "glorious" days of his youth as we were getting ready to go to sleep—"when we were squandering everything we had on drink. Papa and Mama wouldn't give me a penny, but one of my friends had some money. We went to a restaurant and spent everything we had in no time at all. Where to go next? Going home was out of the question. My father wouldn't allow me to come in during the night. Then, all of a sudden, someone came up with a brilliant idea. Why don't we go, he says, to the Uspensky Cathedral and attend the archdeacons' matins there.[3] So off we went.

"I stood, leaning against a pillar. It was warm there. A choir of birds was singing; I stood there, beginning to doze off, when someone tapped me on the shoulder from behind. I looked around and saw someone's hand passing me two copper five-kopeck pieces and a sacramental wafer. As I understood the situation, someone was asking me to pass these things up to the altar for the repose of the soul of some dead person. I took the Host in my hand, but I had the urge to gulp it down myself, like a dog. I thought about it for a moment and then devoured the wafer and pocketed the money. Then I began to doze off again, but once more there was a tapping on my shoulder, and a hoarse whisper: 'Set up a candle to the Virgin Mary for me; here's fifteen kopecks; and pass the Host to the altar.' I looked behind me, strained my eyes, but no one was there. I ate the wafer and put the money in my pocket. Then I stood there, praying, just as if nothing had happened. . . ."

"Ai-yai-yai, what a sin, what a sin!" said the pleasant-looking old man who had rendered me a service on the first day, shaking his head. "You sinner! You'll burn in the flames of Gehenna! Without fail!"

"Just cut out that talk of yours about Gehenna! Don't interrupt me!" said Strepetov, waving him away. "Anyway, in this manner I managed to collect two rubles and sixty kopecks. I ate to my heart's content. In the end, I was stuck in that position—with hardly anyplace to go at night, I now could go to the matins at the Uspensky Cathedral. I could get food there and some money. . . . Well, next thing I did, if you can imagine, was to put out two promissory notes in my father's name. As soon as my father learned of this, he threw me out once and for all. I began to go downhill, to go to hell. . . ."

Much more so than the common criminals, more than the inmates who came from the "base" classes, these "rejects from the nobility" loved to recall the good old days. But in reality, these recollections were almost always overgrown with a pretty thick layer of improbable legends, stories that the narrators themselves had begun to believe were true.

My next stop with the convoy was at the Iaroslav transit prison, filthier still than the Butyrskaya prison, and even more saturated with every conceivable kind of parasite. Nothing noteworthy happened during my six-day stay there. It was a prison like any other, striking only by virtue of its antiquity and its delapidated condition.

I was held in a communal cell with the common criminals, and there, right before my eyes, scenes were performed from several homosexual novels, with all the usual features—courtship, gifts, the torments of jealousy, and so on.[4] One of these novels almost ended with a knifing. But the prison administration intervened in this affair just in time, and isolated the love object of the two prison "Ivans" who had been fighting over their "sweetheart," a pretty little fellow who was either a pickpocket or a burglar by profession. Both "fiancés" were strong, robust fellows. One had spent nearly eight years in prison, except for some brief intervals, and the other about ten. All the criminal scum of the prison submitted to their authority without questioning. They were the prison dictators, feared even by the prison administration.

I arrived in Arkhangelsk in August. It was the last station on the railroad line. The weather was rainy and foul. It smelled like autumn. Steeped in filth, our convoy went on to the local provincial prison. There they kept five of us, all political prisoners, in one cell. Our joy was unbounded. We all got to know one another very quickly, and there was a constant stream of conversations, stories, arguments. . . . Who had been arrested for what? Who had been accused by the gendarmes of what crimes? What did each of us contemplate doing while in exile? . . .

Among my cellmates, Bukhanevich stands out in my memory. He was a typesetter from Kiev, and a lively, cheerful fellow. I later encountered him at the Stockholm congress of 1906, by which time he had become a Menshevik.[5] Then I remember Kirill Kapustin, a Social Democrat who was a teacher from Cherepovets,[6] who rather prided himself before us, the workers, on his education. When I asked him just where this Cherepovets was located, he was very insulted, and began to expose my ignorance, my lack of knowledge of our country's geography. Then it was my turn to get angry, and I asked him:

"Look, I'm from Volokolamsk, myself; can you tell me the location of that town?"

Kapustin gave it a great deal of thought, but was still unable to answer, which left him feeling very dejected.

"For me, a worker, it is forgivable not to know where Cherepovets is, but for you, an educated teacher, not to know such things is completely inexcusable," I reproached him, eliciting general laughter.

Another of our cellmates was Iakov Fedorovich Dubrovinsky (Innokenty's brother), who was shot by the Czechoslovaks in 1918 in Krasnoyarsk.[7] He was a serious, thoughtful young man, who had just graduated from a technical high school.

We experienced the first relaxation of our prison routine with enormous pleasure. We were now permitted to go to town accompanied by a prison guard and to make purchases of food products. We even forgot that an even longer stage of the journey— on foot and on horseback—still lay before us.

For about a week we awaited our instructions from the local governor. To what remote, out-of-the-way regions would he send us?[8] There was no reason to imagine we'd be permitted to remain here. In any case, Arkhangelsk was overflowing with exiles, and one could arrange to stay only through special connections. But none of us had any connections at all. We were all unmarried men, bachelors, and from this it followed that they could send us to some isolated backwater.

Finally, the governor's instructions arrived: Kapustin and Dubrovinsky—to the village of Ust-Tsylma, on the Pechora River; Bukhanevich—to Onega; and me—to the village of Izhma.[9] We quickly began to prepare for our departure under escort to our respective places of exile. We questioned the guards and the other prisoners—how many miles to this location, how large were the settlements where we were supposed to spend many long years, what kind of work did the local population do there, and so on. But no one could give any clear, intelligible answers to the questions that were of interest to us. And information about my new place of residence—the village of Izhma—was particularly scanty. No one could even say how far it was from Arkhangelsk. Some said that there weren't any roads leading to Izhma at all, others said that it was more than 600 miles away. In short, I was about to play the role of Columbus—to discover a new world. Kapustin managed to get hold of a geography textbook somewhere, and we all devoured it eagerly. But all that I was able to learn was that Izhma was inhabited by Zyrians, who professed the Orthodox faith, were very clever and very honest, and left their houses without locking the doors. . . .[10]

Soon, on a clear, sunny morning, when a light fog covered the dirty streets of the city, we were taken out of the prison and surrounded by a convoy of soldiers with naked swords; then, wallowing in filth, we started off in the direction of Kholmogory.[11] Two or three peasant carts were drawn along the road behind us; they carried our meager household goods, the sick prisoners, and two women from the ranks of the common criminals.

As soon as we were beyond the city limits, the soldiers sheathed their swords and began walking along casually. The road away from town became drier, and we walked in wide-open spaces. Immense greenish meadows extended all around us, the woods were growing dark in the distance, streams and rivulets rushed by, while the clear sky and the pink morning sun looked down on us. After the terrible, stuffy air of the prison, we now breathed easily, and our gait was merry and gay. Jokes and witticisms abounded, and fresh, lively laughter could be heard. We ran about, frolicked, and delighted in our "freedom" as if there hadn't been any onerous experiences and difficult struggles behind us and as if nothing but happiness and a carefree life lay ahead of us.

We were supposed to travel twenty to thirty miles a day, a distance we traversed effortlessly. And if one of us got tired, he would ride in the cart. Part of the military convoy also rode with us.

In this manner we managed to cover the 50 miles to Kholmogory in two days. On the third day we were to have a one-day rest stop in Kholmogory, but they locked us up again in the halting-station. No one was allowed in town, not even under escort. The reason for this strictness was that two political prisoners had escaped from here during the previous convoy, and, as a consequence, several soldiers had been court-martialed and sentenced to three-year terms in punitive battalions. The convoy troops were irritable and particularly vigilant.

When we arrived, they had placed the political prisoners in one cell, the criminals in another. However, apparently to make it easier to guard us, the convoy command decided to herd us together with the criminals into one cell. We began to protest. They threatened us with force. We became still more enraged. They surrounded our cell and ordered us to clear out. We refused to give in. Some of the troops tried to seize us by the arms. We armed ourselves with whatever we could lay hold of. I remember picking up a big bread ring and flinging it at a soldier. He tried to jab me with his bayonet, but missed. . . . An unbelievable racket, a huge hubbub, broke out, and the criminals began to get agitated as well. The soldiers drew back. They must have been of two minds in this regard, for to tie us down would have been of no value to them. They had trouble agreeing on an approach. For a long time we were agitated and nervous, fearing an attack, and we began to take precautionary measures in earnest. But the convoy commanders were evidently afraid of a scandal, and they decided to leave us in peace.

After we left Kholmogory, the weather changed radically. The endless dark forest stretched before us, interrupted now and then by tall hills and rapid rivers, large and small, abounding in water. Bridges were nowhere to be seen. Sometimes we crossed the rivers on ferryboats, sometimes we simply went across on large fishing boats. On the road we ate mainly fish; we purchased Arkhangel herring, which was sold by weight and was incredibly cheap.

Thus we reached the town of Pinega, situated some 150 or 200 miles from Arkhangelsk.

> Here are Arkhangelsk and Pinega—all swamp and forest!
> Disappear, there, my cart—all four wheels. . . .[12]

There really was a lot of forest, but we still hadn't encountered any swamps. In Pinega the convoy turned us over to the district police chief; we were to complete the trip unescorted, except for one village police agent.[13] There were three of us left.

While in Pinega we encountered some political exiles. With the permission of the police chief, to whom they pledged their word of honor, they took us off to treat us to a good dinner. We learned a good deal about the latest political news; they showed us an issue of *Iskra*, but they didn't let us take it along. We read the courtroom speeches of the convicted Rostov demonstrators,[14]

as well as some newspapers. It was only here that we really felt
ourselves to be free. Irrespective of faction and political tendency,
the comrades—there were about eight of them—gave us a
hearty welcome, fed us a magnificent meal, and saw us off with
an invitation to write to them about our needs.

Each of us was assigned a horse for the remainder of the journey. For economy's sake, they put us together in a single, spacious
covered wagon, yoked the troika of horses with a belled harness,
and, with whooping and jingling, drove us on to the next station.
Then they reharnessed the horses and we sped onward. The village policeman accompanied us for two or three stations, but
after that he apparently grew tired of this long, tedious task (in
any case there was nowhere for us to flee), so, at one of the settlements, we were given our "secret" convoy papers and allowed to
go on alone.

After Pinega the dense, silent forest stretched before us like an
unbroken dark-green wall. Extravagantly thick, the giant pines
and firs were so tall that they seemed to touch the clouds with
their shaggy tops. Coveys of wildfowl were rushing about between the trees. Every now and then, woodcocks, grouse, and
partridges flew out from under the feet of our horses, rose lazily
in the air, and landed again a short distance away. Full-grown
gray hares ceaselessly ran across our path. Once in a while the
fluffy tail of a fox gleamed in the sunlight, then quickly disappeared into the thick green forest. We had the driver lead the
horses by foot, while we ourselves strolled by the road, never ven-
turing to penetrate into the depths of the taiga.

At one of the stops we bought two "chukars" (the local word for
grouse), each weighing about ten pounds, for a total of only 25
kopecks. We roasted them, and we ate them for three full days.

The grouse is a beautiful bird. It flies in, settles down on the
top of a fir tree, and, looking like a huge black rooster, peers
around on all sides. We throw knots and lumps of dry clay at it,
but it won't even honor us with its attention.

The wildness and the stillness that surround us are broken only
by the occasional tinkle of the bell under the shaft-bow of the
horse's yoke. The gentle autumn sun generously pours its slanting rays on the gray top of the virgin forest. The horses move
along quietly. The early, light frosts have killed the gadflies,
horseflies, and mosquitoes, which had drifted in swarms in the

sultry summer heat, driving animals into a frenzy. We are tired of traveling—we climb into the wagon, the driver pulls on the reins, hits the lead horse with his whip; frightened by the crack of the whip, the side horses catch up and the troika speeds along, "flies away to a place where Makar has never driven his calves."[15]

The farther we go, the fewer villages we see, and human beings are now beginning to disappear altogether. The coniferous forest is ending, the trees are growing thinner, and we encounter more and more swamps. We are riding into the limitless, dismal tundra. A yellowing marsh without any edges, covered with withered vegetation, extends from both sides of the road. The small pines are meager, dwarflike, no thicker than your hand, with long scrawny legs. Every once in a while there are some bushes and moss, through which rusty puddles emerge everywhere. In the summertime, neither man nor beast can take a step here. Even birds are not to be seen over the tundra. What we have before us is a kind of continuous dead sea. One must travel fifteen or twenty miles just to reach a station house, inhabited by a guard and the drivers. And that is the pattern for nearly 80 miles. Out there, they call this the "little tundra." Then comes an interval— a wooded plain with scrawny little trees, followed in turn by the "big tundra," which extends for well over 150 miles.

The tundra becomes inhabitable only in the winter, when the fierce frosts weld together the soil, and the profuse atmospheric precipitation dresses it in a thick shroud of snow. It is then that the habitual inhabitant of the area—the Samoyed, herding his fleetfooted deer—becomes the lord of the tundra.[16]

It is best to hurry up and quickly leave this melancholy, dismal desert, with no visible end or edge, behind you. You want to weep when you look around at this unpopulated, sinister plain.

We travel day and night without stopping, without rest. We push the drivers; we ask, we beseech the station keepers to give us fresh horses right away, just so we can leave this accursed desert as quickly as possible.

By the end of August we finally reached the village of Ust-Tsylma, the administrative center of the Pechora region and the place of exile of my comrades Kapustin and Dubrovinsky. We received a hearty welcome from the political exiles there, and I practically felt I was at home. I walked all around the village, got acquainted with different people, and inspected the surrounding area.

Ust-Tsylma was a large village, with 450 homesteads, situated on a bank of the copious Pechora River. According to tradition, the village was created by fugitives around the time of Ivan the Terrible; later, in the days of Patriarch Nikon, schismatics were banished there. Hence the population of Ust-Tsylma consisted entirely of Old Ritualists, who crossed themselves with two fingers and refused to recognize Orthodox priests.[17] The basic occupations of the population were fishing, hunting, trapping, and various kinds of seasonal work away from home. The peasants kept cows and horses, but grain, mainly barley, grew badly here. Except for potatoes, no vegetables were grown in the area.

Once a year, in the springtime, merchants and tradesmen would come by water from Cherdyn or from Perm,[18] their barges loaded with grain and other goods, which they exchanged for furs, sturgeon, and wildfowl, all of which they were able to obtain for a mere trifle, thereby enslaving the poor villagers for a whole year. They enticed the poor peasants, the women, and the young girls with spirits, with vodka, and they spread syphilis. Family ties that had been built up for centuries began to break apart; the solid foundations of the Old Ritualist faith now grew weak.

Thus it should come as no surprise that you could often encounter there, on the one hand, the observance of all the rituals of the Old Belief—everyone eats from his own dish, tobacco smokers are severely persecuted—and, on the other hand, husbands selling their own wives and fathers selling their own daughters to tradesmen, government officials, visiting merchants, and purchasing agents, and with no one condemning the practice.

I stayed in Ust-Tsylma for three or four days. Then one day a guard came up to me and very tactfully asked me when I was thinking of leaving for my place of exile. I must admit that I was sick of the nomadic way of life, the moving from station to station under guard; I wanted to alight at a definite place, where I could just rest. So I said I was prepared to depart on the following day. In the summertime there were no land routes to Izhma; you could only get there by boat, sailing against the current.

They supplied me with a covered police boat (it was also the mail boat). The police chief handed me my "secret" documents, provided me with two village policemen—not to watch me, but to pull the boat—and off we went.

It was some 70 miles to Izhma. The policemen, alternating with each other, walked along the riverbank and pulled the boat—in which I was sitting—with a rope. It was dark and cold in the boat. I would sometimes climb out onto the embankment, harness myself to the rope, and take my turn at pulling the policemen. But if a favorable wind was blowing, we would all sit in the boat and use the oars. And when it was time to eat, the policemen would tie up the boat, make a fire on the riverbank, cook some soup or fish chowder or fry up some salted fish. The voyage lasted about five days. I remember distinctly that we sailed into Izhma on the morning of September 5, and that the first snows fell that very evening.

46

In Exile Again

IZHMA WAS a large village, with 250 homesteads, located on the right bank of the Izhma River (a tributary of the Pechora), and populated by Zyrians, who spoke Russian very poorly. The men could speak it a little, but the women understood no Russian at all. The breeding of reindeer, fishing, and trapping were the basic occupations of the population. Agriculture was only a subsidiary occupation at that time. As was the case in Ust-Tylma, the villagers planted mainly barley and rye, but neither crop could thrive. The wealthy proprietors, the big reindeer-breeders, each had herds of 10,000 deer and hired many hands. Moreover, for all practical purposes they also owned the herds of the little reindeer-breeders, who were completely in debt to the rich ones. The entire area was held in the palms of the hands of two wealthy Zyrian families—the Filippovs and the Noritsyns. They were involved in an extensive trade in reindeer hides and pelts, they bought up wildfowl and fish, and they owned their own stores, as well as tanneries for the primary processing of leather. In the summertime their steamboats sailed the Pechora River and pulled barges laden with cargo.

Beginning in the spring, these "spiders" would "generously" distribute their goods on credit, in order to collect for them in kind—highly valued furs, hides, wildfowl, and fish—at incredibly low prices in the fall and winter. When they had to, these wheeler-dealers gladly sold goods from their stores to the political exiles on credit, since they were confident that not a single kopeck could be lost to them from such transactions.

The Zyrians were a rather industrious people, trustful and honest, but they had already been powerfully affected by the "culture" of the merchant-civilizers. The young girls and the women were modest; the girls would not even kiss their boyfriends at parties. On the other hand, the men drank a great deal, especially on holidays. They also had a tremendous passion for judicial litigation. The chambers of the local justice of the peace were always overloaded with all manner of petty cases. In the winter I would occasionally look into his courtroom. I recall one occasion when I observed the disposition of a case in which a certain Zyrian had lodged a complaint. The plaintiff had asked that charges be brought against his neighbor for having threatened him.

"And what did your neighbor's threat consist of?" asked the judge.

"My neighbor had been drinking vodka; he came to the window of my cottage, raised his fist, and said: 'I'm gonna wipe you out.'"

It took enormous efforts on the part of the justice of the peace to persuade the plaintiff to resolve the case through conciliation.

Most Zyrian families bore the name of the mother, rather than the father. My landlord, the man whose home I lived in, was called Ust-Vasya, which meant Vasily Ustinin, although this Ust-Vasya was 72 years old.[1]

All the Zyrians professed the Orthodox faith. On every holiday, the church was filled with people, although the women, being ignorant of the Russian language, were unable to understand the service.

It was evident that the Zyrians had been converted to Christianity at a time when they were still at a very low level of cultural development, for they had not even been able to preserve their own folklore. Except for their tales of the "forest sprite" and "forest nymph," I heard no legends recounted by them. The forest creature played approximately the same role in their lives as the household spirit or wood spirit played in the life of the Russian peasant.[2] To be sure, I heard them tell many stories of the adventures of Saint Nikolay, and the tricks he played on people who were insufficiently attentive to him. For example, during a winter's journey, he would raise a blizzard or snowstorm or would knock down the reindeer on which a poor little peasant was riding. But it is obvious that this was the Zyrian's same old native "forest sprite," transformed into Saint Nikolay when they accepted Christianity.[3]

One winter morning I was awakened by the sound of some

strange liturgical chant. I stepped up to the window and this is what I saw: a crowd of Zyrians, dressed in their holiday best, singing:

> *Holy God, holy and mighty,*
> *Holy, eternal—forgive us!*

At first I thought it was a funeral, but it turned out to be a wedding procession. Later, when I had rather frequent occasion to attend weddings or other evening festivities myself, people frequently sang: "Oh Lord, save Thy people," "Our Father," or couplets such as "Under a skirt, skirt, skirt, a sheep and a goat were playing. . . ." But since the singers couldn't understand their own words, did it really make any difference what they sang?

At the time of my arrival in Izhma, the colony of political exiles consisted of six or eight people. I can recall the Social Democrat Savchenko, a tall, temperamental man from the Caucasus; Charnetsky, "The Proletarian," a Pole from Warsaw who was a shoemaker by trade, who was very involved in Christology, and who once even read us a report on that theme; the SR Bulyuk, a joiner, a very gray fellow; the Social Democrat Vasily Starkov, a joiner, somewhat elderly; a religious sectarian from the Volga region, a shoemaker, who knew the Gospel and the Bible almost by heart—a very lively, gifted person who saw everything good in the world as being merely a manifestation of "love"; and, finally, Ivan Korablev, a medical assistant without political affiliation.

Each of the politicals lived separately; they gathered together now and then when a new prisoner arrived. When they heard that a new arrival was coming, they all went down to the riverbank to await the boat. They took the newcomer to their quarters, stuffed him with food and drink, and then helped him get organized. There were shipments of mail every two weeks, but in the spring and fall, when the roads were becoming impassable and the rivers were overflowing, the mail came less than every two months. In the wintertime there were about two months of nearly uninterrupted darkness; without a flame to read by, it was possible to read for only two or three hours a day.

Each of us people of the "base" classes received a government stipend of eight rubles a month, whereas those of the "wellborn" ranks got eleven to thirteen. For a person to live by himself on this amount of money, even given the low cost of goods, was impossible. So as soon as we found the right person to take on the task of preparing our meals, we immediately organized a communal dining room. That person was a 40-year-old Ukrainian peasant from some border village, who had been exiled here for three years as a political criminal for having smuggled illegal literature across the border.[4] Just what kind of literature he had transported, even he didn't know, since he was illiterate. Later, we were able to liquidate his illiteracy.

This "smuggler," whose name was Vasily Alekseevich, was distinguished for his unusual organizational and culinary skills, and it was he who bore the burden of organizing our dining commune. At the time, meat cost five kopecks a pound if you bought it from a tradesman. But Vasily Alekseevich would buy a calf or a cow, slaughter it himself, cut it in pieces, and sell the hide, so that the cost per pound of the meat would come to only three to four kopecks. Venison was cheaper—two pounds for five kopecks. Whenever we ran out of money, we switched to venison, or else we ate skinned partridges.

The way it worked was that the tradesmen would buy up the white partridges for stuffing animals. They would strip off the skin, together with the plumage, and sell the meat for five kopecks per two partridges. The rest of our food was very monotonous—soup made with meat, served with potatoes or groats, and roasted or stewed meat, also with potatoes. There were no other vegetables; even cabbage was never brought in. There was fish, but only rarely.

We held all kinds of meetings in our dining commons—there were lectures, reports, and debates. But they failed to arouse much interest, for the audience was too diverse, and our speakers weren't very good.

I had to give several lectures myself—on the Decembrists, on Populism and Marxism, on the Great French Revolution. I had brought along quite a few books, mainly on history. In addition, our colony received almost all the liberal newspapers and the thick journals—*God's World, Russian Wealth, Education, Truth*; we also received the newspapers *The Russian News, Northern Land*, and others.[5] In most cases the publications were sent to us without charge by their liberal editors at our collective request. Now and then one of the newcomer-politicals would arrive with a copy of *Iskra* or some other illegal literature.

I first learned of the Second Party Congress and of the splitting of the Party into Majority and Minority factions from letters from Matvey Aleksandrovich Fisher.[6] I had been conducting a correspondence with him while in exile. As the reader will recall, we left Fisher in Saratov, where he was working as a turner at the Gantke factory and where he'd joined our workers' group. Here is what had subsequently become of him.

In Saratov he was serving out his term of "restriction,"* having already spent ten months in prison and three years in exile in Arkhangelsk. Fisher was a German, but his father had died in Russia when Fisher was still a child. After he'd finished serving his sentence, the Russian government banished him from Russia, calling him a "foreigner." But he had no ties to Germany whatever, so he decided to move to England.

In Saratov he had married a woman who worked as a medical assistant, a Social Democrat, who was also an active participant in our workers' group. Long before his exile abroad, he had begun to study the English language. And now Fisher lived in England together with his wife. He worked in a factory, joined a trade union, kept in contact with the Russian emigration, met with Lenin and with Nadezhda Konstantinovna.[7] He was well informed about our revolutionary life and he sent detailed letters to me in Izhma about the Party split, the life of English workers, and his own day-to-day existence.

I was unable to grasp from his letters just what the essence of the disagreements between the Majority and the Minority had been, but for me one thing was clear: that I would go along with those who carried forward the line of the old *Iskra*, for in my mind *Iskra* was linked with my basic revolutionary education, and from it I had assimilated the principles of organizational centralism. This is why when I returned to Russia from exile and my comrades put the question to me: whom was I with, the Majority or the Minority—I had already decided the question. I went with the Majority without hesitation.[8]

My quarters in Izhma were in the home of Ust-Vasya, a Zyrian of average means. As I have already said, he was a man of 72, but he had a cheerful, fresh appearance—even his large beard was barely touched with gray.

* "Restriction" was loss of the right to reside in the capitals or in other university towns. (Author's note.)

Ust-Vasya's two-storied house was made of wood. He lived on the ground floor, together with his son and two grown daughters; the upper floor he gave to us. He had two horses, three cows, and 250 reindeer. His son lived with the deer almost all year round— in the winter, out on the tundra, in a tent made of reindeer skins, and in the summer, in the big meadowlands in the direction of the sea. Despite his ostensible prosperity, Ust-Vasya was in debt. He was in debt to the Noritsyns, the Filippovs, and the Cherdynsk merchants. Reindeer hides, carcasses, and antlers—all were taken from him by those voracious sharks. The only satisfaction that ever befell him was to get himself drunk from time to time.

I shared my large upper room, which had a creaky floor, with the medical assistant Korablev. He was a small blond man with broad shoulders—cheerful, gay, and kindhearted. He loved to drink, eat, sing, and woo the girls, and he was completely uninterested in politics. He had worked as a medical assistant in the Tambov hospital, and had many friends and acquaintances among the student youth. Students, young women from the special courses, and upper-level seminarians had often gathered of an evening in his room. Vanya Korablev would light up the samovar, cook up a bucketful of sausages—sometimes he also bought some vodka—and the merriment would go on at his place all night long: they folk-danced, they argued about politics, they read proclamations.

To his misfortune, Korablev was a passionate collector. He collected stamps, cigarette cases, postcards, old coins—in short, anything, whether or not it was worthy of attention. Hence he began to collect proclamations as well. Whether he actually read them is hard to say, but he gathered them very meticulously, smoothed them out, collated the signatures and the text to be sure there were no duplicates, and piled them all together in his writing desk. In this manner he collected 43 samples of all possible kinds of proclamations.

Then, difficult times descended on Tambov. The gendarmes began to launch massive raids; there were many arrests and forays. During one of these raids, the gendarmes suddenly appeared at Korablev's. They found his collection of proclamations. Since he was unable to prove that he wasn't involved in the dissemination of the proclamations, but was merely collecting them, they arrested him. They held him in prison for six months, and then exiled him to Arkhangel province under police supervision, for a period of three years.

There, he grew extremely sad and terribly bored from idleness. He didn't like to read, and, as a political prisoner, he wasn't permitted to practice his profession of medical assistant. All day long he would idle about the village. Occasionally, he would go hunting. Every morning he would sing melancholy, mournful songs, or else he would ask me for some still uncut books and journals, sit down at the table, and, armed with a knife, begin to slit them. He was able to carry on this "intellectual" activity for days on end, provided that I had enough uncut books to supply him.

Now and then his relatives would send him one or two ten-ruble notes, whereupon he would disappear from the house for a whole week. He would wander from one haunt to another, gather a band of spongers around him, drink, make merry, and engage in debauchery. . . . And only after he had squandered everything he had on drink would he reappear, feeling guilty and humbled, and begin to ask my forgiveness, swearing solemnly that it would never happen again.

Members of our colony began to accuse him of discrediting our calling—that of political exile. We jealously guarded the high calling of the revolutionary and strictly punished anyone who sullied and abased it. We felt even stronger about this insofar as we were the first political prisoners to come here, and, in the beginning, the local population had confused us with common criminals. We had to expend a great deal of energy in order to draw a sharp and distinct line between ourselves—political people who were struggling for an idea and suffering for our convictions—and the ordinary criminal offenders.

A court was set up to hear Korablev's case. I rose to his defense a couple of times, in the hope that he would straighten himself out and I would be able to rehabilitate him. Korablev repented, solemnly swore that he had acted that way for the last time, that he would never again engage in that kind of disruptive behavior. He was given a public reprimand or censure, but was permitted to remain in the colony. However, just as soon as money fell into his hands again, he would drink himself into a stupor, vanish for yet another week, and the very same story—with all the remorse, with all the solemn pledges, and so on—would repeat itself.

I finally backed away from him. And when he again squandered 25 rubles on drink, a sum that was given to us by the government once a year for the purchase of our winter clothing, we excluded him from the colony.

A severe and gloomy winter arrived, with temperatures around −40 degrees Celsius, and furious blizzards and snowstorms. Once in a while, in the company of some hunter-entrepreneur, we would don a pair of snowshoes covered with "kanys"[9] and head out to the taiga on a hunt. We did very little shooting; mainly, we avoided stepping into snares and animal traps of various kinds and we removed the game that had been trapped in them. There were specialized "entrepreneurs" who went after the foxes of this area; these trappers traveled a long distance toward the seacoast, and lived in our region for months at a time.

On several occasions, Ust-Vasya took me out to the tundra. I'd put on a "malitsa," then a "savik" over that, and, to cover my feet, I'd put on deerskin boots with "lipty."* We fastened ourselves to our sleigh and dashed across the virgin land at full speed. When we reached the tent-station we would unharness our reindeer, and they, breaking through the deep, soft snow with their hooves, would find themselves some grass and moss.

In the course of the winter I was invited to Ust-Tsylma a couple of times. The winter trail along the frozen river was in excellent shape, and we were able to travel seventy miles in a day and a half. Many new political exiles had arrived in Ust-Tsylma. A strong barrier now divided them—the SRs stuck to themselves, and the SDs grouped themselves apart, in their own residence. Much self-education work was taking place. Many workers had arrived from Rostov-on-the-Don, from the Caucasus, and from Ekaterinoslav,[10] and they had a strong desire to utilize their free time to expand their knowledge. They would study *A Short Course in Economic Science*, by A. Bogdanov, and *The Erfurt Program*.[11] News of the disagreements between Lenin and Martov on organizational problems reached the people here, but their meaning was poorly grasped and absorbed. People here didn't want a schism in the Party.[12]

One SD in the Ust-Tsylma colony who was particularly strong on matters of theory was S. L. Vainshtein, later a member of the Menshevik Central Committee.[13] He gave lectures, spoke out

---

* A malitsa is a long shirt made of reindeer fur; a savik is a deerskin coat with a hood; lipty are fur stockings. (Author's note.)

against the SRs, and conducted a study circle on political economy. Even out here, however, disagreements drawing a line between intelligentsia and workers would not abate. There were arguments about questions of principle, but often they also involved some of the problems of day-to-day existence. As a rule, the intelligentsia maintained closer ties in the outside world with members of the propertied strata, who sent them money, food, and other goods when they were in exile. Not all of them were tactful enough to keep from being conspicuous in this regard, or from holding themselves aloof, for this reason, from their comrades in struggle. Thus, tense relations developed between the haves and the have-nots, and this tension carried over into questions of principle as well.

The Socialist Revolutionaries in Ust-Tsylma were grouped around Boris Bartold.[14] He was a tall, rather thin man, with a long, pampered face, which was "decorated" by his magnificent, sparkling whiskers. He spoke through his nose, lisped, and gave himself airs. He always dressed irreproachably, spotlessly, foppishly. He loved to play the role of leader and protector, and he was talkative and boastful. He always spoke with an air of mystery about his party's secret, grandiose, terrorist plans; he took great pride in his intimacy with the Party leadership and with the old veterans of the People's Will, and he liked to recount every conceivable entertaining story and anecdote from their lives. In Social Democratic circles he was called Khlestakov.[15] He came from a wealthy family, and he received 200,000 rubles while in exile—an inheritance from a deceased aunt. He lived in grand style, rented a large two-story house previously occupied by the police chief, and maintained a cook and a servant. The following anecdote used to be told about him: when he was looking for a servant, it was claimed, every girl who applied presented him with an unconditional demand—to sleep with her employer. But because he always turned down this condition, for a long time he was unable to find himself a suitable servant, so he was forced to turn to another village.

Bartold shared his house with his fellow SRs. He lived in Ust-Tsylma for over a year. When the "spring" of Minister of Internal Affairs Sviatopolk-Mirsky began in Russia,[16] Bartold escaped, together with Vainshtein. This was the only successful escape from Ust-Tsylma. But even then, it only succeeded because Bartold gave a big bribe to the police chief, who agreed to keep quiet until they got to the railroad.

I always returned to Izhma from Ust-Tsylma in high spirits. I would gather my comrades together and share my news with them. Sometimes I brought back some illegal literature, and we'd organize a reading and discussion session.

When I was still living with Korablev, the local peasants' superintendent came by to chat with us.[17] He was a man of some fifty years. He had lived here for a long time, and had apparently been assigned to this region because of some kind of unseemly conduct, which he was careful never to mention. He lived as a bachelor in a separate home, where he kept a beautiful cook; she had children, and everyone knew that they were the children of the peasants' superintendent, though he wouldn't acknowledge them as his own. He also had progeny in other villages, places that he had to visit as part of his official duties. The peasants' superintendent loved to talk with cultured people who could maintain intellectual conversations with him and, most important, who would appreciate the breadth of his views. He was a partisan of the preservation of the peasant commune, and in the course of his conversation he often referred to himself as a populist.[18] Having said that, it's true, he would immediately correct himself:

"I'm a 'populist' myself, gentlemen, but a conservative 'populist'; I believe that it's through the commune that we can best preserve the good, honest, traditional customs of times gone by, respect for the elderly, for property, for religion, for the law, and for the past. The gentleman-landowner is the father, and the peasants are his children—that is what should lie at the foundation of the morality of the people!"

In addition to everything else, the peasants' superintendent was a designer of great schemes. He dreamed about breeding salmon in ponds; he designed a conductor of underground steam-heating in the tundra, in order to make the tundra more fertile—and so on.

All these dreams of the zealous administrator were without any real foundation, and conversations with him were dull and monotonous, since he neither enjoyed listening to others nor had the capacity to do so. And yet we were reluctant to send him packing.

The real reasons for his visits to us became clear soon after we had had several conversations. Out in the quiet, uninhabited taiga, some 250 miles or more to the north of Izhma, in an area the Zyrians called Balban, he had discovered a new settlement, consisting of thirteen homesteads. This settlement had apparently been organized by poor people who had fled from the oppression and the excessive taxes imposed on them by government functionaries and kulaks. Their main occupations were hunting, fishing, and reindeer-breeding. They paid no taxes or levies to anyone, predator-tradesmen were not yet there to suck their blood, no tsarist officials were there to ridicule them, and they lived in clover.

For all these reasons, the population of this northern Arcadia had increased with each passing year, up to the time when it was discovered by our enterprising Columbus. It goes without saying that he wished to assist the "unenlightened" inhabitants of the America he had discovered. He began his civilizing mission by collecting a rich tribute of furs, hides, and fish from the population, which was steeped in ignorance. His next civilizing act was to send them a priest and a rural police officer. After a while, an order was issued to change the name of Balban to Petrun, that is, to name it after the peasants' superintendent, who was called Petr Georgievich.

Nor did the authorities' benevolent care for their newly discovered subjects stop here. Petr Georgievich now saw it as his basic task to implant sanitation and enlightenment among the backward savages. It was precisely in pursuit of these goals that he had begun to bless us with his visits. He began circuitously, without revealing his secret intentions. He began by describing with inspiration the charms and natural beauties of Petrun, and then its rich natural resources.

"There's an unbelievable amount and variety of game there! All you need is an ordinary stick and you'll be able to find dozens of woodcocks to stuff," he said. "And you wouldn't believe the number of foxes! They're not even afraid of people. You don't even need a gun there; they walk into your traps all by themselves."

Then he began to describe the rich stock of good qualities that characterized the population, and the low cost of living there. And finally, only after the third or fourth visit, he explained his plans for us in great detail. At the same time, his speech was accompanied and embellished by a multitude of compliments of all kinds, addressed to us. In short, he was conducting himself like the agent of a large company, trying to recruit slaves for settlement in some uninhabited colonies. He offered me the position of teacher in Petrun, and Korablev the post of medical assistant. And he promised to get us each a monthly salary of 30 rubles plus government-subsidized living quarters.

". . . And you'll live in real style there!" he concluded his flattering offer.

We had already heard of the charms of that happy Arcadia from local villagers. We knew that communication with Balban was possible only in the winter, by deersled, and that no other roads led there. And even by deersled you were lucky to get there. For this reason, we turned down the peasants' superintendent's offer without any hesitation.

"The charms of one exile are quite enough for us. Why would we, of our own free will, arrange a second exile for ourselves, an exile within an exile, and an even worse one at that?" I said. "Why don't we just let the gendarmes worry about that!"

This time the peasants' superintendent was quite discouraged when he left us. Yet it appeared that he still hadn't given up his hopes to persuade us. He came by about two more times, but the results were the same.

The story of Balban continued long after my period in exile.

Having failed in his efforts to organize a voluntary exile settlement there, the zealous administrator apparently decided to embark upon the path of forced settlement of political exiles on his newly discovered land. He wrote an official report to his superiors, in which he recommended that they convert Balban into a settlement for new exiles, from which escape would be completely impossible.

His superiors eagerly accepted his proposal, and the very next party of political exiles to arrive in the village of Izhma under escort was ordered to go on to Balban. This happened in the fall, during the season when roads were impassable. The political exiles, who were still lodged in Izhma, began to ask the governor to rescind the order exiling them to Balban. The governor refused, and when the time came to prepare for the sleigh route, the police official asked the exiles to gather at the halting-place. The exiles declared that they categorically refused to go on to Balban and demanded to remain in Izhma. The officer threatened to use force on them. The politicals declared that they would defend themselves, and they would be sent to Balban only over their dead bodies.

The entire colony, down to the last man, rose to their defense. They quickly got organized, collecting whatever hunting guns and flintlocks they could find; some of them even turned up with revolvers, daggers, and Finnish knives. Having armed themselves, they occupied Ust-Vasya's house, where two other comrades had been living since we moved out. They barricaded themselves in, stored up provisions, and began to await an attack.

The police officer did not decide to attack right away. First he got together with the police from the surrounding villages, made preparations with them, and only then, on the second or third day, did he begin his assault. The politicals opened fire. The police officers fell back and scattered. The local population followed the heroic struggle of the political exiles with rapt attention and obvious sympathy, and even gave them some support. Heartened by their initial success, the comrades began to prepare for the next attack. They stood watch at the barricades day and night, and slept with their clothes on.

An entire week passed in this state of tense anticipation. Their spirits began to falter. Rumors began to spread that the police officer was awaiting help from a company of soldiers from Arkhangelsk. To crown it all, one morning they found one of the comrades suspended in a hayloft—he had hanged himself. It was Kalman Krapivnikov, a member of the Jewish Bund.[19] Having served two years in prison, he had arrived in Izhma with extremely unsettled nerves. He was also in a depressed state for another reason. He had been waiting impatiently for the arrival under police escort of his betrothed, whom he loved passionately, but she had married one of his comrades while en route, and had gone with him to another village. This had further intensified Kalman Krapivnikov's already very troubled condition, and so it was that now, at the most difficult moment of a life-and-death struggle with the tsarist police, unable to bear up, he hanged himself. His faint-hearted exit from life had a depressing effect on the others, who had already marked themselves for death. But it didn't break their resistance; no one thought of surrendering; everyone was ready to die with honor and to sell his life at a high price.

In the ranks of the attackers, however, there was relatively little enthusiasm. The policemen came from the local population, they had lived in harmony with the political exiles, and who among them was eager to risk his life for something he didn't understand? And to this must be added the fact that news was arriving from European Russia of continuous working-class unrest and a mounting revolutionary movement.[20]

The police made no more attempts to attack the house, and before long they even received an order from the government to allow the political exiles to reside in Izhma and other nearby villages.

Thus did this tragic struggle end with the victory of our comrades.

With the coming of spring, our life became easier and merrier. The harsh northern nature awoke. The evergreen coniferous forest began to sparkle more brightly in the sunlight, while continuing to maintain its majestic silence. Northern birds do not fill the air with their singing, and the rare flowers with bright coloring are not aromatic. Wherever you look, you see a rich emerald verdure, noisy rivers abounding in water, and forest, endless forest. In the summertime there are one and a half to two months of almost uninterrupted daylight. The scorching sun burns mercilessly. There are swarms of mosquitoes, horseflies, and gadflies in the air; you cannot go beyond the confines of the village without the risk of being stung to the point of bleeding. But comes the evening, when the sun has just barely descended and is moving toward the horizon, and an icy breeze has begun to blow in from the north, then the insects will temporarily vanish, you'll begin to feel cold even in your coat, and the local residents will bundle themselves up in their warm deerskin mantles without a twinge of conscience.

I decide to turn the night into my day, since it's a more comfortable, more peaceful time; I read and I write without a lamp, by the light of the dusk and the dawn; I wander through the meadows and forests, undisturbed by bothersome insects. I sleep in the daytime, covering the windows with newspapers.

The woods are filled with countless numbers of raspberry, huckleberry, and blackberry bushes. We go to the forest in a noisy crowd, gather berries, and sink into the swamp. The peasants gather whole buckets and barrels of raspberries. We return home with swollen faces, bitten and stung all over our bodies, bloodstained, but still merry and cheerful.

During the summer we had difficulty with food. Fresh meat turned bad very quickly, dairy products disappeared, and we found the sour fish inedible. When we woke up in the morning our room would be filled with such a foul odor that it became difficult to breathe, just as if someone had spilled a barrel of garbage under our feet. It was our landlady baking a large fish pie with sour fish. It fed the entire family.

They begin preparing the sour fish in the fall. They pickle it in large barrels, but they use very little salt, with the idea that the fish will then decompose very gently and emit an aroma. That's the state it is in when they eat it. The local doctor affirms that fish prepared like this is completely harmless, for during all his long years of practice he has never seen a single case of stomach poisoning from the fish. Doctor Martynov, a well-known liberal activist in the zemstvo movement who was then in exile in Arkhangelsk,[21] conducted a statistical investigation of the Pechora region and came up with the following hypothesis on this subject.

It is likely that in earlier times, Doctor Martynov suggests, when the roads were in even worse condition, very little salt could be brought into the area, so the population was unable to effect a normal salting of its fish. The fish, of course, would get spoiled, and the people would eat it that way. Since this was repeated year after year, the population grew accustomed to it, and the organism developed an immunity against poisoning.

It may well be that this hypothesis is plausible, but we still couldn't eat the foul-smelling, putrid fish. So in the summer our basic food was pickled venison, which was dry and tasteless.

One of the exiles came up with the idea of smoking the reindeers' "backsides" (i.e., their hams). This is very tasty, but it was also very expensive, fifteen kopecks a pound, which we couldn't afford.

That summer, the water in the Izhma River got warm enough to swim in. That river is rather wide and, like all northern rivers, very rapid. I often went swimming there with Efim Bulyuk; we always swam across to the other shore without any difficulty, and warmed ourselves for a long time on the sandy shoal. One day, however, while we were swimming back, we were caught in the path of a powerful current. For a long time we thrashed about and exerted all the strength we had, trying to swim to calmer waters. After a determined struggle, Bulyuk was finally able to swim away, but I was trapped in the current and carried downstream. No longer capable of struggling with the elements, I abandoned myself to their power, while still trying to stay on the surface. I had the feeling that I lacked the strength to do even that for very much longer. . . . I was slowly immersed in the water. . . . It was suffocating me, squeezing my throat. . . . What a stupid, senseless way to die. . . . Better to die in battle . . . from a bullet. . . .

But then, suddenly, my foot touched something hard. I gathered all my remaining strength and stretched my body. . . . One more instant—and I could already feel sand beneath my feet. . . . It carried me up to a sandy spit. I coughed up lots of water, inhaled the air with my entire chest, and then looked behind me. I could see Efim, still far away, running toward me along the riverbank.

Our comrades would spend a good deal of time scolding us for our needless bravery.

The short northern summer was soon behind us. It was followed by a clear, frosty autumn, and then by a cold, dark winter. I was often seized by gloomy thoughts. It seemed to me that it would be hard, virtually impossible, to live through one more winter like this. For days on end I thought agonizingly of flight. But how? In the winter it was only possible by crossing the tundra by deersled. . . . And where would I get the money? I shared my thoughts with my comrades, who shook their heads and cited dozens of incontrovertible arguments against my plans. Joyful, cheering news came to us from the outside world, which simply reinforced my awareness of the meaninglessness of my existence in this cursed snowy desert.

And then, in this dark and difficult period, not only for me but for our entire colony as well, we suddenly received a notification from the police chief, addressed to Gavrilov—a recently arrived, very young fellow with SR inclinations—saying that he was released from exile by Imperial order and was free to go wherever he liked. We were all perplexed by this news, and he most of all. There were soon many rumors, arguments, and discussions about this in our colony. In the last analysis, we reached the conclusion that he'd probably been amnestied on the occasion of the birth of Alexis, the heir to the throne, because Gavrilov was still under age (he was twenty).[22]

After receiving his transit pass, Gavrilov departed.

But the discussions and excitement surrounding Gavrilov's departure had barely begun to abate when a second notice of the same kind suddenly arrived, and this time it was directed at me: I was unconditionally released from the public supervision of the police in Arkhangel province, and was free to go wherever the wind might blow.

This news literally drove me to despair. How was I to explain such "kindness" to me on the part of the tsarist authorities? I was clearly an adult, and I had provided no pretext to them for this act of "mercy," and yet, all of a sudden? . . . If a revolution had taken place in the heart of Russia, then everyone would have been amnestied. My comrades were equally troubled, and the colony decided that I should go to Ust-Tsylma and consult with the colony there.

After gathering all my belongings and taking leave of my comrades, I abandoned Izhma.

When I got to Ust-Tsylma I encountered enormous excitement. There were several more people there who found themselves in the situation of having been "pardoned" by order of the highest authority. In accordance with the decision of their colony, they had gone to the police chief and attempted to protest against this unsolicited Imperial "mercy." After listening to their protest, the police chief said:

"I am not forcing you to accept your Imperial pardons; you may stay right here and live wherever you please. That's your business. Your public police supervision will simply be removed. But as for this gentleman," he said, pointing to the Jewish Bundist Zalmanzon, one of the group, "I am obligated by law, since he does not have the right to reside here, to send him away to the Jewish Pale of Settlement."[23]

The comrades expressed to the police chief their indignation over the insolence of the tsarist government, and then they left.

The question elicited some impassioned speeches at our meeting. This "mercy" was viewed as an attempt by the tsarist regime to create a schism in the ranks of the revolutionaries who were struggling against autocracy. Still, to refuse the amnesty would have been irrational. It was necessary to take advantage of this concession by the authorities and to turn it against them. Our final resolution was roughly in this spirit.

After that I went to the police chief and handed him the following protest-declaration:

TO THE MINISTER OF INTERNAL AFFAIRS
FROM SEMËN IVANOVICH KANATCHIKOV

Declaration

I deem it necessary to bring to your attention, as the highest representative of the central administrative authority, my attitude toward the decision, communicated to me by Imperial decree, that I be released from public police supervision; I deny categorically that the autocratic government of Russia has any right whatever to judge and to inflict any punishments on any citizens who are placed under investigation or brought to trial as state criminals. And if I have submitted to my sentence, it is only because physical force was on the side of the government.

In response to the order releasing me from public supervision, I feel obliged to say that I view it as nothing but an act of necessity on the part of the state as well as a sign of the weakness of the autocratic government.

November 13, 1904
Semën Kanatchikov*

Escorted and sent off with all kinds of good wishes, we—three of us in all—traveled by sleigh to Arkhangelsk. It was the dead of winter. Giant pine and fir trees dressed in snow and hoarfrost stretched out in an endless column. We drove day and night, almost without stopping. Each of us was anxious to return to his native region, to hear the latest political news, and to get involved in the thick of revolution himself. Here and there we did stop to rest in colonies of political exiles. They greeted us cordially, expressed their envy, told us some fresh news, and, with longing gazes, accompanied us to the edge of the settlement, where we took our seats in the sleigh and began to speed along the rolling, snow-covered road.

In one of the colonies, I heard the following conversation:

"Lenin is a little autocrat, a Napoleon. He copies the autocracy in everything. His organizational plan is just the hierarchical ladder of the autocratic government. . . ."

* The original document is located in the files of the Department of Police in the Central Archive in Moscow. (Author's note.)

The speaker was a tall, stout man with the appearance of a lawyer, who had been abroad—he was apparently up-to-date on the disgreements within the Party. His views were challenged by a comrade of sickly mien, a man who had evidently been subjected to the tortures of prison and prisoner convoys: "That's a lie! Lenin is a true revolutionary, an unyielding one.... Making a revolution is different from charity work. It's time to put an end to the sentimental idealism of the intelligentsia. ..."[24]

The discussion continued—I can no longer remember the rest; but my memory has retained these words about a name that was just beginning to become popular in our circles....

Again we're in Arkhangelsk, again we meet old comrades, who have also been amnestied. In the governor's office, we are given free railroad tickets.

I travel to Saratov. In the railroad cars I hear open discussions about politics, and I hear of the Black Hundreds for the first time.[25] Someone was recounting in minute detail the outrages they had committed at the meeting of a zemstvo board. The rest of the people listened sympathetically, conversing freely and with animation.

The revolutionary wave was growing, and rising ever higher. . . .

47
The Liberal Spring

I GOT TO SARATOV right in the thick of the revolutionary turmoil. All my comrades there were up to their necks in propaganda activity, agitation, circle work, and cultural-educational legal projects. Their ties with workers had increased significantly and were now much stronger. Evening and Sunday schools, legal and charitable societies—all were overflowing with workers. There were lectures for them on political economy, on history, on the trade-union movement in Western Europe, on literature, on the history of Russian serfdom, and so forth. In most cases the speakers and lecturers were Marxists or our comrades from the Social Democratic Party. Liberal lawyers, zemstvo activists, physicians, and people from the literary and artistic worlds organized noisy banquets and delivered beautiful, magnificent speeches about freedom, about constitutions, about the parliamentary system, about whether that system of government should have one or two Houses, about the four-tailed suffrage, and so on.[1]

The Socialist Revolutionaries, now at the zenith of their glory, were extolling terror and the heroes who engaged in it, were speaking at banquets about the all-suffering Russian people, and, in general, were merging with the talkative mass of liberals.[2]

The Social Democrats kept themselves apart, and when they did appear at combined meetings or banquets, they would try to emphasize their own particular position. The division of the Party into Bolsheviks and Mensheviks was an accomplished fact, but there were no sharp clashes between them, and the local Social Democratic committee was a joint one. Its Menshevik members included V. M. Obukhov and I. M. Liakhovetsky; its Bolsheviks, Iosif Petrovich Goldenberg (using the pseudonym of Meshkovsky), and the worker Melsitov.[3]

There can be no doubt whatever that the most remarkable and

outstanding figure among the Saratov SDs was I. P. Goldenberg. Tall, thin, and handsome, he had a small beard, a forehead that looked as if it had been carved out of ivory, and intelligent black eyes. As an emigrant, he had lived in France for a long time. He had a good command of both the French and German languages, a broad education, and a good knowledge of Marx. He always spoke about Lenin with great enthusiasm, and he was considered one of the best orators in our party, an honor he fully deserved. Later, he moved to Piter, where he was repeatedly elected to our Central Committee. In the most lifeless period of reaction, as a member of the Central Committee, he was in charge of Bolshevik work in Russia and in our Duma faction, and so on.[4] He served time in exile and in prison. He left us at the time of the February Revolution, but he returned to the Party in 1920. Vladimir Ilich Lenin had a high opinion of him in his time. Goldenberg died in 1922.[5]

When I returned to Saratov from exile, I stayed with Elena Ia-kovlevna Arkhangelskaya, with whom I had been corresponding. She was already a dedicated Bolshevik, and she was conducting propaganda among the workers. I met with Goldenberg frequently, and had conversations with him about fundamental questions of principle; he told me a great deal about life abroad and about the disagreements with the Mensheviks. It was from him that I heard my first thorough and enthusiastic portrayal of Lenin.

"He is a remarkable and outstanding man, a true and worthy leader of our Party," Goldenberg would say. "It's just a pity that he's too direct. That will hinder the overcoming of our factional differences."[6]

I. P. Goldenberg was a very gentle man by nature, and at the time his orientation toward certain of the Mensheviks, especially Plekhanov, was conciliatory; he thought that our differences with the Mensheviks were only temporary. Apparently he did not wish to impose his views upon me, and he provided me with both Bolshevik and Menshevik literature. I read Lenin's *One Step Forward, Two Steps Backward*, the protocols of the Second Party Congress, and articles from the Menshevik-controlled *Iskra*.[7]

When I had read all of this literature, Comrade Goldenberg asked me: which side was I on? As I have already said, my answer to this question had already been decided for me by my entire previous education in the spirit of the old *Iskra*. The Bolshevik literature that I now read fixed me even more firmly on this path and made me into a "rock-hard Bolshevik," as people used to put it then.

During that sojourn in Saratov, I had an unpleasant experience that I was unable to forget for a long time.

In the middle of December the liberals organized a big banquet. The Social Democrats were also invited to attend. Our Party committee decided that Comrade Goldenberg and I would speak at this banquet.

I had never spoken in front of a large audience before, especially such a refined one. I protested and categorically declined. But Goldenberg put pressure on me and began to persuade me that I had no right to refuse.

"First, you're a worker, and second, you're very well known, and you've just returned from exile," he listed my qualities for me.

"But you're forgetting the most important thing: I'm simply incapable of speaking before a large audience," I retorted.

"That's nonsense; you have a whole week at your disposal to get yourself ready. . . . And what difference does it make whether you're speaking before a large audience or a small one? The important thing is to have courage, and look past their heads, just the way Tsar Nicholas gives his speeches."

After some prolonged arguments, I finally agreed, and I set to work reading more literature. I read through a whole series of brochures on the history of the revolutionary movement and on the current situation. I prepared an outline, and it seemed to me that I had complete mastery over the question I was to speak on: the struggle of the working class with the autocracy and the bourgeoisie, its special role as an oppressed and exploited class, and its relations with the liberal bourgeoisie, which we Social Democrats supported insofar as it conducted a struggle against the autocracy, while at the same time exposing its half-heartedness and lack of perseverance. Each section of my speech was clearly and distinctly arranged in my mind, and I was able to repeat it to myself by heart.

When I arrived at the banquet on the evening of the appointed day the hall was already filled to overflowing; it was brightly illuminated by chandeliers, and its cold white walls were shining. Nearly a thousand people were in attendance, for the most part splendidly attired, well-fed, finely groomed men and women. The smartly dressed ladies gave off a fragrant aroma; their bare arms, shoulders, and ample busts were shiny white, and their precious adornments sparkled. After my three years of separation from normal life, all of this had such a stupefying effect on me that I completely lost my head, and I didn't know what to do with myself.

I located some of my friends and took a seat in a corner. Sitting in the chairman's seat was a middle-aged gentleman whose face seemed very familiar to me.

"Who is presiding?" I asked my neighbor.

"Count Nesselrod."

"Oh my! That must be the very same "liberal" whose furniture I repaired when I first came to Saratov! . . . I've already had a clash with his dog," I almost exclaimed.[8]

A rather unpleasant feeling about him stirred within me when I recalled the details of my first encounter with this "liberal." And now he was playing a prominent role in articulate liberal society, and was one of the pillars of the "Liberation" movement organized by Petr Struve.[9]

A whole file of brilliant orators appeared on the platform before me, competing with one another in the orator's art and in the wit and sarcasm of their attacks on the autocratic government. Among the speakers were Rossov, an artist; the SR Anikin, later a member of the State Duma; the brilliant lawyer Kalmanovich; and a doctor who was a well-known zemstvo activist. I remember Kalmanovich's speech particularly clearly. He likened the autocracy to the principal of a secondary school, and the Russian people to the school watchman, whom the principal addresses in an edifying tone with the words: "Nikita, how many times have I told you that when you're talking with me, you're supposed to keep quiet."

The audience laughed infectiously. As I listened to these clever orators, who conducted themselves so freely and naturally on the platform, almost as if they'd been born there, I began to tremble and to grow even more agitated. What could I possibly have to say to such polished, educated people, who, as the saying goes, had forgotten even more than I knew?

With these thoughts in mind, I went up to Goldenberg and made yet another attempt to withdraw.

"It's too late now. I have given your name to the chairman. Just calm down! Everything will be just fine," he assured me.

Soon Goldenberg himself took the lectern. Tall and calm, he

spoke with confidence, boldness, and great pathos. I was the next speaker in line.

Goldenberg finished his speech to the accompaniment of prolonged applause. Muddling my name, Count Nesselrod summoned me to the podium. I mounted the platform in a state of panic. All my ideas suddenly fled from my head, and I was unable to utter a single word. I picked up the decanter that was on the podium, poured some water into a glass, and began to drink. This fortified me somewhat. I managed to spew out a word or two of salutation—something like "gentlemen" or "citizens." I spoke haltingly, stammeringly—I stopped, resumed, paused. . . . Then someone cried out from the back: "That's enough!" A solitary whistle resounded. Severely and imposingly, the chairman called the audience to order and asked me to continue. I completely lost my head. Crumpling up my speech, I walked off the platform. Goldenberg and some other friends came up to me. I was ashamed to look them in the eye, just as if I had committed some kind of terrible crime. What had I said? How had I said it? I was unable to remember a single word of my speech.

After I had calmed down a bit, my friends informed me that I'd spoken for about twenty minutes, and that the content of my speech was pretty good, but the form was just impossible.

Apparently the Saratov gendarme who reported to the Department of Police on my performance at the banquet had a higher opinion of my speech—he called it "agitational" and "outrageous."

After this unsuccessful performance, I was unable to make myself speak before a large audience for a long time to come. But the struggle with our class enemies eventually taught me how to be brave and to make good use of every weapon in this struggle.

I didn't stay in Saratov very long. I wanted to get a job in a factory as a pattern-maker, but evidently the "spring" existed only for the liberal bourgeoisie, and there was no intention to extend it to the workers. In the eyes of the employers, I still remained an "unreliable" who must not be allowed in the factory, and I was refused work everywhere I went.

Taking along some addresses and references, I left for Moscow to face the revolutionary storm. There I chose a new specialization—I became a professional revolutionary.

EDITOR'S POSTSCRIPT

EDITOR'S POSTSCRIPT

As HE TELLS US in his closing paragraph, Kanatchikov left Saratov for Moscow on the eve of the 1905 Revolution to "face the revolutionary storm."[1] In Moscow, the city where his decade-long Odyssey through the perils of adolescence, manhood, and social and political self-awareness had begun, he quickly joined the Bolshevik-controlled Moscow Committee of the RSDLP, adopted the revolutionary *nom de guerre* "Egorov," and began his career as a full-time "professional revolutionary." However, his sojourn in Moscow was to last only a few months. In the summer of 1905 Kanatchikov was dispatched by his Party superiors to St. Petersburg, the second city of his earlier voyages, to serve the revolution as a member of the Bolsheviks' Petersburg Committee (which temporarily reunited with its Menshevik counterpart in November). There he was given responsibility for agitational activity among the factory workers of the important industrial area near the Narva Gate, at the city's southwestern frontier. There too he composed his first Bolshevik leaflet, a polemic against alleged liberal attempts to divert the labor movement from its true course.

Between the suppression of the revolutionary movement in St. Petersburg at the end of 1905 and Kanatchikov's arrest (the third of his career) in 1910, the Bolsheviks entrusted him with a variety of assignments that took him to the Ural region and back to Moscow and St. Petersburg. Much of Kanatchikov's Party work in this period was spent as an officer of the legal but harried trade-union movement of St. Petersburg, where he seems to have lived for the better part of 1908–10. Beginning in 1908 he worked for the tanners' union (where he encountered some minor difficulties in keeping the union's financial records), and in 1909 he was named secretary to the woodworkers' union and member of the editorial board of the union's newspaper. The evidence strongly suggests that, in his capacity as a Bolshevik union leader, Kanatchikov favored open competition with the Mensheviks rather than the strict emphasis on illegal, underground activity advocated by the extreme wing of Bolshevism.

The year 1906 was marked by Kanatchikov's first sojourn beyond the borders of the Russian Empire, an experience he could only have greeted with the greatest excitement. He visited Stockholm in April of that year as a delegate to the RSDLP's so-called Unity Congress, where the Bolshevik and Menshevik factions temporarily set aside their differences in an ill-fated effort to reunite a badly divided party. His appointment as one of the 45 or so Bolshevik delegates to this Menshevik-dominated congress was a measure of Kanatchikov's quiet rise to a minor position of prominence in the Bolshevik movement. Later, his participation as a worker-delegate (representing the tanners' union) to the First All-Russian Congress on Combating Alcoholism (held in St. Petersburg in December 1909–January 1910), where he delivered a major address on the problem of alcoholism viewed from a socialist perspective ("The Workers and the Temperance Society"), bore witness to his growing confidence in his ability to face a largely middle-class, professional audience.[2] Thus Kanatchikov's budding career as a "professional revolutionary" had begun to grow in the daylight of open public activity when it was suddenly cut short by a police dragnet.

After a prolonged period of imprisonment in St. Petersburg—I have been unable to determine the precise dates—Kanatchikov was exiled to southern Siberia (Irkutsk, near Lake Baikal), where he was kept under surveillance from late 1911 until his release in February 1917, at the time of the overthrow of the tsarist regime. Despite his release, he remained in southwestern Siberia (mainly around Novonikolaevsk, on the Trans-Siberian Railroad, and Tomsk, a little to the north) and in the Ural region (Perm province), where he carried out various organizational and propaganda functions for the embattled Bolsheviks in 1917 and 1918, and on through the first year or so of the Civil War. (It is interesting to speculate about the role he might have played in 1917 had he chosen, as did so many other exiled revolutionaries, to return to the familiar territory of Petrograd or Moscow.)

In the years that followed, Kanatchikov's activity was concentrated in the fields of political education and journalism. Returning to Moscow in 1919, at the age of 40, he helped organize a special university-level Party school for the training of Communist agitators and propagandists, where he also delivered a series of public lectures on the history of the Party, a testimony to his long and painstaking efforts to overcome his oratorical inhibitions. This was followed in 1920 by brief administrative and educational assignments in the Tatar Republic, the Ural region, and Siberia, and in 1921 by appointment to the prestigious rectorship of the Communist University in Petrograd, a post he held for the next three years. In 1924 Kanatchikov headed the Press Bureau of the Communist Party's Central Committee, and in 1925–26 he served as director of that Committee's Department of Historical Research (the so-called *Istpart*). These were rapid promotions to sensitive and difficult positions for a man with only five years of formal education.

The year 1925 appears to have been something of a turning point in what had hitherto been Kanatchikov's unblemished career as a trusted and reliable professional Communist. Prior to that year, there are no indications that he ever drifted from the mainstream of Party ideology or policy, or that he associated himself with any of the factional heresies that challenged the Party leadership between 1920 and 1924. His authorship of a highly polemical anti-Trotsky political brochure, *Istoriia odnogo uklona* (*The History of a Deviation*, Leningrad, 1924), at the height of the Party leadership's anti-Trotsky campaign, was emblematic of his conformity to the Party line in the first years of the decade.

In 1925, however, we begin to see signs of some of that rebelliousness and independence of spirit we have seen and admired in Kanatchikov's recollections of his earlier years. In the fall of that year, when the top Party leadership had already split and reassembled in a manner that saw two members of the old "triumvirate," Lev Kamenev and Grigory Zinoviev, transformed into "left" deviationists, opposed to the dominant "right" positions of Stalin and Nikolay Bukharin, Kanatchikov indirectly but unmistakably identified himself with the opposition. Writing in his capacity as director of Istpart, Kanatchikov boldly criticized those Party historians who, as he saw it, were underestimating

Lenin's 1905 doubts about the reliability of the peasantry. "Historical" criticisms of this kind were correctly understood as attacks on what was now the official Bukharin-Stalin view of the peasantry, and they earned Kanatchikov the dubious distinction of denunciation by Bukharin a few months later (July 1926), quickly followed by dismissal from his Istpart position, the only significant crack in the armor of Kanatchikov's professional success preserved in the public record. Important though the immediate circumstances of this episode may have been, as students of Kanatchikov's early years we must surely take special note of the issue on which he chose to break ranks: the importance of distinguishing clearly between the unstable peasantry and the trustworthy, steadfast proletariat.

Just how deeply involved with Zinoviev's "Leningrad Opposition" Kanatchikov actually became is still unclear. It may well be that he restricted himself to participation in the kind of historiographical debate just described. According to one Soviet source, he abandoned the opposition very quickly, "having announced his errors to the Central Committee."[3] Be that as it may, he suffered only the mild sort of punishment for his deviation that would hardly be thinkable a decade later: removal from his post and reassignment to a two-year stint as TASS correspondent in Czechoslovakia. (This was the time when Kamenev was "punished" by appointment as ambassador to Italy, and when other oppositionists were conveniently assigned to positions abroad or in remote corners of the Soviet Union.)

Kanatchikov returned to Russia in 1928, ostensibly "rehabilitated." His new, literary assignments were important ones — membership on the editorial boards of the literary journals *Krasnaia nov'* (*Red Virgin Soil*), whose "fellow travelers" were about to come under attack by Stalin for "right" deviations, and *Literaturnaia gazeta* (*Literary Gazette*), the new journal (starting in April 1929) of the Federation of Organizations of Soviet Writers, an organization that had been similarly challenged in recent months. Sensitive assignments of this kind leave no room for doubt that Kanatchikov was once again in relatively good standing. This view is also confirmed by the repeated republication of his memoirs between 1929 and 1934, and by his authorship (or at least the printing under his name) of a short propagandistic account of the 1905 mutiny of the battleship *Potemkin* and a

straight Party-line pamphlet, written in semifictional form, glo-
rifying collectivization, the machine tractor stations (MTS), and
"our chief *kolkhoznik*" and "glorious leader Comrade Stalin."[4]
Yet something may have gone awry for Kanatchikov, who, as an
"old Bolshevik" of the first lineage, would have been a prime can-
didate for victimization during the "Great Purge" that began in
1936. The evidence, however, is strictly *ex silentio*: the absence of
any reference to Kanatchikov's activities during that period in any
Soviet sources, the absence of even his name in Soviet reference
works published between 1936 and Stalin's death in 1953.

We now know that Kanatchikov died on October 19, 1940. At
61, it may have been a natural death.

REFERENCE MATTER

NOTES

INTRODUCTION

1. M. I. Brusnev, "Vozniknovenie pervykh sotsial-demokraticheskikh organizatsii. (Vospominaniia.)" (The Rise of the First Social-Democratic Organizations. [Recollections.]), *Proletarskaia revoliutsiia*, no. 2/14 (1923), p. 20. Brusnev (1864–1937), a Marxist student, was an organizer of workers' circles in St. Petersburg at the beginning of the 1890's. August Bebel (1840–1913) was a German craftsman who was instrumental in founding the German Social-Democratic Party; he was one of its principal leaders throughout most of his adult life.

2. V. I. Lenin, *Collected Works* (4th ed.), vol. 4 (Moscow, 1964), pp. 280–81.

3. These comments on Kanatchikov's obscurity apply primarily to the years described in his memoirs, which end in 1905. His role in the Bolshevik trade-union movement after 1905, and, to a much greater extent, the various middle-level but conspicuous posts he held during the early years of the Soviet regime (see the summary in the "Postscript" below) left many more traces in the historical record than his activities during the years illuminated by his memoirs. Hence our only major source of information about the young Kanatchikov is the autobiography itself, read, of course, in the context of the rich sources of knowledge of Russian working-class life in this period that are now available.

4. These two institutions are explained below, Chap. 2, notes 1 and 3, respectively.

5. See, for example, Zelnik, "Populists and Workers."

6. Zelnik, "Russian Bebels," pp. 439–43.

7. See "Editor's Postscript," pp. 387–91.

8. Pierre Pascal, *The Religion of the Russian People* (trans. Rowan Williams; Crestwood, N.Y., 1976), p. 33.

CHAPTER 1

1. Volokolamsk was the westernmost of Moscow province's thirteen administrative districts. It was located approximately 75 miles to the west of the city of Moscow, and bordered on Tver province to the north and northwest and Smolensk province to the west and southwest.

2. "War Communism" was the name of the economic policy pursued by the Bolshevik (Communist) government throughout most of the period 1918–21, when the "Red" regime was locked in civil war with its "White" enemies. It began as an effort to mobilize the resources of a badly shattered economy in order to pursue the war more effectively, but it was soon transformed into a more ideologically motivated program to advance the construction of a radically new kind of socialist or even communist society, as this vague notion was then understood by Lenin and others. The policy gave rise to great discontent and even resistance among peasants and workers, and was abandoned by Lenin early in 1921.

3. NEP, or the New Economic Policy, replaced War Communism beginning with the Tenth Congress of the Communist Party in March 1921. Utopian schemes to build a new kind of communist society were temporarily replaced by concessions to the private sector of the economy in general and to the peasantry in particular. NEP remained in force until 1928. A "show trial" was a public trial the main purpose of which was to convey a particular political message to the population. It usually entailed the uncovering of an alleged "conspiracy" by enemies of the regime to engage in sabotage, espionage, or "wrecking." Such trials grew in number and importance at the end of the 1920's and especially in the 1930's, but minor show trials took place at the beginning of NEP as well.

4. The period of the author's childhood was one of extreme poverty and want in the overpopulated, agriculturally backward Russian countryside, still weighted down by the legacy of serfdom, which had been abolished only in 1861.

5. Although the social structure of the Russian village was very complex, and varied regionally, both scholars and political activists tended to view the peasant population as consisting of three basic components: the poor (*bedniaki*), the middle stratum (*seredniaki*), and the well-off (*kulaki*, or kulaks). The author frequently refers to kulaks in the pages that follow. The literal meaning of "kulak" is "fist," and the word suggests a person who is miserly, greedy, and acquisitive. The middle peasants— the stratum to which the author's father belonged—were by far the most numerous of the three groups, though boundaries were extremely difficult to draw, and the terms were often used polemically.

6. Under serfdom it was very common for peasants, young men especially, to leave their villages temporarily to seek by-employment to supplement their families' meager earnings. Such travel required the permission of the serfowner. Serfs who sought work away from their villages, known generically as *otkhodniki*, were often attracted to major cities such as Moscow or St. Petersburg, in part because of the employment opportunities, but also because of less tangible factors such as the excitement surrounding the myth of the great city.

7. At this time there were still many small villages in Russia with no schools of their own. When this was the case children could be sent to a larger village (*selo*) in the region for elementary education. This amounted to little more than the most primitive introduction to reading,

writing, and arithmetic, and repeated exposure to religious instruction, required in all schools. Instruction usually began at the age of seven or eight, and rarely lasted for more than two or three years. Instructors were often only a few steps ahead of their pupils in their own educational level. For a good summary and analysis, see Brooks, "The Zemstvo and the Education of the People," in Emmons and Vucinich, eds., *The Zemstvo in Russia*, pp. 243–78. See also his *When Russia Learned to Read*, Chap. 2.

8. In the original, the word translated here as "schooled" is *bityi*, which has the literal meaning "beaten," the implication being either that the schooling was routinely beaten into the pupil or that the pupil was subjected to scheduled weekly beatings.

9. Church Slavonic is the liturgical language of Russian Orthodox Christianity. As a very rough approximation, its relation to modern Russian may be compared to the relation of Church Latin to modern Romance languages.

10. The original "three-handed" (*troeruchitsa*) icon of the Virgin, dating back to the mid-fourteenth century, was located in a monastery in Athens. Variants of this Byzantine icon, in which Mary holds the Christ child on her right arm, were especially revered in Russia.

11. *Rodnoe slovo*, an extremely successful primer for peasant children by Konstantin D. Ushinsky (1824–70), the prominent Russian educator, was first published in two parts (first and second grades) in St. Petersburg in 1864. (A volume for third-year pupils was published in 1870.) In part, the book is a collection of Russian folk tales, rendered by the author in a lively, engaging style. By the eve of the First World War, parts 1 and 2 had already gone through well over a hundred editions. (The title could also be translated as *The Mother Tongue*.)

12. Dmitry Karakozov was a radical student who attempted to assassinate Tsar Alexander II in 1866, an event that accelerated the tempo of the reformer-tsar's fitful retreats from the spirit of reform. Osip Komissarov was an artisan of peasant origin who happened to be in the vicinity when the attempt took place. Although it is almost certain that Komissarov's presence was irrelevant to the failure of the assassin's shot to find its mark, an officially encouraged rumor was soon abroad that he had saved the Emperor's life, and he was quickly transformed into a national hero. Komissarov died an alcoholic. See Venturi, *Roots*, pp. 244–50. The word "nahilist," both here and later, is meant to convey the father's mispronunciation of "nihilist."

13. Sofya Perovskaya and Andrey Zheliabov were two of the most notorious radicals of the 1870's, most well known for their involvement in the attempts on the lives of Alexander II and other government officials in the years 1878–81. Both were executed for the successful attempt on the tsar on March 1, 1881. Neither were nihilists in any strict sense of the word, and Perovskaya, the daughter of an army general who held several important posts in the Russian government, was certainly not a "Jewess." Here and in the paragraphs that follow, the author is trying to show how his father had credulously accepted the common prejudices of his milieu. On Perovskaya, Zheliabov, and their roles in the assassination

plots, see Venturi, *Roots*, pp. 480–81, and Chaps. 21–22. See also David J. Footman, *Red Prelude: A Life of A. I. Zhelyabov* (London, 1944) and, on Perovskaya and her female comrades, Stites, *The Women's Liberation Movement*, Chap. 5.

14. Here the father was both misusing and mispronouncing a term. He wishes to say "Freemasons," which he corrupts into *farmazony* in Russian, and his simplistic definition of their beliefs reflects a common bias of the time.

15. Hence Kanatchikov completed approximately five years of formal schooling, considerably more than most peasant children of the period.

16. These so-called *lubochnye knizhki* and their age-old attractiveness to the semiliterate peasant reader are ably discussed in Brooks, "Readers and Reading."

17. The List factory, founded in 1863, was a moderately large machine-construction plant (550 workers in 1890, 800 in 1897), located on the southern bank of the Moscow River, just below the Kremlin. It specialized in the production of steam engines, fire-fighting pumps, and scales.

CHAPTER 2

1. With regard to the chapter's title, the artel (*artel'*) was an ancient Russian folk institution with roots dating back to the medieval period. The term is sometimes rendered in English as "cooperative," but by the end of the nineteenth century it was applied to such a wide variety of institutions as to defy any single, uniform translation. In this chapter the author is using the term to describe a cooperative living arrangement among workers, some of whom came from the same village or region. Members of such artels usually shared the cost of rent, food, fuel, and the cook's wages.

2. This was probably from coal tar that had accumulated in the yard.

3. The Russian term translated as "countryman" here is *zemliak*, the equivalent of the German *Landsmann*. Normally the term was used to refer to persons who hailed from the same village, clearly the meaning intended here. But it could also be used for natives of different, usually neighboring villages in the same region. For a discussion of the importance of the community bonds linking immigrant countrymen residing in Moscow, see Johnson, *Peasant and Proletarian*, Chap. 4. One such link, the case in point, was the custom whereby workers employed in urban factories assisted their newly arrived countrymen, either by prearrangement or upon their arrival, to gain employment at the same enterprise. An organized community of "countrymen" was sometimes called a *zemliachestvo*.

4. The hair of village boys was frequently cut *pod kruzhok*, i.e., by placing an inverted bowl or comparable round object over their heads and trimming all around beneath the rim.

5. A diminutive form of Ivan.

6. A diminutive form of Avdotya.

7. According to strict Russian Orthodox observance, believers were

expected to eat no meat or dairy products on Wednesdays (the day of the betrayal of Christ) and Fridays (the day of the Crucifixion). Hence the cook prepared the soup with fish instead of meat and the gruel (*kasha*) with vegetable oil instead of butter, animal fat, or milk.

8. Payday in Russian factories almost always fell on a Saturday afternoon (a six-day week was the norm, with Saturday as a half day), either once or twice a month.

9. St. Basil the Blessed (*Vasilii Blazhennyi*): one of Moscow's most prominent and remarkable cathedrals, constructed on Red Square in 1555–60 under Tsar Ivan the Terrible. Its location was only a short walk from the List factory and, it follows, from Kanatchikov's apartment. "St. Nicholas on the Drops" (*Mikola na kapel'kakh*) was probably the popular name for a small, local church. "Mikola" is a folksy version of Nikolay (St. Nicholas), and "on the drops" may refer to the church's location near some ponds.

10. The Khitrov market, or labor exchange, popularly known as the Khitrovka, was a lower-class neighborhood centered around the large Khitrov square in the northeast quadrant of the inner city (Miasnitskaya district), perhaps a mile from Kanatchikov's quarters. It was notorious for its high rates of crime and disease and was frequented by a multitude of prostitutes, beggars, pickpockets, ragpickers, drunkards, and street urchins, as well as by the sundry casual laborers, migrant peasants, and other poor people who wandered in and out of the area in search of casual employment. Given the dangerous and even debauched character of the neighborhood, it is not surprising that Korovin would admonish the boys to keep their distance from it, especially in the company of a drunkard like Stogov. In Henri Troyat's semifictional account of an English traveler's voyage to Moscow in 1903, the Englishman's guide refuses to take him to the Khitrovka because of the perils there, though the traveler eventually gets to the area and provides us with a rich and vivid description. (See Troyat, *Daily Life*, pp. 56–62.) The Soviet Academy of Sciences' history of Moscow cites an investigation of the Khitrovka's health and sanitary conditions, conducted at the end of the 1890's, which concluded that the area was the most horrible sore spot of the entire city, and that it was "pointless to try to remove the deeply ensconced evils of the Khitrov market by any partial improvements. . . ." (Quoted from *Istoriia Moskvy*, vol. 4, p. 544; see also pp. 260, 274, 398, 542–43.)

11. For an explanation of "graters," see Chap. 11, note 1, below.

12. Despite the formal abolition of serfdom in 1861, peasants were still subject to an internal passport system that restricted their freedom of movement to and from their villages, and made it easy for the municipal police, who controlled the passports, to send migrant peasants back to their villages if their presence in the city was deemed undesirable. This was a simple administrative procedure in which the word of an employer, a landlord, or the senior member of an artel was often sufficient to trigger the action. If the peasant was considered particularly unreliable, a recidivist, violent, or politically dangerous, he might be sent back under police or military escort (*po etapu*, from the French *étape*), a

fate that would later befall Kanatchikov. Unless the offense was considered very serious, however, the period of banishment was usually of short duration, and permission to leave the village again was not hard to come by, as witness the case of Stogov.

13. Literally, "hornless cattle" (*skotina bezrogaia*).

14. The Butikov factory was a large mechanized textile mill specializing in the weaving of woolen cloth. It employed some 1,100 workers in 1890. *Istoriia Moskvy*, vol. 4, pp. 76n, 96.

15. *Moscow Sheet (Moskovskii listok)*, published from 1881 to 1917, was a "scandal-mongering paper that covered the family affairs of prominent merchants, advertised pianos and tools," and attracted subscriptions mainly through its serialized novels, which were "potboilers." (Brooks, "Readers and Reading," p. 144.) Brooks describes the main clientele for such papers as "merchants, the petty bourgeoisie, and the service people with whom they had contact," but Kanatchikov's account suggests that factory workers were not immune to the papers' attractions. Bogdan Khmelnitsky, the subject of the novel in question, was a renowned Cossack military leader who led Ukrainian Cossacks in a series of uprisings against their Polish overlords in the mid-seventeenth century, which led indirectly to the incorporation of the Left Bank Ukraine (east of the Dnieper) into Russia in 1667. The novel serialized in *Moscow Sheet* probably presented Khmelnitsky as a larger-than-life Russian Orthodox hero struggling against Polish Catholic domination.

16. The Rumiantsev Art Museum was located on Tver Street, the site of Moscow's main administrative and cultural institutions. The Tretiakov Gallery housed the country's greatest collection of Russian paintings, donated to the city of Moscow by the wealthy Moscow merchant and art collector Pavel M. Tretiakov in 1892. It was located within easy walking distance of Kanatchikov's living quarters. On wealthy Moscow merchants as patrons of the arts, see Owen, *Capitalism and Politics*, pp. 153 ff.

CHAPTER 3

1. The next seven paragraphs are absent from the 1929 edition of volume 1 of Kanatchikov's memoirs. They are taken from the one-volume 1932 edition, pp. 28–30.

2. As in many other countries, Mondays were frequently very unproductive days in the Russian factory; workers often returned to work late, badly hung over from their weekend drinking and carousing. This was the cause of numerous petty conflicts between workers and their supervisors.

3. Nikifor was clearly attempting to make the "tea" (i.e., the alcohol-based varnish) more palatable to the workers who would soon be drinking it.

4. 1877–78.

5. The German foreman speaks in broken Russian in the original text. The broken English here is meant to suggest the flavor of the original.

6. The next six paragraphs are absent from the 1929 edition. They are taken from the 1932 edition, pp. 34–35.

7. "Vanka the Steward" (*Vanka kliuchnik*): the 1888 adaptation of a popular song by the poet Nikolay A. Panov. Sokolov, *Russian Folklore*, p. 570. For a version of the Russian text, see D. M. Balashova, ed., *Narodnye ballady* (Popular Ballads) (2d ed., Moscow, 1963), pp. 354–55. The song tells the story of a young steward who sleeps with the wife of his prince and is hanged when the prince gets wind of the affair. Once caught, Vanka displays courage and honor. The song ends with the suicide of the princess.

8. Adventure stories of daring bandits and brigands who lived outside the normal social order were extremely popular among the lower-class reading public of this period. For a subtle discussion of this complex phenomenon—the tales were fraught with moral ambiguity—see Brooks, *When Russia Learned to Read*, Chap. 5.

9. The next five paragraphs are absent from the 1929 edition. They are taken from the 1932 edition, pp. 36–37.

10. Here Kanatchikov is referring specifically to *political* consciousness. See my discussion in part ii of the Introduction, above.

11. In the spring of 1896 a citywide strike of unprecedented tenacity took place in the St. Petersburg textile industry. It was followed by a similar strike in January 1897. One of the strikers' principal demands was the introduction of a ten-and-a-half-hour workday. Although this demand was never met, the strikes did lead indirectly to the promulgation of the law of June 2, 1897, which limited the length of the workday for adult male factory workers to eleven and a half hours on normal workdays and to ten hours on Saturdays and on the eves of official holidays. These strikes and their historical significance are discussed in Wildman, *The Making of a Workers' Revolution*, Chap. 3, and Pipes, *Social Democracy*, Chap. 6. Kanatchikov is suggesting that List, frightened by the news from St. Petersburg, introduced a shorter workday to head off a possible strike movement in his own plant. By the end of the year, several other Moscow factories had done this, either under pressure from their own workers or in anticipation of such pressure.

CHAPTER 4

1. An archaic liturgical term suggesting that which *is* or which *exists*. The use of such language by the workers with reference to a deeply religious comrade, though employed in a lighthearted, teasing manner, is an indication of the extent to which they were still culturally and linguistically entangled in their religious backgrounds. There are several examples of the use of such terminology, which defies smooth translation into English, in this and later chapters.

2. The placing of illuminated icons in a workshop, whether at the initiative of the owners or of the workers themselves, was a common practice.

3. *Aleksandrovsky sad*: a large public garden, built in 1819–22 as part

of the restoration of Moscow after the great fire of 1812 at the time of Napoleon's invasion of Russia. The garden is located on the northwest side of the Kremlin, at the present site of the Tomb of the Unknown Soldier.

4. Stepka is addressing Sushchy by his formal first name and patronymic.

5. The Russian terms translated here as "sin" and "harlot" are again laden with old religious import, giving them very solemn connotations.

6. Riazan was a province located just to the southeast of Moscow province. Many Riazan peasants worked in Moscow city.

7. Many Russian factory owners, especially in traditional centers of Orthodox Christianity such as Moscow, liked to infuse their workers with religiosity by holding religious ceremonials on the factory premises. At such events the factory owners themselves sometimes became the objects of homage and veneration.

CHAPTER 5

1. The Gopper factory was a fairly large metalworks (600 workers in 1905 according to Engelstein, *Moscow, 1905*, p. 85) located in Moscow's Serpukhov district in the southernmost part of the city.

2. The equation of "student" with "revolutionary" stemmed from the 1870's, when the revolutionary populist movement first caught on among students in Russia's major university centers. Students remained a prominent element in the revolutionary movement in the decades that followed.

3. A military fortress in St. Petersburg, located on an island off the northern shore of the Neva River. It was constructed by Peter the Great in the early years of the eighteenth century. Because the fortress was used to incarcerate people considered politically dangerous by the government, it was looked upon by many as a symbol of political oppression. Some of Russia's most prominent revolutionaries served time there.

4. A complex system of universal (male) military service had been introduced in 1874 as part of a larger overhaul of the Russian military establishment, discredited since the Crimean War of 1853–56.

5. The jewel-studded Iversky (Iberian) icon of the Mother of God, located in a chapel at the entrance to Moscow's Red Square, was deeply venerated by the people of Moscow. "Not a day passed but it was taken in a [horsedrawn] carriage, at a high fee, to the bedside of a sick person, or to a newly installed apartment, or to a family feast. . . . All along the road the passers-by uncovered and crossed themselves, and when the carriage stopped in front of a 'client's' house a crowd formed to witness the 'descent' of the image. The faithful followed it to the door, while others devotedly kissed the seat on which the ikon had rested. . . ." Troyat, *Daily Life*, pp. 65–66. Ioann (or John) of Kronstadt (1829–1908) was a renowned Orthodox spiritual leader widely revered for his healing powers. Calling him by the diminutive name of "Vaniukha" was like calling him "Johnny," and was intended to show disrespect.

6. The Monastery of the Caves near Kiev (*Kievo-Pecharskaia lavra*), Russia's oldest monastery, was an extremely important Orthodox religious shrine and a major destination for pilgrims.

7. The State Historical Museum, located near the Kremlin on Red Square, was opened in 1883.

8. Alexander III succeeded Alexander II to the throne in 1881 and ruled until his premature death at the age of 49 in 1894, when he was succeeded by his son Nicholas II. Whether or not it was actually brought on by drink, his death was apparently caused by a severe kidney disease.

9. The importance to Orthodox Russian culture of relics in general and bones of saints in particular was based on the popular belief in their curative powers. Parts of the saint's body were thought to be incorruptible. See Nina Tumarkin, *Lenin Lives! The Lenin Cult in Soviet Russia* (Cambridge, Mass., 1983), p. 5.

10. The influence of a vulgarized version of Darwinian evolutionary theory is evident here. Darwin's influence on Russian intellectual, cultural, and political life had been enormous since 1861, when his theory of evolution was first introduced to Russia. It was particularly attractive to "nihilists" and other radicals, including Marxists, who sought to combine their socialist ideas with atheism and a scientific world view. See Vucinich, *Science in Russian Culture*, Chap. 4, esp. pp. 104–8, and Chap. 9. On Russian Marxism and Darwinism, see Vucinich, *Social Thought in Tsarist Russia*, pp. 186–91. Radical propagandists who designed political education programs for Russian workers often included Darwinian evolution as one of the units. Kanatchikov's story illustrates the corrupted but nonetheless significant ways in which evolutionary theory managed to work its way down to the lower rungs of the educational ladder.

11. The Dukhobors (literally, "Spirit Wrestlers") were members of a militant religious sect dating from the early eighteenth century that rejected earthly pleasures and secular authorities in the name of a higher spirituality. They were often in conflict with the Russian government over their refusal to serve in the military.

12. The almost mythical attraction of St. Petersburg for provincial peasants and workers, especially those who had never been there before, was noted in Chap. 1, note 6, above. The attraction remained strong well past the abolition of serfdom. For a fictionalized portrayal of the ways in which it functioned, see F. M. Reshetnikov's 1868 novel *Gde luchshe?* (Where Is It Better?), in his *Izbrannye sochineniia* (Moscow, 1956).

13. *Die Weber*, a play in five acts by the German writer Gerhart Hauptmann (1862–1946), was completed in 1892, but its performance was repeatedly prohibited by the Berlin police and Prussian judicial authorities. Nevertheless, it had been performed in several German cities by 1894, thanks in part to successful litigation. The play depicts the exploitation of Silesian linen weavers and the bloody uprising that resulted in 1844. Two illegal Russian translations appeared under the title *Tkachi* in 1895, and they soon enjoyed enormous success in radical circles. The translation printed by the "People's Will Group" (*Gruppa narodovol'tsev*) frequently appeared among the brochures confiscated from workers'

groups during police raids in 1895 and the years that followed. See, for example, *Rabochee dvizhenie v Rossii v XIX veke*, vol. 4, part 1, pp. 33, 35, 75, 319, 321, 680, 713.

14. The "song of the weavers," repeated in various sections of Hauptmann's play, was considered particularly provocative by the German authorities because of its open call for vengeance against employers. The passage cited here appears in Acts 2 and 3 of the original play. (I have translated directly from the Russian, which has only a loose resemblance to the German.) For the full text of the German folksong from which Hauptmann borrowed the song of the weavers, see Hans Schwab-Felisch, *Gerhart Hauptmann, Die Weber* (Frankfurt am Main, 1975), pp. 115–18.

15. The original Russian translation of this Polish pamphlet, *Chto nuzhno znat' i pomnit' kazhdomu rabochemu?*, was hectographed in 1893, but was printed for the first time (by the Union of Russian Social Democrats in Geneva) only in 1895. (There were slight variations in the Russian title.) Like *The Weavers*, it was widely used to propagandize workers and was frequently confiscated by the police. (See *Rabochee dvizhenie v Rossii v XIX veke*, vol. 4, part 1, pp. 130, 284, 319–21, 325, 443, 492, 708, 725, for examples from the years 1895–97.) The original author was the Polish anarcho-Marxist Edward Abramowski (1868–1918).

16. Georgy V. Plekhanov (1857–1918), the most prominent representative of the Russian Marxist intelligentsia from the mid-1880's to the turn of the century, published the partially autobiographical *Russkii rabochii v revoliutsionnom dvizhenii* first in his Geneva periodical *Sotsial-Demokrat* (1890–92), and then as a separate pamphlet (1892). One of his purposes was to inspire working-class militants by demonstrating that they had had heroic predecessors in the 1870's, when Plekhanov had been active in propagandizing St. Petersburg workers. It is not at all clear in what way Plekhanov's booklet would have shed any light on the biases of Kanatchikov's father or the distortions in his stories.

17. The cult of St. Nicholas (Nikolay-ugodnik), originally a Greek saint, was brought to Russia from Constantinople by merchants and soldiers, and the much-revered saint entered the spiritual world of the Eastern Slavs at least a century before Kiev's official conversion to Christianity in 988. With time, in the popular imagination Saint Nicholas became the spiritual protector of the Orthodox Christian population against marauding infidels such as the Tatars. For a brief summary, see Konrad Onasch, *Icons* (London, 1961), p. 347. The militant revolutionary and student of peasant life Sergey Kravchinsky (1851–95) wrote: "Of all the saints, St. Nicholas is perhaps the most popular with the Russians." Stepniak (Kravchinsky's pseudonym), *The Russian Peasantry*, p. 360. The author recounts some of the popular tales about St. Nicholas on pp. 365–68.

CHAPTER 6

1. Nicholas II succeeded his father, Alexander III, in the fall of 1894. His coronation in Moscow, however, was scheduled for May 1896, more

than a year and a half later. The events described in this chapter center around the notorious Khodynka affair, a great human tragedy that marred Nicholas II's reign and contributed heavily to the discrediting of the regime. There is a vivid account of these events, based mainly on an eyewitness report by Vladimir Nemirovich-Danchenko (printed in the magazine *Niva* [*The Cornfield*]) in Salisbury, *Black Night, White Snow*, Chap. 7. See also Lincoln, *In War's Dark Shadow*, pp. 280–83.

2. Janitors and building superintendents were frequently used by the police as informers and unofficial agents.

3. On the liberal daily paper *Russian News* (*Russkie vedomosti*, sometimes translated as *Russian Gazette*), see Chap. 41, note 3, below.

4. Sergey Vasilevich Zubatov (1864–1917) was chief of the Moscow security police (*Okhrana*) from 1896 to 1902. Early in 1901 he introduced a controversial program that came to be known, after its founder, as the *zubatovshchina*, or, more ironically, as "police socialism," an attempt to divert the workers of Moscow and several other towns from the path of revolution and socialism to the path of moderation and monarchism. Under his plan, factory workers were encouraged to organize, under police supervision, to work toward the improvement of their lot by peaceful means. At first the program enjoyed some success, but it soon succumbed to the simultaneous attacks of panicky industrialists and their sympathizers within the government and of almost all elements of the Russian Left. In 1903 Zubatov was dismissed from government service in disgrace, and by 1904 the Zubatov experiment as such was effectively finished (though the remnants of Zubatov's organizations still played a fairly important role in Moscow in the early months of the 1905 Revolution). For a thorough study of these developments see Schneiderman, *Sergei Zubatov and Revolutionary Marxism*; for shorter summaries, see Bonnell, *Roots*, pp. 80–86; Engelstein, *Moscow, 1905*, pp. 59–62; Lincoln, pp. 206–11.

Mikhail Afanasev's name is mentioned several times in Schneiderman's account. He is cited as an initiator among his fellow Moscow metalworkers of the mutual-aid society that became the first Zubatov organization in 1901. He was also its first chairman. Schneiderman describes him as part of the "small but highly significant worker-intelligentsia" that was capable of communicating with the average worker much more effectively than people from the educated classes could. Afanasev's involvement with Zubatov, according to Schneiderman, should be dated to his arrest by Zubatov in July 1896, which conflicts somewhat with Kanatchikov's claim that the initial arrest took place on the eve of the coronation. (See Schneiderman, pp. 100–104.) Despite his involvement with Zubatov, Afanasev was a very militant agitator who earned no gratitude from Moscow industrialists.

5. The reference here is to two different categories of cavalry officer. They are "shelling little seeds," probably sunflower seeds, in order to chew them, a common Russian habit.

6. The song "Down Along the Mother Volga" (*Vniz po matushke po Volge*), one of the more famous Russian folksongs, is usually categorized as a "robber song." It describes young men, probably brigands, sailing

freely along the river, then putting in to shore and meeting a young girl. (See V. Propp, "The Russian Folk Lyric," in Reeder, ed., *Down Along the Mother Volga*, pp. 35–36; an abbreviated English translation of the song may be found on pp. 196–97 of the same volume.) The "Kamarinskaya" was a lively Russian folkdance.

7. The factory legislation of the early 1880's included regulation of the workday of minors and women only. As indicated in Chap. 3, note 11, above, limitations on the working hours of adult males were finally introduced in 1897, about a year after the events described here. An eight-hour day was, of course, way beyond reach at this time, but it had enormous symbolic meaning as a slogan of the international labor movement.

8. The Khodynka field, scene of the catastrophe that gives this chapter its name, was located on the northwest outskirts of Moscow. The site of various military barracks, the field's rugged and treacherous terrain was marked by ditches and ravines.

9. Not surprisingly, a precise calculation of the number of deaths and injuries at Khodynka has never been made. The official estimate of about 1,400 dead and 1,300 injured was clearly much too low (see Lincoln, pp. 282–83), but Smirnov's figure of 30,000, proclaimed in rage, was much too high.

10. See Chap. 3, note 11, above.

11. The Russian words *stachka* and *zabastovka*, used almost interchangeably, are usually translated as "strike." *Stachka* has more of a connotation of conspiracy, hence my choice of the English "combination" to avoid having to say ". . . the words 'strike' and 'strike.' . . ."

12. The figure 30,000 is often cited as the approximate number of participants in the 1896 Petersburg textile strike. Recently, however, some Soviet historians have revised this figure downward to approximately 16,000. (See *Istoriia rabochikh Leningrada*, vol. 1, p. 206 and 206n.) Although Kanatchikov refers to the strikers as "weavers," spinners and other textile workers were heavily involved as well.

13. Reference here is to the Manège (riding school), which was constructed in 1817 opposite the Alexander Garden. A massive building with spacious grounds, it was used as an army barracks and as a training ground for cavalry.

CHAPTER 7

1. This is his first name and patronymic.

2. It was an unwritten rule among Russian factory workers that a newly hired or newly promoted worker should treat his fellow workers to drinks. A number of jocular expressions were used to describe this rite of passage, including, as in the present case, the metaphor of taxation. The term employed, *prival'noe*, was originally the word for the fee paid for docking a boat at a pier, and later referred to the vodka or tea given to barge haulers as tips for bringing a boat safely to port. Dal', *Tolkovyi slovar'*, vol. 3, p. 401.

3. That is, it had an underlying radical propaganda purpose.

4. "Khaz [or 'Khas'] Bulat the Daring": a song based on a poem by A. N. Ammosov (1823–66) called "Elegy" (1858). The lyrics, which are reprinted in Ivan N. Rozanov, *Russkie pesni XIX veka* (Russian Songs of the Nineteenth Century) (Moscow, 1944), pp. 384–86, have virtually nothing in common with Sergey Petrovich's song.

CHAPTER 8

1. Mozhaisk was an administrative district in the western part of Moscow province, immediately to the south of Kanatchikov's home district of Volokolamsk, a fairly easy distance from Moscow city (roughly 75 miles). Tula and Riazan were neighboring provinces to the south and southeast of Moscow province, respectively. At their borders, they were located at about the same distance from Moscow city as Mozhaisk and Volokolamsk.

2. This was obviously a genital examination. The practice was widespread in Russian industry, and the attendant humiliation was sometimes the cause of unrest among affronted workers.

3. This is the festive holiday or Yuletide period from Christmas Eve to January 6. For a description of the typical procedures and ceremonials that surrounded a marriage in the villages of the Moscow region, see Matossian, "The Peasant Way of Life," pp. 25–29. Matossian also describes the intense celebrations and other activities of the Yuletide season (pp. 32–33). The "striking of hands" mentioned in the text refers to the final sealing of the marriage bargain by the fathers of the bride and groom.

4. His formal first name and patronymic, indicating that the marriage had earned him new respect from his neighbors.

5. According to the existing factory legislation, both employer and employee were required to give two weeks' notice in order to terminate a contract. If the employer wished the worker to leave immediately, he was required to give the worker two weeks' additional salary as severance pay.

6. Egorych is the shortened, conversational form of the patronymic Egorevich. Dropping the syllable "ev" or "ov" is the most common way to turn a Russian patronymic into conversational form; thus Ivanovich becomes Ivanych, etc.

7. The Bromley Brothers' engineering works (founded in 1857), often called the "Old Bromley" to distinguish it from a second Bromley factory, was one of the largest engineering works in Moscow, with over 900 workers at the end of 1896. It was located close to the Moscow River, in the western part of the Serpukhov district, the southernmost part of the city.

CHAPTER 9

1. It is very unlikely that Kanatchikov is using the term "independent" to suggest an intent to set up his own shop. More likely, he is trying to

convey the skilled or "qualified" worker's sense of having attained a relatively high degree of autonomy. Successful completion of the kind of test of the quality of his workmanship described here by the author was another important rite of passage, leading from youthful apprenticeship to professional adulthood. Distant echoes of the medieval guild notion of completion of a *chef d'oeuvre* can be heard in this factory ritual.

2. Another reference to the "unwritten rule" described in Chap. 7, note 2, above.

3. *Raschetnye knizhki* (paybooks or workbooks) were partially modeled on the French *livrets d'ouvriers*. They contained the terms of the worker's contract, his official title or grade, a running record of all financial transactions that affected him, and a list of all the factory regulations. Although formally required by law since 1835, they were not really made mandatory until the important factory law of June 4, 1886. For the background and further details, see Zelnik, *Labor and Society*, pp. 33–34, 125–29, 141, 358–59, and Tugan-Baranovsky, *The Russian Factory*, pp. 327–32.

4. Zamoskvoreche (literally, "beyond the Moscow River"): one of the six major divisions of the city of Moscow, located south of the Moscow River at the point where it bends across the center of the city; the area was heavily populated by industrial workers. The Serpukhov district, where the Bromley factory was located, constituted the southernmost part of Zamoskvoreche. There is a clear and concise sketch of this area in Engelstein, *Moscow, 1905*, pp. 46–47. For a sense of the conservative, tradition-bound, Muscovite character of the neighborhood on which the factories of the Zamoskvoreche were superimposed, one should also consult Robert Whittaker, "'My Literary and Moral Wanderings': Apollon Grigor'ev and the Changing Cultural Topography of Moscow," *Slavic Review*, 42, no. 3 (1983), pp. 390–407.

5. The author uses the Russian word *meshchanka*, the feminine form of *meschanin*, a member of the lowest and most numerous legally constituted segment of the urban population. The term corresponds roughly to the concept of petty bourgeois, and was sometimes used with the same negative connotations. Here I translate *meshchanka* as "city girl," since this appears to be the point the author wishes to stress.

6. The Russian slang word *fonar'*—here translated as "shiner"—literally means "lantern."

7. The weekly visit to the public steam baths, usually on Saturday afternoons (when work ended earlier than on weekdays), was an almost universal practice among Russian workers. More luxurious bathhouses were also available to the upper classes. There is a nice description in Troyat, *Daily Life*, pp. 51–54.

8. Sukharevka was a large open-air market situated on Sukharevskaya Square along the outer ring of boulevards on the north side of the city center. It included a "respectable section for the sale of real and imitation antiques, books, and the like, and a plebeian [section] . . . where petty profiteers bought and sold all sorts of old clothing and miscellaneous trash." Gohstand, "The Internal Geography," vol. 2, p. 538.

9. "Black" clergy were members of the monastic clergy, who took vows

of celibacy; "white" clergy were members of the secular clergy, who were expected to marry. The white clergy constituted the rank and file of Russia's parish priests.

10. Ivan Ia. Franko (1856–1916), an outstanding and very popular Ukrainian poet and publicist who combined socialist with Ukrainian nationalist aspirations. The Russian title of his fable is *Khvostik*.

11. Reference is to the *kulich*, a very rich, sweet cake, and the *pashka*, a rich mixture of sweetened curds, white cheese, butter, eggs, and raisins. At Eastertime, believers would have these ritual cakes and their colored Easter eggs blessed by their parish priest.

12. Labor contracts were customarily drawn up to expire with the coming of the Easter holidays, in part because workers with close ties to the countryside often wished or were obligated to return to agricultural work at that time of year. Since the contract had expired, the Bromley factory was not bound at this time by the law requiring two weeks' notice (see Chap. 8, note 5, above), and the dismissals were therefore legal. Technically, in fact, they were not dismissals at all; the administration would simply refuse to rehire the "undesirables" whose contracts had expired.

13. The Mytishchensk factory was located near the village of Mytishchi, about thirteen miles northeast of Moscow. In 1903 the factory employed well over 1,300 workers.

CHAPTER 10

1. The author's precise expression here is "tradition of . . . *tsekhovshchina*," by which he means an excessive devotion to or pride in one's workshop, craft, or some other limited, parochial unit.

2. *Niva* (*The Cornfield* or *The Grainfield*, suggesting in this case a field in which the seeds of knowledge are planted) was a popular weekly magazine, published in St. Petersburg since 1869. It specialized in escapist literature for the common reader, but also published major authors of the stature of Tolstoy and Chekhov. By the mid-1890's its circulation had reached the enormous figure of 200,000. Billington, *The Icon and the Axe*, p. 439.

3. A diminutive form of Semën.

4. Stenka Razin, a Don Cossack, was the leader of a major peasant uprising in 1670. He was captured and executed in 1671. Emelyan Pugachev, also a Don Cossack, led a similar rebellion in 1773–74 and was executed in 1775. Both men, but Razin in particular, became the heroes of Russian folktales and ballads, and both were incorporated into the ideologies and mythologies of Russian radicalism, especially its "populist" variant. For a concise introduction to the history of the two uprisings, see Paul Avrich, *Russian Rebels: 1600–1800* (New York, 1972), Chaps. 2 and 4; see also Avrich's comments on the legacies of these uprisings in the nineteenth and early twentieth centuries (in Chap. 5).

5. Reference is to the great German radical poet and critic Heinrich Heine (1797–1856). The verses cited here were very popular among the socialist workers of Germany. The Russian lines cited by Kanatchikov

combine parts of the ninth and tenth stanzas of Heine's "Winter Tale" (*Wintermärchen*, 1844). A direct translation of Heine's original lines (stanza 10) would read: "The lazy belly shall not waste in its gluttony/ That which diligent hands have earned." The reference to a heavenly kingdom on earth is from the previous stanza. See Wolfgang Emmerich, ed., *Proletarische Lebensläufe: Autobiographische Dokumente zur Entstehung der Zweiten Kultur in Deutschland*, vol. 2 (Reinbek bei Hamburg, 1975), pp. 69–70 (from the memoirs of the Berlin metalworker Karl Retzlaw).

6. Alexander Pushkin (1799–1837) is universally recognized as nineteenth-century Russia's greatest poet. I have been unable to locate this aphorism among his writings.

7. Kanatchikov is hinting at a recurrent theme in the history of the Russian labor movement: generational conflict between older workers with a history of revolutionary experience, who no longer wish to take great risks, and younger workers who are more impetuous and fearless, and are prepared to burn their fingers in the fires of revolutionary politics. More specifically, the older men Kanatchikov encounters in the 1890's and later must have been veterans of the radical workers' circles of the 1870's (and possibly the 1880's), some of whom had been closely involved with the radical students who launched the revolutionary movement of that period. On the first known contacts of this type, see Zelnik, "Populists and Workers."

8. See Chap. 12, note 4, below.

9. See Chap. 12, note 2, below, as well as Kanatchikov's description of the Nevsky Gate region of St. Petersburg in chapters 12 and 14.

10. The short-lived Soviet of Workers' Deputies was perhaps the most important revolutionary institution generated by the Revolution of 1905, and served as a model for the famous soviets that appeared in 1917. "Factory elder" (*starosta*) refers to legislation introduced in 1903 whereby factory workers were permitted for the first time to elect their own representatives. The implementation of the law was left in the hands of management, and very few factories had elected elders by the beginning of 1905. See Bonnell, *Roots*, pp. 96–97.

11. The contrast between the attitudes and conduct of revolutionaries from the working class and revolutionaries from the educated elite or intelligentsia is one of the major themes to which Kanatchikov will return again and again. For an analysis of Kanatchikov's approach to this problem, see Zelnik, "Russian Bebels," especially pp. 424–39.

12. Nikolay V. Shelgunov (1824–91) had been one of Russia's most well-known radical political writers since the 1860's. His St. Petersburg funeral procession in 1891, attended by some one hundred workers, turned into an important and impressive political demonstration. See Pipes, *Social Democracy*, pp. 31–32, and Naimark, *Terrorists and Social Democrats*, p. 166.

13. Shelgunov's article, first published in the radical Petersburg journal *Sovremennik* (*The Contemporary*) in 1861, was actually called "The Working Proletariat in England and France." The article was an attempt

to expose the sufferings inflicted on the working classes of Western Europe under capitalism, and it drew heavily on Friedrich Engels' 1845 study, *The Condition of the Working Class in England.* (Note that Kanatchikov blends the two titles.) Shelgunov's purpose was to argue against the value of capitalist development in Russia—essentially an anti-Marxist, populist position. (For further discussion of the article, see Zelnik, *Labor and Society*, pp. 109–10.) This explains the confusion experienced by the young Kanatchikov when he read the article, as suggested in the paragraphs that follow.

14. Iaroslav (or Yaroslav) province was located about a hundred miles to the northeast of Moscow province, and contained the northernmost bend of the Volga River. As in other parts of the Volga region, it was common there to give the vowel "o" its full value when speaking, whereas most Russians weaken this sound unless the syllable containing the "o" is stressed.

15. By shifting the stress on Oslopov's name from the first to the second syllable, Kanatchikov and his friends made it sound like the Russian word for an ass (*osël*).

16. As indicated in Chap. 9, note 9, above, members of the clerical estate (excluding monks) married and had children.

17. The clear implication is that Kanatchikov had been "set up." The real reason he was fired was his effort to propagate his radical religious and political views.

CHAPTER 11

1. The Russian word *rashpil'* (also *rashpel'*) comes from the German *Raspel*, and can be translated as either "grater" or "rasp," a kind of rough-edged filing tool. The term is used here pejoratively, in reference to a notoriously hard-nosed type of small employer in specialized crafts who worked on subcontract for factories or larger workshops.

2. The author is referring to the factory of Vartse and McGill, located near the Krestovsk Gate, the old northern gate of the city.

3. "Piter" was the popular, colloquial, and even somewhat affectionate term for the capital city, St. Petersburg. Kanatchikov uses it frequently in the chapters that follow.

4. Nikolay A. Nekrasov (1821–77), a radical poet and editor, enjoyed enormous popularity among Russia's left intelligentsia and politically sensitized workers. As the following paragraphs suggest, the plight of Russia's impoverished masses was one of the central themes of Nekrasov's "civic" poetry.

5. From Nekrasov's long poem "Knight for an Hour" (*Rytsar' na chas*), written in 1860. For the full text, see Nekrasov, *Polnoe sobranie sochinenii i pisem*, vol. 2, pp. 92–97.

6. As Kanatchikov goes on to say, the full title of Nekrasov's satirical poem, written in 1858, is "Reflections at the Main Entrance" (*Razmyshleniia u paradnogo pod"ezda*). Like so many of Nekrasov's verses, the poem is meant to evoke compassion for the long-suffering Russian peas-

ant. The title refers to the entrance to a government office building, where the poet observes poor peasants being turned away from the door. For the full text, see *ibid.*, pp. 52–55.

7. "People's libraries" (*narodnye biblioteki*) and reading rooms, accessible to the urban lower classes at no cost or for only a nominal fee (thanks to the subsidies of philanthropists), were first organized in the late 1880's. By the 1890's the government was carefully supervising the choice of books and magazines available at such institutions.

8. Russia's Factory Inspectorate was established in 1882 and confirmed and expanded by the major factory legislation of 1886. It was the job of the inspectors to listen to the complaints of workers, report on violations of the labor laws, and maintain surveillance over other aspects of factory life, such as working conditions and labor disturbances.

CHAPTER 12

1. Address bureaus or offices were introduced in St. Petersburg and Moscow in 1809 and in other Russian cities soon thereafter. In addition to assisting in the location of residents, the bureaus performed certain police functions such as surveillance over the domicile, employment, and movement of the temporary, migrant population (mainly peasants) of the city. See Zelnik, *Labor and Society*, p. 20.

2. The region beyond the Nevsky Gate (usually called the Nevsky or the Nevsky Gate region) was the large and at times politically explosive industrial and working-class neighborhood located at the southeastern extreme of the city of St. Petersburg and extending southeastward beyond the city limits along the Neva River and the Shlisselburg Road or Highway. The part of the region that was within the city limits also overlapped parts of the Aleksandro-Nevsky police-administrative district or borough. The Nikolaev railroad station, where Kanatchikov arrived by train from Moscow, was in that district, but at its northernmost point, almost in the inner city; hence he had to take the local steam train to head back out to the working-class neighborhood at the outskirts of town.

3. The Maxwell (Maksvel') or Spassko-Petrovsky cotton-spinning and -weaving factory (founded in 1843) was located on the Shlisselburg Road a short distance beyond the city limits. Its workers had played a prominent role in the Petersburg textile strikes of 1896 and 1897. The factory (actually a complex of two factories with the same owners) employed between 2,700 and 3,000 workers at the time of the strikes.

4. Here and elsewhere Kanatchikov follows the custom of Petersburg workers and other residents of the capital (including, at times, government officials) by referring to the factory in question by the name "Semiannikov," one of its original owners. Its correct name was the Nevsky (or Neva) shipbuilding and machine-construction factory (founded in 1857). Like the Maxwell factory, it was located near the Shlisselburg Road in the village of Smolenskoe, a short distance beyond the city lim-

its. One of the city's giant enterprises, the factory had upwards of 3,000 workers at this time. It had been known as a hotbed of worker activism ever since the 1870's.

5. A very small plant that specialized in the manufacture of bullets. It was located in the Aleksandro-Nevsky district, on Kiev Street.

6. The Vyborg side refers to the administrative district of the city immediately to the north of the Neva River after its sharp westward bend toward the sea. The district was heavily industrialized and had a large working-class population, which became increasingly militant in the decade leading up to the revolutionary upheavals of 1917. Vasilevsky Island was also an administrative district. It was a large island, also north of the river, but further to the west, and separated from the Vyborg side by the Petersburg district. The population and character of the island were heterogeneous and complex; it contained a few large factories, many smaller workshops, the stock exchange, the university, and several shipyards and docks.

7. The adjective "gray" (also used as a noun) was the term most commonly applied to urban workers who still maintained close ties to the countryside. It had strong connotations of ignorance and backwardness, and is therefore not quite captured by the comparable use of "green" in English. For this reason, I will continue to use "gray" whenever the Russian (*seryi*) occurs.

8. The Okhta region of St. Petersburg was on the right bank of the Neva River, immediately to the south of the southeastern tip of the Vyborg district; hence it was the easternmost section of the city. It was underpopulated and by almost any standard was the most "backward" area within the city limits.

9. On the significance of the two weeks' notice, see Chap. 8, note 5, above.

10. See Chap. 6, note 2, above.

CHAPTER 13

1. See Chap. 12, note 6, above.

2. The pseudonym of Sergey Kravchinsky (see Chap. 5, note 17, above). *Underground Russia (Podpol'naia Rossiia)* was published first in Italian in 1881–82, then in English (under the title *Underground Russia: Revolutionary Profiles and Sketches from Life*), and then in Russian (translated from the English) in 1883. Several illegal Russian editions appeared in the following years. Essentially, the book was a highly subjective glorification of the Russian revolutionary intelligentsia of the 1870's—to which the author had belonged—approached through biographical sketches of heroic individuals.

3. In December 1904, a militant oil workers' strike in the Caspian port city of Baku grew into a citywide general strike, one of the events that sparked the Revolution of 1905. The strike was led mainly by a group of dissident Social Democrats with some ties to the Menshevik faction of

the Russian Social Democratic Party. The group was dominated by the three Shendrikov brothers and was usually referred to as the "Shendrikovites." (On the splitting of the Party into Menshevik and Bolshevik factions in 1903, see Chap. 46, note 12, below.) The most popular and talented of the brothers was Ilya, who was generally seen as the hero of the strike. In calling him a traitor, Kanatchikov is lapsing into the standard Communist historiographical line, in part a reflection of the fact that the role of the Bolsheviks in Baku was eclipsed by the successes of the Shendrikovites for about a year. (Note, however, the author's tone of admiration in the text itself.) For two detailed and somewhat conflicting discussions of the Baku strike and the role of the Shendrikovs, see Schwarz, *The Russian Revolution of 1905*, pp. 129–30, 301–14; and Ronald G. Suny, *The Baku Commune, 1917–1918* (Princeton, N.J., 1972), pp. 33–42. As to Shendrikov's having been an "outright villain" in Siberia in 1917–18, Kanatchikov is probably referring to the fact that in 1917 Shendrikov became an official of the Provisional Government that the Bolsheviks overthrew in October of that year, and that he later fought on the "White," anti-Communist side of the Civil War that began in 1918.

4. The Council of State or State Council (*Gosudarstvennyi sovet*), created by Tsar Alexander I in 1810, was a prestigious government body whose members—usually high-ranking dignitaries with long records of state service—were appointed by the tsar to advise him in the preparation of legislation.

5. The correct Russian word for "pharmacist" was *farmatsevt*. Here Kanatchikov depicts himself stumbling over this difficult word and mispronouncing it as *farmatsent*, which I have Anglicized in translation.

6. *Russian Wealth* (*Russkoe bogatstvo*) was a monthly literary and political journal published in St. Petersburg from 1880 to 1918. In the mid-1890's this moderately radical populist journal devoted a great deal of space to attacks against Marxist social theory, which is why Kanatchikov, who clearly liked the journal at the time, alludes apologetically here to his political ignorance.

7. The Cheshire (Chesher, also called the Nikolsky) cotton-weaving factory (founded by an English weaver named Joseph Cheshire in 1866) was located in the Vyborg district on the right bank of the Bolshaya Nevka, the small tributary of the Neva that separated the Vyborg and Petersburg districts. It was a fairly small factory, with perhaps 200 workers, mainly women, in this period.

8. I have been unable to find any further information about either of the women from the Cheshire factory.

9. As the head of the family household in his village, the elder Kanatchikov still had the right, subject to the approval of local administrative authorities, to control the movement of his children by approving or disapproving issuance of the temporary internal passport Russian peasants were required to carry when traveling or working away from their homes. A vestige of the days of serfdom, the passport system had been a major source of controversy in Russia since 1861, when its retention partially

undermined the goal of emancipation. (Note also the elder Kanatchikov's difficulty with the word "passport.")

CHAPTER 14

1. On the Nevsky factory, see Chap. 12, note 4, above. The Aleksandrovsk machine works (founded in 1843) was a very large factory (well over 4,000 workers in 1897, and expanding rapidly) that specialized in the production of locomotives and rolling stock. The Obukhov steel mill (founded in 1863), owned by the Naval Ministry, had 4,300 workers in 1898. Located a short distance south of the city limits, it played a central role in the upsurge of violent labor unrest that would sweep sections of the capital in the late spring of 1901. (See Surh, "Petersburg Workers," pp. 86–99.) The Pal (or Aleksandro-Nevsky) cotton-weaving factory (founded in 1879) had some 1,500 workers when it participated in the citywide strike of 1896. On the Maxwell factory, see Chap. 12, note 3, above. The final reference is to the Nevsky stearine factory, founded in 1851, which had about 500 workers at the turn of the century.

2. The first theatrical performances for the working-class population of the Nevsky Gate area were launched in the late 1880's by civic-minded notables and enlightened industrialists who wished to raise the cultural and, as they saw it, the moral level of the local population. In 1891 their organization, known as the "Nevsky Society," created a permanent, enclosed theater, seating 258, where performances were given by both amateur and professional troupes, presenting mainly a classical Russian repertoire. The working-class audience appears to have been extremely receptive. (These developments are briefly summarized in *Ocherki istorii Leningrada*, vol. 2, pp. 520–22. For a broader discussion, see Gary Thurston, "The Impact of Russian Popular Theatre, 1886–1915," *Journal of Modern History*, 55, no. 2 [1983], pp. 237–67, esp. pp. 258–62.) Kanatchikov's sneering reference to "shabby theaters" is clearly an overstatement.

3. Pskov province was located about 200 miles to the northwest of Moscow province, immediately to the south of St. Petersburg province. *Pskopskie*, the Russian term described here as a slang expression for men from Pskov, is probably a play on the word *skoptsy*, meaning "eunuchs" or "castrati"; the second "p" replaces the letter "v" in the correct term, *pskovskie*.

4. Kanatchikov actually uses the untranslatable terms *zavodskoe* and *fabrichnoe*, adjectives derived from the two basic Russian words for factory: *fabrika* and *zavod*. The distinction between the two is much more complex than is suggested by my choice of "metalworkers" for *zavodskie* and "textile workers" for *fabrichnye*, though these expressions render the meaning intended by the author in the present context. For further discussion see Bonnell, ed., *The Russian Worker*, p. 73n.

5. In this period there were almost no women in the Russian metalworking industry, but the proportion of women in the textile industry

surpassed 44 percent, and was even higher in St. Petersburg. See Glick-man, *Russian Factory Women*, pp. 80, 82.

6. "Pharaoh" and "archangel" were popular terms of reproach for po-lice officials.

7. A Biblical reference to baptism in the Jordan River.

8. On the SRs, see Chap. 35, note 22, below. The point the author is making here is that impatient workers turned to those radical groups whose emphasis was on heroic revolutionary deeds rather than slow pre-paratory work.

9. It is not clear to whom Bykov is referring here.

10. *Workers' Thought* (*Rabochaia mysl'*) was a worker-oriented jour-nal that was critical of the mainstream Russian Social Democratic move-ment for allowing nonworkers, i.e. the intelligentsia, too great a leader-ship role. Its first issue, which appeared in October 1897, contains a basic statement of the journal's political philosophy. There is a transla-tion of this editorial in Pipes, *Social Democracy*, pp. 128–31. (See also Wildman, *The Making of a Workers' Revolution*, esp. Chap. 5.) The jour-nal, which was published first in St. Petersburg (illegally) and then in Berlin, was one of the main objects of attack by Lenin (in his famous 1902 pamphlet *What Is to Be Done?* and elsewhere), who took it to task for downplaying the importance of political as opposed to economic struggle, although by this time *Workers' Thought* had modified its posi-tion and had become quite political in orientation. The last issue was published in December 1902.

11. I have been unable to identify this poem.

12. See Chap. 7, note 2, above.

13. The Union of Struggle for the Emancipation of the Working Class—or simply the "Union of Struggle" (*Soiuz bor'by*), as it was com-monly called—was founded in St. Petersburg in 1895 and existed until 1897. It was an illegal organization of revolutionary Marxists, including the future Bolshevik leader Lenin and the future Menshevik leader Iuly Martov.

14. From Nekrasov's short untitled 1869 poem that begins "It is suf-focating! without happiness or freedom . . ." (*Dushno! bez schast'ia i voli* . . .). For the full text see his *Polnoe sobranie sochinenii i pisem*, vol. 2, p. 318. The poem contains the thinly veiled threat of a popular uprising.

15. The "era of reaction" refers to the period 1907–11, when Petr A. Stolypin (1862–1911) was chairman of the Council of Ministers (roughly, the prime minister). Stolypin dealt very severely with the revo-lutionary movement, which he succeeded in suppressing—albeit tem-porarily—until his assassination in September 1911. The implication of Kanatchikov's remark is that "Vadim" abandoned his comrades out of cowardice. Kanatchikov is referring to D. S. Postolovsky, a leading ad-vocate of greater worker participation in the Party leadership during the Social Democratic (really Bolshevik) Party Congress of 1905, when he was elected to the Party's (i.e., the Bolshevik) Central Committee. See Schwarz, *The Russian Revolution of 1905*, pp. 218–20, and Keep, *The Rise of Social Democracy*, pp. 167, 211–12.

16. On Razin and Pugachev, see Chap. 10, note 4, above.

17. Professor Sergey D. Lvov was a prominent Soviet plant physiologist. He was elected corresponding member of the Soviet Academy of Sciences in 1946. Although the author goes on to take note of Lvov's "extreme youth" at the time under discussion, he was actually born in the same year as Kanatchikov, 1879.

18. In circles of this kind, "political economy" was often used as a euphemism for Marxism.

CHAPTER 15

1. Nekrasov is identified in Chap. 11, note 4, above. Aleksey N. Apukhtin (1841–93) began his writing career as a protégé of Nekrasov's, writing for the radical journal *The Contemporary*. At the beginning of the 1860's, he echoed many of Nekrasov's "civic" themes, but in the 1880's his poetry became more personal, psychological, nostalgic, and even pessimistic. (See M. P. Alekseev et al., eds., *Istoriia russkoi literatury* [A History of Russian Literature], vol. 9, part 1 [Moscow, 1956], pp. 487–96, and Mirsky, *A History of Russian Literature*, p. 361.) Ivan S. Nikitin (1824–61) was a minor poet whose main theme was the day-to-day suffering of the poor people of Russia. He is briefly discussed in Mirsky, p. 238.

2. Nekrasov's satirical poem "The Railroad" (*Zheleznaia doroga*) was written in 1864. The full version was forbidden by the censor that year, but a slightly abbreviated, toned-down version appeared in *The Contemporary* the following year (No. 10, 1865). The poem depicts the travails of the railroad workers who constructed the line between Moscow and St. Petersburg between 1842 and 1852, and the indifference of the authorities to their plight. For the full text, see Nekrasov, *Polnoe sobranie sochinenii i pisem*, vol. 2, pp. 202–6. The poem "Reflections at the Main Entrance" is discussed in Chap. 11, note 6, above.

3. Mikhail E. Saltykov (1826–89), who wrote under the pseudonym N. Shchedrin, was probably nineteenth-century Russia's most beloved satirist. He was a close collaborator of Nekrasov's, whose radical social and political views he generally shared. "The Nag" (*Koniaga*) was part of Saltykov's 1880–85 cycle of stories in the genre of the fable or folktale (*skazka*), a marked departure from his satirical works. It uses the image of a worn-out horse to symbolize the fate of the poor peasant. See Mirsky, p. 294.

4. "The Little Tail" (*Khvostik*) is identified in Chap. 9, note 10, above.

5. I have been unable to identify the play *The Workers' Suburb* (*Rabochaia slobodka*).

6. Vladimir G. Korolenko (1853–1921) was a very popular writer of stories that evoked sympathy for Russia's poor and oppressed. After arrest and several years of exile for having joined a revolutionary organization, he remained very close to the nonrevolutionary wing of the populist intelligentsia, and was a leading collaborator on the populist journal *Russian Wealth*. He was widely admired for his unremitting op-

position to the injustices committed by the government. His moral authority in Russia was extraordinary. See Mirsky, pp. 355–58, for further details.

7. The controversial actress L. B. Iavorskaya was the founder in 1901 of St. Petersburg's "New" (*Novyi*) Theater, a theater that flirted with revolutionary ideas and incurred the wrath of the government. *Ocherki istorii Leningrada*, vol. 3, pp. 712–14, and 714n.

8. Kazimir S. Barantsevich (1851–1927) was the author of stories and novels about the poor and the oppressed, especially the poor folk on the peripheries of St. Petersburg.

9. Nevsky Prospect was St. Petersburg's main boulevard. It stretched from the Admiralty building on the south bank of the Neva through the city center to the Aleksandro-Nevsky monastery on the river's west bank, just north of the Nevsky Gate region. Liteiny Prospect bisected Nevsky Prospect on the north-south axis, so that their intersection might be thought of as the epicenter of fashionable St. Petersburg. Although this was an élite area, people of the lower classes often strolled there, rubbing shoulders with their social superiors.

10. Ivan Nikitin's poem "The Boat Hauler" or "The Barge Hauler" (*Burlak*) was published in 1855.

11. This disdainful attitude toward Pushkin had been fairly common among Russian radicals since the 1860's.

12. The local governing council or *zemstvo* was introduced in 1864 as part of the Great Reforms of Alexander II. *Zemstva* (the plural) existed at the local and provincial levels in 34 provinces by the years Kanatchikov is writing about. Although elected on the basis of a highly restricted franchise, the zemstva were in frequent conflict with the central government over questions of jurisdiction and competence. Around the turn of the century zemstva were becoming one of the main centers of liberal activity and sentiment, usually of a moderate, cautious variety, and Kanatchikov uses them here and later as a symbol of Russian liberalism and, usually, its inadequacy. In the pages that follow I normally use the term "zemstvo" in my translation, but I sometimes use a more descriptive phrase (as in the present case) depending on the context.

13. Onegin, Lensky, Tatiana, and Olga are the main characters in Pushkin's famous novel in verse *Eugene Onegin* (completed in 1831). All are members of the privileged gentry—though, notwithstanding Langeld's sardonic remarks, Pushkin often depicted the Russian gentry in rather unflattering terms.

14. Dmitry I. Pisarev (1840–68) was one of the most famous radical thinkers of the 1860's and the one for whom the term "nihilist," in its most precise historical sense—the denial of traditional values, the rejection of conventional ethics and aesthetics, the exaggerated belief in science—is most appropriate.

15. Petr B. Struve (1870–1944) was a leading Marxist intellectual of the 1890's who by the end of that decade had begun his evolution toward a more moderate constitutional liberalism and away from his earlier commitment to revolutionary Marxism. Mikhail I. Tugan-Baranovsky

(1865–1919), like Struve, was a Marxist thinker who made important contributions in the fields of economics and economic history in the 1890's. While he remained somewhat closer to Marxism in the years that followed than did Struve, Tugan-Baranovsky's Marxism became increasingly unorthodox, eclectic, and attenuated.

16. The Petersburg side: an informal designation for the city's Petersburg district, the northern borough situated between the Vyborg district and Vasilevsky Island (see Chap. 12, note 6, above). It had a sizable working-class population.

17. University-level students often wore student uniforms during this period, which is why the author distinguishes them from civilians. The female students he alludes to here and elsewhere were the so-called *kursistki* (sing., *kursistka*), students from the "Bestuzhev Courses" or, more formally, the Petersburg Higher Women's Courses, then located on Vasilevsky Island. Founded in 1878, this special women's college—women were not allowed to enroll in the regular universities—was the only one of its kind to survive the reactionary educational policies of the 1880's. (Similar courses in Moscow, Kiev, and Kazan had been closed down by the end of that decade.) For further details see Stites, *The Women's Liberation Movement*, pp. 82–83, 168.

18. By stressing that this socialist was a "populist" (*narodnik*), that is, a socialist who saw the simple peasant as the bearer of Russia's revolutionary future, Kanatchikov seems to be suggesting that the story was about the socialist's difficulty communicating with the peasant.

19. The humor here, somewhat lost in translation, is based on the juxtaposition of the solemnity of the Biblical creation story with a free-wheeling, folksy peasant idiom, further enhanced by the imitation of intoxicated speech. In the original, Adam uses the archaic Russian word *bobyl'*, which evokes the image of a very poor Russian cottager without any family ties.

20. This is certainly a reference to M. M. Filippov, an expert on Marx and Hegel, their influence on Russian thinkers, and related questions. In the 1890's he contributed to *Russian Wealth* and other journals of the left intelligentsia, including *The Scholarly Review* (*Nauchnoe obozrenie*), which he edited from 1894 to 1903 in a more or less Marxist spirit. See Leikina-Svirskaia, *Intelligentsiia v Rossii*, p. 229.

21. "Dubinushka" ("The Cudgel") was a popular protest song that dated from the 1860's, when it existed in several versions. But it was the version published by the poet A. A. Olkhin (1829–97) in 1885 in the radical Geneva-based journal *Obshchee delo* (*The Common Cause*) that became the basis for the song's enormous popularity. The theme of the song, which follows the formal structure and rhythm of the songs of the Volga and Don boatmen, is that the cudgel has always been used to beat down the poor Russian people, but the day will come when the people will turn the cudgel on their oppressors. The Olkhin version is printed in *Pesni russkikh rabochikh*, pp. 84–85 (see also the editor's comments on p. 256). There is another variant in *Agitatsionnaia literatura*, pp. 466–68; an English translation of a prototypical barge-haulers' song that be-

gins "Cudgel, little cudgel" may be found in Reeder, ed. and trans., *Down Along the Mother Volga*, pp. 193–94. See also the discussion of these songs in V. Propp, "The Russian Folk Lyric," in *ibid.*, pp. 33–34.

22. The satirical song "Nagaechka" ("The Whip") had many variants. A version dating from the revolutionary year 1905, five years after the year recalled here by Kanatchikov, is printed in *Pesni russkikh rabochikh*, pp. 171–72 (see also the editorial comment on p. 273).

CHAPTER 16

1. The Kornilov (or Smolensk) evening and Sunday school for workers, located in the Nevsky Gate region, was founded in 1883 by a group of local industrialists and philanthropists. Its volunteer teaching staff was dominated by liberal and radical intelligentsia of various persuasions, with an increasing proportion of Marxists in the 1890's (e.g., Nadezhda Krupskaya, the future wife of Lenin), who weaved their various ideologies into their teaching of reading and other basic subjects. In the early 1890's the school was accepting about 1,000 pupils a year and turning away many more applicants. The Kornilov school was one of 36 evening and Sunday schools for workers in St. Petersburg in the mid-1890's (and there were many more in the country's other industrial centers). See *Ocherki istorii Leningrada*, vol. 2, pp. 677–79. On the first, ultimately unsuccessful effort to organize Sunday schools for workers, see Reginald E. Zelnik, "The Sunday-School Movement in Russia, 1859–1862," *Journal of Modern History*, 37, no. 2 (1965), pp. 151–70.

2. The older workers are using "student" as a synonym for "revolutionary." See Chap. 5, note 2, above.

3. The reference is of course to the great Russian writer Maxim Gorky (1868–1936). By 1900, when Kanatchikov was taking the class described here, Gorky's reputation both as a writer and as a radical champion of the oppressed was already well established, although his major creative work still lay before him. "Chelkash," one of Gorky's first stories, was written in 1894 and published in *Russian Wealth* in 1895 on the recommendation of Korolenko. As Kanatchikov indicates in the pages that follow, the principal characters are Chelkash and Gavrila, and the action revolves around the conflict between these two men. Chelkash is an intrepid criminal who hires the greedy but frightened peasant Gavrila to assist him in a smuggling endeavor on the Black Sea. The characterization of the two men and their relationship is subtle and ambiguous, leaving open the possibility of the conflicting interpretations and evaluations that Kanatchikov will describe later in the chapter.

4. The nouns "populism" (*narodnichestvo*) and "populist" (*narodnik*) have already been introduced in the text and partially explained in the notes (see Chap. 15, note 18, above). What needs to be added here is that Populism (which I capitalize only when the specific political ideology rather than the vague tendency is at issue, though the line between them is often unclear) was the dominant ideology of the Russian Left in the 1870's, and, though it had many variants and mutations over the

years, continued to compete with Marxism up to 1917 and even beyond for the allegiance of radicals and, to some degree, of liberals as well. The core beliefs that separated Populism from Marxism, both of which purported to be socialist ideologies, were (1) Populism's emphasis on the primacy of the peasantry rather than the industrial proletariat as a popular revolutionary force (or at least the equal importance of the two social groups as component parts of a single "people" [*narod*]), and (2) Populism's commitment to the preservation of some version of the traditional peasant commune, which Marxists viewed as archaic and anachronistic, as an essential part of any future socialist order. Apart from these core beliefs, Populism, like Marxism, had many profound internal conflicts and cleavages over tactics, strategy, and even matters of principle.

5. The Atlas (or German) machine-construction works (founded in 1872) was located in the Nevsky Gate region, on the Shlisselburg Highway, close to the Obukhov works. It was a fairly small factory specializing in machine parts.

6. The ideas of the SRs are briefly discussed in Chap. 35, note 22, below. In the present context it should be noted that the SRs were the political embodiment of the updated, early-twentieth-century version of populist ideology summarized above in note 4. Thus the author is suggesting that Tolmachev had reservations about the emphasis placed on the peasantry by revolutionaries with populist leanings.

7. The speaker is referring to the famous "Movement to the People," the high point of which was the summer of 1874, when nearly 3,000 students fanned out to the villages of Russia to educate or propagandize the peasants, and in some cases to incite them to rebellion. Not only was the movement largely unsuccessful, there were times, as the speaker indicates, when the peasants reported their unwanted student visitors to the police, resulting in their arrest and trial.

8. A reference to the fact that Gorky's pen name is the Russian word for "bitter" (*gor'kii*). His real name was Aleksey Maksimovich Peshkov.

9. The story takes place in the port city of Odessa, on the Black Sea.

10. Probably the first wife of the famous radical publicist and bibliographer Nikolay Rubakin (see Chap. 37, note 8, para. (g), below).

11. Aleksandr S. Griboedov (1795–1829) was a prominent playwright of the early nineteenth century. His great comedy *Woe from Wit* (*Gore ot uma*), written in 1823, satirizes Russian high society of that period. Aleksandr N. Ostrovsky (1823–86), an extremely prolific playwright, is considered the real father of Russian realist drama. One of his beloved subjects was the traditionalism, backwardness, and low morality of the old merchant class of Moscow and other provincial towns. The play *Poverty Is No Vice* (*Bednost' ne porok*) (1854) belongs to this category.

12. As works of literature, most of these books were quite mediocre, even "potboilers"—albeit potboilers, as Kanatchikov indicates, of a subversive political rather than purely escapist character. Their heroes were generally rebels against constituted authority. Of the books mentioned, probably the most popular in revolutionary circles (see the references in

Pearl, "Revolutionaries and Workers") was *At Dawn* (*Na rassvete*) by T. T. Ezh (pen name of the Polish writer Zygmunt Milkowski), a story about the resistance of Bulgarians to Turkish oppression in the 1870's.

13. *The Albigenses* could not have depicted "the Netherlanders' struggle." See note 15, below.

14. The point here is that the poem actually contained no revolutionary sentiment, but merely the vision of a better, peaceful future, yet Kanatchikov and his comrades heard it as a call to arms.

15. Bruno was a sixteenth-century Italian heretic and utopian thinker who defended Copernicus's heliocentric view of the universe. He refused to recant his views before the Venice Inquisition, which burned him at the stake in 1592. The Albigenses (or Cathars) were twelfth-century religious heretics in southern France who practiced a mystical and ascetic form of Christianity. They favored the communalization of property and the elimination of the Catholic Church. Most of them were persecuted and destroyed in a bloody crusade during the first third of the thirteenth century. Garibaldians were followers of the revolutionary Italian nationalist military leader Giuseppe Garibaldi (1807–82) who attempted to unite Italy, an effort that attained partial success by the 1860's. Bulgarian nationalists carried on a bloody struggle for independence from the Ottoman Empire throughout much of the nineteenth century. With the assistance of Russian arms, an independent Bulgaria was established in the early 1880's, but Russia went on to oppose the southward expansion of the new Bulgarian state in the years that followed. The romantic infatuation and identification of militant young Russian workers with these diverse heroic movements and individuals is a theme that deserves further investigation.

16. Prince Petr D. Sviatopolk-Mirsky (1857–1914) occupied several important positions in the Russian government. He reached the zenith of his career in August 1904, when he was appointed minister of internal affairs, but his moderate, conciliatory policies came too late to avert the outbreak of the 1905 Revolution and his own resignation in January 1905. At the time Kanatchikov is describing, Sviatopolk-Mirsky occupied the dual post of chief of gendarmes and deputy minister of internal affairs (1900–1902), which effectively made him the government's chief law enforcement officer. He was especially concerned with the labor question.

17. This quotation is the first of several passages that the author will cite directly from unpublished archival documents to which he had access in preparing his memoirs in the 1920's. In most other cases he will give the location of his source. The parenthetical phrase "the gendarme adds soothingly" is obviously Kanatchikov's own addition.

CHAPTER 17

1. *Kak derzhat' sebia na doprose*: an illegal pamphlet by V. Bakharev (pseudonym for Vladimir P. Makhnovets or Akimov, 1872–1921), a leading spokesman for the "Economist" trend in Russian Marxism and

an editor of the journal *The Workers' Cause* (see Chap. 30, note 6, below). The pamphlet was published in Geneva in 1900 by the editors of that journal.

2. In 1826, when Tsar Nicholas I (r. 1825–55) created a special Corps of Gendarmes to serve as the main arm of his new political police, he had them dressed in bright, sky-blue uniforms to single them out from the rest of his uniformed officials.

3. The site of a theater for the working-class population. See Chap. 14, note 2, above.

CHAPTER 18

1. The Petersburg House of Preliminary Detention (*Dom Predvaritel'-nogo Zakliucheniia*) was the jail where political prisoners were housed pending the disposition of their cases by trial or other means. This "preliminary" period was often a lengthy one. The prison was located in the interior of the city, near the left bank of the Neva opposite the Vyborg side.

2. The Russian is *sobach'ia nozhka*.

3. Literally, "in a dog box" (*sobachii iashchik*).

4. *God's World* (*Mir Bozhii*) was a leading monthly literary-political journal of liberal and to some extent radical—a hybrid of populist and Marxist—orientation. It was founded in 1892 and was published until 1906, when it was closed down by the government. G. Chelpanov was a Russian interpreter of European philosophical thought who had published a history of ethics in 1897. The German philosopher Arthur Schopenhauer (1788–1860) was still widely read by Russian intellectuals in the period under discussion.

5. Ivan Turgenev (1818–83) and Fedor Dostoevsky (1821–81) were, of course, two of the great novelists of the nineteenth century. Gleb Uspensky (1843–1902) was an influential populist writer whose most well-known and controversial work, *The Power of the Land* (*Vlast' zemli*) (1882) was a semifictional account of peasant life that challenged conventional populist optimism regarding the peasantry. There is an excellent account of his troubled life and work in Richard Wortman, *The Crisis of Russian Populism* (Cambridge, Eng., 1967), Chap. 3. Friedrich Spielhagen (1829–1911) was a highly prolific German writer of romantic novels, stories, and plays with a liberal to radical political and social orientation. *Odin v pole ne voin* (One Man in the Field Is Not an Army), an 1874 Russian translation of his 1866 novel *In Reih und Glied*, was often read by Russian radicals in the years that followed. (See Pearl, "Revolutionaries and Workers," pp. 80, 135–36, 488, and 515 for specific instances. For an illuminating analysis of Spielhagen's work, see Leo Löwenthal, *Schriften*, vol. 2 [Frankfurt am Main, 1981], Chap. 5.) A very inexpensive 23-volume collection of Spielhagen's works was published in Russian translation in 1896. On Saltykov-Shchedrin, see Chap. 15, note 3, above.

6. Saltykov-Shchedrin's satirical work *Letters to Auntie* (*Pis'ma k teten'ke*) was published in 1882.

7. The Hospital of St. Nicholas the Wonderworker (*Nikolay-chudotvorets*) was a well-known Petersburg mental hospital.

8. Ferdinand Lassalle (1825–64) was perhaps the most prominent German socialist of the mid-nineteenth century, and an immediate ancestor of the German Social Democratic Party. Although his bitter rivalry with Karl Marx has prevented any balanced evaluation of Lassalle in Soviet historiography, the record shows that his writings, which were available in Russian translation from the 1870's onward, enjoyed great popularity among Russian radicals, including politicized workers who considered themselves Marxists. Pisarev is identified in Chap. 15, note 14, above.

9. Vissarion Belinsky (1811–48) was the outstanding Russian literary critic of his times, and one who continued to exert a profound influence on Russian literary criticism long after his premature death. He also cut a striking figure by virtue of his modest social origins, unusual among the Russian intelligentsia of that period. Belinsky believed in the social and political mission of literature, while at the same time maintaining high aesthetic standards in his evaluation of contemporary writers. Kanatchikov's reference to Belinsky's "correspondence with friends" is somewhat confused. He is probably conflating *Selected Passages from Correspondence with Friends* (1847), a reactionary apology for serfdom and the existing political order by the great writer Nikolay Gogol (1809–52), with Belinsky's furious response to that work, "Letter to Gogol" (also written in 1847). Although Belinsky's letter was not published legally until 1905, copies were readily available throughout the intervening half century. Kanatchikov may also have been confused by the title of Belinsky's "Letters to V. P. Botkin" (1840–41). For English translations of some of Belinsky's more typical works, including a slightly abbreviated version of the "Letter to Gogol," see James M. Edie, et al., eds., *Russian Philosophy* (Chicago, 1965), vol. 1, pp. 273–320 (includes a valuable commentary by the editors).

10. This appears to be a compressed paraphrase from memory of a longer paragraph in Belinsky's "Letters to V. P. Botkin."

11. In 1881 the People's Will (*Narodnaya Volya*), the revolutionary organization that assassinated Tsar Alexander II in that year, formed an auxiliary organization called the Red Cross (*Krasnyi krest*) society to assist political prisoners and their families by providing them with money, food, reading material, and other amenities. The society, whose special link to the People's Will soon weakened, was also involved in organizing escape attempts. The significance of the name "Elskaya" is unclear, but probably was related to a word beginning with the letter "l."

12. Ilya Shendrikov: see Chap. 13, note 3, above.

13. The American philosopher William James (1842–1910) published his first major work, *The Principles of Psychology*, in 1890. His works began to appear in Russian translation in 1896.

14. This was probably V. M. Piramidov, a high-ranking officer of the political police.

15. Kanatchikov is being transported from his prison to the offices of the political police, a very short ride.

16. Probably Fadey F. Zelinsky (1859–1944), a St. Petersburg University philology professor.

17. Kanatchikov seems to be unaware of several examples in Russian literature of stories or novels attentive to the way in which factory workers "live and think," among them Reshetnikov's long novel *Where Is It Better?*, which appeared as early as 1868 (see Chap. 5, note 12, above). A large section of the novel explores the lives of Petersburg factory workers.

18. Gorky's romantic prose poem "The Song of the Falcon" (*Pesnia o sokole*) was first published in 1895. The original was a broad hymn to freedom without any narrow political posture. Later editions, subsequent to the time under discussion, contained changes that turned the poem into a more partisan political statement.

19. The brother's letter contains several grammatical and orthographic errors, which do not lend themselves to translation. My misspelling of "inform" is meant to suggest one category of those errors.

20. Avdotya is referring here and below to her husband.

21. In Russian, *mukha* is a fly and *tarakan* is a cockroach. The humor would be obvious to a Russian reader.

22. The municipal governor (*gradonachal'nik*) of St. Petersburg was a very high-ranking and sometimes very influential appointed official. At this time the position was held by General Nikolay V. Kleigels (1850–1916), who occupied the post from 1895 to 1903. Gorokhova Street ran through the middle of the city center, beginning (like Nevsky Prospect) at the Admiralty building; the governor's office was located directly behind the Admiralty.

23. The Strelka (literally, "The Little Arrow") was the easternmost tip of Vasilevsky Island, just across the river from the Admiralty building.

CHAPTER 19

1. Chapters 19 through 23 are absent from the 1929 edition of volume 1 and the 1934 edition of volume 2 of Kanatchikov's memoirs. (Chronologically, the events described in these five chapters fall between the two volumes.) The text is taken from the one-volume 1932 edition, pp. 217–61. I have added the chapter title, "Departure."

2. Under customary law, property in land was vested in the village community rather than in the individual peasant, and the primary unit used by the community to determine allocations and reallocations was the household, not the individual. At the time of the death of his father, Ivan, Kanatchikov's brother had taken over the position of head of household, but Kanatchikov was still in a position to bring claims on some of the family property before the village council.

3. Reference here is to the fact that Kanatchikov now had, in effect, a criminal record as a politically dangerous person, though he had never been convicted by a court of law.

4. Klin was the northwesternmost district of Moscow province and the first part of the province one entered on the train from St. Petersburg to Moscow city. Tambov province was some 200 miles southeast of Moscow

province, and Saratov province was immediately to the southeast of Tambov, bounded on the east by the Volga River. Kanatchikov apparently transferred in Klin to a local train to his native district of Volokolamsk (immediately southwest of Klin), while his friends remained on the train to Moscow city, en route to their respective homes in Tambov and Saratov.

5. The "Saratov student organization" (*zemliachestvo*) refers to students from the Saratov region who had been studying at St. Petersburg University. It was common for university students to organize into social (and sometimes even political) groups according to their place of origin.

6. The song that moved Kanatchikov to tears, beginning with the words "Along the dusty road" (*Po pyl'noi doroge*) may be found in *Pesni russkikh rabochikh*, pp. 86–87. It is a sentimental song about a prisoner who craves his freedom, and is probably of Polish origin. (See the editorial comment in *ibid.*, p. 256.)

7. Part of the humor here lies in the familiar tone the smuggler adopts in addressing the tsar. Sasha, for example, is the diminutive form of Alexander; the smuggler also uses "ty," the familiar form of the pronoun "you," a locution that cannot be translated.

8. French President Sadi Carnot had been murdered while in office in 1894, which was also the year of Alexander III's death.

9. These were all measures that had been introduced as part of the "counterreforms" of Alexander III's repressive reign. The "land captains" (*zemskie nachal'niki*), an office created in 1889, were district officials appointed by the minister of internal affairs. Chosen from among the local landed gentry, they were given wide-ranging administrative and judicial powers. Their creation was widely viewed as a serious blow to the already fragile autonomy of the peasant community and the already restricted competence of the zemstvo (see Chap. 15, note 12, above). Flogging and other forms of corporal punishment had been effectively abolished in 1863 for all social groups except the peasants (who of course constituted the vast bulk of the population), for whom it was not formally abolished until 1904 (though it continued to be administered under emergency decrees thereafter). During the reign of Alexander III the use of corporal punishment against the peasantry increased, in part because of the actions of the land captains. The issue of corporal punishment was one of the most burning questions that divided Russian society during these years. See the informative discussion in Frieden, *Russian Physicians*, pp. 185–92.

10. I have substituted "swine" for the original "cattle," as more expressive of the tone the original song conveys.

11. The unambiguously positive attitude toward revolutionary students expressed in this paragraph is quite out of step with several passages in later chapters of Kanatchikov's memoirs.

12. At the time when this debate was taking place, the working-class movement was experiencing a brief lull in Russia, whereas students and other members of educated society were beginning to show signs of increased militance. However, workers were about to reassert their mili-

tance—the most dramatic instance being the armed resistance of the Obukhov workers in St. Petersburg in the spring of 1901. (See Surh, "Petersburg Workers," pp. 86–99.)

13. Under the military reform of 1874 (see Chap. 5, note 4, above), the normal term of active duty for a new recruit was six years, beginning at the age of twenty. Kanatchikov's term, however, would have been four years, in recognition of his completion of elementary school. Whether or not a particular individual would actually have to serve was determined by lot, as was the time when one's active duty actually began.

CHAPTER 20

1. On the fortress, see Chap. 5, note 3, above.

2. Old Believers or Old Ritualists were one of Russia's oldest and most important religious sects, dating back to the 1660's. Under the leadership of the "heretical" Archpriest Avvakum, they had split from the Russian Orthodox Church in protest over certain changes that had been introduced into the traditional Russian ritual. The Old Believers' opposition to the established church soon grew fierce, the more so in that they were the victims of relentless persecution by the authorities for many years to come. Although this persecution dissipated in the course of the nineteenth century, Old Believers still stood out as a marginal, dissident group, albeit culturally a very conservative one, at the beginning of the twentieth century.

3. The term "kulak" is discussed in Chap. 1, note 5, above.

4. When younger members of a peasant family left their village to take employment elsewhere, usually in an urban center, they were expected to send part of their earnings back to their households as a contribution to the family's tax payments and other financial obligations.

5. It was customary for Orthodox believers to cross themselves upon rising from a meal.

6. "Police agents," my rough translation of the author's "*oprichniki,*" does not capture the full flavor of the original. *Oprichniki* were members of the *oprichnina,* an administrative institution founded in 1564 by Tsar Ivan IV ("the Terrible") that amounted to a state within the state. The *oprichnina* had its own territorial jurisdiction, and its leaders answered directly to the ruler. At times the *oprichniki,* acting as Ivan's personal police agents, would conduct a reign of armed terror against those segments of the population that Ivan wished to persecute. Although the *oprichnina* was abolished after a few years, it remained a symbol of government persecution and oppression, as suggested by Kanatchikov's use of the term here.

7. The forced transfer of gentry-owned lands to the peasantry, popularly known as "black repartition," was a deeply rooted aspiration of many Russian peasants, and was intensified by the peasants' disappointment that the 1861 emancipation had left much of the best land in the hands of their former masters. Although the vision of black repartition would fuel the fires of revolutionary upheaval in 1905 and 1917, here the villagers are thinking of the confiscation and redistribution of gentry

land by a benevolent tsar, an equally powerful peasant myth. For further discussion, see Daniel Field, *Rebels in the Name of the Tsar* (Boston, 1976).

CHAPTER 21

1. Peasants were accustomed to working with axes and other simple tools.

2. The typical Russian village (*derevnia*) did not have a church of its own with resident clergy. A larger village (*selo*) that did have a church would service the religious (and other) needs of the nearby smaller villages. See Matossian, "The Peasant Way of Life," p. 3.

3. On the office of land captain, see Chap. 19, note 9, above. The village meeting (*skhodka* or *skhod*) was a communal assembly consisting of all the heads of household or, less frequently, the entire populace of the village. Although it was traditionally a self-governing body, note that it is the land captain who summons the meeting.

4. See Chap. 1, note 5, above, for an explanation of these categories.

5. A reference to the emancipation of the serfs by Tsar Alexander II in 1861, for which he was often called the "Tsar-Liberator" (*tsar-osvoboditel'*).

6. A reference to Alexander's famous 1856 statement to the Moscow gentry that it would be better to begin to abolish serfdom from above than to wait until it began to abolish itself from below (i.e., by means of peasant rebellion). "And then they'll take all of the land away from you" was not part of the tsar's statement, but it is a reasonable inference.

7. The "black coach" (*temnaia kareta*) was a common reference to a carriage used by the political police to transport their prisoners.

8. Livna was a town in Orel province (about 250 miles south of Moscow) that specialized in the manufacture of a particular kind of accordion.

9. The normal preparation for the Russian Orthodox priesthood consisted of completion of a church school and graduation from a clerical seminary, where the curriculum was narrow and the atmosphere was generally stifling. Although it was difficult for someone whose father was not a priest to take this path, the priesthood had recently become less of a closed caste than it once had been, and for someone like Kuzma it represented the possibility of modest upward social mobility for his son. For background to this kind of situation and to the conversation that follows, see Gregory L. Freeze, "Caste and Emancipation: The Changing Status of Clerical Families in the Great Reforms," in Ransel, ed., *The Family in Imperial Russia*, pp. 124–50.

10. Iaropol (or Iaropolets) was a town located just to the northwest of Volokolamsk.

11. The chorus of a popular revolutionary song. For the full text, see *Russkie pesni*, comp. N. A. Usov (Gorky, 1940), p. 286.

12. Because he is an officer, the army doctor uses the familiar form of address when he speaks to Kanatchikov.

CHAPTER 22

1. I have taken the minor liberty of dividing a long chapter, which bears the same title in the original as Chapter 21 of my translation, into three chapters (21 through 23). I have added simple descriptive titles to Chapters 22 and 23.

2. The Lefortovo district was located at the northeastern periphery of the city.

3. Gvozdev assumes that Kanatchikov is a student from either St. Petersburg University or the Petersburg Technical (or Technological) Institute, the city's main school of engineering.

4. D. N. Mamin-Sibiryak (1852–1912) was a minor writer whose stories described the harsh lives of workers in the Ural Mountains mining region.

5. Eduard Bernstein (1850–1932), one of the leaders of the German Social Democratic movement, created a storm among German Marxists in 1898 when he began to call for the transformation of the Social Democratic Party into an openly reformist, evolutionary party, an approach that soon was given the name "Revisionism." The heated debate had almost immediate repercussions on the Russian Left, where it added fuel to the raging arguments over "Revisionism" and "Economism," "heresies" (in the eyes of Lenin and others) that were tearing Russian Marxism apart around the turn of the century.

6. Streets located in fashionable Moscow neighborhoods.

7. "Smail's" (Smiles?): I have been unable to identify this author.

CHAPTER 23

1. A boyar (*boiarin*) was a high-ranking nobleman who served in the retinue of a Russian prince. More specifically, the author is probably alluding to the boyars of Muscovite Russia in the sixteenth and seventeenth centuries, the most important and influential military and civil servitors of the tsar.

2. Seasonal religious holidays played a very important part in the lives of Russian Orthodox villagers. Most of these holidays honored particular saints—Nicholas, George, Peter, Philip, etc. The relative importance of saints' days varied by region and even by village, but they often marked important transitions in the agricultural work cycle.

3. The last sentence is clearly meant to be ironical, the implication being that the "gentleman" landowner had no wish to mix with his social inferiors.

4. The card game they played is identified as *stukolka* (or *stukalka*— literally, "cudgel").

CHAPTER 24

1. Thus opens the first chapter to volume 2 of Kanatchikov's memoirs, entitled simply "Introduction."

2. See Chap. 10, note 4, above.

3. Here the author is referring to the period from the emancipation of the serfs in 1861 to the beginning of the twentieth century.

4. The author has listed, either by name or indirectly, the major European revolutions and popular uprisings from 1789 through the Paris Commune of 1871. The last reference in the paragraph is evidently to Paris in 1848.

5. The German Social Democrats were doing increasingly well in the Reichstag election campaigns of the late 1890's and early 1900's. In England, the Independent Labour Party (ILP), founded in 1893, engaged in a rather unsuccessful Parliamentary electoral campaign in 1895. The Labour Representation Committee (LRC, renamed the Labour Party in 1906), which was founded in 1900 by the ILP and other organizations, proved much more successful; it was able to elect only two MPs in 1900 and a few more in subsequent by-elections, but managed to elect 29 members to the House of Commons in the general election of 1906. Kanatchikov, whose chronology here is very vague, could be referring to either the 1900 or 1906 elections, or possibly to the by-elections of 1902–3.

6. August Bebel is identified in note 1 to the Introduction, above. Keir Hardie (1856–1915) was a prominent British labor leader whose checkered career took him from the Lanarkshire coalfields, where he led the miners' union, to membership in the House of Commons as a representative of the ILP—he was one of its founders and its first president—and the LRC. As Kanatchikov mentions, both men were of working-class background, hence they were "tied to us by class."

7. *Iskra* (*The Spark*) was a Social Democratic newspaper founded by Lenin, Martov, and others in 1900 to combat the alleged influence of "Economism" on the movement. It was published in Munich and smuggled into Russia, where it was widely read by members of illegal Social Democratic groups, for whom it soon became a sort of unifying organizational center. Note how Kanatchikov falls into the language of hero worship when mentioning Lenin's role.

8. The city of Saratov was the capital of the Volga River province that bore the same name. The population of the city at the time of the Empire-wide census of 1897 was roughly 137,000, and it was expanding rapidly (to nearly 203,000 in 1904), thanks in part to the intensive growth of industry. (Here and elsewhere, specific information on the city of Saratov is from Raleigh, *Revolution on the Volga*, Chaps. 1 and 2.) Despite this industrial growth and the presence of a relatively large working class, however, Saratov was not so much an industrial city as a mixed and diverse center of commerce, transportation (both rail and steamship), administration, small-scale manufacturing, and, as Kanatchikov indicates here, educational institutions (though it still had no university at this time). According to official statistics cited by Raleigh, in 1903 there were 186 industrial enterprises (excluding small artisanal workshops) in the city, with a total of some 9,200 workers, a figure that Raleigh finds somewhat too low. Hence Kanatchikov's figure of 10,000 appears to be a reasonable approximation.

9. On the "zemstvo" in general, see Chap. 15, note 12, above. See also Thomas S. Fallows, "Forging the Zemstvo Movement: Liberalism and Radicalism on the Volga, 1890–1905" (Ph.D. dissertation, Harvard University, 1981). The Saratov provincial zemstvo was known for its liberalism.

CHAPTER 25

1. The author is apparently quoting from a document in the files of the Saratov or Moscow gendarme office.

2. Department of Police was the formal name of the subdivision of the Ministry of Internal Affairs charged with responsibility for security matters.

3. On the special courses for women students (*kursistki*), see Chap. 15, note 17, above. The allusion to medical assistants and midwives underlines the point that women still had no access to the regular Russian medical schools as full-fledged medical students. There were just over 600 female physicians in the Russian Empire in 1900 (as compared to nearly 20,000 males), mostly graduates of the Women's Medical Institute in St. Petersburg (opened in 1897) or of the special medical courses for women given under the auspices of the Military Medical-Surgical Academy in St. Petersburg between 1872 and the early 1880's, when they were ended. (See Frieden, *Russian Physicians*, p. 323 [Appendix I.A], and Stites, *The Women's Liberation Movement*, pp. 85–87, 174). It is possible that Kanatchikov is using the term *kursistki* loosely, to include medical students from the Women's Medical Institute or other schools of this kind that were beginning to open in university towns.

CHAPTER 26

1. The chapter title refers to the notion of Leo Tolstoy (1828–1910), the great Russian writer and moralist, that evil should not be resisted by force, a notion he derived from the Gospel According to Matthew. Other tenets of Tolstoy's social and moral philosophy, including his dietary strictures, are mentioned in the course of the chapter.

2. The Forestry Institute (*Lesnoi Institut*) was a university-level technical school in St. Petersburg.

3. The years 1899–1901 were marked by student riots and demonstrations at St. Petersburg University, Kiev University, and other institutions of higher education. This unrest, which contributed heavily to political ferment among other elements of Russian society, is sometimes seen as the first link in the chain of political activity that eventually led to the 1905 Revolution. The specific reference in this passage is probably to the demonstrations by university students and others that took place in St. Petersburg in March 1901.

4. The reference is of course to the great Russian composer Petr Ilich Tchaikovsky (1840–93). Auntie's "salon" is described by the author in Chap. 28, below.

CHAPTER 28

1. A neighboring province; see Chap. 19, note 4, above.
2. The Russian word is identical to the French *salon*, and has the same upper-class connotations. Note that Kanatchikov is so sensitive on this score that he continues to use quotation marks each time he employs the word, which is very often.
3. Nikolay A. Dobroliubov (1836–61) was a radical literary critic who wrote for the journal *The Contemporary* until his premature death. Pisarev and Belinsky are identified above in Chap. 15, note 14, and Chap. 18, note 9, respectively.
4. The meaning of this assertion is difficult to decipher, since Kanatchikov and his worker-comrades belonged, more or less, to the same chronological generation as these students. The absence of relations between the two groups is more readily explained by reference to education and social class than to age.
5. Another reference to the fact that Kanatchikov has examined the archives of the gendarme office in preparing his memoirs of this period.
6. Some of the people listed either were or would soon become moderately important figures in the history of the Russian revolutionary movement. Martin N. Liadov (1872–1947), whose real name was Mandelshtam (the N. N. Mandelshtam mentioned by Kanatchikov may have been his brother) became an "*Iskra*-ite" delegate from Saratov to the Second Congress (in effect the founding congress) of the RSDLP in 1903 and a member of the Bolshevik Moscow Committee during the revolutionary events of the fall of 1905. In subsequent years his relations with Lenin and mainstream Bolshevism became erratic, but he served the Communist regime in the 1920's. "S. M." Baramzin may refer to Egor V. Baramzin, then the official agent of *Iskra* in Saratov. V. F. Gorin-Galkin (1863–1925), like Liadov, became an *Iskra*-ite delegate from Saratov to the Second Congress, where he too joined the Bolshevik faction. He lived abroad for many years, but returned to Petrograd (St. Petersburg) in time to play an active role in the revolutionary events of 1917. Pavel A. Lebedev, a young Marxist who was exiled to Saratov in 1900, became a leading Bolshevik activist. Although the A. A. Bogdanov mentioned here might be the Aleksandr A. Bogdanov who became famous as a controversial and troublesome "left" Bolshevik intellectual and a leading theoretician of "Proletarian Culture," this is fairly unlikely (see Chap. 37, note 4, below). On A. I. Rykov, the most famous of the names listed by Kanatchikov, see Chap. 36, note 31, below. (Some of the above information is taken from Raleigh, *Revolution on the Volga*.) On Liadov's activity as a leader of a Marxist-oriented propaganda circle in Moscow prior to his arrest in 1895, see Johnson, *Peasant and Proletarian*, pp. 105–10.
7. The reactionary statesman Viacheslav K. von Plehve (or Pleve) served as minister of internal affairs from April 1902 until his assassination in the summer of 1904 by the SR terrorist Egor Sazonov.
8. L. P. Bulanov was an older SR who had belonged to one of the first

Populist organizations, "Land and Liberty" (*Zemlia i Volia*), in the late 1870's. Pavel P. Kraft had been active in its successor organization, the "People's Will," in the 1880's, and was involved in attempts to propagandize the peasantry in the late 1890's. He was one of the original organizers of the SR Party. N. I. Rakitnikov, another founder of the SR Party, headed one of the main revolutionary circles in Saratov. He was one of the most prominent SR leaders for many years. On Breshko-Breshkovskaya and Kocherovsky, see below, Chap. 36, notes 26 and 10, respectively.

9. The SR-oriented student Stepan V. Balmashev assassinated Minister of Internal Affairs Dmitry S. Sipiagin, Plehve's predecessor, in April 1902.

10. By "Saratov organization," Kanatchikov apparently means the RSDLP's Saratov Committee, an organization that existed only in embryo at the time he is writing about. SD and SR activities in Saratov in this period are the subject of an unpublished paper by Michael Melancon of Auburn University.

11. Probably the Petersburg Technological Institute.

12. The reference may be to the Smolny Institute in St. Petersburg, a special boarding school for the education and cultivation of young ladies of the nobility (founded by Catherine the Great in 1764), but there were other, less prominent "institutes" of this kind in other parts of the country. For further discussion, see Stites, *The Women's Liberation Movement*, pp. 4–6, 51, 167.

13. *Krasivka*: roughly, "The Beauty."

14. The Volga city of Samara, the capital of Samara province (the province just to the east of Saratov), was a little more than 200 miles upstream from the city of Saratov.

15. The theme of this story—the well-meaning landowner who tries by means of some experiment to help or uplift the peasants who depend on him, only to fall victim to their greed, mistrust, or misunderstanding—was almost a commonplace in the literature and lore of post-Emancipation Russia. That the beneficiaries of the stillborn cooperative turn out to be "kulaks" may be viewed as a particularly Marxist twist to the story.

16. This is a vague reference to the fact that after the February Revolution of 1917 Lenin and the Bolsheviks began to prepare for the overthrow of the new Provisional Government, a goal that was accomplished with the October Revolution eight months later. However, Kanatchikov's laconic statement fails to do justice to the tortuous path that was followed or the internecine strife that had to be overcome before the "seizure of power" could be achieved.

17. The Civil War refers to the bloody conflict between "Reds" and "Whites" (i.e., between Bolsheviks and anti-Bolsheviks) that devastated Russia roughly from the summer of 1918 to the end of 1920. It is sometimes defined more broadly to encompass the entire period from late 1917 to 1922, when the last front was definitively liquidated.

18. The VTsIK is the abbreviation of the Russian term for the All-Russian Central Executive Committee of the Congress of Soviets, which

was headed by Iakov M. Sverdlov (a close associate of Lenin's) from November 1917 until his premature death in March 1919. Being head of the VTsIK was tantamount to being head of state. In 1919 Kanatchikov was one of the organizers of short, intensive courses for Communist agitators and instructors that were established in Moscow under the auspices of that committee. Later that year, these courses were transformed into a "Communist" university—a university-level Party school—which was named in memory of Sverdlov, their initiator.

19. The Merchants' Club had been the main social and entertainment center of well-to-do Moscow merchants in the nineteenth century.

20. Earlier in the chapter Adrian himself is identified as "Auntie's" oldest son. Possibly Iurka was the oldest son from her second marriage.

21. Tambov province was a major center of peasant resistance to the Soviet regime during the latter part of the Civil War period and beyond. Adrian's identification of the Bolsheviks' enemies in Tambov with the SR Party oversimplifies a complex situation—an oversimplification that conforms with official Communist historiography. The accuracy of the quotation is open to challenge on several grounds, although it is certainly true that Tambov province was an old SR center.

22. The SR political and intellectual leader Viktor M. Chernov (see Chap. 35, note 21, below) was not born in Tambov province, but he was very active there in the late 1890's, when he was banished there by the police.

23. In this paragraph Kanatchikov continues to present the official Party version of peasant resistance to the regime in the Tambov region. By 1920–21 peasant dissatisfaction in that province had flared up into a full-scale, bloody popular insurrection—hardly reducible to a "kulak uprising"—under the leadership of Aleksandr S. Antonov. Adrian Diakov is not mentioned in Oliver H. Radkey, *The Unknown Civil War in Soviet Russia: A Study of the Green Movement in the Tambov Region, 1920–1921* (Stanford, Calif., 1976), our most thorough study of the uprising and its suppression; his role in those events was probably less prominent than is suggested by Kanatchikov.

CHAPTER 29

1. Kolpino: an industrial suburb of St. Petersburg, located a few miles southeast of the city limits, past the Nevsky Gate region. It was the site of a large industrial complex that belonged to the Naval Ministry.

2. The Volga steel mill and iron foundry was founded in 1897. It was located in the Saratov district (*uezd*), not far from Saratov city. It had between 600 and 700 workers.

3. Matvey (alias Andrey or Genrikh) Fisher (1871–1935) was one of the most prominent worker-revolutionaries of the 1890's and the author of one of the most interesting worker autobiographies. His life and his memoirs are analyzed in Zelnik, "Russian Bebels," Part II.

4. At this time, the Czech people, located mainly in Bohemia and Moravia, were still subjects of the Austro-Hungarian Empire, and were particularly resentful of what they saw as German domination.

5. On Ezh's *At Dawn*, see Chap. 16, note 12, above.

6. The performance of *The Smugglers* (*Kontrabandisty*), a one-act play by A. Z. Serpoletti, and the attendant protest demonstration are also described in Fisher's autobiography. See Fisher, *V Rossii i v Anglii*, p. 52.

CHAPTER 30

1. Ivanovo-Voznesensk was one of Russia's major textile production centers; it was located in Vladimir province, immediately to the northeast of Moscow province. The State Duma (or simply Duma) was the lower chamber of the national parliamentary body introduced by Tsar Nicholas II in 1906 as a concession to the revolutionary movement of 1905. The "Third" Duma, elected on the basis of a highly restricted, indirect, conservatively weighted suffrage, existed from the fall of 1907 to the summer of 1912. Semën A. Voronin, representing the workers' curia of Vladimir province, was one of five Bolsheviks elected to that Duma in 1907.

2. Among the names on this list (apart from Kanatchikov and Fisher) I have been able to locate Grigoreva, who is discussed in note 5, below, Denisov (see Chap. 41), Efimov (see Chap. 32), Shepelev, Retling (or Reitling), Fominykh, and Fofanov in other sources. All were active SDs.

3. Presumably, Kanatchikov has in mind that the name of his group was not formally registered with *Iskra*.

4. As should be evident by now, these were the same difficult questions that had vexed and divided the Russian Left for several years. (Some of them even dated back to the 1870's.) They were questions that drew a line not only between SDs and SRs—the division emphasized here when Kanatchikov refers to the question of terrorism—but between different tendencies within each party as well, as will emerge when he goes on to discuss the questions of intelligentsia versus worker and political struggle versus economic struggle that divided his own group.

5. A. N. Grigoreva is clearly a reference to Natalya Grigoreva, a seamstress from St. Petersburg whose involvement in radical workers' circles dated back to the beginning of the 1890's. After serving time as a political exile in Siberia, she was sent to Saratov in 1901. There, as Kanatchikov indicates, she attempted to bridge the gap between SDs and SRs, between workers and the intelligentsia. All this is confirmed by Fisher (*V Rossii i v Anglii*, pp. 47, 49), who knew her well and frequently argued with her about politics.

6. The journal *The Workers' Cause* (*Rabochee delo*), founded in 1899 as the organ of the Union of Russian Social Democrats Abroad, represented the more moderate element of the "Economist" tendency within Russian Marxism, a tendency that placed less emphasis on the need for political struggle than did Lenin, Plekhanov, and other "orthodox" Marxists. Advocates of the "Workers' Cause" position found themselves in sharp conflict with *Iskra* and the *Iskra*-ites when that paper was founded in 1900. *Iskra* eventually gained the upper hand; *The Workers' Cause* folded early in 1902 and the proponents of its position walked out

of the Second Party Congress in 1903. Since the *Iskra*-ite position was unquestionably the "correct" position in official Soviet historiography, Kanatchikov's admission that "several of us" leaned in the other direction and his judicious presentation of anti-*Iskra*-ite sentiments in the following paragraphs were extremely daring on his part.

7. The Russian term in the original is *chistaia politika*.

8. The Russian phrase in the original is *kopeechnye i piatashnye interesy*, a more literal translation of which would be "penny and nickel interests."

9. In what was by then a fairly typical maneuver in debates of this kind, The Artist was using the Marxist notion of surplus value (the value of the labor power expended by workers beyond what was necessary for their own subsistence and biological reproduction, and hence the measure of their exploitation) as a polemical weapon against the workers' intelligentsia allies, many of whom came from socially and economically privileged families.

10. The term "fellow traveler" (*poputchik*) was widely used in the 1920's, with both positive and negative overtones, to designate writers and other intellectuals who sympathized with the Soviet regime but did not fully identify with the principles of the Communist Party. Kanatchikov's analogy is apposite to a degree, but it should be noted that The Artist made no distinction between Party and non-Party intelligentsia in his critical remarks, which were meant to apply to all radicals from privileged backgrounds. The effect (and probably the intent) of Kanatchikov's analogy is to soften the impact of the words he has attributed to The Artist, which could otherwise be seen as critical of Lenin and other representatives of the Marxist intelligentsia.

11. Kanatchikov's point here is that the Social Democratic intelligentsia's neglect of the workers' economic aspirations drove the workers in the direction of the SRs and compelled the workers to conduct their economic struggle on their own. It should be noted, however, that the terrorist-oriented joint SR/SD organization (formed in 1902) mentioned by Kanatchikov included the majority of neither SRs nor SDs in Saratov.

12. See Chap. 24, note 7, above.

13. *The Workers' Newspaper* (*Rabochaia gazeta*), not to be confused with the 1898 Kiev paper of the same name, was founded in Saratov in 1901. Several issues appeared. It was an illegal, independent, worker-run paper, and at first was viewed askance by the Marxist, *Iskra*-ite intelligentsia for its alleged "Economist" tendency, a point that Kanatchikov makes only obliquely. *The Workers' Newspaper* was also critical of *Iskra*, which it viewed as too intellectual a paper for a mass audience; but when *Iskra* reproved it for its criticisms, *The Workers' Newspaper* chose not to respond in kind. (Fisher, p. 48.) Raleigh's study (Chap. 2) generally confirms Kanatchikov's picture of the Saratov workers' conversion to loyalty to *Iskra*, although this seems to have happened less rapidly and much less smoothly than Kanatchikov suggests. *Iskra* also encouraged the SD intelligentsia to draw closer to the workers.

14. This was the standard (and, on the whole, quite accurate) litany of accusations against *Iskra* between 1900 and 1903.

15. In other words, *Iskra* was expressing pleasant surprise that *The Workers' Newspaper* was not taking a narrowly "Economist" position, though by July 1901, when the sixth issue of *Iskra* appeared, very few Social Democratic groups were. (There are no italics in the original.)

16. The polemical pamphlet *Kto chem zhivet?* (Who Lives from What?), written by the Polish Marxist S. Dikshtein (Szymon Diksztajn, 1858–84), was first published in Polish in 1883. A Russian translation was published in Geneva in 1885. Fisher (p. 19) mentions having read and reread it in his Petersburg workers' circle at the beginning of the 1890's. (For further evidence of the influence of this popularization of Marxist political economy on the workers' circles of the late 1880's and beyond, see Pearl, "Revolutionaries and Workers," pp. 303, 315–16, 338, 342, 396, 412–13, 486, 490, and 515.) It was reissued several times thereafter. The other book mentioned here is almost certainly Carl August Schramm's *Osnovy ekonomicheskoi nauki* (Principles of Political Economy) (St. Petersburg, 1900), a translation from the German of *Grundzüge der Nationalökonomie*, his popularization of Volume 1 of Marx's *Capital*.

17. The hectograph was an imperfect device for duplicating written or typed material in multiple copies by pressing a carbon-backed sheet of paper against a glycerin-coated sheet of gelatin. It was commonly used by revolutionaries who did not have access to a printing press for the duplication of their leaflets and proclamations.

18. In this context, "agitation" refers to efforts on the part of revolutionaries to reach a much larger population of workers than could be influenced in a small propaganda circle. This was done by focusing attention on the workers' economic, workplace grievances and aiding them in their strike activities. Since the so-called shift from propaganda to agitation began in St. Petersburg in the middle of the 1890's, it is noteworthy that this debate appears to be reaching Saratov only in 1901.

19. The year 1900 marked the end of a decade of dynamic industrial growth for the Russian economy and the beginning of several years of industrial stagnation.

CHAPTER 31

1. Nikolay G. Chernyshevsky (1828–89) was the most prominent representative of the radical intelligentsia in the early years of the reign of Alexander II. His career as a revolutionary publicist, which included editorship of the radical journal *The Contemporary*, was cut short by his arrest and imprisonment in 1862. Most of his remaining 27 years were spent in prison and Siberian exile. *What Is to Be Done? (Chto delat'?)*, a novel that first appeared in 1863, was his most famous work. A fictionalized polemic that purported to portray the lives of a new generation of radical youth, it continued to inspire young Russians, including the

young Lenin, for decades to come. Lenin borrowed the title of Chernyshevsky's novel for his famous 1902 pamphlet. (See Chap. 35, note 23, below.)

2. "Tsar Akhreyan": a reference to an anonymous tale in verse called "How Tsar Akhreyan Went to God to Complain." (There were variations in the Russian title.) This popular satirical work was first printed illegally in St. Petersburg in 1883 by the "People's Will"; several more editions appeared in Paris and Geneva in the 1890's. Although the name A. K. Tolstoy appeared on some editions, the actual author was Anna P. Barykova (1839–93).

3. *Neprimirimyi (The Intransigent)*: an ultraradical publication that appeared briefly in Saratov in 1901.

CHAPTER 32

1. This statement is slightly misleading insofar as it implies that the workers who read and admired *Iskra* in these years were exclusively Bolsheviks. There were, of course, no Bolsheviks or Mensheviks before 1903, and even the editors of *Iskra* in this period included future Mensheviks as well as future Bolsheviks—as did the readers.

2. A man whose official legal estate was that of townsman (*meshchanin*, defined in Chap. 9, note 5, above) was inscribed in the rolls of that estate in his city of permanent residence. The island city of Kronstadt (or Kronshtadt) was primarily a naval base. It was located in the Finnish Gulf, about eighteen miles to the west of St. Petersburg.

3. The Russian government jealously guarded the right to punish political criminals by administrative or police means, that is, without a trial, bypassing the judiciary. The penalty was often exile for a fixed period, under police supervision, either to one's village or town of origin or to another designated location. Kanatchikov's own banishment to Saratov had also been by administrative means.

4. Nizhny-Novgorod (renamed Gorky in 1932) was the capital of the province of the same name. Located at the confluence of the Volga and Oka rivers, on the right bank of the Volga, the city was one of Russia's major commercial centers.

5. Article 318 of the Russian Criminal Code (*Ulozhenie o nakazaniiakh ugolovnykh i ispravitel'nykh*, pp. 109–10) made it a crime for anyone to belong to an organization whose goal it was to oppose the orders of the government, promote disobedience to the constituted authorities, destroy the principles of the social order (religion, the family, property), arouse enmity between classes or between workers and their employers, or promote the organization of strikes. The punishment could be as severe as six years' exile at hard labor, depending on the defendant's degree of involvement and various other circumstances.

6. *Iskusnik*, a play on the Russian word for "skilled."

7. It was not uncommon for a skilled worker to set himself up as an individual garret-master, plying his trade from his own apartment. See Bonnell, *Roots*, p. 27n.

8. This school was founded in 1876 or 1877 by the wealthy and influential banker-industrialist Baron Aleksandr L. Shtiglits (or Stieglitz, 1814–84) for the purpose of training draftsmen and designers for jobs in industry as well as teachers of design and related subjects in secondary schools. The correct name of the school, which began instruction in 1879 and functioned until 1924, was Baron Shtiglits' Central School of Technical Drawing.

9. The Biblical prophet Elijah (Ilya in Russian), who ascended to heaven in a chariot of fire (2 Kings 2.11), was widely revered as a saint by Russian Orthodox believers.

10. See Chap. 28, note 9, above.

11. The official government service rank of councillor of state (*statskii sovetnik*) was the fifth highest of the fourteen civilian ranks.

12. Diogenes-the-Cynic (412?–323? B.C.E.) was the Greek philosopher who, the story goes, was approached by Alexander the Great while he was sunning himself and, when requested by Alexander to ask any favor he wished, replied "Please move out of my sunlight," to which Alexander responded in turn: "If I were not Alexander, I would like to be Diogenes."

13. Xanthippe: the proverbially ill-tempered, shrewish wife of Socrates. The speaker is making light of Socrates' drinking of the hemlock and consequent death. The entire exchange presented here, with its learned references to classical antiquity, is the author's way of bearing witness to the high level of sophistication of the workers in his group.

14. The location of Samara is given in Chap. 28, note 14, above.

15. "Days of freedom" refers to the brief period in the fall of 1905 (between the government's manifesto of October 17 and the beginning of December) when, with the revolutionary movement at its peak and the regime in seemingly desperate straits, the government virtually abandoned all attempts to enforce its laws against the SDs and other revolutionary groups, and freedom of speech, assembly, and the press was temporarily at hand. According to Bonnell, *Roots* (p. 126), the Petersburg woodworkers' union was actually initiated a few months before that period.

16. The Moscow district of St. Petersburg was located immediately to the west of the northernmost sector of the Aleksandro-Nevsky district. (See Chap. 12, note 2, above.) On the Vyborg district and the Okhta, see Chap. 12, notes 6 and 8. There is a brief discussion of Kanatchikov's activities in St. Petersburg in 1908–10 in my "Postscript," below.

17. The "recallists" (*otzovisty*) were an extreme left faction within the Bolshevik wing of the Social Democratic Party in 1908–9. They criticized Lenin and others for having supported participation in the elections to the Third Duma and demanded that SD delegates to the Duma be recalled. The phrase "anti-Party activity" was a Stalinist political shibboleth, quite uncharacteristic of the general tenor of these memoirs, that was used to denigrate any "deviation" from an official Party line, whether contemporary or historical.

18. The Central Committee was the organizational center of the So-

cial Democratic Party between Party congresses. At the time Kanatchikov is discussing, the Bolshevik faction had effective control of the Central Committee. The Bolshevik-Menshevik feud was now in full swing, and was characterized by the publication of rival periodicals, including the two journals mentioned here. *Professional Herald* (*Professional'nyi vestnik*) was published in St. Petersburg in 1907–9; *Herald of the Professional Movement* (*Vestnik professional'nogo dvizheniia*) was published in St. Petersburg in 1908. (In this context, the adjective "professional" actually means "trade-union.") As for the other editors of *Herald of the Professional Movement* listed by Kanatchikov, Grigory E. Zinoviev (or Zinovyev, 1883–1936) was a Bolshevik leader, member of the Central Committee, and close adviser to Lenin, and Nikolay A. Rozhkov (1868–1927) was a Marxist economic historian and revolutionary activist. Zinoviev was executed as part of Stalin's Great Purge.

19. The "February days" refers to the period in 1917 from February 23, the beginning of several days of strikes and street demonstrations in the capital, to the abdication of Nicholas II on March 2.

CHAPTER 33

1. The author offers no explanation for the appearance of the word "collaborator" or "co-worker" (*sotrudnik*) in the chapter title. Possibly it was the workers' nickname for the Bering factory.

2. The Bering works, founded in 1888, was a medium-sized machine-construction factory with 300 to 400 workers.

3. Kvass (*kvas*) was a popular Russian drink, especially among peasants. It was a slightly alcoholic home-brewed sour beer, made from rye, oats, or barley.

4. It was a common practice in Russian factories for angry workers to bundle an unpopular foreman or other supervisor into a sack, dump him into a wheelbarrow, wheel him away, and abandon him at the factory gate or at some more remote location. See, for example, Bonnell, ed., *The Russian Worker*, p. 108.

5. On the Factory Inspectorate, see Chap. 11, note 8, above.

6. In this period there was still no formal mechanism for setting up and carrying out negotiations between the two sides in a labor dispute. Workers were often asked by management to choose representatives or negotiators at the height of a strike, but since strikes were illegal and strikers (especially leaders and "instigators") were subject to criminal prosecution, the position of a delegate entailed considerable risk.

7. Despite Kanatchikov's purported rejection of the views of the "Economist" wing of Russian Social Democracy, what he presents in this paragraph is essentially the position of moderate Economists regarding the process whereby economic struggle naturally evolves into political struggle.

8. Note the customary isolation of "instigators," as indicated in note 6, above.

9. The Makarov factory: a small machine-construction factory with 60 to 100 workers.

10. The Department of Police is identified in Chap. 25, note 2, above. The two documents that follow are further selections from archival files of the gendarmes to which the author had access.

11. Reference is to a partially successful strike of 1,200 workers at the Saratov workshops of the Riazan-Ural railroad line on June 6–9, 1901.

12. On the 1902 May Day demonstration, see Chap. 40, below.

CHAPTER 34

1. See Chap. 36, note 31, below.

2. There are several minor errors in this list, mainly in the titles. Julius Lippert (1839–1909) was a German anthropologist of a materialist bent. His most famous work, *Kulturgeschichte der Menschheit in ihrem organischen Aufbau* (1887), does not seem to have been translated into Russian. Kanatchikov is probably referring to a shorter work, *Istoriia kul'tury* (History of Culture), which was published in St. Petersburg in 1894 and went through several editions in the years that followed. Vasily O. Kliuchevsky (1841–1911) was a brilliant history professor. Kanatchikov may be referring to his *Kurs russkoi istorii* (Course of Russian History), but the first volume appeared only in 1904. More likely, he has in mind the *Kratkoe posobie po russkoi istorii* (Short Guide to Russian History), a summary of Kliuchevsky's Moscow University lectures, which went through several editions in the early 1900's. Kliment A. Timiriazev (1843–1920) was a renowned plant physiologist. Deeply involved in liberal academic politics and positively inclined toward Marxism, he was dedicated to the popularization of Darwinism. The book in question was probably *Charlz Darvin i ego uchenie* (Charles Darwin and His Teachings). The Kiev University economics professor V. Ia. Zheleznov published several editions of his *Ocherki politicheskoi ekonomiki* (Survey of Political Economy), a lively, readable book with lengthy sections on the labor question, in the early 1900's. Lenin's book *Razvitie kapitalizma v Rossii* (The Development of Capitalism in Russia), begun in Siberian exile in 1896, was published legally under the pseudonym V. Ilin (or Ilyin) in 1899.

3. The name Erckmann-Chatrian actually stood for two French authors, Emile Erckmann (1822–99) and Alexandre Chatrian (1826–90), who wrote popular historical novels together. Among their novels translated into Russian, the most popular was *Histoire d'un paysan, 1789*, the book Kanatchikov refers to as *The Peasant*, the full Russian title of which was *Istoriia krest'ianina* (The Story of a Peasant; St. Petersburg, 1870–72). It was written in the form of a memoir of a French peasant, set in the period of the French Revolution. An extremely condensed and altered Russian version, giving the story a more revolutionary thrust and inviting comparisons between the plight of the French people and that of the Russians, was published in Geneva by Russian populists in 1873 under the title: *Istoriia odnogo frantsuzskogo krest'ianina* (The Story of a French Peasant). The main title was followed by the words: "This book was written by a French peasant as a sign of brotherly love for the Rus-

sian peasants." For further details see Zakharina, *Golos revoliutsionnoi Rossii*, pp. 67–76.

4. A reference to one of the committees for the advancement of literacy that had been formed in the 1880's, mainly by members of the liberal intelligentsia, to provide the lower classes with appropriate reading materials. These committees were harassed and partially taken over by the government in the mid-1890's.

5. The word *poganyi* means putrid, rotten, or disgusting; it is also one of the words for heathen or pagan.

CHAPTER 35

1. On *Iskra*, see Chap. 24, note 7, above.

2. On Schopenhauer, see Chap. 18, note 4, above. The Artist is poking good-humored fun at Schopenhauer's notion that the satisfaction of the passions can often lead to unhappiness.

3. The German philosopher Friedrich Nietzsche (1844–1900) was probably the most admired and certainly the most discussed European thinker in Russia at the turn of the century. The speaker is alluding here to Nietzsche's famous work *Beyond Good and Evil* (1886), where he denigrates the morality of the "herd" and celebrates the passion and the "will to power" of the "masters." The speaker's tone is light-hearted, however, and is probably meant to display his fleeting acquaintance with Nietzsche's extremely complex ideas, which he seems to be deliberately trivializing.

4. A reference to Horatio in Shakespeare's *Hamlet*, again with the probable purpose of displaying the speaker's recently acquired literacy.

5. The "zemstvo" (local governing council) is discussed in Chap. 15, note 12, above.

6. The Social Democratic journal *Zarya* (*The Dawn*), published in Stuttgart, Germany (1901–2), was a high-level theoretical organ of the *Iskra*-ite SDs. It was meant to be the more scholarly, sophisticated counterpart to the more worker-oriented, popularly written *Iskra*.

7. The reference is to Aleksandr V. Amfiteatrov (1862–1938), a popular author of novels and adventure stories dealing with themes of contemporary Russian life, a literary critic, and, as a journalist, a strong advocate of the rights of women and national minorities. His "story" "Messrs. Obmanov-Romanov" (*Gospoda Obmanovy-Romanovy*)—the root of the name Obmanov means "fraud" or "deceit," and Romanov was of course the surname of the Imperial dynasty—was a satirical attack on the tsarist regime (published in St. Petersburg in 1901). The title might also be translated as "The Cheaters Romanov."

8. Apparently an institution of the Sunday-school variety, somewhat like the one in St. Petersburg discussed in Chap. 16, note 1, above. However, as the author goes on to suggest, the organizers were particularly cautious not to risk running afoul of the police by permitting political discussion to penetrate the classroom.

9. The future Menshevik Petr P. Maslov (1867–1946) was a Marxist economist who specialized in the agrarian question. Vasily S. Golubev

(1866–1911) was a former participant in Marxist intelligentsia-worker propaganda circles in St. Petersburg who had been exiled to Saratov, where he became involved in liberal zemstvo work. (See the brief biographical sketch in Pipes, *Social Democracy*, p. 136.) Kanatchikov is mistaken in identifying these men with so-called Legal Marxism, essentially a pejorative term for the reformist Marxism of people like Struve and Tugan-Baranovsky (see Chap. 15, note 15, above).

10. On Kocharovsky and Rakitnikov, see respectively Chap. 36, note 10, below, and Chap. 28, note 8, above. Kanatchikov is using "populist" as a loose synonym for SR, since the SRs saw themselves and were seen by others as heirs to the populist tradition.

11. Leonid N. Andreev (or Andreyev, 1871–1919) was a very popular, vaguely radical writer of short stories and melodramatic plays that usually had bizarre and pessimistic twists. His "Story of Sergey Petrovich" (*Rasskaz o Sergee Petroviche*) was published in October 1900 in the Marxist-oriented literary review *Zhizn'* (*Life*), with the aid and encouragement of Gorky.

12. The quotation is a condensed paraphrase of a longer passage from Nietzsche's *Thus Spake Zarathustra* (First Part, 1883). In the chapter entitled "On Free Death" (*Vom freien Tode*), Zarathustra says: "There are some for whom life is failure: a poisonous worm eats away at their hearts. May they see to it that their deaths be that much more successful."

13. This is a list of some of the major figures of the early years of the French Revolution. The political reading of Andreev's story presented here, though perhaps a very questionable interpretation, was typical of the approach of Kanatchikov and his comrades to literature.

14. Thermidor: a reference to the period in the French Revolutionary era between the Jacobin Reign of Terror in 1794 and the coup d'état of Napoleon in 1799. It was characterized by a return to moderation and conservatism, especially with respect to the sanctity of private property. Hence it became a negative symbol in the eyes of militant revolutionaries.

15. Nikolay A. Berdiaev (or Berdyaev, 1874–1948), later a prominent Christian religious thinker, was then in a period of intellectual transition from his rather idiosyncratic Marxism of the 1890's to a new phase of philosophic idealism, but he was still a sympathizer with the revolutionary cause. His article "The Struggle for Idealism" (*Bor'ba za idealizm*), published in the journal *Mir Bozhii* (see Chap. 18, note 4, above), was an expression of this transitional, eclectic phase in Berdiaev's political-philosophical thinking. For a concise overview of Berdiaev's life and thought, see George L. Kline, *Religious and Anti-Religious Thought in Russia* (Chicago, 1968), pp. 90–102.

16. Lassalle and Bernstein are discussed above in Chap. 18, note 8, and Chap. 22, note 5, respectively.

17. The writer and social critic Nikolay K. Mikhailovsky (1842–1904) was widely acknowledged as the chief theoretician of Russian Populism. For a perceptive analysis of his social thought, see Vucinich, *Social Thought in Tsarist Russia*, Chap. 2.

18. An ironic reference to the fact that Tsar Alexander III liked to play

the trombone, occasionally playing it in a quartet during entertainments for his friends at his country residence. See Florinsky, *Russia*, p. 1087.

19. The names are those of three of the more well-known representatives of "Utopian" socialist thought, the pejorative term used by Marx, Engels, and their followers to contrast their own "scientific" socialism with that of thinkers who, so they claimed, failed to understand the process of class struggle scientifically and constructed artificial social utopias on the basis of humanitarian ideals and intellectual fantasies.

20. The influential Moscow journal *Russian Thought (Russkaia mysl')* was a moderate liberal monthly, founded in 1880. Viktor Goltsev was a senior member of its editorial board from 1885 to 1906. The role of the individual in history was one of the problems Plekhanov addressed in his Marxist theoretical writings, especially his 1898 book of that name (*O roli lichnosti v istorii*), where he argued that the so-called great man or genius was not someone who changed the course of history, but someone who grasped and expressed the historical moment and the needs of his social class. (Plekhanov is discussed briefly in Chap. 5, note 16, above.)

21. Viktor M. Chernov (1873–1952) was the most prominent leader of the SR Party and the leading theoretician of the movement. Though as an SR Chernov was a rival of the SDs in general and, with time, of Lenin and the Bolsheviks in particular, Kanatchikov makes no attempt to conceal the respect he and his comrades had for Chernov. The complete title of the collection in which Chernov's article appeared was *On Honorable Duty (A Literary Collection Dedicated to N. K. Mikhailovsky)* (*Na slavnom postu* [*literaturnyi sbornik posviashchennyi N. K. Mikhailovskomu*], St. Petersburg, 1900).

22. This discussion (including the paragraphs that follow) provides a neat illustration of the theoretical differences between SDs and SRs with respect to the peasant question. To most SDs, landowning peasants, no matter how impoverished, no matter how tiny their holdings, were small producers—"petty bourgeois," according to Marxist criteria (i.e., they were owners of the means of production)—and were therefore not to be counted as allies of the working class in a proletarian revolution. To most SRs (including Chernov), such peasants were an essential part of the "people" (*narod*)—the broad mass of exploited villagers and factory workers—on whom the socialist revolution must be based. Apart from the question of terrorism, this was the issue that most separated the two major radical parties. For a detailed analysis of this and related problems, including their evolution in subsequent years, see Esther Kingston-Mann, *Lenin and the Problem of Marxist Peasant Revolution* (New York, 1983).

23. On the conflicts between "Economists" and *Iskra*-ites, which had begun to subside well before the appearance of Lenin's 1902 pamphlet, see Chaps. 24, note 7, and 30, note 6, above. Lenin's *What Is to Be Done?*, probably his most famous work, argued, among other things, that workers were capable of coming to "political class consciousness" only

under the guidance of professional revolutionaries from the Marxist intelligentsia.

CHAPTER 36

1. Strictly speaking, the SRs did not adopt an official program until their First Party Congress in January 1906, but Kanatchikov's statement is correct in that provisional programs had been published by the SRs by the beginning of 1902. See Perrie, *The Agrarian Policy*, esp. pp. 46–48.

2. Chernov's *Memoirs (Zapiski sotsialista revoliutsionera)*, published in Berlin in 1922, cover only his early revolutionary experience (up to the turn of the century). The time Chernov is describing in this passage (pp. 335–36 of the original) is probably 1899, a couple of years before the period Kanatchikov is discussing. As Kanatchikov goes on to explain, Chernov's quotation about cavalry and infantry is taken from Pushkin's historical poem "Poltava" (1828), which depicts the famous battle in which Peter the Great's army destroyed the army of King Charles XII of Sweden in 1709.

3. Kanatchikov's rather mean polemical thrust against the SRs includes an untranslatable pun on the words *zapevala* (the first singer in a choir) and *podpevala* (a bootlicker or toady).

4. Lenin's basic position vis-à-vis the SRs was that, despite their claim to be socialists, they represented the interests of the small-peasant proprietors, and were therefore a petty bourgeois and not a socialist party. But there was a plethora of conflicting corollaries to this position over the years, and at times it was compatible with close tactical cooperation between Lenin and the SRs, especially their left wing.

5. Astrakhan: a town on the lower Volga, about 60 miles upstream from the Caspian Sea.

6. Klitchoglu (1878?–1928) was one of the leading SR women in Saratov from the turn of the century until 1902, when she moved to St. Petersburg to evade the police. She was imprisoned shortly thereafter for her involvement in assassination plots, escaped, was rearrested, and was exiled to the Far East, where she became a schoolteacher. She returned to European Russia in 1917.

7. A reference to the Women's Medical Institute in St. Petersburg, identified in Chap. 25, note 3, above. On the Bestuzhev courses, see Chap. 15, note 17, above.

8. On Kraft, see Chap. 28, note 8, above.

9. On Bulanov, see Chap. 28, note 8, above.

10. Kocharovsky is clearly the same man whose name is spelled Kocherovsky in Chap. 28. But Kanatchikov may be in error both times, for the person who best fits this description is K. R. Kachorovsky, author of the 1900 study *The Russian Land Commune (Russkaia obshchina)*.

11. Sofya (or Sonya) Perovskaya is identified in Chap. 1, note 13, above. Vera N. Figner (1852–1942), like Perovskaya, was a leading figure in the terrorist organization the People's Will. Arrested in 1883, she

was still in prison at the time the author is describing. Here Kanatchikov is mocking the hostess for referring to these revolutionary heroines in such intimate terms.

12. The Decembrists: In December 1825 there was an abortive attempt by a group of gentry military officers to overthrow the Russian government and replace it with a more liberal political system, either a constitutional monarchy or a republic. Although many of the revolutionaries were themselves serf-owners, the abolition of serfdom was one of the uprising's major goals. See Anatole G. Mazour, *The First Russian Revolution, 1825: The Decembrist Movement* (Berkeley, Calif., 1937; 2d ed. Stanford, Calif., 1961).

13. Ponty's claim that the Decembrists feared to provoke a peasant upheaval was essentially correct.

14. Here Ponty's history is way off the mark. First, during his 1812 invasion of Russia Napoleon never attempted to free the serfs. (Whether this would indeed have been an effective tactic remains an open question.) Second, the Russian peasantry, with very few exceptions, rallied to the flag in 1812.

15. A nickname for Serafima, i.e., for Klitchoglu.

16. Zot Sazonov was the brother of Egor Sazonov (see Chap. 28, note 7, above).

17. Both these Volga provinces, which were adjacent to Saratov, were centers of intense SR propaganda work among the peasants in this period. Much of this illegal activity was organized in Saratov and radiated outward to the other provinces. See Perrie, *The Agrarian Policy*, pp. 38–40, 71–72. Klitchoglu is asking Kanatchikov to participate in this activity.

18. A reference to the activity described in the previous note.

19. Chernov's activity in Tambov province had taken place in 1896–97. Kanatchikov uses the expression "gone to the people" (*khodil v narod*) to evoke the movement of that name that had taken place in the early 1870's. It is discussed in Chap. 16, note 7, above.

20. This sentence is from Chernov's *Memoirs* (see note 2, above), p. 320; the entire quotation is on pp. 320–21, and the entire story to which it relates is on pp. 310–27. (See also Perrie, *The Agrarian Policy*, pp. 20–22.) Briefly, a radical student (a disciple of Chernov's), taking advantage of peasant discontent with the abuses of local authorities, had managed to organize a secret organization consisting of seven men to lead a sort of resistance movement against those authorities and gain control of the local offices. The organization scored an important tactical victory when Ivan Popov, a well-to-do peasant to whom many poorer villagers were in debt, went over to its side. The quotation begins at the point when Popov appears before his former enemies to ask if he might join their ranks. (There are some very trivial deviations from the original text in Kanatchikov's version.)

21. The parenthetical comment is obviously Kanatchikov's. Here and in subsequent paragraphs, Kanatchikov shows little generosity to Popov, who, after all, had sacrificed his wealth to the cause and kept his word. The readiness of the other peasants to forgive the repentant "kulak" once

it was clear he had changed his ways was quite consistent with customary peasant practice.

22. The peasant leader of the secret organization.

23. Kanatchikov fails to relate the rest of the story. According to Chernov's account, Popov's defection made it possible for the peasants to achieve their goals by peaceful means. Moreover, within the secret organization, Popov actually became the "most passionate and wild," albeit unsuccessful, advocate of even greater militancy, including the confiscation of the land of the local landlord (Chernov, pp. 326–27). In addition to ignoring these aspects of the story, Kanatchikov also introduces two details (in the following paragraph) for which there is no evidence, one way or the other, in Chernov's account: that Popov became a member of the SR Party (which did not even exist at the time of the incident) and that he retained all his property.

24. The SRs were not, of course, a "kulak" organization, and there is no reason to believe that Klitchoglu's purpose was to deprive Kanatchikov and his comrades of their "Marxist spirit." Though the obvious political reasons for Kanatchikov's extreme interpretations of these and related matters cannot be ignored, his vehemence should also be read in the context of his periodic efforts to distance himself from his peasant background. In a sense, Chernov's story, notwithstanding Kanatchikov's gloss, was an unwelcome reminder of some of the positive features and values of the village milieu Kanatchikov had abandoned, and Klitchoglu's request had the threatening appearance of an attempt to return him to that milieu.

25. See note 31, below.

26. Ekaterina K. Breshko-Breshkovskaya (1844–1934), a major figure in the SR Party, was at the time Kanatchikov encountered her a seasoned veteran of years of revolutionary activity, arrests, imprisonments, and escapes. Richard Stites is correct to point out that her nickname, *Babushka*, is more accurately conveyed as "The Grand Old Lady" than as the more commonly used "The Grandmother" or "The Little Grandmother" (usually followed by the phrase "of the Russian Revolution"). (See Stites, *The Women's Liberation Movement*, p. 140n, and, for a concise summary of her early career as a revolutionary, pp. 140–41.) However, for the sake of consistency and economy, I have elected to use the traditional English variants of her nickname. She arrived in Saratov late in 1900 (hence Kanatchikov is referring to the winter of 1900–1901). Her activities there are described in Perrie, *The Agrarian Policy*, pp. 35–38.

27. Although she was undoubtedly a sympathizer, it is highly unlikely that Breshkovskaya, who was in prison for most of the period of the People's Will's existence, was ever an active member of that organization.

28. The "Trial of the 193" took place in St. Petersburg in the winter of 1877–78. Most of the defendants, including Breshkovskaya, were young radicals who had taken part in the movement "to the people" in 1874 or related activities in the years 1872–75. Although there were numerous acquittals, Breshkovskaya was convicted and sentenced to five years of

exile and hard labor (*katorga*) in the Siberian mining settlement of Kara, the first woman revolutionary in Russian history to undergo such a stiff punishment. See Vera Broido, *Apostles into Terrorists*, pp. 157–60.

29. This term is explained in Chap. 20, note 6, above.

30. Taking into account both Kanatchikov's avowed fascination with Breshkovkaya and the embarrassing position it would have placed him in to admit there was any truth to this anecdote, the possibility that he actually considered asking for her blessing cannot be excluded.

31. The revolutionary Marxist Aleksey I. Rykov (1881–1938), a native of Saratov, was soon to become a leading Bolshevik. However, Rykov had a consistent tendency to favor conciliatory approaches to and friendly relations with rival revolutionary groups such as the SRs and the Mensheviks, a posture that would at times strain his relations with Lenin. Although Rykov held high government and Party positions in the 1920's, he ended up a victim of the Great Purge in 1938. On Rykov's early years as a revolutionary, see Oppenheim, "The Making of a Right Communist." (According to Oppenheim [p. 421], Rykov returned to Saratov from Kazan early in 1902, not in the autumn of 1901.)

32. As the author maintains here, Rykov's attitude toward "Economism" was very negative and his work against those in Saratov who wished to emphasize the economic struggle was very effective. (See Oppenheim, p. 422. Note that Kanatchikov is effectively conceding that his own attraction to the economic struggle was still strong at the time. This may even be the reason he prefers to backdate his first encounter with Rykov.)

33. In most respects *Iskra* and its followers (though themselves seriously divided, as it turned out) dominated the Second Party Congress. *Iskra* maintained a sharply critical attitude toward the SRs. Since the Saratov SDs were quite firmly in the *Iskra*-ite camp by 1903, it is not surprising that their attitude toward the SRs would now be in line with *Iskra*'s.

34. Nadezhda K. Krupskaya was now Lenin's wife.

35. The demonstration is described in Chap. 40, below.

36. A familiar form of Stepan.

37. See Chap. 28, note 9, above.

38. Sipiagin's assassin.

39. The journal *Revolutionary Russia* (*Revoliutsionnaya Rossiia*) was then the official organ of the SR Party. The journal was published, mainly abroad, from 1900 to 1905. Chernov was one of its editors and chief contributors.

40. Though it is difficult to say which side of this esoteric quarrel was closer to the truth, it should be noted that even the letter Kanatchikov goes on to quote concedes that Balmashev could not have acted entirely on his own.

CHAPTER 37

1. As should be clear from their titles, some of the items listed were contemporary revolutionary political leaflets. What follows is an expla-

nation of the other items on the list that I have been able to identify, in order of their appearance in the text:

(a) *How the Minister Took Care of the Workers (Kak ministr zabotilsia o rabochikh)*: a propaganda pamphlet, anonymous, but written by the young Marxist Nikolay A. Vigdorchik (1874–1954) and published by Plekhanov's Union (or League) of Russian Social Democrats in Geneva in 1896. The brochure was basically an attack on Finance Minister Sergey Witte's "secret" circular to the factory inspectors (December 5, 1895, published in the revolutionary press on December 9), in which Witte argued (quite disingenuously) that Russia's paternalistic industrialists generally treated their workers with Christian solicitude, and instructed his inspectors to be tough with striking workers.

(b) *Explanation of the Law on Fines Levied on Workers in Factories and Mills (Ob"iasnenie zakona o shtrafakh, vzimaemykh s rabochikh na fabrikakh i zavodakh)*: an agitational pamphlet by Lenin, first printed illegally in St. Petersburg in 1895, and reissued by the Union of Russian Social Democrats in Geneva in 1897. The purpose of the pamphlet was to demonstrate to the broad mass of workers that existing labor legislation facilitated their exploitation by their employers.

(c) *The Russian Political System and the Workers (Russkii politicheskii stroi i rabochie)*: a short pamphlet published in Geneva by the Union of Russian Social Democrats Abroad in 1901. Although the Union was now in the hands of supposed "Economists," and was in a state of conflict with Plekhanov, Lenin, and the "politically" oriented wing of the SD movement, the pamphlet called unequivocally for the abolition of autocracy and the introduction of a constitutional order in Russia, hardly evidence of a very extreme "Economist" perspective.

(d) *The Workers' Cause (Rabochee delo)*: see Chap. 30, note 6, above. It was the official organ of the Union of Russian Social Democrats Abroad.

(e) "The Marseillaise" *(Marsel'eza)*: a popular revolutionary workers' song/poem modeled on the famous French revolutionary anthem of that name. There were several variants of these workers' Marseillaises. For one of the most popular, probably the one in question, see *Pesni russkikh rabochikh*, pp. 189–90.

(f) "Varshavianka" ("The Warsaw Song"): another very popular song among militant workers in this period. The lyrics, Gleb M. Krzhizhanovsky's adaptation of an 1883 poem by the Polish writer Waclaw Swiecicki, were written by Krzhizhanovsky (a close collaborator of Lenin's) in 1897, while he was in prison. They are available in *Pesni russkikh rabochikh*, pp. 192, 194 (see also the editorial comments on p. 277). "Into Bloody Battle" *(Na boi krovavyi)*, identified by Kanatchikov as a separate poem, is actually the first line of the chorus to "Varshavianka."

2. Of the items on this list, I have been able to identify the following (listed in order of appearance):

(a) "Vankovsky's (sic) Reform" *(Reforma Generala Vannovskogo* [General Vannovsky's Reform], 1st ed. 1901, 2d ed. 1902): an anonymous pamphlet written by Grigory A. Gershuni (1870–1908), a founder of the SR Party, soon to become a leading SR terrorist. The pamphlet deals with the university disorders that began in 1899 and the ensuing (mainly abortive) educational reforms of the new minister of education (1901–2), General Petr S. Vannovsky (1822–1904). On Vannovsky's brief and frustrating tenure as minister, see Alston, *Education and the State*, pp. 160–66.

(b) "The Demolished Pier" (*Razrushennyi mol*): a short ballad published in Berlin in 1902 and attributed at the time to Maxim Gorky; it was actually written by Grigory Gershuni.

(c) *On Crimes Against the Property of Private Parties* (*O prestupleniiakh protiv sobstvennosti chastnykh lits*): a secret circular of the ministry of internal affairs (June 17, 1898) on the suppression of peasant unrest that fell into the hands of SR-oriented revolutionaries, who exposed its contents in a brochure published in London in 1900. The cover displayed the deliberately misleading title noted above, as well as the false information that the pamphlet was an 1899 publication of the Russian Ministry of Internal Affairs. The pamphlet, which was prepared by Nikolay Rubakin (see note 8g, below), was also known under the title *Kak ministr zabotitsia o krest'ianakh* (How the Minister Takes Care of the Peasants).

(d) *Conversations About Land* (*Besedy o zemle*): an anonymous pamphlet published in Geneva in 1901 by the Agrarian Socialist League (founded in 1900), an important populist-oriented émigré group that anticipated the SR Party and federated with it in 1902 (for details, see Perrie, *The Agrarian Policy*, pp. 28–34, 66–69). The pamphlet was written by Leonid E. Shishko (1852–1910), a founder of the League, whose revolutionary career dated back to the early 1870's.

(e) Tolstoy, "On the Subject of My Excommunication" (*Po povodu moego otlucheniia*): Tolstoy was formally excluded from the Russian Orthodox Church—which he had vehemently rejected in any case—by an act of the Holy Synod in 1901. "On the Subject . . . " was his public response to his excommunication.

3. The Grand Duchy of Finland, though part of the Russian Empire since 1809, had been granted a constitution and autonomous status within the Empire. At the end of the nineteenth century, however, the Russian government began a policy of Russification of the Finns and partial withdrawal of Finnish autonomy, a policy that was intensified in the first years of the twentieth century. Hence the image of the two-headed eagle (the Russian Imperial seal) ripping the constitution from the hands of Finland. Count (General) Mikhail N. Muravev (1796–1866), after suppressing the Polish uprising of 1863, was appointed governor-general of Vilna (the Lithuanian provinces). For the next two years he ran the region with an iron hand, persecuting and even executing many Polish landowners, and pursuing a cruel and vigorous policy of Russification. L. Melshin was a pseudonym for the minor revolutionary writer Petr F. Iakubovich (1860–1911), who spent eleven years as a political prisoner and exile and described his life as a convict in a moving book of stories called *In a World of Outcasts* (*V mire otverzhennykh*, 2 vols., St. Petersburg, 1896–99). He is briefly discussed in Mirsky, *History*, p. 353.

4. By now we are very familiar with Ponty Denisov. Lebedev and Bog-danov are discussed briefly in Chap. 28, note 6, above, although here Kanatchikov gives "Alekseevich" as Bogdanov's patronymic, whereas the patronymic of the Bogdanov I identify in that note was "Aleksandrovich." For this reason, and because there is reason to doubt that the more fa-mous Bogdanov was in Saratov at this time (see Vucinich, *Social Thought*, p. 206), the person mentioned here was almost certainly some-one else. Golubev is identified in Chap. 35, note 9, above.

5. It is unclear to which member of the group this refers, but it is probably Bogdanov.

6. This clearly refers to Golubev.

7. Tolstoy's *Must It Really Be Like This?* (*Neuzheli tak nado?*) contains his moving observations of the long, tedious, and backbreaking toil of the mining and foundry workers at an unnamed metallurgical complex and the peasants and road-workers who labor nearby. A party of privi-leged, well-to-do passersby in a horse-drawn carriage display their in-difference to the plight of these people while showing great concern for their dog. The ending does suggest the workers' and peasants' pained and passive toleration of their torments, but it is incorrect to describe this work as advocating nonresistance. For the full text, see Tolstoy's *Polnoe sobranie sochinenii* (Complete Collected Writings), vol. 41 (Moscow, 1957), pp. 388–91.

8. I identify these works in the order listed:

(a) Chernyshevsky, *What Is to Be Done?*: see Chap. 31, note 1, above.

(b) Innokenty V. Omulevsky (1836–83), *Step by Step* (*Shag za sha-gom*): a popular radical novel, first published in serial form in 1870 and as a separate book in 1871. The author, whose real name was Ivan V. Fedorov, was also a poet and translator.

(c) Emile Zola (1840–1902), *Germinal* (in Russian, *Uglekopy* [The Miners]): Zola's great French novel (1885) of life among the coal miners, which enjoyed a large reading public in Russia. (A Russian translation of Zola's complete works—48 volumes—appeared only two years after his death.) There were both abridged and complete Russian translations of this long novel.

(d) A translation of Karl Emil Franzos' 1882 novel *Ein Kampf um's Recht* (A Struggle for Justice) was serialized under the title *Bor'ba za pravo* in the Petersburg journal *Zagranichnyi vestnik* (*Foreign Herald*) in 1882. The novel relates the adventures of "Taras Barabola," a Ruthenian peasant in Eastern Galicia who forms a band of armed avengers who seek to restore justice to the victims of oppression; in the end Taras re-nounces violence and turns himself in to the authorities to be executed.

(e) Johann Baptist von Schweitzer (1833–75), *Emma*: a Russian trans-lation of a popular, artistically mediocre political novel of the 1860's by an eccentric but influential German Lassallean socialist politician and author. The novel—in large part a polemic against capitalism and in favor of working-class cooperatives—first appeared in Russian in the populist journal *Otechestvennye zapiski* (*Notes of the Fatherland*) in 1871. For evidence of *Emma*'s frequent use in Russian revolutionary propaganda circles, see Pearl, "Revolutionaries and Workers," pp. 116, 135–36, 261, 287, 316, 384, and 488.

(f) Ezh, *At Dawn*: See Chap. 16, note 12, above.

(g) Nikolay A. Rubakin (1862–1945), *Little Sparks. Essays and Sketches of a Publicist (Iskorki. Ocherki i nabroski publitsista)*: a collection of topical essays and stories, published in 1901, by a leading radical bibliographer and advocate of popular literacy and adult education. For a short overview of Rubakin's fascinating career, see Alfred Erich Senn, *Nicholas Rubakin: A Life for Books* (Newtonville, Mass., 1977).

(h) L. Melshin, *In a World of Outcasts*: see note 3, above.

(i) A. I. Faresov, *In Solitary Confinement (V odinochnom zakliuchenii)*: a novel published in St. Petersburg in 1900, with a second edition in 1903.

(j) On Nekrasov and his poetry, see Chap. 11, notes 4–6, and Chap. 15, note 2, above.

(k) On Uspensky and his work, see Chap. 18, note 5, above.

(l) Nikolay E. Petropavlovsky, also known as S. Karonin (1853–92): a populist writer of the late 1870's and the 1880's, whose short stories dealt mainly with village life in post-Emancipation Russia. Many of them were written in prison or Siberian exile.

9. Aleksandr V. Panov (1865–1903) was a populist-oriented bibliographer and journalist and, like Rubakin, a promoter of adult education for workers and peasants.

10. Lebedev and Liadov are identified in Chap. 28, note 6, above.

11. The citation that follows is excerpted (with some minor changes) from *Iskra*, No. 34, Feb. 15, 1903, pp. 3–4. The original article was actually a letter to the editors signed *Severianin* ("a Northerner"). At the end of the letter, the editors of *Iskra* enthusiastically endorsed "a Northerner's" views.

12. March 1, 1881, was the date of the People's Will's assassination of Tsar Alexander II. It is true that the fortunes of this highly centralized revolutionary organization waned after that date, and that its leaders and many other activists were soon arrested or forced to flee the country. Nevertheless, recent scholarship has demonstrated that the People's Will, while no longer a well-defined, unified revolutionary party, continued to exist as a "hazily defined" movement with considerable vitality, especially at the local level—a movement that proved remarkably capable of finding hundreds of new members in the years that followed. See Naimark, *Terrorists*, Chap. 2, esp. p. 42.

13. A synonym for Marxism.

CHAPTER 38

1. The artel is discussed in general terms in Chap. 2, note 1, above. In the present context it refers to a kind of cooperative workshop, run by and for the worker-members. Such endeavors were generally frowned upon by Marxists, who dismissed them as "Utopian." They were more in line with the thinking of Populists and SRs.

2. The contemporary slang expression Kanatchikov uses for the gendarmes' swords is *seledki*, literally "herrings."

3. See Chap. 37, note 3, above.

4. Kanatchikov's reference to workers who did not belong to the artel is obscure. The people he goes on to name are identified earlier in the chapter as members.

CHAPTER 39

1. Oppenheim ("The Making," p. 421) dates the founding of the committee to the spring of 1901, i.e., before the strike wave mentioned in the following sentence. Raleigh (*Revolution on the Volga*), however, dates it to "late 1901."

2. "Amateurism" is my very approximate translation of *kustarnichestvo*, a term of derision used by Lenin to counterpose the allegedly unprofessional and narrow ways of local Marxist groups to his own professional, centralized, ambitious approach to party organization. A *kustar'* was a peasant engaged in cottage industry or handicrafts, and the literal sense of the longer term could be rendered (clumsily) as "kustarism." Keep (*The Rise of Social Democracy*, p. 90) translates it as "particularism."

3. Golubeva was also known as Golubeva-Iasneva. In the early 1890's, before converting to Marxism, she had belonged to a revolutionary group that favored a seizure of state power by conspiratorial means. (See Polevoi, *Zarozhdenie*, p. 374.) Obukhov may have been the Petersburg metalworker of that name who was arrested for his role in the 1896 labor unrest. (See *Rabochee dvizhenie*, vol. 4, part 1, p. 330.)

4. *The Old Bolshevik* (*Staryi bol'shevik*) was a Moscow journal that specialized in the publication of revolutionary memoirs and related materials. It was published from 1930 to 1934. Liadov wrote several accounts of his political experience in addition to the one cited by Kanatchikov.

5. This paragraph should be supplemented by consulting Raleigh, *Revolution on the Volga*.

6. See Chap. 36, above.

7. The Mariinskoe Agricultural School (or College) was located in the village of Nikolaev, some twenty miles from Saratov. According to Perrie (*The Agrarian Policy*, p. 36), "most of the pupils were the sons of peasants from the neighboring villages." Perrie mentions the role of these pupils as links between Saratov SRs and the inhabitants of those villages (pp. 36, 40), but she makes no mention of any SD contacts with them. Raleigh (Chap. 2) connects both the SRs and the SDs with the school, but his source on the SD connection is Kanatchikov himself. It is likely that both groups had sympathizers at the school, but that the SRs were more involved there than the SDs (Kanatchikov's assertions in the following paragraph notwithstanding).

8. The Enisey (or Yenisey) was a river in central Siberia that divided

Siberia on a south-north axis. Large parts of the surrounding province, which bore the name of the river, were held by "White," i.e., anti-Bolshevik, forces during the first half of the Civil War, and "Red" partisans, many of them peasants, were engaged in a bloody guerrilla war with the Whites in 1919. Kravchenko is identified in note 9, below.

9. A. D. Kravchenko (1880–1924) was an agronomist who came from a peasant family. As Kanatchikov indicates, Kravchenko became an important leader in the 1919 partisan campaign against the Whites; but Kanatchikov fails to mention that Kravchenko was then an SR by conviction.

10. Although it is true that some of the more prominent SRs at times sacrificed systematic organization on the altar of terrorism, Kanatchikov's extravagant claims for the influence of the SDs in general and the Bolsheviks in particular on the agrarian movement of 1905, and his correspondingly negative assessment of the role of the SRs, are unconvincing. For a very different point of view, see Radkey, *The Agrarian Foes*, pp. 57–64, and especially Perrie, Chaps. 10 and 11.

11. As will soon become clear, the Saratov demonstration of May 5, 1902, was actually a May Day demonstration. May 1 had been proclaimed an international labor holiday by the inaugural congress of the (Second) Socialist International in Paris in 1889. The Russian labor movement began to observe the holiday in the 1890's, and began celebrating it with renewed vigor at the turn of the century. Because the Russian "Old Style" (Julian) calendar was thirteen days behind the (Gregorian) calendars of other European countries in the twentieth century, Russian socialists were faced with the problem of whether to select April 18 (Old Style) for their "May Day" activities (thereby celebrating on the same day as their foreign comrades) or May 1 (Old Style). Apart from this problem, there was also the tactical question of whether to celebrate on May Day when the day fell on a workday (i.e., Monday through Saturday), thereby risking direct confrontation with employers, or whether to shift May Day activities to the nearest Sunday, as was done on this occasion.

12. The first May Day celebration in Russia proper, in St. Petersburg in 1891 (there had been a major one in Russian Poland in 1890), took the form of a secluded outdoor social gathering that combined the aspect of a small political rally with that of a picnic. (It is briefly described in Pipes, *Social Democracy*, pp. 33–34.) In the following years such celebrations, designed as outings in part to conceal their true character from the police and in part because they were indeed holiday excursions, would continue to take place on May Day and other holidays in many industrial centers. Holiday excursions in the countryside were a common form of working-class entertainment in Russia, and there are examples of their use as clandestine political meetings as early as the 1870's.

13. On Stenka Razin, see Chap. 10, note 4, above.

14. Bashibazouks: irregular troops of the Ottoman Empire, with a rep-

utation in the nineteenth century for unusual cruelty. The author is actually referring (pejoratively, of course) to the Russian gendarmes.

15. Kolpino: see Chap. 29, note 1, above.

16. A paraphrase of the famous formula of the First International (The International Workingmen's Association, 1864–76) that ". . . the emancipation of the working class must be won by the workers themselves . . ."(from para. 1 of the preamble to the organization's statutes, drafted by Karl Marx in 1864).

17. "Tailism" (*khvostizm*): a term used by Lenin in *What Is to Be Done?* to describe the alleged tendency of the Economists to subordinate themselves to the spontaneity of the working class, that is, to the narrow aspirations of workers at a given moment, rather than using Marxist "science" as a guide.

18. The lines are from the last section of Nekrasov's 1858 poem "Reflections at the Main Entrance" (see Chap. 11, note 6, above), a part of the poem that became a popular song among radical students.

19. Except for the SD League (or Union) of Artisanal Workers (*Soiuz remeslennykh rabochikh*), these groups have already been mentioned above. They are all identified in Raleigh, *Revolution on the Volga*. The short-lived League of Artisanal Workers was organized in early 1902.

20. Balmashev is identified in Chap. 28, note 9, above; for the context in which Kanatchikov views the story of Balmashev, see the last pages of Chap. 36.

21. In 1902, there was a series of strikes and massive workers' demonstrations and protest marches in and near the town of Rostov-on-the-Don. The demonstrations, accompanied by a citywide general strike, were strongly influenced by local SDs, who addressed thousands of railroad workers and others at mass meetings, although other revolutionary groups participated as well. (For a brief summary, see Keep, *The Rise of Social Democracy*, pp. 71–72; there is a thorough account in Henry Reichman, "The Rostov General Strike of 1902," *Russian History*, 9, part 1 [1982], pp. 67–85.) The 1902 labor unrest spread to several other provincial towns, including the Volga port of Nizhny-Novgorod and its suburbs.

22. The paragraphs that follow were excerpted, with minor changes, from *Iskra*, No. 43 (July 1, 1903), p. 8. Though probably more or less accurate in its broadest outlines, the letter should be read as part of the ongoing rivalry between SDs and SRs. SR participation in the demonstration is surely understated here.

CHAPTER 40

1. To call the Saratov May Day demonstration the first demonstration in the history of the Russian revolutionary movement is a gross exaggeration. That honor is usually reserved for the Kazan Square demonstration in St. Petersburg on December 6, 1876; depending on one's definition of a revolutionary demonstration, even earlier examples could be

found. Moreover, there were several important revolutionary political demonstrations between the time of the Kazan Square demonstration and 1902.

2. See the discussion in Chap. 39, note 11, above.

3. A major famine swept the Russian countryside in 1891–92, with a death toll that has been estimated at between 300,000 and 650,000. Many of these deaths were from virulent cholera and typhus epidemics that, in 1892–93, ravaged a population already weakened by hunger and malnutrition. (See Frieden, *Russian Physicians*, Chap. 6, and Richard G. Robbins, Jr., *Famine in Russia, 1891–1892: The Imperial Government Responds to a Crisis* [New York, 1975], esp. pp. 169–71.) In the words of Frieden (p. 144), "The cholera epidemic triggered popular riots of such dimensions that medical work became extremely hazardous"; popular actions against medical personnel were "irrational and even murderous," and the popular mood was one of "mass hysteria." Both the epidemic and the consequent mass hysteria moved northward up the Volga River, striking Volga towns like Saratov and the surrounding countryside with particular force. (This occurred in 1892, however, not, as Kanatchikov asserts, in 1891.) "Pogrom" refers to the anti-Jewish riots that began to take place in southwestern Russia in the early 1880's and continued intermittently well into the twentieth century.

4. A Judicial Chamber (*sudebnaia palata*) was a district tribunal with both criminal and civil divisions. It served both as the appellate (second) instance for certain criminal cases tried by the circuit courts and as a court of first instance for the trial of some serious criminal cases, including political crimes. (See Kucherov, *Courts*, pp. 43–44, 49, 201–2.)

5. "Black Hundreds" (*chernosotentsy*): extremely reactionary, nationalistic, virulently anti-Semitic political groups that began to emerge in the early twentieth century. The label "Black Hundreds" was often used very loosely.

6. The young foundry worker P. I. Voevodin had already participated in revolutionary Marxist circles in Ekaterinoslav—a center of the iron and steel industry in the southern Ukraine—in the late 1890's. He is discussed briefly in *Rabochii klass Rossii*, pp. 327, 377–79, where his age at the time of his courtroom speech is given as nineteen.

7. F. A. Volkenshtein was a St. Petersburg lawyer who frequently acted as defense attorney in political cases. He is mentioned briefly in Leikina-Svirskaia, *Russkaia intelligentsiia*, p. 80.

8. In other words, some of the defendants—the author is saying polemically—would later become Bolsheviks.

CHAPTER 41

1. Both the editorial remarks and the full text of Denisov's speech (which Kanatchikov reproduces in its entirety) are in *Iskra*, No. 43 (July 1, 1903), pp. 3–4.

2. The newspaper *Petersburg Sheet* (*Peterburgskii listok*) was a popular

"boulevard newspaper" that contained sensationalized (though sometimes fairly accurate) news stories about crime, vice, and other aspects of city life.

3. *The St. Petersburg News* (*S.-Peterburgskie vedomosti*) was Russia's oldest newspaper. It was founded (under another name) by Peter the Great in 1703. Since the 1860's its politics had been moderately liberal. The Petersburg newspaper *New Times* (*Novoe vremia*) adhered to an extreme right, ultranationalist, monarchist position, closely allied to the views of the Black Hundreds (see Chap. 40, note 5, above). Its editor from 1877 to the end of his life was the conservative journalist and publisher Aleksey S. Suvorin (1834–1912), a disillusioned liberal. *The Russian News* (*Russkie vedomosti*), a daily paper published in Moscow from 1864 to 1918, was one of the most liberal of Russia's legal newspapers. Beginning in the 1880's, many of its most prominent contributors were university professors.

4. The self-defense fighting squad or combat team (*boevaia druzhina*) was an armed unit of militant workers or students formed in order to resist physical attacks by Black Hundreds and other right-wing groups. Although such squads began to appear before 1905, they proliferated in Russian cities only during the 1905 Revolution, when they sometimes played a more aggressive revolutionary role. (For examples, see Engelstein, *Moscow, 1905*, pp. 147–48, 197–201, and Chap. 11.) A member of such a unit was called either a *druzhinnik* or a *boevik* (the term used by Kanatchikov).

5. A flying meeting (*letuchka*) was a quick "hit-and-run" meeting of revolutionary workers, usually called in order to deal with an emergency matter or hand out a leaflet. The term *letuchka* could also refer to a "flier" in the sense of a short leaflet, usually one with a very specific message.

6. On October 21, 1905, a government decree extended full or partial amnesties to various categories of political prisoners.

7. Apparently a sample of the satirical revolutionary verse that greeted the proclamation of Tsar Nicholas II's Manifesto of October 17, 1905, granting civil liberties and other concessions to the Russian people. See also Chap. 32, note 15, above.

8. I.e., Lenin.

9. The "period of reaction" began with Prime Minister Petr A. Stolypin's "coup d'état" of June 3, 1907 (the arbitrary dissolution of the unmanageable Second Duma and the promulgation of a new, unconstitutional electoral law aimed at guaranteeing a more pliant, conservative majority in the new Duma). In a larger sense, however, a period of reaction, replete with arrests, courts-martial, executions, etc., had been under way since 1906.

10. Admiral Aleksandr V. Kolchak (1870–1920) was head of the White forces in Siberia during much of the first half of the Civil War, and for a short period was considered the "Supreme Ruler" of Russia by leaders of the anti-Bolshevik side. He was defeated by the Reds at the

end of 1919 and executed in early 1920. Ekaterinburg was a major center of mining and metallurgy in western Siberia, on the eastern slopes of the Ural Mountains.

11. The metalworker Ivan V. Babushkin (1873–1906) is still the most famous Russian revolutionary worker of his generation, in part because he was befriended and praised by Lenin and in part because of his very valuable posthumous *Memoirs* (*Vospominaniia*) of the 1890's (first published in Leningrad in 1925, republished in Moscow in 1951 and 1955 and in English translation in 1957). He was shot without trial by a government punitive expedition in 1906. The quotation from Lenin is from an obituary originally published in 1910 and republished in the various editions of Lenin's works as well as in the various editions of Babushkin's memoirs.

CHAPTER 42

1. The first volume of Karl Marx's *Das Kapital* (1869) was translated from German into Russian by Nikolay F. Danielson (1844–1918) in 1872. This was the first translation into any language. It was published legally, having been approved by the Russian censors, who viewed the work as too scholarly and complex to present any political danger.

2. The economist V. Ia. Zheleznov is identified in Chap. 34, note 2, above. Professor Aleksandr I. Chuprov (1842–1908) of Moscow University was an eminent political economist and statistician who specialized in agrarian questions. He was a political liberal and a defender of the peasant commune. Tugan-Baranovsky is identified in Chap. 15, note 15, above. His major work, *The Russian Factory, Past and Present* (*Russkaia fabrika v proshlom i nastoiashchem*), first published in St. Petersburg in 1898, went through several subsequent editions and translations. It is a detailed study of the historical development of Russian industry, written from a Marxist perspective. The book by Ilin (i.e., Lenin) is identified in Chap. 34, note 2, above. All told, Kanatchikov was examining books on political economy and Russian economic history by authors representing a broad spectrum of political views.

3. See Chap. 34, above.

4. Aleksandr A. Makarov (1857–1919) succeeded Stolypin as Minister of Internal Affairs in September 1911 and remained in that office through most of 1912. He had been a deputy minister in 1906–9, but was full minister at the time of the inquiry into the Lena goldfields massacre. The massacre of striking workers in the Lena goldfields of western Siberia (April 1912) marked the beginning of a two-year period of explosive labor unrest in urban Russia. See Haimson, "The Problem of Social Stability in Urban Russia."

5. Addressing the Second Duma on March 13, 1907, Stolypin said: ". . . When a house burns, gentlemen, you break into a strange apartment, you break the doors, you break the windows. When a person is sick, he is treated by poisons. When a murderer attacks you, you kill him . . ." (as quoted from the stenographic record of the Duma session in

Kucherov, *Courts*, p. 207). Stolypin was attempting to defend the use of field courts-martial, which had been lavish in their pronouncements of death sentences against the government's political enemies.

6. General Dmitry F. Trepov (1855–1906) served as military governor of the city of St. Petersburg, with emergency powers, for most of the revolutionary year 1905. It was then that he issued the famous order cited by Kanatchikov. See Lincoln, *In War's Dark Shadow*, p. 301.

7. In April 1895 there was a major strike at the "Great" (*Bol'shaia*) Cotton-Spinning and -Weaving Factory in Iaroslav province (in north-central Russia), a huge manufacturing complex with some 12,000 workers. At the height of the strike thousands of workers were actively involved. The provincial authorities had to summon several companies of the army's Phanagorya Regiment to repress the extremely militant strikers, some of whom actually engaged the troops in hand-to-hand combat, hurled rocks at them, and attempted unsuccessfully to seize their weapons. One of the companies fired a volley of shots in the direction of a crowd of hostile workers, killing one man and wounding eleven, thereby dispersing the crowd. Other workers suffered bayonet wounds and other injuries. (There is a documentary history of this important incident in *Rabochee dvizhenie v Rossii v XIX veke*, vol. 4, part 1, pp. 131–57.) When the young Tsar Nicholas II, who had ruled for barely six months, got wind of these events, he wired a personal message of congratulations to the Phanagorya Regiment expressing his gratitude to those "good lads" or "brave lads" (*molodtsy*) for their actions, thereby angering workers and the liberal intelligentsia throughout the country. See Dan, *The Origins of Bolshevism*, pp. 195–96.

CHAPTER 43

1. In this chapter the author returns to the period in Saratov just prior to his imprisonment.

2. Karl Kautsky (1854–1938) was the leading "orthodox" or centrist theoretician of German Social Democracy and a major figure in the German SD Party. At the beginning of the twentieth century he was greatly admired by Russian Marxists.

3. Tsarev is referring here to what was still the standard position of "orthodox" Russian Marxists, including Lenin and future Bolsheviks as well as future Mensheviks: that there would be two revolutions in Russia—first a "bourgeois" revolution that would sweep away the remnants of "feudalism" and replace the autocracy with a liberal-democratic polity, and only later a "proletarian" or workers' revolution that would overthrow the capitalist order and usher in the age of socialism. Notwithstanding Kanatchikov's derision of his ideas (in the following paragraph), Tsarev was expressing a viewpoint found among many of his contemporaries when he spoke skeptically of working-class participation in a bourgeois revolution that would benefit the middle classes at the workers' expense.

4. On Zubatov, See Chap. 6, note 4, above.

5. See Chap. 35, note 6, above.

CHAPTER 44

1. Tsaritsyn (renamed Stalingrad in 1925 and Volgograd in 1961): a town on the right bank of the lower Volga, located near the southern tip of Saratov province.

2. Mikhail I. Sokolov (also known as "The Bear") was an agricultural student who later became a terrorist. (See Perrie, *The Agrarian Policy*, pp. 40, 91, and note 7, below.)

3. Tantalus: in Greek mythology, the son of Zeus who was doomed to perpetual hunger and thirst while remaining in the presence of fruit and water that were just out of reach.

4. The Sorbonne professor François Alphonse Aulard (1849–1928) was the author of several scholarly works on the political history of the French Revolution, some of which were translated into Russian around the turn of the century. He was a defender of the rationality and humanity of the revolutionary tradition that began in 1789. The English Fabian socialists Sidney and Beatrice Webb (1859–1947 and 1858–1943) authored and co-authored numerous works on labor and politics. Here Kanatchikov is referring to their *Industrial Democracy* (translated as *Teoriia i praktika angliiskogo tred-iunionizma*; 2 vols., St. Petersburg, 1901–2), much of which was translated into Russian by Lenin, and their *History of Trade Unionism* (translated as *Istoriia rabochego dvizheniia v Anglii*, St. Petersburg, 1899). The main work of the English writer and materialist interpreter of history Henry T. Buckle (1821–62) was his two-volume *History of Civilization in England* (1857–61; Russian edition 1862–64); three Russian editions had appeared by the year that Kanatchikov is discussing. The works of the famous English empiricist philosopher and liberal political thinker John Stuart Mill (1806–73) had attracted the attention of Russia's left intelligentsia since the 1860's. Here Kanatchikov is referring to Mill's most important formal philosophical work, *A System of Logic* (1st ed. 1843; 1st Russian ed. 1865–67). The novels of Charles Dickens (1812–70) enjoyed enormous popularity among all literate strata of the Russian population. By the beginning of the twentieth century, there were many Russian editions of Dickens' works, including his complete works and some very inexpensive popular editions.

5. *Sadko*: one of the major operas of the famous Russian composer Nikolay A. Rimsky-Korsakov (1844–1908). This romantic opera, which was first performed in 1897, takes its subject matter from early Russian history and legend and borrows many of its musical themes from traditional Russian folk music. The Varangians were Norse warriors who descended on the region that would soon be known as Kievan Rus, the cradle of the first Russian state in the valley of the Dnieper River, in the ninth century. It was often claimed (on the basis of a short section of the *Russian Primary Chronicle*) that in 862 the Varangians were invited by the quarreling Eastern Slavic tribes who inhabited the area to come and rule over them, but that story is now widely regarded as mythical.

6. Iakov P. Polonsky (1819–98) was a lyric poet and short story writer who generally avoided political themes.

7. Maximalists (*maksimalisty*): an ultraradical splinter group that broke with the SRs over questions of tactics (especially terror) and program in 1904, although it did not become a formally separate organization until 1906. Mikhail Sokolov was a leading member of the group. For details, see Perrie, *The Agrarian Policy*, pp. 153–59.

8. The Moscow armed uprising of December 1905 is discussed in Engelstein, *Moscow, 1905*, Chap. 11; on the bloody fighting in the working-class district of northwest Moscow known as Presnya, see especially pp. 214–21.

9. Assassinations and "expropriations" (e.g., armed robberies of banks) were characteristic tactics of the Maximalists. The unsuccessful attempt on Stolypin's life—a bomb explosion in which over 30 people perished—took place in August 1906 at his Petersburg summer home; Fonarny Lane was the location in St. Petersburg of a 1906 armed robbery of some 600,000 rubles that were being transported from the city's customs office to the State Bank. For his role in these affairs, Sokolov was executed without trial on December 2, 1906. (See Perrie, p. 158.)

10. The Franco-Russian factory (formerly the Baird factory, founded in 1792): a large government-owned shipyard and engineering works in St. Petersburg, located in the Kolomensky district, to the west of the city center, on the southern bank of the Neva River. It had about 2,000 workers at the time under discussion.

11. "Sectarians" (*sektanty*) refers to any one of several dissident religious sects, mainly of mystical Protestant origin or inspiration, that emerged in Russia in the late seventeenth and eighteenth centuries, and were often the object of official persecution in the years that followed. In the late nineteenth and early twentieth centuries, some revolutionaries viewed sectarians, especially sectarian peasants (who numbered in the millions), as potential allies against the tsarist regime. The sectarians should not be confused with the Old Believers (see Chap. 20, note 2, above), who, though they broke with the Orthodox Church, saw themselves as representing the pure Russian Orthodox Christian faith.

12. The Dukhobors, perhaps the most important of the sectarian groups described in the previous note, are identified in Chap. 5, note 11, above.

13. Arkhangel (or Arkhangelsk) province: one of European Russia's northernmost provinces, located on the White and Barents seas. Because of the region's remote location, the Russian government used it as a relocation point for exiled prisoners, including politicals. (To distinguish the province's capital city from the province itself, I shall refer to the city as Arkhangelsk and the province as Arkhangel.)

CHAPTER 45

1. The Butyrskaya prison (also known as Butyrki or Butyrka): a notorious prison complex located in the northwestern part of the city of Moscow.

2. Sakhalin: a large island off the Pacific coast of eastern Siberia, just north of Japan. It was used by the Russian government as a settlement for convicts.

3. The Uspensky (Assumption) Cathedral, site of the Imperial coronations, was located on the central square at the heart of the Moscow Kremlin. It was constructed in the 1470's.

4. Erotic novels with sexual (including homosexual) themes became increasingly available and popular in Russia in the decade or so before the First World War.

5. At the RSDLP's Stockholm congress (the Fourth Party Congress, by Bolshevik reckoning), held in the spring of 1906, the Bolshevik and Menshevik factions of the Party attempted to reunite. The attempt was nominally successful, but the success proved short-lived.

6. Cherepovets: a town in the northeastern part of European Russia, on the Vologda side of the border between Novgorod and Vologda provinces.

7. Innokenty F. Dubrovinsky was a rather well-known Bolshevik who was elected to the Party Central Committee in 1908; he favored a conciliatory policy toward the Mensheviks. His brother Iakov was apparently killed in the town of Krasnoyarsk, in the Enisey region of central Siberia (see Chap. 39, note 8, above), when the Czechoslovak Legion—consisting of some 40,000 Czech prisoners of war—seized large portions of the Transiberian railroad line at the beginning of the Civil War.

8. "Remote, out-of-the-way regions" is my rather conventional translation of a much more colorful Russian expression: *medvezh'i ugly*, literally, "bear's corners."

9. The Pechora River winds northward from the western slope of the Ural Mountains to the Barents Sea; the village of Ust-Tsylma (or Tsilma) was about 200 miles upstream from the mouth of the river. Onega was a town near the mouth of the Onega River, where it empties into the White Sea. Izhma was a village on the Izhma River, just south of the northernmost stretch of the Pechora and west of the Urals.

10. The Zyrians (also known as Komi) were a Finnic-speaking people who inhabited the basin of the Pechora River and adjoining areas. They were converted to Orthodox Christianity by Russian monks in the late fourteenth century.

11. Kholmogory: a village on the Northern Dvina River, about 50 miles upstream from Arkhangelsk.

12. Pinega was a town on the Pinega River, which runs parallel to the Northern Dvina, about 100 miles to the east. I have been unable to determine the source of the couplet. (The lines are rhymed in the original.)

13. This was an elected village policeman known as a *desiatskii*, an adjective derived from the Russian word for "ten." In theory, at least, one such official was chosen by every ten households in the village.

14. The reference is either to arrested workers who had taken part in the general strike and demonstrations in Rostov-on-the-Don in 1902 (see Chap. 39, note 21, above), or, more likely, to the arrested leaders of a large protest demonstration that had taken place in that town on March 2, 1903, some of whom were tried, convicted, and sentenced to death.

15. An old Russian proverb contains the expression "to drive in [cattle] where Makar did not drive the calves" (Sokolov, *Russian Folklore*, p.

259). It suggests a visit (either real or metaphorical) to a remote, inaccessible, difficult area, one that even a poor devil would avoid. See also Dal', *Tolkovyi slovar'*, vol. 2, p. 290: "Makar."

16. The Samoyeds were a group of seminomadic peoples who kept and herded reindeer in this region. The Samoyed is also a large, powerful Siberian dog, usually used for herding reindeer or pulling sleds.

17. On Old Ritualists (or Old Believers), see Chap. 20, note 2, above. Nikon (1605–81) was the Orthodox Patriarch of Moscow from 1652 to 1658 (though he would not be formally removed from that post until 1667). It was the changes in the Orthodox ritual introduced by him as part of a systematic ecclesiastical reform that precipitated the schism in the church. Among those changes was the making of the sign of the cross in the "Greek" manner, i.e., with three fingers instead of two, a reform that was fiercely resisted by the Old Ritualists.

18. Cherdyn was a settlement on the northernmost bend of the Kama River, about 400 miles south of Ust-Tsylma. Perm, the main industrial and administrative center of the northwestern Urals, was also located on the Kama, nearly 200 miles to the south of Cherdyn. Part of the voyage between the Kama and the Pechora was overland.

CHAPTER 46

1. The point here is obscure. It may simply be that the landlord was addressed familiarly despite his venerable age.

2. The household ancestral spirit (*domovoi*) and the wood or forest spirit (*leshii*), both dating back to pre-Christian belief systems, were important figures in Russian peasant lore. Henri Troyat (*Daily Life*, pp. 209–10) describes them as follows. The *domovoi*—"old and dishevelled, with a hairy body and a tail. He protected the family, shared in its daily life, amused himself in provoking a sleeper's snores, tangling a flirtatious woman's hair, hiding the master's boots . . . ; but on the other hand he often healed the sick and appeased domestic quarrels." The *leshii*—"a spirit with a bluish skin, protruding eyes, and long hair. This spirit protected criminals, imitated birdsong, and wandered through his realm laughing, whistling, and clapping his hands. . . . A mocking creature, he often amused himself by leading men astray in the woods."

3. On St. Nikolay (Nicholas), see Chap. 5, note 17, above.

4. Illegal literature printed in Western Europe was often smuggled across the border between eastern Galicia in the Austro-Hungarian Empire and the western Ukraine in Russia.

5. *God's World*, *Russian Wealth*, and *The Russian News* are identified above in Chap. 18, note 4, Chap. 13, note 6, and Chap. 41, note 3, respectively. *Education* (*Obrazovanie*), a left-liberal monthly journal of literature and politics with SD sympathies, was published in St. Petersburg from 1892 to 1909. *Truth* (*Pravda*), a Moscow journal with Menshevik political leanings, published in 1904–6, may not have been available yet at the time the author is describing. The liberal daily newspaper *Northern Land* (*Severnyi krai*) was published in Iaroslavl from 1898 to 1905. Its columns were open to SD contributors.

6. Fisher is identified in Chap. 29, note 3, above.

7. I.e., Nadezhda K. Krupskaya, Lenin's wife.

Note that Kanatchikov fails to indicate that after Fisher moved to England in 1901, he maintained a neutral, conciliatory position in the struggle between Bolsheviks and Mensheviks, possibly even tilting slightly toward the latter in the wake of the 1903 split (see Zelnik, "Russian Bebels," pp. 443–44). Fisher's memoirs (*V Rossii i v Anglii* [In Russia and England], published in Moscow in 1922) were certainly available to Kanatchikov at the time he was writing.

8. Some of the weaknesses in this explanation of Kanatchikov's decision to go with the "Majority" (i.e., the Bolsheviks) are discussed in Zelnik, "Russian Bebels," pp. 439–43.

9. The correct word is not *kanys* but *kamys*, an old Siberian term for the skin taken from the leg of a reindeer. See Dal', *Tolkovyi slovar'*, vol. 2, p. 83.

10. All were scenes of general strikes in November 1902 (Rostov) or the early summer of 1903 (Ekaterinoslav and some of the major cities near the Caucasus Mountains, i.e., Baku, Batum, and Tiflis).

11. Aleksandr A. Bogdanov is identified in Chap. 28, note 6, above. His book *A Short Course in Economic Science* (*Kratkii kurs ekonomicheskoi nauki*; 1st ed. Moscow, 1897) was a sort of Marxist alternative to liberal ("bourgeois") political economy texts, intended for the use of SD propagandists. It went through at least ten editions; Kanatchikov is probably referring to the third (Moscow, 1902). The Erfurt Program (composed mainly by Karl Kautsky) was the official program of the German Social Democratic Party; it was adopted in the town of Erfurt at the Party congress of October 1891 and remained in force until 1918. It was printed in Russian, in whole or in part, several times between 1894 and 1903.

12. The immediate cause of the Bolshevik-Menshevik split in 1903 was a disagreement over Party organization, and especially over how narrowly one should define the obligations of a Party member. In the Russian version of the last sentence of this paragraph, the grammatical structure leaves open the question of whether Kanatchikov intended to include himself among those who "didn't want a schism in the Party"; the Russian contains no noun or pronoun, just a verb form that implies either "they" or "we" as its subject.

13. Semën L. Vainshtein (1876–1923), also known as V. Zvezdin, had been arrested in Moscow—where he was a member of the Moscow Committee of the RSDLP—in 1902 and sentenced to four years in exile. He was a member of the Petersburg Soviet in 1905.

14. I have not been able to obtain further information on Bartold.

15. Khlestakov was the central character in the great 1836 comedy *The Inspector General* (*Revizor*), by Nikolay V. Gogol (1809–52).

16. On Sviatopolk-Mirsky and his brief tenure as minister of internal affairs (known as a "spring" because of its relative mildness and moderation), see Chap. 16, note 16, above.

17. A "peasants' superintendent" (*krest'ianskii nachal'nik*) was an ap-

pointed official in Siberia and other remote areas whose power over the peasantry was roughly equivalent to that of the land captain (see Chap. 19, note 9, above).

18. The term is explained in Chap. 16, note 4, above.

19. The Bund was the short name for the General Jewish Workers' Union in Lithuania, Poland, and Russia, founded in Vilna in 1897. The Bund was one of the constituent groups that formed the RSDLP in 1898, but its relations with that party became strained and complex in the years that followed. For a thorough study of the Bund's early years, see Henry J. Tobias, *The Jewish Bund in Russia: From Its Origins to 1905* (Stanford, Calif., 1972).

20. The reference is clearly to the Revolution of 1905, probably to its earliest phase.

21. This is Dr. S. V. Martynov, whose activities are briefly noted in Frieden, *Russian Physicians*, pp. 239, 258.

22. The Tsarevich Alexis (Aleksey), heir apparent to the throne, was born on July 30, 1904. This was the child whose incurable hemophilia was to leave its mark on Russian history.

23. With some exceptions, Jews in Russia were permitted to reside only in the so-called Pale of Settlement (*cherta osedlosti*), corresponding roughly to the boundaries of the old Kingdom of Poland and the provinces of western and southwestern Russia, and stretching southwestward from the Baltic coast to the northern shores of the Black Sea. Hence the irony of a situation in which the police chief, having "freed" the prisoners, is obliged to banish the Jewish prisoner to the Pale.

24. "Sentimental idealism" is meant as a very approximate translation of the difficult Russian term *prekrasnodushie*, which in turn was a literal translation of the German expression *Schönseeligkeit* (sometimes translated more formally as "subjective aestheticism"), adopted from the great German writer Friedrich Schiller (1759–1805). The expression entered the vocabulary of the Russian intelligentsia in the 1830's.

25. The Black Hundreds are identified in Chap. 40, note 5, above.

CHAPTER 47

1. The author is referring to the "banquet campaign" of November–December 1904, when militant liberals, especially lawyers and other professionals, taking advantage of the weakening of restraints on civil liberties during Sviatopolk-Mirsky's brief political "spring," used a variety of pretexts to organize a series of political banquets in Russia's major cities. The "four-tailed" suffrage refers to one of the most important demands put forth at the banquets: the election of a constituent assembly on the basis of (1) universal, (2) equal, and (3) direct suffrage, and (4) the secret ballot. For a close analysis of the banquet campaign, see Terence Emmons, "Russia's Banquet Campaign," *California Slavic Studies*, 10 (1977), pp. 45–86.

2. Although Kanatchikov is correct when he asserts that there was cooperation between liberals and SRs during the banquet campaign, and

certainly more cooperation than there was between liberals and SDs (see Shmuel Galai, *The Liberation Movement in Russia, 1900–1905* [Cambridge, Eng., 1973], pp. 218–19), to say that the SRs were merging (*slivalis'*) with the liberals is a gross exaggeration.

3. The Bolshevik leader Iosif P. Goldenberg (1873–1922, also known as Meshkovsky) was the outstanding SD intellectual in Saratov at this time. As Kanatchikov goes on to explain in his generally accurate portrait of Goldenberg in the following paragraphs, he stood for cooperation and conciliation between Bolsheviks and Mensheviks, which was then a popular position among Saratov SDs.

4. Actually, in the period of the Third Duma (1907–12), the period to which Kanatchikov is referring, both Bolshevik and Menshevik Duma delegates were united in a single "faction," and the two groups cooperated reasonably well. In the Fourth Duma, elected in 1912, this cooperation continued to obtain until the fall of 1913. See Schapiro, *The Communist Party of the Soviet Union*, pp. 133–35.

5. Note that this is yet another occasion where the author seems at pains to reveal, albeit gently and obliquely, his sympathy for those of his comrades who took conciliatory positions with regard to divisions within the movement.

6. "Direct" is my translation of the Russian word *priamolineinyi*, the literal meaning of which is "rectilinear." Although Kanatchikov is quoting another speaker, the appearance of even this mild a criticism of Lenin in a book published as late as 1934 is quite extraordinary, the more so in that it appears without any rebuttal by the author or the editors.

7. Lenin's long 1904 pamphlet *One Step Forward, Two Steps Backward* (*Shag vpered, dva shaga nazad*) was an attempt to justify his conduct at and before the Second Party Congress (1903), where the Bolshevik-Menshevik split took place, and to set forth his views on what he considered to be the pivotal question of party organization. It was partially a response to criticisms of Lenin published in *Iskra*, which was now in Menshevik hands, at the end of 1903 and the beginning of 1904. The actual protocols of the Congress of course contained the arguments of both sides. For a lucid analysis of these extremely tangled matters, see Haimson, *The Russian Marxists*, Chap. 10.

8. See Chap. 27, above.

9. The "Liberation" movement centered around the newspaper *Liberation* (*Osvobozhdenie*), published abroad from mid-1902 to 1905 by Petr Struve (see Chap. 15, note 15, above), and the similarly oriented, largely overlapping Union of Liberation (*Soiuz Osvobozhdeniia*), an illegal political organization founded in July 1903 (though its first congress was in January 1904). It was the most important locus of left-liberal constitutionalist thought and politics prior to the formation of the Kadet (Constitutional Democrat) Party in October 1905, when the Liberation movement was effectively absorbed into that party. The Social Democrats were generally hostile to the Liberationists (who figured

prominently in the banquet campaign), but the Bolsheviks—and Lenin in particular—much more so than the Mensheviks.

EDITOR'S POSTSCRIPT

1. This Postscript is a revised and updated version of the Postscript to my essay "Russian Bebels" (pp. 443–47), except that the original Postscript includes information on the fate of the worker Matvey (or Andrey) Fisher that is not relevant to the life of Kanatchikov. The new information included here pertains mainly to events of 1925–26, when Kanatchikov briefly served as director of the Communist Party's Department of Historical Research (*Istpart*). It comes entirely from a short but very informative unpublished article by William Burgess, "S. I. Kanatchikov: A Half-Rehabilitated Old Bolshevik" (1980), which the author was kind enough to share with me. Except where indicated in the notes that follow, the rest of this Postscript is based on the Russian-language sources listed in "Russian Bebels," note 54 (p. 445).

2. Kanatchikov's report to the Congress on Combating Alcoholism is noted in a very useful unpublished paper by George E. Snow, "Socialism, Alcoholism, and the Russian Working Class Before 1917" (1983), p. 35. For Kanatchikov's participation in the 1906 Stockholm Congress, see *Chetvertyi (Ob"edinitel'nyi) S"ezd RSDRP, aprel' (aprel'–mai) 1906 goda: Protokoly* (The Fourth [Unity] Congress of the RSDLP, April [April–May] 1906: Protocols) (Moscow, 1959). Although Kanatchikov's underground name, Egorov, appears at least twenty times in this verbatim record of the congress (he is almost always listed as voting on the same side as Lenin on contested issues), there is only one entry that shows him as actually speaking, briefly and on a fairly minor point: summarizing the views of peasants in the Ural region on land seizures and the confiscation of mineral deposits (p. 143).

3. These are the words used by the editors of *Chetvertyi . . . S"ezd RSDRP* (cited in the previous note) in their index of names mentioned in the protocols of the congress. See the entry "Kanatchikov, S. I.," p. 657.

4. For the full references to these works, see "Russian Bebels," note 59 (p. 447).

SELECTED BIBLIOGRAPHY

WHAT FOLLOWS is a list of most of the works cited in the Notes. Omitted are works mentioned only once, which are cited in full where they occur, and works mentioned in the course of my explanatory discussions of Kanatchikov's literary allusions.

Agitatsionnaia literatura russkikh revoliutsionnykh narodnikov: Potaennye proizvedeniia 1873–1875 gg. (Agitational literature of the Russian revolutionary populists: The clandestine works of the years 1873–75). Prepared by O. B. Alekseeva. Leningrad, 1970.

Alston, Patrick L. *Education and the State in Tsarist Russia.* Stanford, Calif., 1969.

Bonnell, Victoria E. *Roots of Rebellion: Workers' Politics and Organizations in St. Petersburg and Moscow, 1900–1914.* Berkeley, Calif., 1983.

———, ed. *The Russian Worker: Life and Labor Under the Tsarist Regime.* Berkeley, Calif., 1983.

Broido, Vera. *Apostles into Terrorists: Women and the Revolutionary Movement in the Russia of Alexander II.* New York, 1977.

Brooks, Jeffrey. "Readers and Reading at the End of the Tsarist Era," in William Mills Todd III, ed., *Literature and Society in Imperial Russia, 1800–1914.* Stanford, Calif., 1978.

———. *When Russia Learned to Read.* Princeton, N.J., 1985.

Dal', Vladimir. *Tolkovyi slovar' zhivogo velikorusskogo iazyka* (Interpretive dictionary of the living Great Russian Language). 4 vols. Moscow, 1978–80 (from the 2d ed., 1880–82).

Dan, Theodore. *The Origins of Bolshevism.* Edited and translated by Joel Carmichael. New York, 1964.

Emmons, Terence, and Wayne S. Vucinich, eds. *The Zemstvo in Russia: An Experiment in Local Self-Government.* Cambridge, Eng., 1982.

Engelstein, Laura. *Moscow, 1905: Working-Class Organization and Political Conflict.* Stanford, Calif., 1982.

Fisher, A. *V Rossii i v Anglii: Nabliudeniia i vospominaniia peterburgskogo rabochego (1890–1921 gg.)* (In Russia and in England: The observations and recollections of a Petersburg worker [1890–1921]). Moscow, 1922.

Florinsky, Michael T. *Russia: A History and an Interpretation*. Vol. 2. New York, 1953.

Frieden, Nancy M. *Russian Physicians in an Era of Reform and Revolution, 1856–1905*. Princeton, N.J., 1981.

Glickman, Rose L. *Russian Factory Women: Workplace and Society, 1880–1914*. Berkeley, Calif., 1984.

Gohstand, Robert. "The Internal Geography of Trade in Moscow from the Mid-Nineteenth Century to the First World War." Ph.D. diss., Univ. of Calif., Berkeley, 1973.

Haimson, Leopold H. "The Problem of Social Stability in Urban Russia, 1905–1917," *Slavic Review*, 23, no. 4 (Dec. 1964), and 24, no. 1 (Mar. 1965).

———. *The Russian Marxists and the Origins of Bolshevism*. Cambridge, Mass., 1955.

Istoriia Moskvy (History of Moscow). Vol. 4. Edited by B. P. Koz'min and V. K. Iatsunskii. Moscow, 1954.

Istoriia rabochikh Leningrada (History of the Leningrad workers). Vol 1. Edited by V. S. Diakin et al. Leningrad, 1972.

Johnson, Robert E. *Peasant and Proletarian: The Working Class of Moscow in the Late Nineteenth Century*. New Brunswick, N.J., 1979.

Keep, J. L. H. *The Rise of Social Democracy in Russia*. Oxford, 1963.

Kucherov, Samuel. *Courts, Lawyers, and Trials Under the Last Three Tsars*. New York, 1953.

Leikina-Svirskaia, V. R. *Intelligentsiia v Rossii vo vtoroi polovine XIX veka* (The intelligentsia in Russia in the second half of the nineteenth century). Moscow, 1971.

———. *Russkaia intelligentsiia v 1900–1917 godakh* (The Russian intelligentsia in the years 1900–1917). Moscow, 1981.

Lincoln, W. Bruce. *In War's Dark Shadow: The Russians Before the Great War*. New York, 1983.

Matossian, Mary. "The Peasant Way of Life," in Wayne S. Vucinich, ed., *The Peasant in Nineteenth-Century Russia*. Stanford, Calif., 1968.

Mirsky, D. S. *A History of Russian Literature: From Its Beginnings to 1900*. New York, 1958.

Naimark, Norman M. *Terrorists and Social Democrats: The Russian Revolutionary Movement Under Alexander III*. Cambridge, Mass., 1983.

Nekrasov, N. A. *Polnoe sobranie sochinenii i pisem* (Complete collection of writings and letters). 2 vols. Moscow, 1948.

Ocherki istorii Leningrada (Essays on the history of Leningrad). Edited by B. M. Kochakov et al. Vol. 2. Moscow, 1957. Vol. 3. Moscow, 1956.

Oppenheim, Samuel A. "The Making of a Right Communist—A. I. Rykov to 1917," *Slavic Review*, 36, no. 3 (Sept. 1977).

Owen, Thomas C. *Capitalism and Politics in Russia: A Social History of the Moscow Merchants, 1855–1905*. Cambridge, Eng., 1981.

Pearl, Deborah Lee. "Revolutionaries and Workers: A Study of Revolutionary Propaganda among Russian Workers, 1880–1892." Ph.D. diss., Univ. of Calif., Berkeley, 1984.

Perrie, Maureen. *The Agrarian Policy of the Russian Socialist-Revolutionary Party, from Its Origins Through the Revolution of 1905–1907*. Cambridge, Eng., 1976.

Pesni russkikh rabochikh (XVIII–nachalo XX veka) (Songs of the Russian workers [from the eighteenth to the beginning of the twentieth century]). Prepared by A. I. Nutrikhin. Moscow, 1962.

Pipes, Richard. *Social Democracy and the St. Petersburg Labor Movement, 1885–1897*. Cambridge, Mass., 1963.

Polevoi, Iu. Z. *Zarozhdenie marksizma v Rossii, 1883–1894 gg.* (The origins of Marxism in Russia, 1883–94). Moscow, 1959.

Rabochee dvizhenie v Rossii v XIX veke: Sbornik dokumentov i materialov (The labor movement in Russia in the nineteenth century: Collection of documents and materials). Vol. 4 (1895–1900), parts 1–2. Edited by L. M. Ivanov. Moscow, 1961.

Rabochee dvizhenie v Rossii v 1901–1904 gg.: Sbornik dokumentov (The labor movement in Russia in 1901–1904: Collection of documents). Edited by L. M. Ivanov et al. Leningrad, 1975.

Rabochii klass Rossii ot zarozhdeniia do nachala XX v. (The working class of Russia from its birth to the beginning of the twentieth century). Edited by M. S. Volin et al. Moscow, 1983.

Radkey, Oliver H. *The Agrarian Foes of Bolshevism: Promise and Default of the Russian Socialist Revolutionaries, February to October, 1917.* New York, 1958.

Raleigh, Donald. *Revolution on the Volga: The Russian Revolution of 1917 in Saratov.* Ithaca, N.Y., forthcoming.

Ransel, David L., ed. *The Family in Imperial Russia.* Urbana, Ill., 1978.

Reeder, Roberta, ed. and trans. *Down Along the Mother Volga.* Philadelphia, 1975.

Salisbury, Harrison E. *Black Night, White Snow: Russia's Revolutions, 1905–1917.* New York, 1978.

Schapiro, Leonard. *The Communist Party of the Soviet Union.* New York, 1964.

Schneiderman, Jeremiah. *Sergei Zubatov and Revolutionary Marxism: The Struggle for the Working Class in Tsarist Russia.* Ithaca, N.Y., 1976.

Schwarz, Solomon M. *The Russian Revolution of 1905: The Workers' Movement and the Formation of Bolshevism and Menshevism.* Translated by Gertrude Vakar. Chicago, 1967.

Sokolov, Y. M. *Russian Folklore.* Translated by Catherine Ruth Smith. Detroit, 1971.

Stepniak [Sergey Kravchinsky]. *The Russian Peasantry: Their Agrarian Condition, Social Life, and Religion.* London, 1905.

Stites, Richard. *The Women's Liberation Movement in Russia: Feminism, Nihilism, and Bolshevism, 1860–1930.* Princeton, N.J., 1978.

Surh, Gerald. "Petersburg Workers in 1905: Strikes, Workplace Democracy, and the Revolution." Ph.D. diss., Univ. of Calif., Berkeley, 1979.

Troyat, Henri. *Daily Life in Russia Under the Last Tsar.* Translated by Malcolm Barnes. Stanford, Calif., 1979.

Tugan-Baranovsky, Mikhail I. *The Russian Factory in the 19th Century*. Translated by Arthur Levin and Claora S. Levin. Homewood, Ill., 1970.

Venturi, Franco. *Roots of Revolution: A History of the Populist and Socialist Movements in Nineteenth Century Russia*. Translated by Francis Haskell. New York, 1960.

Vucinich, Alexander. *Science in Russian Culture, 1861–1917*. Stanford, Calif., 1970.

————. *Social Thought in Tsarist Russia: The Quest for a General Science of Society, 1861–1917*. Chicago, 1976.

Wildman, Allan K. *The Making of a Workers' Revolution: Russian Social Democracy, 1891–1903*. Chicago, 1967.

Zakharina, V. F. *Golos revoliutsionnoi Rossii: Literatura revoliutsionnogo podpol'ia 70–kh godov XIX v. "Izdaniia dlia naroda"* (The voice of revolutionary Russia: Literature of the revolutionary underground of the 1870's. "Publications for the People"). Moscow, 1971.

Zelnik, Reginald E. *Labor and Society in Tsarist Russia: The Factory Workers of St. Petersburg, 1855–1870*. Stanford, Calif., 1971.

————. "Populists and Workers: The First Encounter Between Populist Students and Industrial Workers in St. Petersburg, 1871–74," *Soviet Studies*, 24, no. 2 (Oct. 1972).

————. "Russian Bebels: An Introduction to the Memoirs of Semen Kanatchikov and Matvei Fisher," *The Russian Review*, 35, nos. 3 (July 1976) and 4 (Oct. 1976).